Drawing on a wide range of unpublished sources from archives in Albania and Greece, Ardit Bido's book provides a fascinating journey into the interplay between Orthodox Christianity, nationalism and political power in Albania. His meticulous and thought-provoking study focuses on key events and religious and political figures in the making of an independent Albanian Orthodox Church. The book is summarised in a key sentence, as Bido has eloquently argued: 'the newly established Albanian nation desired to create its own symphony between Church and state in the hope of consolidating the nation-state'. This is the first detailed study on the Albanian Orthodox Church challenging the relationship between Orthodox churches and state authorities, and more broadly, between religion and nationalism in South-eastern Europe.

— Lucian Leustean, Reader in Politics and
International Relations, Aston University,
United Kingdom

One of the best analyses of the history of the Albanian Orthodox Church and the fight for autocephaly. It is a succinct, readable and learned study based on primary sources of a "peripheral" Orthodox Church in a predominantly Muslim nation. The study is a gem for the specialist in Eastern Christianity, the student of Eastern Orthodoxy, and all those interested in the history of modern autocephalies and in the political history of Balkans in general. Highly recommended.

— Ines Angeli Murzaku, Professor of Ecclesiastical
History and Director of Catholic Studies Program,
Seton Hall University, New Jersey, USA

Ardit Bido's monograph is a special historiographical contribution dedicated to the issue of autocephaly of the Albanian Orthodox Church. The innovative approach analyses crucial periods of the troubled path of the foundation on national basis of the Albanian Orthodox Church: the origins within the *Rilindja* movement (1878–1918); the decade 1918–1929 of the affirmation and proclamation of Albanian ecclesiastical autonomy; the twenty years (1929–1945) of the consolidation preceding the Communist dictatorship. Of each of the three phases identified, Bido carries out an in-depth critical scan, which allows his historical and political reconstructions to be embedded in an interpretative framework that is as objective as it is convincing. The results of this research, thanks to the use of various archival sources, will undoubtedly constitute the subject of further debate among contemporary historians.

— Matteo Mandala, Full Professor of Albanology and
Director of the Albanology Laboratory,
University of Palermo, Italy

The Albanian Orthodox Church

Religion in Albania has had a complicated history, with Orthodoxy, Bektashi and Sunni Islam, and Catholicism coexisting throughout much of the history of this Balkan nation. This book traces the rise of the Albanian Orthodox Church from the beginnings of Albanian nationalist movements in the late nineteenth century to the end of the Second World War and the Communist takeover. It examines the struggles of the Albanian state and Church to establish the Church's independence from foreign influence amid a complex geopolitical interplay between Albania and neighbouring Greece and its powerful Ecumenical Patriarchate as well as the Italian and Yugoslav interference, and the shifting international political circumstances. The book argues that Greece's involvement in the Albanian "ecclesiastical issue" was primarily motivated by political and territorial aspirations as Athens sought to undermine the newly established Albanian state by controlling its Orthodox Church through pro-Greek bishops appointed by the Patriarchate. With its independence finally recognized in 1937, the Albanian Orthodox Church soon faced new challenges with the Italian, and later German, occupation of the country during the Second World War: the Church's expansion into Kosovo; the Italian effort to place the Church under papal authority; and, the ultimate threat, the imminent victory of Communist forces.

Ardit Bido is General Director of the Archives of Albania and Lecturer at the Metropolitan University of Tirana, Albania.

Routledge Religion, Society and Government in Eastern Europe and the Former Soviet States

Series Editor
Lucian Leustean is Reader in Politics and International Relations at Aston University, Birmingham, United Kingdom.

This Series seeks to publish high quality monographs and edited volumes on religion, society and government in Eastern Europe and the former Soviet States by focusing primarily on three main themes: the history of churches and religions (including, but not exclusively, Christianity, Islam, Judaism and Buddhism) in relation to governing structures, social groupings and political power; the impact of intellectual ideas on religious structures and values; and the role of religions and faith-based communities in fostering national identities from the nineteenth century until today.

The Series aims to advance the latest research on these themes by exploring the multi-facets of religious mobilisation at local, national and supranational levels. It particularly welcomes studies which offer an interdisciplinary approach by drawing on the fields of history, politics, international relations, religious studies, theology, law, sociology and anthropology.

For more information about this series, please visit: https://www.routledge.com

The Albanian Orthodox Church
A Political History, 1878–1945

Ardit Bido

GENERAL DIRECTOR OF THE ARCHIVES OF ALBANIA,
LECTURER AT THE METROPOLITAN UNIVERSITY OF TIRANA

LONDON AND NEW YORK

First published 2021
by Routledge
2 Park Square, Milton Park, Abingdon, Oxon OX14 4RN

and by Routledge
52 Vanderbilt Avenue, New York, NY 10017

Routledge is an imprint of the Taylor & Francis Group, an informa business

British Library Cataloguing-in-Publication Data
A catalogue record for this book is available from the British Library

Library of Congress Cataloging-in-Publication Data
A catalog record has been requested for this book

ISBN: 978-1-138-35472-2 (hbk)
ISBN: 978-0-429-42459-5 (ebk)

Typeset in Times New Roman
by codeMantra

Contents

Figures

x *Figures*

Acknowledgements

I would like to thank the publishers of UET Press for their permission to reproduce parts of my original book, *Kisha Ortodokse Shqiptare: një histori politike, 1878–1937* (Tirana: UET Press, 2016), in this revised translation of the work. It would have been impossible to publish this volume without the outstanding help of the Routledge editorial board, especially Lucian Leustean and Peter Sowden, and my good friends, associates, and relatives: Prof. Ilira Çaushi, Prof. Ferit Duka, Besmira Çako, Vasil Jançe, Aleksandra Kola, Thomas Logoreci, and Rawley Grau. The photographs used as illustrations in this book can be found in the Phototheque of the General Directorate of Archives of Albania, Niko Kotherja's private collection, and Andrea Llukani's private collection, all of whom I thank for their generous help. I dedicate this book to the memory of my late mother, Roza Bido, whose unconditional support over the years contributed in no small part to who I am. I thank God for bringing her into my life.

Abbreviations

AMFA   Archives of the Ministry of Foreign Affairs of Albania
AQSH   Central State Archives of Albania *(Arkivi Qendror Shtetëror)*
ELIA   Greek Historical and Logotechnical Archives
GAK   Central State Archives of Greece *(Genika Arxeia tou Kratous – Γενικά Αρχεία του Κράτους)*
IBE   Northern-Epirotic Research Foundation (Idryma Voreiohpeirotikon Erevnon – Ίδρυμα Βορειοηπειρωτικών Ερευνών)
IDAYE   Historical and Diplomatic Archives of Greece *(Istoriko kai Diplomatiko Arxeio tou Ypourgieou Eksoterikon – Ιστορικό και Διπλωματικό Αρχείο του Υπουργειου Εξωτερικων)*
MFA   Ministry of Foreign Affairs
MIA   Ministry of Interior Affairs
MJ   Ministry of Justice
OACA   Orthodox Autocephalous Church of Albania
PMO   Prime Minister's Office

The archival indication initials are
f   File
F   Fonds
Y   Year

Introduction

On 10 June 1878, 48 representatives of the Albanian elite gathered in a small, white, mud-brick house in the fortress town of Prizren in Kosovo Vilayet and created the first Albanian national institution: the League of Prizren.[1] This momentous undertaking occurred four centuries after the Ottoman Empire occupied the short-lived medieval Albanian principalities. The 1878 gathering marked the rise of Albanian nationalism, which was the last nationalist movement to succeed in the European part of the Ottoman Empire, a patriotic revival senior only to a similar failed venture by the Vlachs. The inception of the Prizren League was triggered by the Ottoman Turkish defeat in the war against Russia, a defeat finalized by the Treaty of Berlin only a few months before. Following the Russian victory, the independent Balkan states of Greece, Serbia, and Montenegro had annexed many ethnic Albanian territories in the Ottoman Empire. The Treaty of Berlin also established the Principality of Bulgaria as a vassal state of the Ottoman Empire, albeit a de facto independent one. Thus, the Albanians – who lived in a compact territory informally known as Ottoman Albania[2] – were the last nation in the European part of the Ottoman Empire that had neither a state nor any national institutions.

This book focuses on the struggle of the Albanian people to create an independent Orthodox Church amid the complex political interplay between the emerging Albanian state, the Greek state, and the Ecumenical Patriarchate. The analysis begins in 1878, a pivotal year marked by three coinciding decisive factors. First, the League of Prizren, as a catalyst for Albanian nationalism, invigorated the concept of a common Albanian identity with language as its sole criteria, regardless of allegiance to any of the region's four main religious groups – Sunni Islam, Bektashi Islam, Eastern Orthodoxy, and Roman Catholicism. Second, the Ecumenical Patriarchate, which ruled over the Orthodox Church in Albania, was gradually coming under the guidance of the Greek state in the second half of the nineteenth century and thus also came into conflict with the Albanian national movement. Third, the Greek irredentist concept *Megali Idea* (The Great Idea, 1844), which sought the expansion of Greece, overlapped with Albanian, Bulgarian, and Vlach territorial claims and thus brought those three nations into opposition with Greece and the Ecumenical Patriarchate. These combined factors mark the year 1878 as the start of the Albanian struggle for an independent Orthodox Church and the political interplay that followed.

The analysis covers two distinct political periods. Before the First World War (1914–1918), the Albanian ecclesiastical issue was part of the overall "Eastern Issue" during the period of the Concert of Nations. This resulted in a dispute between the post-Prizren League Albanian national movement on the one hand and the Greek state and the Ecumenical Patriarchate on the other. This clash took place against a background of explicit Greek territorial claims, which continued until Albania's frontiers were solidified in the wake of the Paris Peace Conference of 1919.

Albania's independence (declared in 1912, recognized in 1913, with the Principality of Albania established and dissolved in 1914, and the government re-established in 1920) brought a new approach to the ecclesiastical issue: the question of the status of the Orthodox Church in Albania. This became a diplomatic struggle between the two countries, each seeking to prevail. During this period, the ecclesiastical issue followed the trajectory of Albanian–Greek relations, with the whip hand alternating between Albania and Greece. These developments were due to unexpected events during the interwar period (1918–1939) and influenced by the shifting political circumstances in the Balkans and in Europe more generally. The Albanian Orthodox Church declared its autocephaly in 1922,[3] only months after the final settlement of Albania's borders. The Church, however, was not formally recognized until 1937, which marked the end of the struggle for ecclesiastical independence. The Albanian Orthodox Church then faced the challenges brought by the Second World War: the Axis occupation of neighbouring Kosovo in Yugoslavia and its incorporation into Albania, the pressure of the Italian occupation forces to place the Albanian Church under the pope's authority, the consequences of the Greek–Italian War, and finally the growing strength of Communism.

The analysis concludes in 1945, when Communist forces assumed control in Albania, which marked the end of the nationalist struggle with regard to the Albanian Orthodox Church. The post-war period witnessed the use of religion in the broader Cold War power dynamic, resulting in the complete abolition of religion in Albania in 1967. The period after 1945, while of great importance, would require a totally different scholarly approach, as the political interplay surrounding the Orthodox Church went beyond any bilateral relations, becoming instead an ideological battle between the two camps of the Cold War.

The events are presented chronologically, with the first chapter detailing the development of the ecclesiastical issue from the rise of Albanian nationalism in 1878 to the re-establishment of the Albanian state in 1920. The second chapter chronicles the declaration of autocephaly and the initial reactions of Greece and the Ecumenical Patriarchate, which coincided with Greece's momentous defeat in the Greco-Turkish War of 1919–1922.

The next three chapters follow the curve of Albanian–Greek relations until 1929, a period when the Albanian Church twice came close to winning recognition of its autocephaly before internal political developments in both Albania and Greece reversed the situation. The sixth and last chapter describes the final negotiations that led to the Patriarchate's endorsement of Albanian autocephaly and discusses the developments that occurred during the Second World War.

This study is based on archival sources from Albania and Greece[4] as well as a number of published archives,[5] the personal archives and memoirs of Albanian and Greek hierarchs, and newspaper accounts from the time. This book is the first overall discussion in English of the issue of the Albanian Orthodox Church before the Communist regime came to power, as the various existing chapters in other works do not focus on the struggle for autocephaly.[6]

Regarding this topic, some historical research exists in Albanian and Greek, but most of these discussions follow their respective national narratives, and some do not draw on archival sources and lack a sustainable scientific approach.[7] Apart from these works and Dhimitër Beduli's short, but landmark, contemporary history of the Albanian Orthodox Church written in 1944,[8] there are two Albanian monographs[9] and a number of papers in a volume published by the Albanian Academy of Sciences in 1993.[10] All of these, however, lack Greek political and ecclesiastical archival sources and are influenced by the communist narrative, in which religion was viewed unimportant to Albania's social and political history. As such, they underestimate the role the Church played in international relations and the nationalist support of such Albanian hierarchs as Ierothe Jaho (the metropolitan of Korça, 1922–1929), Kristofor Kisi (the metropolitan of Berat, 1922–1929; then metropolitan of Korça, 1933–1937; and finally archbishop of Tirana and all Albania, 1937–1949), and Evlogji Kurilla (the metropolitan of Korça, 1937–1941). Overall, these papers downplay the role of the Albanian state in the ecclesiastical issue by attributing the religious movement to a few patriotic priests and the "Orthodox population" in general.

Although there has been some superficial treatment of the Albanian ecclesiastical issue in Greek historiography,[11] it is the scholarly work of the historians Mihail Tritos and, especially, Apostolos Glavinas that stands out.[12] Glavinas's findings are of great importance, providing a full picture of the Albanian Church as gleaned from archival sources from the Ecumenical Patriarchate and the Orthodox Church of Greece. However, his work lacks Albanian archival sources as well as Greek political references. Thus, Glavinas presents the Albanian ecclesiastical issue as stemming from the presence of numerous minorities – although, in fact, the minorities among the Orthodox in Albania were inconsiderable. Due to his lack of Greek political sources, Glavinas fails to acknowledge the bilateral diplomatic background, treating the issue purely as an ecclesiastical dispute between the Patriarchate and Albania's Orthodox population, whom for Glavinas were under the pressure of the Albanian state. Glavinas also emphasizes what he believes was the impact of Albania's Muslim population on the ecclesiastical issue.

This study attempts to reconstruct events in a way that is faithful to the broad spectrum of archival sources from both Albania and Greece. Ultimately the book challenges both earlier approaches, and especially Glavinas, whose work has so far been the most important and noteworthy on the Albanian ecclesiastical issue. As we shall see, the Albanian Orthodox Church came about as the direct result of the political interplay between the Albanian and Greek states, with all but one of the Albanian metropolitans taking an Albanian nationalist approach. Although the Albanian ecclesiastical movement was supported by the vast majority of Orthodox Albanians, it was the determination and crucial role of Orthodox Albanian political leaders, the Albanian state, and the Albanian hierarchs that overcame the obstacles created by the Greek state. Finally, Orthodox Albanians had a greater nationalist sensitivity towards the ecclesiastical issue than did the Muslim political leaders, as there were cases when the latter were momentarily willing to back Greece on the issue, only to be blocked by political leaders of the Orthodox faith.

Nation and church: the Balkan paradigm and the Albanian exception

The Orthodox Churches in the Balkans were prime actors in the nation-building process. Lucian Leustean notes that, with the exception of Bulgaria (whose national movement took place in the second half of the nineteenth century), "other countries in the region showed the active support of the church for nation-state building".[13] Moreover, most scholars agree that religion played a key factor in the process of consolidating the national identity. Yet nearly all these historians leave aside the Albanians, whose national movement was the only one in the Ottoman European territories that does not fit into any of the categories noted above. The Albanian national movement was purely ethnic-based, in contrast to the ethno-religious movements of the other nations in the region. In the Balkans, the nationalist ideas inspired by the French Revolution intermingled with the Ottoman Empire's *millet* ("nationality") system. The ecumenical patriarch of Constantinople was the religious and political leader for the *Rum millet* ("the Roman nation") – the Orthodox community living under the rule of the Ottoman Empire. Until the first half of the nineteenth century, the Ecumenical Patriarchate was highly influenced by the ethnically diverse (albeit mostly Greek) Phanariots, who were named after Phanar, the Orthodox quarter of Istanbul. The Phanariots held a number of important positions within the empire, as well as nearly all the main offices of the Ecumenical Patriarchate.[14]

The first nationalist movement that shook the European part of the Ottoman Empire was the Greek Revolution (1821–1830). Backed by Russia,

France, and Great Britain, this upheaval resulted in the independence of Greece, in what is today the southern part of the country's mainland. The Greek national identity was based on the *Rum millet*, along with the perennial belief that Greek identity was a continuum dating back to antiquity.[15] Thus, the first Greek constitution stated that every believer of the Great Church of Constantinople (i.e. every Orthodox inhabiting the territory where the revolution succeeded) should be considered Greek, even though a considerable portion of this population was made up of Albanians (Arvanites),[16] Vlachs (in Boeotia), and other groups. Greek-speaking Muslims, on the other hand, were not considered to be Greeks, but Turks. The same thinking would apply to populations in Greece's future expansions, including the Turkish-speaking Orthodox of Turkey who were deported to Greece in the Greco–Turkish population exchange of 1923. This ethno-religious national identity was a direct product of the *Rum millet*, the only institution in the Ottoman Empire that was comparable to a national institution. The Greek Revolution was proclaimed by the Orthodox hierarch Metropolitan Germanos III of Old Patras (1771–1826) on the Feast of the Annunciation, 25 March 1821, and was supported by the majority of the clergy. The Ecumenical Patriarchate did not officially support the revolution, but after its success, notable Phanariots and the ecumenical patriarch himself, Gregory V (in office 1797–1798, 1806–1808, and 1818–1821), were accused of treason and executed by the Ottoman government. In 1833, the newly established Greek state convened an assembly of the clergy, excluding the hierarchs, and declared the autocephaly of the Orthodox Church of Greece. The Church was recognized by the Ecumenical Patriarchate in 1850.[17]

The Serbs had preceded the Greeks in their struggle for independence. Through a series of Russian-backed uprisings (1804–1817), a semi-independent Principality of Serbia was created in 1815, gained de facto independence in 1867, and was eventually recognized by the Treaty of Berlin in 1878. Orthodoxy was considered to be the guardian of the Serbian national identity.[18] The ethno-linguistic group of Serbo–Croats was divided along religious lines. Only the Orthodox Serbs were considered to be part of the Serbian nation. This religious factor separated the Serbs not only from the other ethnicities, enabling them to establish a strong religious and national bond, but also distinguished them from Muslims and Roman Catholics who spoke the same language as they did. The Orthodox Serbs had a strong religious tradition going back to the Patriarchate of Peć,[19] which had been abolished by the Ottomans in 1766. Within the newly established principality, a religious jurisdiction was formed at the beginning of the nineteenth century. The Ecumenical Patriarchate granted autonomy to the metropolitanate of Belgrade in 1831 and full autocephaly in 1879. Even the Montenegrins, Serbia's neighbours to the south-west, created their distinct identity within their own Serbian Orthodox diocese, the metropolitanate of Cetinje, which shared the same borders as the autonomous Prince-Bishopric of Montenegro.[20]

The history of Romania was quite different from that of the other Balkan countries. Located between three of Europe's Great Powers – the Ottoman, Russian, and Austrian Empires – the lands that comprise modern-day Romania were at one time or another ruled by one of these powers either directly or as a vassal principality. The union of two of these principalities in 1859, to form what was nominally a vassal state of the Ottoman Empire, marked the first step towards Romanian independence. The unification of Romania would probably have been impossible without the role of the Romanian clergy.[21] The new united principality declared the autocephaly of the Romanian Orthodox Church in 1865. After independence and the establishment of the Kingdom of Romania in 1881, the Ecumenical Patriarchate granted the tomos of autocephaly to the Romanian Orthodox Church in 1885.[22]

The Bulgarian national movement in the second half of the nineteenth century brought about the creation of the Principality of Bulgaria in 1878. The Bulgarian religious tradition, however, traced its roots back to the powerful archbishopric of Ohrid, which before its suppression in 1776 had often been led by Bulgarian clergy.[23] The rise of Greek nationalism resulted in the banning of the Bulgarian language from the liturgy and schools, which contributed to the weakening of the religious traditions practised by many Bulgarians.[24] Nonetheless, Bulgaria preserved a strong Orthodox tradition that allowed it to build its national identity on an ethno-religious foundation. Bulgarian Muslims were therefore excluded from the new national identity, which comprised only those Bulgarian speakers who were Orthodox. As Carsten Riis notes, for Bulgarians, being Christian "was one of their most distinctive qualities".[25] The Bulgarians succeeded in creating their own *millet* as an ethno-religious jurisdiction within the Ottoman Empire. The Bulgarian *millet* was recognized unofficially in 1847 and received official recognition from the sultan after the creation of the Bulgarian Exarchate in 1872. This development, aided by the Russian Empire, brought fierce opposition from the Ecumenical Patriarchate, which condemned the establishment of the Exarchate as the heresy of ethnophyletism, that is, the overemphasis on ethnic identity with regard to religion.[26]

The last ethno-religious movement in the European part of the Ottoman Empire was the Vlach (or Aromanian) movement. The Vlachs lived in territories in what is today north-western Greece, small portions of southern Albania and southern North Macedonia. Owing to their proximity to the Romanian nation and the intervention of Austria–Hungary and Romania, the sultan recognized the Vlachs as separate *millet* on 22 May 1905. But the Ecumenical Patriarchate did not recognize any form of religious autonomy for the ethnic group. The outbreak of the First Balkan War (1912–1913) halted any significant development in the Vlach religious movement.[27]

The Ecumenical Patriarchate thus reacted differently to each of these complicated Balkan paradigms. On the one hand, it recognized the autonomy and, later, autocephaly of the Serbian Church as soon as they were requested, respectively, by the Principality and then by the Kingdom of Serbia. On the other hand, the Patriarchate first opposed but ultimately recognized the autocephaly of the Church of Greece (declared 1833, recognized 1850) and the Church of Romania (declared 1865, recognized 1885). The Patriarchate's reaction to the Bulgarian Church was much harsher: when the Bulgarian Exarchate was declared in 1872, the Patriarchate condemned it, defrocked its leaders, and, until 1945, viewed the Bulgarian Church as schismatic and heretical.

According to Pachalis Kitromilides, the reasons for such differences in the Ecumenical Patriarchate's approaches were based almost exclusively on religious considerations, mainly the unilateralism of the declarations of autocephaly in the newly established Balkan states. Kitromilides argues that this is why the Ecumenical Patriarchate immediately recognized the Serbian Church, while delaying recognition of the Greek and Romanian Churches, as the latter two did not fulfil the formalities required by canon law. Kitromilides further argues that the Patriarchate was consistent even in regard to the Bulgarian Church. He maintains that, because the Church had declared itself autocephalous prior to the establishment of the Bulgarian state, it did not meet one of the primary criteria of canon law, namely, that an independent Church could only be established in an independent state.[28]

The present book partially challenges this assumption. The religious reasons behind the attitude of the Ecumenical Patriarchate fully explain the cases of the Serbian Church, the Church of Greece, and the Romanian Church. But as we shall see, the case of the Albanian Orthodox Church supports the idea that, from the latter half of the nineteenth century on, religious considerations were secondary to political concerns in the reluctance of the Ecumenical Patriarchate to recognize autocephaly in nations with overlapping territorial claims with Greece. A comparison of the different outcomes in the Romanian and the Bulgarian cases makes this clear. In both cases, the Ecumenical Patriarchate cited the need to fulfil the standard requirements of canon law as its reason for withholding recognition. Yet, while the tomos of autocephaly was granted to the Romanian Orthodox Church just four years after the establishment of the Kingdom of Romania, the establishment of the Kingdom of Bulgaria in 1908 had no impact on the Patriarchate, which continued to view the Bulgarian Church as schismatic for another 37 years. This period coincides with the shared Greek and Bulgarian territorial claims to Ottoman Macedonia during the period of the Balkan Wars and the First World War, which brought about the dissolution of the Ottoman Empire.

This book illustrates that, with regard to the Albanian Church, the actions of the Ecumenical Patriarchate corresponded closely to the will of the Greek state. The Patriarchate nearly recognized the independence of the Albanian Church in 1923 and 1926, but both times reversed its stance, until it finally granted the tomos of autocephaly in 1937 – all decisions made at the request of the Greek government. The Patriarchate also replaced hierarchs in Albania, appointing those who had been requested by the Greek state in order to advance Greece's political aims. Furthermore, the Patriarchate's official ban on the Albanian and Bulgarian languages in the churches during the second half of the nineteenth century coincided with Greece's desire to annex the southern parts of Ottoman Albania and Ottoman Macedonia, arguing that every Orthodox in Albania and every Bulgarian-speaking *patriarchalist*[29] were in fact Greek.

After Greek independence in 1830, the end of the Phanariots' influence left the Ecumenical Patriarchate under the direct economic and political sway of the Greek state. According to Steven Runciman, the loss of the ecumenical character of the Patriarchate and its Hellenization had begun even earlier, in the second half of the eighteenth century with the abolition of the Serbian and Bulgarian autocephalous Churches, and was then reinforced when the Ottoman Empire purged the Phanariots in response to Greek independence.[30] Kitromilides attributes the Patriarchate's alignment with Greek *cultural* policies and Greek nationalism to a pastoral need for a new generation of hierarchs.[31] During this period, however, Orthodoxy grew weaker in Bulgaria and Albania, thus creating the opportunity for Byzantine Catholics (or Uniates)[32] to spread their faith among the Orthodox – the very opposite of tending to the pastoral needs of Orthodox believers. Byzantine Catholics began performing the liturgy in Albanian in an attempt to convert nationalist Orthodox Albanians.[33] The reasonable explanation, consequently, is that, from the mid-nineteenth century on, Kitromilides's theory applies only to cases in which Greece had no national interests. Thus, after the establishment of the Church of Greece, the Ecumenical Patriarchate came under the direct political influence of the Greek state and began undermining the ecclesiastical movements of Orthodox Albanians, Bulgarians, and Vlachs because these groups served as the main pretext for Greece's territorial aims. In contrast to the Serbian, Romanian and Greek cases, the decisions of the Patriarchate here were based on Greek political and nationalist considerations and not on religious grounds.

The Orthodox *symphony* principle helps to explain this crucial concept. The notion *symphony* was a doctrine that defined the rule of the people in the Byzantine Empire as a fusion between the political role of the state and the spiritual role of the church. According to this principle, the Church should not interfere in matters of the state and the state should not interfere in dogmatic issues.[34] As a result of this principle, the nationalist movements of the nineteenth century did not impact any dogmatic issue for the Ecumenical Patriarchate. Ethnophyletism – the emphasis of ethnic identity over the church – had been condemned as heretical, as it challenged the universal (catholic) nature of the Orthodox Church. However, support for the nation is the undeniable obligation of an autocephalous Church, so long as its believers are deemed part of a nation-state.[35] The role of the Ecumenical Patriarchate as the spiritual and administrative head of the *Rum millet* during the Ottoman Empire was religiously in line with the *symphony* principle, which is the chief reason why, initially, the Patriarchate officially denounced the Greek Revolution. The change occurred with the establishment of the Greek state and the Patriarchate's subsequent recognition of the autocephaly of the Church of Greece. This created a new paradigm for the Patriarchate. Gradually, the Orthodox Church's *symphony* with the Ottoman Empire shifted towards the Greek state, creating an unprecedented situation in which the Orthodox Church was aligned to a foreign state and not to the one in which it served. The Albanian, Bulgarian, and Vlach examples, which clearly illustrate the Patriarchate's realignment, were confirmed by the Greek state itself as it officially recognized the patriarch as the governor of the Greek nation within the Ottoman Empire.[36] Consequently, the Greek desire to keep the Albanian Church under its control clashed with the concept of *symphony*; meanwhile, the newly established Albanian nation desired to create its own *symphony* between Church and state in the hope of consolidating the nation-state.

Unlike the other Balkan peoples, the Albanians did not have an Orthodox majority. Although all the other ethnic groups in the Balkans included significant Muslim populations, they were minorities and so were excluded altogether from the nation-building process. In the case of Greece, this process was based entirely on the notion of the *Rum millet*, which comprised all Orthodox ethnicities living in the territories of the independent state. While in all other cases (the Bulgarians, Romanians, Serbs, and even the Montenegrins), the process included only the inhabitants within their respective areas who spoke the language of that ethnicity and adhered to the Orthodox faith, the Albanians were different because their various religious groups overlapped. The southern part of Albania had a strong Orthodox presence, which made up almost half the population there, with the others being mainly Bektashi Muslims. Central and north-eastern Albania was overwhelmingly Sunni Muslim, with a sizeable Orthodox minority and a small number of Catholics. In the north-western part of the country, the Catholics were the majority. Overall, during the nineteenth century, two-thirds of Albanians[37] were Muslim and one-third Christian. Moreover, no single religious group formed a majority, as two-thirds of the Muslims were Sunni and the rest Bektashi, while two-thirds of the Christians were Orthodox and the rest Catholic; there were also small Protestant and Jewish populations. Albanians thus had a double affiliation: they were simultaneously members of a religious *millet* and ethnically indivisible among themselves.[38]

This composition influenced the late rise of Albanian nationalism for a number of reasons. First, the religious makeup of their territory deprived the Albanians of foreign support. The Russian backing of Romania, Bulgaria, and Serbia had been of great importance in these Balkan states' achievement of their national goals, while the overall support of the Great Powers had been crucial for the Greek independence. However, the Great Powers were reluctant to let the Ottoman Empire collapse. The expansion of Russia's influence into the Balkans was seen as a threat by the other Great

Powers. Nor was the increase of Austro–Hungarian influence acceptable to the other powers. So the Ottoman Empire was left alive but weakened, and the Albanians, with their Muslim majority, were thought to be better off under the sultan. Only when the rise of South Slav nationalism, in the wake of the Treaty of Berlin, created the prospect of a unified Yugoslav state – to the alarm of both Austria–Hungary and Italy – did the Albanian national movement find allies among the Great Powers.[39]

Second, the Albanians were reluctant to back an armed movement. Nationalist Albanians of all religions feared that, without the support of one of the Great Powers, an Ottoman retreat would leave them unable to protect their lands from the encroachment of Serbs, Greeks, Bulgarians, and Montenegrins, all of whom had organized armies and foreign support. In addition, there were a minority of Muslims throughout the province who remained loyal to the Ottoman Empire. The Treaty of Berlin, however, became the catalyst for the rise of Albanian nationalism, as it clearly showed that existing under the umbrella of the Ottoman Empire was no longer a viable option for protecting Albanian lands, some of which the Treaty had awarded to neighbouring countries.

Finally, unlike other Balkan nations, there was no political, cultural, or religious organization within Albania that predated the incipient national movement. The Albanian Sunni and Bektashi Muslims were under the direct authority of the sultan, in his capacity as caliph, and so had no existing national institution available to them. The Orthodox Albanians, as nationalism developed in the Balkans based on different nation-defining criteria, seemed to belong to two nations: they were ethnic Albanians, and yet as part of the *Rum millet* they were counted among the Greeks. This double affiliation in the years before the National Renaissance later became the central controversy dominating Albanian–Greek relations. Greece hoped to assimilate the Orthodox Albanians if they came under its authority, despite the fact that Orthodox Albanians were at the vanguard of the ecclesiastical issue and the Albanian nationalist movement.[40] The situation resembled the division in Bulgaria between *patriarchalists* and *exarchists*.

Christianity in Albania and the lack of a religious linguistic tradition

The Albanians were one of two nations in the Balkans with no religious-linguistic tradition in the Orthodox Church prior to their national revival; the Romanians were the other. Whereas the Romanians managed to create religious-national institutions before they attained independence, the Albanians were unable to do this due to three factors. First, their national movement did not begin until the second half of the nineteenth century, when the Ecumenical Patriarchate was unwilling to tolerate national religious movements on those territories that were claimed by Greece. After 1878, the Ecumenical Patriarchate replaced all the metropolitans in lands inhabited by Albanians, due to their inability to counter the challenge of Albanian nationalism among the Orthodox. Second, the plurality of religious faith among the Albanians differentiated them from the largely homogeneous Orthodox Romanian nation. The third factor was the mixed religious-linguistic traditions among the Orthodox Albanians: while most followed the Greek tradition, a minority adhered to the Slavonic tradition.[41] Thus, the Orthodox Albanians differed from every other case in the Balkans.

The lack of an Orthodox Albanian religious-linguistic tradition and the Albanians' religious plurality, which caused their delayed national revival and the late emergence of the ecclesiastical issue, were the result of several complex factors, of which the common denominator was that Albanians lived in a territory with different rites and linguistic traditions. Ironically, although Albania was the second oldest evangelized territory in Europe, it had become a nation without a Christian majority and was only beginning its national revival. The Church in Albania had been founded in the first century by the Apostle Paul, who is mentioned as having travelled to Illyria, passing from Apollonia to Nicopolis.[42] The Albanian port of Durrës was an important hub of early Christianity and has had bishops and Christian communities since the middle of the first century. The first bishop of Durrës, St Caesarius, was succeeded by St Astius, who was crucified by the city's governor in AD 98 during Trajan's persecution of the Christians.[43] With the exception of the Greeks, all other nations in the Balkans were evangelized centuries after the ancestors of the Albanians.

During the first half of the first millennium, Albania was divided by the separation line of the Byzantine East and the Latin West, which later created a division between the Roman Catholics and the Eastern Orthodox. Although the lands of what is today Albania had been under the rule of the Eastern Roman Empire since 379, the churches in these lands remained under the Church of Rome until 732, when the Byzantine Emperor Leo III the Isaurian (ruled 717–741) put these dioceses under the authority of the Patriarchate of Constantinople. But the changing boundary between the two Roman empires also affected the ecclesiastical order. At times, the Church of Rome would extend its borders into several ecclesiastical districts, due to Western invaders such as the Normans, the Venetians, etc. The only place where the Catholic Church maintained uninterrupted influence was north-western Albania, where it exercised direct rule under the archdiocese of Bar. Among other things, the four Eastern Patriarchates (Constantinople, Alexandria, Antioch, and Jerusalem) differed from the Patriarchate of Rome by the language they used in the liturgy: they used Greek, while the Roman Church used Latin. Thus, changes in the ecclesiastical order affected not only the leadership in an ecclesiastical district but also which linguistic tradition it used.[44] The same bishops would change the ecclesiastical tradition whenever their political dependence changed. This was one reason why ecclesiastical institutions became weaker in territories where the Church of Rome bordered on the Church of Constantinople. The split between the Eastern Churches and the Church of Rome was formalized in 1054 by mutual anathema.[45] As a result, Albania found itself caught in the middle of Christianity's Great Schism.

Before Islam spread to the Balkans, the Orthodox experienced yet another divide in their religious linguistic traditions. The establishment in the Middle Ages of, first, the Bulgarian and, later, the Serbian Patriarchate resulted in the Church in Albania having three different linguistic traditions: Greek, Latin, and Slavonic. From the eleventh century until 1776, when the Bulgarian and Serbian Patriarchates were dissolved, most of what are currently Albanian dioceses were under the authority of the archbishopric of Ohrid, which, through most of its existence, used the Slavonic language. Thus, Orthodox in the central and north-eastern parts of the Albanian lands followed the Slavonic religious tradition of the Serbian and Bulgarian patriarchates, while Orthodox Albanians in the south followed the Greek religious tradition of the Ecumenical Patriarchate.

The Bulgarians and the Serbs had been able to create their own religious-linguistic traditions only because they possessed empires. Unlike the Greeks, Serbs, and Bulgarians, the Albanians did not have the historical legacy of a powerful empire that might allow them to create a single unified Church. The rule of the three major Balkan empires – Byzantine, Bulgarian, and Serbian – came to an end in Albanian lands before the conquest by the Ottoman Empire. In the interval, a number of small Albanian principalities emerged. The League of Lezhë, which convened in 1444, united all the principalities under the leadership of Gjergj Kastrioti Skanderbeg (1405–1468) to fight the Ottomans. The main leaders of the principalities belonged to the Orthodox religion, as they were heirs to the great Byzantine families from which they had received both their lands and the status that enabled them to seize power.[46] Skanderbeg, who would ultimately become the Albanians' national hero, was born into an Albanian Orthodox family of the Slavonic tradition. After being converted to Islam at a young age, he reconverted to Christianity when he launched his campaign against the Ottoman Empire. His reign coincided with the period of uncertainty that followed the Council of Florence.[47] Accordingly, he would be named *Athletae Christi* (Champion of Christ) by the pope, even though he was part of the Orthodox bishopric in his capital, the central Albanian city of Kruja. His spiritual father was the Orthodox monk Zaharia, while Skanderbeg, invoking an Albanian tradition, became the spiritual brother of a priest in Kruja, the future St Niphon, who was later elected as ecumenical patriarch (in office 1486–1488, 1497–1498, 1502). Both Zaharia and Niphon were liaisons between Skanderbeg and the archbishop of Ohrid in planning a great anti-Ottoman uprising that never took place.[48] Other Balkan states immediately established their Orthodox patriarchates with the relevant official languages. While their example might have been followed even in the Albanian case, the League of Lezhë was under constant attack from the Ottoman army, which made it impossible to create the kind of genuine state that would have had consequences in the religious sphere. Thus, the Albanians were left without a religious tradition in their own language.

This plurality of religious rites and traditions weakened Christian institutions in the Albanian lands and so facilitated the spread of Islam once the Ottoman Empire had fully overrun region in the late fifteenth century. This situation mirrored the one in Bosnia, another Balkan region where Islam spread on a large scale and was similarly introduced in the borderline of Orthodox and Catholic populations who shared a common language.[49]

The lack of an Albanian ecclesiastical tradition does not mean, however, that the Albanian language was not used in the churches. The Arbëreshë population in Italy[50] provide the first records of the liturgy in Albanian. The Arbëreshë were Orthodox Albanians that had fled Albania in the aftermath of the Council of Florence and maintained ties with the archbishopric of Ohrid until the middle of the sixteenth century. The consolidation of the Ottoman Empire's rule in the Balkans finally left the Arbëreshë under the sole authority of the pope in Rome.[51] Their Albanian liturgies were first reported at the beginning of the seventeenth century, but the tradition must have begun at least in the fourteenth century, when the Albanians still lived in independent principalities. Moreover, writing in Albanian by Arbëreshë missionaries[52] in the southern Albanian town of Himara during the early part of the seventeenth century[53] strengthens the idea that its use had spread as well to Orthodox liturgies in Albania. This proves that Albanian was used early in the churches, although it had no form of an ecclesiastical tradition, as Greek continued to be the main liturgical language. Meanwhile, a codex written in Greek in the fourteenth century includes a single sentence in Albanian. This codex and a baptismal formula from the fifteenth century are the earliest confirmed records of written Albanian.[54]

The use of Albanian in the Orthodox Church flourished in the eighteenth century, especially in Voskopoja and Elbasan.[55] The eighteenth-century manuscript known as *Anonymous of Elbasan* contains parts of the four Gospels translated into the Elbasan dialect using a special alphabet.[56] Meanwhile, in 1731, Nektar Tërpo Voskopojari (1665–1740), the abbot of Ardenica Monastery, wrote in an engraving: *Virgjin dhe Mamë eperndis uro prë nee fajtorët* (Holy Mary, Mother of God, pray for us sinners).[57] Reverend Konstandin of Berat drafted a 152-page prayer book, in which the first 46 pages were written in Albanian using the Greek alphabet.[58] These translations must also have been used in liturgies, as there is no other way to explain their accurate translation.[59] Dhaskal Todri, born Theodhor Haxhifilipi (1730–1805), continuing Konstandin's work, made numerous religious translations, of which the liturgy of St John Chrysostom and parts of the Gospels are all that have survived. The German scholar Johann Georg von Hahn (1811–1869) maintained that Dhaskal Todri had translated both the Old and New Testaments but the manuscripts were burnt in 1832.[60]

Metropolitan Grigor of Durrës was another student and professor at the Voskopoja Academy. In 1768, he translated all four Gospels into Albanian using an alphabet he himself created. During this period, there are a number of attested cases in which the liturgy was performed in Albanian. The most important work in Albanian, published shortly before the Albanian National Renaissance, was the translation of the Gospel of Matthew by Vangjel Meksi (1770–1821) and Grigor Gjirokastriti (metropolitan of Paramythia, 1799; metropolitan of Euboea, 1799–1821; and metropolitan of Athens, 1827–1828); it was published in Corfu in 1824 and republished in Athens in 1858.[61] Grigor Gjirokastriti spent most of his life as the metropolitan of Euboea, the lower half of which was inhabited by Albanians, and as the metropolitan of Athens at a time when Albanians were the overwhelming majority in Attica. He also translated the religious booklets *The Cross of Christ*, *The Life of Saint John the Baptist*, and *The Golden Law*, among others.[62] Moreover, the Ecumenical Patriarchate blessed his work. The Scottish missionary and the head of the Bible Society, Robert Pinkerton (1780–1859), recounts that the Patriarchate of Constantinople asked its clerics to translate the Bible into Albanian during the Orthodox–Protestant rapprochement. Pinkerton wrote on 15 October 1818 that the Patriarchate had "promised to send one or two clerics, skilled in Albanian, in order to assist Dr Meksi in his work and to make the translation as perfect as possible".[63]

The noted Albanian writer Konstandin Nelko Kristoforidhi (1827–1895), born in Elbasan, in central Albania, translated and published the New Testament, the books of Psalms, Proverbs, and Isaiah, and other parts of the Old Testament, as well as *The History of the Holy Scripture*.[64] Unlike the earlier work of Grigor Gjirokastriti, Kristoforidhi faithfully preserved the original form of the sacred text. His translation was considered so accurate that it is still being used two centuries later by the Orthodox Autocephalous Church of Albania.[65]

Apart from the Arbëreshë of Italy, the first voices calling for the establishment of an Albanian nation, prior to the League of Prizren, came from Orthodox Albanians. With the Ottoman Empire in decline, they had nothing to lose; on the contrary, they would benefit from a new order based solely on national affiliation. The person who first expressed the idea of an Albanian nation-state was Naum Veqilharxhi (1797–1846), who, though born in Albania, had moved to Romania as a young man; he may be considered the earliest precursor of the autocephaly movement. In the preface to his alphabet primer, *Evëtar* (1844), Veqilharxhi called for including Albanian in the religious service, as the existing situation did not allow Albanians to pray in their mother tongue. The Albanian activist Thimi Mitko (1820–1890) and the writer Jani Vreto (1822–1900) made similar efforts towards the comprehensive use of Albanian, including in the churches.[66] During his lifetime, Veqilharxhi experienced the two main periods in the transformation of the Church of Constantinople: from the time when it was ecumenical to its gradual development into an extension of the Greek state. Initially, Veqilharxhi's books were distributed by the diocese of Korça in the Orthodox schools of southern Albania.[67] But as the Patriarchate became more dependent on

Greece, attitudes changed and the Patriarchate requested that the Ottoman Empire intervene "to preserve the unity" of the Christian religion, which, it said, was threatened by Veqilharxhi's activities. The Albanians accused the Patriarchate of causing Veqilharxhi's death, which they claimed had occurred under suspicious circumstances.[68] Despite this, Orthodox schools in Albania played an important role in the education of the Orthodox elite – and also a number of Albanian Muslim nationalists – thus contributing to the rise of Albanian nationalism.[69]

These events laid the groundwork for the Albanian ecclesiastical movement, which flourished after the weakening of the Patriarchate's ecumenism and coincided with Greece's irredentist claims on the southern territory of Ottoman Albania and the rise of Albanian nationalism after 1878.

Linguistic conventions

For the purposes of this study, the term *Hellenist* is used in reference to Albanians, both Orthodox and Muslim, who considered themselves part of the Greek nation and worked against Albanian nationalism. They included such individuals as Dr Koço Noçka, Havjer Hrushiti, and Pandeli Kotoko. The term *Hellenophile* is used to describe Albanians who had a keen interest in Greek culture, but did not question their own national identity.

Geographical names are used in their English form if they are well known; otherwise, they appear in their original form. The proper names of hierarchs and other individuals mentioned in the book are rendered according to their national background, regardless of other forms under which they may have been known. For example, Evlogji Kurilla, who spent most of his active life in Greece, is better known in Greece as Ευλόγιος Κουρίλας (Eulogios Kourilas), the name he used when he wrote his Greek-language books. But in line with our convention, the Albanian form of his name is used here, since he was Albanian. In the case of names written in the Greek, Arabic, or Cyrillic alphabets, the "original form" refers to their transliteration into the Roman alphabet.

Notes

1 The League for the Defense of the Rights of the Albanian Nation, better known as the League of Prizren, was an alliance of prominent Albanian intellectuals, landlords, and military personnel, who were committed to resist any attempt to divide Albania among other Balkan countries (Greece, Serbia, and Bulgaria) and to raise the national consciousness of Albanians that they were a nation with a single language and culture, despite their religious divisions.
2 Ottoman Albania included the territories of four administrative divisions of the Ottoman Empire, namely, the vilayets of Iskodra (Shkodra, Albania), Kosovo (based in Skopje, North Macedonia), Yanya (Ioannina, Greece), and Monastir (Bitola, North Macedonia), which together comprised the territories that make up present-day Albania, Kosovo, north-western Greece, southern Serbia, eastern Montenegro, and the western part of North Macedonia. In 1911, the *Encyclopaedia Britannica* (11th ed) defined Albania as "a portion of the Turkish

empire extending along the western littoral of the Balkan Peninsula from the southern frontier of Montenegro to the northern confines of Greece". (James David Bourchier, "Albania", *Encyclopaedia Britannica*, 11th ed., ed. Hugh Chrisholm (Cambridge: Cambridge University Press, 1911)). Compact Albanian populations also lived in what are now southern Greece (the Arvanites), southern Italy (the Arbëreshë), and scattered villages in Thrace (in present-day European Turkey and north-eastern Greece). For the purposes of this book, all references to Albania before 1912 refer to Ottoman Albania or the lands inhabited by Albanians and not the current Republic of Albania.

3   The term *autocephalous Church* refers to an Orthodox Church that is not subject to the authority of another Orthodox Church. Autocephaly is recognized when the tomos of autocephaly is granted by either an ecumenical council, the relevant Church on whose territory the new Church is established, or the Ecumenical Patriarchate, based on various interpretations of canon law. The Church of Cyprus was the first autocephalous Church; it was granted autocephaly by an ecumenical council, a process that is now obsolete. With regard to the Balkans during this period, the other two interpretations amount to one and the same thing, as the territory in which the new Churches were established was that of the Ecumenical Patriarchate.

4   The Central State Archives of Albania (AQSH) and the Archives of the Ministry of Foreign Affairs of Albania (AMFA) are both located in Tirana. The Central State Archives of Greece (GAK), the Greek Logotechnical and Historical Archives (ELIA) are both in Athens, while the Institute of Northern Epirotic Studies (IBE) is in Ioannina, Greece.

5   Vasilios Kondis, *Ελληνισμός της Βορείου Ηπείρου και ελληνοαλβανικές σχεσείς, έγγραφα άπο το ιστορικό αρχείο του Υπουργείου Εξωτερικών [Hellenism of Northern Epirus in Greek-Albanian Relations: Documents from the Historical Archives of the Foreign Ministry]*, 4 vols. (Athens: Estia, 1995); French archival sources are found in Muin Çami, *Lufta e popullit shqiptar për çlirimin kombëtar 1918–1920 [The War of the Albanian People for National Liberation 1918–1920]*, 2 vols. (Tirana: Mihal Duri, 1975 and 1978); and British archival sources have been published in Valentina Duka, *Dokumente britanike për Shqipërinë dhe Shqiptarët, Vëllimi II, 1914 [British Documents of Albania and Albanians, Volume II, 1914]* (Tirana: Toena, 2012).

6   For example, Nicholas Pano, "The Albanian Orthodox Church", in *Eastern Christianity and the Cold War, 1945–91*, ed. Lucian Leustean (London: Routledge, 2010).

7   Nexhmedin Spahiu, *National Awakening Process Among Orthodox Albanians* (Hamburg, 2006); Qani Nesimi, *Ortodoksizmi te shqiptarët [Orthodoxy among Albanians]* (Tetovo, North Macedonia, 2005).

8   Dhimitër Beduli, *Kisha Ortodokse Autoqefale e Shqipërisë gjer në vitin 1944 [The Orthodox Autocephalous Church of Albania until 1944]* (Tirana: OACA, 2006).

9   Andrea Llukani, *Kisha Ortodokse Autoqefale e Shqipërisë: nga vitet apostolike deri në vitet tona [The Orthodox Autocephalous Church of Albania: From the Apostolic Time to Ours]* (Tirana: Trifon Xhagjika, 2005); Dhori Qiriazi, *Krishtërimi në Shqipëri [Christianity in Albania]* (Tirana: Argeta-LMG, 2000).

10   Academy of Sciences, ed. *70 Vjet të Kishës Ortodokse Autoqefale Shqiptare [70 Years of the Albanian Autocephalous Orthodox Church]* (Tirana: Institute of History, 1993), namely: *Koço Bihiku*, "Themelimi i Kishës Ortodokse Kombëtare dhe roli i Nolit [The Establishment of the National Orthodox Church and the Role of Noli]"; Fatmira Rama, "Sinodi i Parë Shqiptar dhe Kongresi i Dytë Panortodoks i Kishës Autoqefale Kombëtare [The First Albanian Synod and the Second Pan-Orthodox Congress of the National Autocephalous Church]";

Aurela Anastasi, "Statuti i Kishës Ortodokse Autoqefale Shqiptare dhe evoluimi i tij [The Albanian Autocephalous Orthodox Church Statute and Its Evolution]"; Muin Çami, "Kleri i Lartë Ortodoks në Shqipëri dhe Lëvizja Kombëtare Shqiptare në vitet 1912–1921 [The Orthodox Hierarchs in Albania and the Albanian National Movement 1912–1921]"; Valentina Duka, "Veprimtaria e Kishës Ortodokse Shqiptare të Amerikës (1912–1920) [The Activity of the Albanian Orthodox Church in the United States (1912–1920)]"; Alqi Jani, "Papa Pano Gjirokastra – Figurë e shquar e Kishës Shqiptare [Reverend Pano Gjirokastra – A Distinguished Figure of the Albanian Church]"; Kaliopi Naska, "Kongresi themeltar i Kishës Ortodokse Autoqefale në Berat [Foundation Congress of the Autocephalous Orthodox Church in Berat]".

11 Gerasimos Kondiaris, *Η Ελληνική Εκκλησία ως Πολιτιστική Δύναμις εν τη Ιστορία της Χερσονήσου του Αίμου [The Greek Church, as a Cultural Power in the History of the Peninsula of Haimos]* (Athens, 1948); Varnavas Tzortzatos (metropolitan), *Η Αυτοκέφαλος Ορθόδοξος Εκκλησία της Αλβανίας και οι βασικοί θεσμοί διοικήσεως αυτής [The Orthodox Autocephalous Church of Albania and Its Basic Managment Institutions]* (Athens, 1975).

12 Mihail Tritos, *Η εκκλησία στο ανατολικό Ιλλυρικό και την Αλβανία [The Church in the Eastern Illyricum and in Albania]* (Athens: Kiriakidi Afi, 1999); Apostolos Glavinas, *Ορθόδοξη Αυτοκέφαλη Εκκλησία της Αλβανίας [The Orthodox Autocephalous Church of Albania]* (Thessaloniki: AISF, 1992); and *Το αυτοκέφαλον της εν Αλβανία Ορθοδόξου Εκκλησίας επί τη βάσει ανεκδότων εγγράφων, [The Autocephaly of the Orthodox Church in Albania, Based on Unpublished Documents]* (Ioannina: Ioanian Foundation, 1978).

13 Lucian Leustean, ed., *Orthodox Christianity and Nationalism in Nineteenth Century South-Eastern Europe* (New York: Fordam University Press, 2014), 9.

14 On the role of the Ecumenical Patriarchate in the Ottoman Empire, see Steven Runciman, *The Great Church in Captivity* (Cambridge: Cambridge University Press, 1968); Leustean, ed., *Orthodox Christianity*, Sabrina P. Ramet, ed., *Eastern Christianity and Politics in the Twentieth Century* (Durham and London: Duke University Press, 1988). Regarding the nation building process in the Ottoman Empire, see Hannes Grandits, Nathalie Clayer, and Robert Pichler, *Conflicting Loyalties in the Balkans: The Great Powers, the Ottoman Empire and Nation-Building* (London: I.B. Tauris, 2011).

15 Leustean, ed., *Orthodox Christianity*, 6–13.

16 *Arvanite* is the exonym for the Albanian population in southern Greece who migrated from Albania beginning in the Middle Ages and once constituted the majority in Attica, Boeotia, the northern Peloponnesus, the Saronica Islands, and the southern part of Euboea. As the Greek Revolution was based within the *Rum millet* and the Arvanites were overwhelmingly Orthodox, they were gradually assimilated into the Greek nation in the nineteenth and twentieth centuries. Today, the Arvanite subdialect of the Albanian language is considered endangered, with only a few hundred native speakers remaining.

17 On the factors that led to the formation of the Greek nation, see Victor N. Roudometof, "From Rum Millet to Greek Nation: Enlightenment, Secularization, and National Identity in Ottoman Balkan Society, 1453–1821", *Journal of Modern Greek Studies*, 16 (1):11–48; and Paraskevas Matalas, *Εθνος και Ορθοδοξια [Nation and Orthodoxy]* (Iraklio: Panepistimiakes Ekdosis Kritis, 2003), 18–42.

18 Vjekoslav Perica, *Balkan Idols: Religion and Nationalism in Yugoslav States* (Oxford and New York: Oxford University Press, 2002), 74.

19 Currently Peja, Kosovo.

20 Runciman, *The Great Church in Captivity*, 84–94.

21 Leustean, ed., *Orthodox Christianity*, 9.

22   Barbara Jelavich, *Russia and the Formation of the Romanian National State,
     1821–1878* (Cambridge: Cambridge University Press, 1984), 287–290.
23   Carsten Riis, *Religion, Politics, and Historiography in Bulgaria* (Boulder: East
     European Monographs, 2002), 70–76.
24   Daniela Kalkandijeva, "The Bulgarian Orthodox Church", in Leustean, ed.,
     Orthodox Christianity, 164–203.
25   Riis, *Religion*, 116.
26   Ibid, 127–129; Paschalis M. Kitromilides, "The Ecumenical Patriarchate", in
     Leustean, ed., *Orthodox Christianity*, 14–33; Selim Deringil, *Conversion and
     Apostasy in the Late Ottoman Empire* (Cambridge: Cambridge University Press,
     2012), 68–75.
27   Arno Tanner, ed., *The Forgotten Minorities of Eastern Europe: The History and
     Today of Selected Ethnic Groups in Five Countries* (Helsinki: East-West Books,
     2004), 216.
28   Kitromilides, "The Ecumenical Patriarchate", 18–20.
29   The Bulgarian-speaking population of the Ottoman Empire was divided be-
     tween the *patriarchalists*, who followed the Patriarchate of Constantinople and
     were considered Greeks by Greece and Bulgarians by Bulgaria, and *exarchists*,
     who followed the Bulgarian Exarchate and were considered Bulgarians by both
     nations.
30   Runciman, *The Great Church in Captivity*, 185–211.
31   Kitromilides, "The Ecumenical Patriarchate", 23–26.
32   The churches referred to as Byzantine Catholic, Greek Catholic, Eastern Catho-
     lic, etc., are all Eastern Rite churches: their rites, traditions, liturgy, etc., are
     similar to those of the Orthodox churches, but they are in full communion
     with the Church of Rome and under the authority of the pope. All major move-
     ments in the Balkans that are the result of breakaway (schismatic) communities
     of Orthodox Churches are called *Uniate* (since they unite with the Church of
     Rome), a term that is often used pejoratively by the Orthodox. Regarding the
     Byzantine Catholics in Albania, see Ines Murzaku, *Returning Home to Rome:
     The Basilian Monks of Grottaferrata in Albania* (Grottaferrata, Rome: Analekta
     Kryptoferris, 2009).
33   Later, after the Albanian Orthodox Church declared its autocephaly, the Byz-
     antine Catholics began conducting the liturgy in Greek in order to attract
     the Hellenists. The Byzantine Catholics in Albania were missionaries from
     the Albanians of Italy, who had their own Italo-Albanian Byzantine Catholic
     Church, as is discussed later in the introduction. The only Byzantine Catholic
     jurisdiction that ever existed in Albania was the Apostolic Administration of
     Southern Albania, which was created in 1939 after the Italian invasion.
34   In Greek, the word *symphony* means "agreement". See Leustean, ed., *Eastern
     Christianity*, 1.
35   See also Joan Pelushi (metropolitan of Korça), "Kisha Ortodokse dhe konflik-
     tet etnike [The Orthodox Church and Ethnic Conflicts]", *Tempulli [Temple]*, 9
     (2004):1–9.
36   Greek Foreign Minister Lambros Koromilas noted in 1912 that the patriarch
     of Constantinople was "the governor of the Greek nation in the Ottoman Em-
     pire", quoted in Vasilios Kondis, *Albania and Greece 1908–1914* (Thessaloniki:
     Institute of Balkan Studies, 1976), 70–71. The Ottoman term *Rum Millet* can be
     translated as "nation of the Romans": the word Romans was often used to refer
     to the Greeks, because of the Greek cultural dominance in the Eastern Roman
     (Byzantine) Empire. Nonetheless, the *Rum millet* per se, included all Orthodox
     believers in the Balkans, regardless of ethnicity, and although the churches used
     Greek as its language, it was ecumenical (i.e. universal) in nature until the nine-
     teenth century. After the establishment of the Greek state, the term "the Greek

nation" as a synonym for the *Rum millet* was used in the sense of the alignment of the Orthodox populations of the Balkans not only with the Patriarchate (as the leader of the *Rum millet*) but also with Greece (as the motherland of that nation), regardless of the fact that these Orthodox populations were of different ethnic backgrounds. Thus, the title "governor of the Greek nation", attributed to the patriarch by the Greek state, implied his role as the extension of Greek national policy within the Ottoman Empire.

37 Excluding the Arbëreshë and Arvanites.

38 A number of anthropologists, writers, travellers, and scholars, who studied and visited Albania before its independence, noted that although Albanians belonged to different religious groups, they all had a strong ethnic identity and considered fellow Albanians from another religion as their kin, while viewing their co-religionists from a different ethnic group as foreigners. See, for example, Edith Durham, *High Albania* (London: Edward Arnold, 1909), 80–99.

39 On the birth of nation states in the Balkans and the attitudes of the Great Powers towards the Ottoman Empire and the nationalist movements within it, see Charles Jelavich and Barbara Jelavich, *The Establishment of the Balkan National States, 1804–1920* (Seattle and London: University of Washington Press, 2000); and Norman Rich, *Great Power Diplomacy, 1814–1914* (New York: McGraw-Hill, 1991).

40 Greece managed to assimilate Orthodox Albanians who remained in the lands it annexed: the Cham Albanians in north-western Greece and the Arvanites in the south. It should be noted that in the nineteenth-century Albanians in Greece did not have a "non-Albanian" identity. On the contrary, Albanian nationalists such as Panajot Kupitori (Panagiotis Koupitoris) and Anastas Kullurioti (Anastasios Koulouriotis) came from Athens, which at the beginning of that century had an Albanian majority.

41 The Slavonic tradition refers to Orthodox Albanians who followed religious traditions provided in Old Church Slavonic in areas once under the jurisdiction of the Archidiocese of Ohrid or the Serbian Patriarchate.

42 Dhimitër Beduli, *Kishë dhe kulturë [Church and Culture]* (Tirana: Institute of Dialogue and Communication, 2006).

43 Metropolitan Iakovos, *Asmatiki akolouthia tou Agiou endoxou ieromartyros Astiou: episkopou Dyrrachiou [Akoluthia of the Saint and Hieromartyr Astius, Bishop of Dyrrachium]* (Istanbul, 1918).

44 Qiriazi, *Christianity in Albania*, 52–72.

45 On the Schism, see Steven Runciman, *The Eastern Schism: A Study of the Papacy and the Eastern Churches during the XIth and XIIth Centuries* (Cambridge: Cambridge University Press, 1955); and Aidan Nikols, *Rome and the Eastern Churches: A Study in Schism* (Edinburgh: T&T Clark, 1992).

46 On the history of the medieval Albanian principalities and the League of Lezhë, see Academy of Sciences, ed. *Historia e popullit shqiptar [History of the Albanian People]*, vol. 2 (Tirana: Toena, 2007).

47 The Council of Florence, also known as the Council of Basel-Ferrara-Florence, was a series of ecclesiastical councils held between 1431 and 1449 that brokered a reconciliation between the Church of Rome and the Eastern Orthodox Churches; it was triggered mainly by the Ottoman offensive towards Constantinople and Byzantine pleas to create a pan-Christian alliance to defeat the Ottoman forces. The reconciliation recognized the supremacy of the bishop of Rome – the pope – and lifted the mutual anathema of 1054. After the fall of Constantinople in 1453, however, the Eastern Churches, in the Synod of Constantinople of 1484, condemned the decisions made by the Council of Florence. In the period between the Council of Florence and the Synod of Constantinople, the Eastern and Western Churches were seen as united. Thus it cannot be said

that Skanderbeg "returned to Orthodoxy" or "converted to Catholicism". The correct assertion is that he returned to Christianity and remained a Christian for the rest of his life – so there is nothing contradictory about the pope naming him the Champion of Christ even though he was in an Eastern Orthodox bishopric.

48 Beduli, *Church and Culture*, 143–156.

49 Peter F. Sugar, *Southeastern Europe under Ottoman Rule, 1354–1804* (Seattle: University of Washington Press, 1977), 52–53.

50 As mentioned in note 2, the Arbëreshë were immigrants from Albania and the Albanian-inhabited areas of southern Greece who settled in Italy after the Ottoman conquest of the Balkans. They retained their Orthodox traditions, but as they migrated during the period of the Council of Florence, when the Churches were reconciled, they came under the authority of the pope without being schismatic. Even today, the Arbëreshë retain their language and traditions in more than 50 villages in Calabria, Sicily, Puglia, and other parts of southern Italy. They played a pivotal role in both the Italian and Albanian national revivals in the nineteenth century and were, indeed, the first proponents of the Albanian Renaissance.

51 Murzaku, *The Basilian Monks*, 37.

52 Ibid., 63–83.

53 Dhimitër Shuteriqi, *Shkrimet shqipe në vitet 1332–1850 [Albanian Writing in the Years 1332–1850]* (Tirana: Academy of Sciences, 1976), 5–28.

54 Joan Pelushi (metropolitan of Korça), "Një vështrim i shkurtër historik mbi përkthimet fetare në Kishën Orthodhokse në Shqipëri [A Brief Historical Overview of Religious Translations in the Orthodox Church in Albania]", *Tempulli [Temple]* 2 (2000):4–25.

55 Evlogji Kurilla Lavrioti (Eulogios Kourilas Lavriotis), *Η Μοσχόπολης και η Νέα Ακαδημία αυτής [Voskopoja and Its New Academy]* (Athens, 1935), 22–24; Evlogji Kurilla Lavrioti (Eulogios Kourilas Lavriotis), *Grigorios, o Argirokastritis [Gregory, the Gjirokastran]* (Athens: Foinikos, 1933), 57–89.

56 Shuteriqi, *Albanian Writing*, 91–92; Nos Xhuvani, *Na flet Visarion Xhuvani [Visarion Xhuvani Speaks to Us]* (Tirana, 2008), 144–145; Kurilla, *Voskopoja*, 22–24.

57 Xhuvani, *Visarion Xhuvani*, 133.

58 Pelushi, "Religious Translations", 3.

59 Dhimitër Beduli, *Gjuha shqipe në Kishë [The Albanian Language in the Church]* (Tirana: Orthodox Autocephalous Church of Albania, 1997), 5.

60 Xhuvani, *Visarion Xhuvani*, 133.

61 Pelushi, "Religious Translations", 3–5.

62 Xhuvani, *Visarion Xhuvani*, 18.

63 This was the last period that the Albanian language enjoyed support from the Patriarchate of Constantinople. Metropolitan Joan Pelushi of Korça, in his recent overview of the history of Albanian religious translations, points out that in the late eighteenth and early nineteenth centuries, "the translation of Holy Scripture and the use of the Albanian language in religious services had developed to a considerable degree". Pelushi, "Religious Translations", 3–5.

64 Llukani, *Orthodox Church*, 34–35.

65 Beduli, *Albanian Language*.

66 Enis Sulstarova, "Lindja e kombeve dhe Naum Veqilharxhi [The Birth of Nations and Naum Veqilharxhi]", *Politika & Shoqëria [Politics & Society]* 2 (2004):91–103.

67 Eleftheria Nikolaidou, *Ξένες προπαγάνδες και εθνική αλβανική κίνηση στις Μητροπωλιτικές Επαρχίες Δυρραχιου και Βελεγράδων κατά τέλη του 19ου και τις αρχές του 20ου αιώνα [Foreign Propaganda and the Albanian National Movement in the Metropolitan Eparchies of Durrës and Velegrad during the Late Nineteenth Century and Early Twentieth Century]* (Ioannina: University of Ioannina, 1978).

68 Academy of Sciences, ed. *History V. 2*, 270. Even Naum Veqilharxhi's family circle was affected. A relative of Veqilharxhi's, a newborn baby, would die from the cold waiting for baptism after the priest refused to perform the service in Albanian. (Stefanaq Pollo, *Në gjurmë të historisë shqiptare, Volumi II [In the Footsteps of Albanian History, Volume II]* (Tirana: Institute of History, 2003), 85).

69 Koli Xoxi, *Shkolla ortodokse në Shqipëri dhe rilindësit tanë [The Orthodox School in Albania and Our Renaissance Men]* (Tirana: Mokra, 2002).

1 Origin of the Albanian ecclesiastical issue, 1878–1918

Ecclesiastical issue during the Albanian National Renaissance, 1878–1908

For Albanians who for four centuries had been living under Ottoman Turkish rule, the short-lived League of Prizren (1878–1879) marked the beginning of a national renaissance that spread through all religious communities, seeking a unified nation based on ethnic affiliation regardless of creed. As the League's philosophy gained support, neighbouring Greece and the Ecumenical Patriarchate began to alter their stance towards the Orthodox communities in Albania. The Orthodox faithful of Elbasan and Korça, the two Albanian cities with the fewest Hellenists, strongly embraced the fledgling nationalist movement and thus created friction with Greece.[1]

In an official 1879 memorandum, the metropolitan of Dryinopolis, based in Gjirokastra, Anthim Gjeci (1876–1880), a Hellenist Albanian, strongly denounced the new Albanian alphabet – devised and published by the prominent nationalists Pashko Vasa, Sami Frashëri, and Jani Vreto – and any books printed in Albanian. Vreto later wrote (in 1892) that Anthim had attached immortal disgrace to his own name by denouncing and cursing his mother tongue, a disgrace a thousand times worse than changing one's faith.[2] The official position of the metropolitanates in Chameria[3] – Ioannina, Preveza, and Paramythia – was even harsher. In this historically contested region, which today is located in Greece, the flourishing patriotic movement failed to overcome the obstacles put by the local Greek bishops. Following the League of Prizren, a Gospel appeared in the Albanian language, most likely the translation of Kostandin Kristoforidhi, which was subsequently used in the province. In 1881, Muslim and Orthodox Albanians living in Chameria assembled in the seaside town of Preveza and requested that the Great Powers recognize the Albanian nation and block Greece from annexing these territories. Even earlier, on 20 June 1880, the Committee of Margëlliç[4] had made a similar plea to preserve the territorial integrity of Ottoman Albania.[5]

The struggle for national identity intensified after nationalists established the first Albanian-language school, in Korça in 1887. Before this, the Ottoman authorities had forbidden the formal teaching of Albanian, in accord with the *millet* principle, by which Orthodox schools used Greek, Catholic schools used Latin, and Muslim educational institutions instructed pupils in Turkish. The Greek metropolitan of Korça, Filotheos Kostandinides (1885–1893), continually pressed Ottoman officials to close the Albanian school. The local authorities, however, denied his request, fearing conflict with the Albanians, with whom they had reached a modus vivendi following the relative failure of the Prizren League. Filotheos then excommunicated Thanas Sina, the school's first headmaster, and threatened to excommunicate all the teachers too, as well as any parents who dared send their children to study there.[6]

Korça would ultimately be at the forefront of the growing Albanian ecclesiastical movement. In 1888, Orthodox patriots in the city's cathedral petitioned the metropolitan to hold the liturgy in Albanian, but Filotheos refused and, in order to continue the liturgy in Greek, had to summon the Ottoman gendarmerie, made up of Muslims.[7] Ten years later, in 1891, tensions rose to the surface in Korça after the death of a man named Suli, a supporter of Sina's successor, Gjerasim Qirjazi. Filotheos refused to bury Suli in any of Korça's Orthodox cemeteries, a decision that led many in the metropolitan's flock to openly oppose the Church. Suli was then buried in a newly built cemetery, which became known as *Varreza e të Padëshiruarve* (the Graveyard of the Unwanted).[8]

Petro Nini Luarasi, the deputy headmaster of Qirjazi's school, played an important role in this conflict. With the aid of local residents, he tried to spread Albanian education to Korça and the surrounding areas. Inspired by Petro Nini Luarasi, a village priest named Stefan Luarasi began holding the liturgy in Albanian and teaching children in their mother tongue. The metropolitan of Kostur[9] excommunicated Stefan Luarasi and, with the help of the Ottoman gendarmerie, forced him into exile.[10] The metropolitan of Kostur wrote that Albanian was not a true language and would twist the conscience of the Orthodox mind.[11]

The situation was different in central Albania. In 1867, the Ecumenical Patriarchate appointed Visarion, an Albanian from Elbasan, as the metropolitan of Durrës. Visarion allowed teaching in Albanian in the schools of Elbasan, Tirana, and Durrës.[12] However, his pro-Albanian approach led the Patriarchate to consider him the worst possible choice for the Durrës diocese, so he was succeeded by Metropolitans Prokopios Lazaridis (from 1899 to 1906) and Ioannis Diakoumakis (from 1906 to 1911). Under Metropolitan Ioannis, pupils in Durrës schools had to pledge, under the threat of grave punishment, not to speak Albanian with each other.[13]

The metropolitanate of Florina, in what today is north-western Greece, also had a significant Albanian population. Negovani[14] was one of three Albanian villages where displaced Albanians from the Konica region had lived for several centuries. Reverend Kristo Negovani, the village priest and teacher, began a concerted effort to spread the use of Albanian in schools and churches, publishing nine educational religious texts in Albanian. He continued preaching and instructing in Albanian until 1905, when the metropolitan was apprised of his activities. On 10 February 1905, Reverend Kristo held the liturgy in Albanian in the presence of the metropolitan, who, cursing the priest, stormed angrily out of the service. Two days later, Kristo was murdered along with his brother and four other Albanian patriots.[15] On 9 September 1906, an armed group led by Albanian revolutionary guerrillas – the brothers Çerçiz and Bajo Topulli – and the activist and poet Mihal Grameno, took revenge by assassinating the metropolitan of Korça, Fotios Kalpidis.

The first substantial push to establish an Albanian Orthodox Church came from the United States of America. Theofan ("Fan") Noli, who was born in an Albanian village near Adrianople, in eastern Thrace,[16] had lived in Greece and Egypt before making his way to the United States. He believed that Albanians could achieve independence only if they united across social classes and religions.[17] In America, Noli's efforts towards the establishment of an Albanian Orthodox Church were done in cooperation with his employer, Sotir Peçi, the founder and publisher of the Albanian-language newspaper *Kombi* (The Nation), and Petro Nini Luarasi, who due to his conflict with the metropolitan of Kostur, had fled to the United States in 1904. The ideas of these three men coalesced after Kristaq Dishnica, an Albanian immigrant in Worcester, near Boston, Massachusetts, passed away in July 1907. Worcester's Greek Orthodox churches did not allow a religious funeral for Dishnica, who had refused to call himself Greek Orthodox and instead joined the Albanian national movement. The American metropolitanate of the Patriarchate of Antioch followed the Greek churches' example, and Dishnica was buried without religious rites.[18] Consequently, the Albanian Orthodox community in Worcester founded the religious association *Nderi Shqiptar* (Albanian Honour), which sought to resolve the ecclesiastical issue. This development caused the Greek Church to send Reverend Zaharia, an Albanian-speaking Greek priest from the villages near Gjirokastra,[19] to Massachusetts to rectify the matter. However, *Nderi Shqiptar* rejected this solution since Zaharia continued to hold the liturgy in Greek, contrary to the wishes of the Massachusetts Albanians.[20]

Nderi Shqiptar set up a commission that selected Fan Noli to be ordained as a priest in the Russian Orthodox Church, which was not subject to any Greek influence. Noli met with the Russian Archbishop Platon Fyodorovich Rozhdestvensky (in office 1907–1914, 1922–1934), who ordained him as a deacon and a priest on 8 March 1908. That same day, Noli performed his first service, baptizing the daughter of the leader of the Arbëreshë association. Two weeks later, as Petro Nini Luarasi sang the psalms, Noli held the first liturgy in Albanian. Noli said that the religious institutions in Albania had prevented his compatriots from uniting and blamed the cunning of Greek politicians who tried to present Albanian as a language cursed by Christ. Noli established Orthodox communities and churches in a number of New England towns and translated the first religious services into Albanian.[21] The Albanian press praised Reverend Theofan, and his name quickly spread to all centres of the Albanian national movement. He received numerous invitations to hold the Orthodox liturgy in Albanian, not only from Albania, but also from Albanian diaspora settlements in the United States and in the Balkans.[22]

The Albanian diaspora in Romania was another important hub for the growing ecclesiastical movement at the turn of the century. In a meeting on 27 May 1900, the *Drita* (Light) association in Bucharest made the establishment of an independent Albanian Church its main objective. *Drita* sought to create an independent Albanian state comprised of the four Ottoman vilayets inhabited by Albanians, with Albanian as its official language; the organization also requested that the words "Christian, Albanian" replace "Greek religion" or "Slavic religion" in the Ottoman passports of Christian Albanians.[23] Among other things, they created an Albanian church choir. In 1908, this choir was the first to sing the future Albanian national anthem, as adapted by Aleksandër Stavre Drenova, the secretary of the Albanian community in Bucharest.[24] These efforts, launched at the beginning of the new century, finally came to fruition on 1 November 1909, when Reverend Harallamb Çallamani, who had left the Ecumenical Patriarchate and joined other patriots in Bucharest, held the first liturgy in Albanian in Romania.[25] Soon after, on 6 December, members of the diaspora established the Albanian Orthodox Community, which would serve the newly created Albanian church of Bucharest, under the auspices of the Romanian Orthodox Church.[26]

Ecclesiastical movement in Albania on the eve of independence, 1908–1912

The Ottoman Empire was irrevocably changed by the Young Turk Revolution of 1908, which sought to restore the 1876 constitution, which had been suspended by Sultan Abdul Hamid. The Albanian nationalists welcomed the change, since initially the revolution allowed ethnic and cultural minorities to establish their own organizations. The Greeks, therefore, no longer enjoyed the Empire's protection in ecclesiastical and educational matters relating to the Albanians, who were now free to act without fear of persecution. The Ecumenical Patriarchate now saw first-hand that the Albanian national movement enjoyed tremendous support, especially among the Orthodox. On 12 September 1908, the Patriarchate sent a memo to 12 dioceses, urging Christians to maintain favourable relations with Muslim Albanians and requiring that the Albanian-speaking Orthodox not join the Albanian national movement, since in the Patriarchate's view they were Greeks. The Patriarchate instructed the metropolitanates to seek the opinions of its believers and introduce the Albanian language into the schools of the Albanian-speaking communities only if they believed this to be inevitable. Nevertheless, Greek remained the only language allowed to be used in the Orthodox Church in Albania.[27]

Greece, too, had not foreseen that support for the Albanian national movement would be so strong among Orthodox Albanians. They were even more shocked when it became evident that the vanguard of the Albanian movement was composed of elite members of the Orthodox community, including within the church elderships. On 21 September 1908, the Greek consul in Bitola expressed his belief that Greek officials had not done their best to strengthen the bond between the Albanian-speaking Orthodox and the Greek nation, thus leaving this population vulnerable to "Albanization". The Greek government blamed the bishops for their incompetent handling of the situation. During this period, many Albanian teachers in Greek schools had become pioneers in the growing national movement, a situation that eventually forced the Patriarchate to replace all bishops in areas with significant Albanian populations, from Preveza to Adrianople.[28]

Korça was the centre of the Albanian ecclesiastical movement. On 1 February 1909, Mihal Grameno, alongside dozens of Albanian patriots, established the Orthodox League, whose goal was the creation of an autocephalous Albanian Orthodox Church. On 10 July, the League began publishing its own newspaper, and in the first issue, in an editorial by Grameno, it announced its intention to spread the word of God to Orthodox Albanians by avoiding any foreign propaganda that tried to violate the ethnic and religious identity of Albanians.[29] Grameno, noting that history showed no other examples of the Gospel and the Cross being used as tools to plant enmity and denial between brothers and towards the motherland, accused the bishops of poisoning Orthodox Albanians with propaganda. He was repulsed by the bishops' curse on the Albanian language and their assertion that Christ was Greek and loved only the Greek language. Grameno noted that Greece had used these tools also against the Vlachs and the Bulgarians and reminded his readers that other nations had separated from the Patriarchate when they realized the danger they faced from its political utilization. He appealed to the Patriarchate to allow every nation to hold the liturgy in its own language and to stop working solely for the benefit of Hellenism. It was only a matter of time, he wrote, before the path paved by Reverend Fan Noli in the United States would reach Albania. Grameno ended with the assertion that the Albanian people would soon establish their own Albanian Orthodox Church.[30]

The Orthodox League met with Metropolitan Gervasios Sarasitis of Korça (in office 1906–1908) and asked him to begin using Albanian in the liturgy, baptisms, and funerals. The metropolitan expressed his support for their demands and vowed he would try to win the Patriarchate's approval.[31] The League's eldership threatened that, if the Patriarchate refused their request, they would bear no responsibility for the consequences.[32] Pandeli Cale, the only member of the League who was also a member of Korça's church eldership, asked the elderships in Elbasan and Berat to press their

own metropolitans to hold the liturgy solely in Albanian.[33] Inspired by
Reverend Theofan Noli's activity in the United States, the League asked all
Albanian priests to join the new ecclesiastical movement. Grameno urged
such priests to demand that the Patriarchate bestow the same rights on Albanians that all the other nations in the region had been given.[34]

The metropolitan of Korça had for many years faced demands from Albanians and Vlachs to hold the liturgy in their respective languages, since there
was no Greek-speaking population in the Korça region. In 1905, through
the intervention of the Romanian government, the Vlachs reached an agreement with the Patriarchate that allowed them to have their own church in
Korça; they were also ardent supporters of the Albanian liturgy, since they
considered themselves to be Albanian Vlachs.[35] But in October 1909, after
the church eldership of Korça began to side with the Albanian patriots, the
metropolitan replaced them with a new eldership that included only two
people from the city of Korça – the Albanian nationalists Vangjel Kota
and Kostandin Lako – while the rest came from the village of Voskopoja,
where there was a minority of Orthodox Albanians who identified as Greek.
Grameno mocked the metropolitan's "proper choice" of excluding several
patriots from the Korça eldership, specifically, Thimi Marko, Rafail Avrami,
and Kol Kaçiroi. Grameno noted that the body's new composition ensured
that Hellenism remained unchallenged, since all of its members were from
Voskopoja.[36]

In other articles, writing on behalf of the League, Grameno requested
support from the Albanian members of the Ottoman Assembly and begged
Patriarch Joachim III (born Xristos Dimitriadis, 1934–1912; in office as
ecumenical patriarch, 1878–1884 and 1901–1912) to review the situation.
He stressed that in a period of four months the Greeks had murdered four
priests – Spiro Tola, Reverend Vasil, Reverend Thoma, and Vasil Negovani –
simply because they had espoused the Albanian national cause.[37] The
League, he wrote, was asking the patriarch to act as any father would
towards his sons and carry out the teachings of Christ by stopping the metropolitans from spreading further hostility among the Orthodox and allowing
the use of the Albanian language. Grameno sought harsh measures against
those who had desecrated Orthodoxy and had turned the Gospel into a
political weapon.[38] The metropolitan of Korça replied to the League's letter
with a petition to the Patriarchate, which stressed that Grameno had lied to
both the government and the Patriarchate when he claimed that there was
any ecclesiastical dispute in Korça.[39] The Holy Synod of the Ecumenical
Patriarchate decided to allow the use of Albanian only in the new churches
that were about to be established. But the Patriarchate then refused permission for these churches to be built. Nonetheless, it allowed the priests to read
the psalms in Albanian as well as certain parts of the Gospels. Thus, for the
first time, after more than half a century of being prohibited, Albanian was
officially permitted in church services.[40] But this practice of holding the
liturgy in Albanian lasted only a few months, for the Young Turk movement

had in the meantime changed its position and was now attempting to turn the Ottoman Empire into a centralized Turkish national state. In February 1910, the Ottoman authorities banned all ethnic associations and outlawed the Orthodox League as an "Albanian community".[41] The League's closure enabled the Korça metropolitanate to restore Greek as the only language allowed in churches.[42]

The other important hub of the Albanian ecclesiastical issue was the metropolitanate of Durrës. Metropolitan Ioannis expressed his despair at the continued growth of the Albanian movement and likened it to an unstoppable stream. On 17 July 1908, the Greek consul in Durrës reported that before the Young Turks reinstated the Ottoman constitution, the Orthodox had identified as Albanians by ethnicity and "Greek Rum" by religion, but after the inclusion of the Albanian language in education, they identified only as Albanians. The metropolitanate expelled Pavllo Terka and Ilia Lavda from the church eldership for having led an Albanian nationalist association. This made it clear to the Orthodox in the Durrës region, all of whom were Albanian, that the Patriarchate and Greece were determined to promote Hellenism and would not support the demands of Orthodox Albanians.[43]

Apart from everything else, the alphabet issue was still creating friction. Albanian did not have a single unified alphabet until 1908, having previously been written in Roman, Greek, Arabic, Cyrillic, and even ad hoc invented alphabets. On 13 August 1908, the Greek government allowed the Orthodox faithful to write in Albanian but insisted that they use the Greek alphabet to do so, regardless of what other Albanian religious communities were doing. The Albanian patriots in Korça and Elbasan, meanwhile, used a Roman-based alphabet created by the Albanian *Drita* association in Sofia, Bulgaria. The Durrës church eldership thanked the Greek government for their missive on 16 August, but they did not follow its instructions; instead, they insisted that the alphabet must be the same for all Albanians.[44]

On 17 July 1908, the Orthodox elite of Tirana demanded that Albanian become the official language of the Orthodox community and be taught in its religious schools. The central town of Elbasan, where the majority of the metropolitanate's Orthodox lived, became a centre of anti-Greek sentiment. Greek officials estimated that the Orthodox of Elbasan displayed more enmity against Hellenism than did the Muslims, despite having been educated in Greek secondary schools and universities. In November 1909, the Greek consul in Durrës reported that all the Orthodox of Elbasan, even a number of teachers and priests who received salaries from the metropolitanate, were staunch Albanian nationalists. Half the teachers in the newly established Albanian-language Normal School of Elbasan had previously taught in Orthodox schools. Meanwhile, without the metropolitan's approval, Albanian began to be included even in the metropolitanate schools in Elbasan – a practice soon followed by schools in Kavaja and Tirana. In early 1912, a number of Elbasan Orthodox sent a letter to the metropolitanate requesting the introduction of Albanian in girls' schools as well. The metropolitanate and the Greek consulate decided to allow one additional lesson in the Albanian language. This was a genuine achievement for the Albanians, although admittedly a small one, since by now persecution by the Young Turks had resulted in a large reduction in the number of Albanian educational institutions.[45]

The Orthodox Albanians in southern Albania had been continually demanding the introduction of the Albanian language in their churches. In the Chameria region, the metropolitan of Ioannina denounced the two Albanian schools in the region, in Filat and Paramythia, and supported the armed Greek mobs attacking Orthodox Albanian villages that backed the national movement.[46] In 1908, a number of residents in Zagoria, Gjirokastra, led by a local teacher named Ilia Dilo Sheperi, sent a letter to the patriarch, in which they proudly proclaimed that they were Orthodox Albanians and demanded that the liturgy be performed in their mother tongue. The Patriarchate excommunicated Dilo, and, at its request, the Ottoman authorities arrested, tortured, and sentenced him to death. The sentence, however, was commuted, and Dilo was only banished from Zagoria.[47] On 12 January 1909, the priests and believers in the metropolitanate of Velegrad, based in the town of Berat, demanded the introduction of Albanian in Orthodox schools. The eldership denied their request and suggested instead that the Albanians establish their own schools.[48]

On 12 May 1910, the Greek government asked the patriarch to oppose any change in the status quo that could favour Albanians.[49] The metropolitans continued their efforts to convince the Orthodox faithful to turn their backs on the Albanian movement.[50] The Greek government estimated that there were around 200,000 Orthodox Albanians.[51] It instructed both its consulates and the metropolitanates to publicly refer to them not as Albanians but as Albanian-speaking Greeks.

The Greeks received strong support from the Ottoman authorities. The Ottoman foreign minister, Adil Haci, visited Korça in 1911 and was satisfied that the city had a "Greek community" that used only the Greek language, and that the Albanian movement was not spreading. Mihal Grameno nevertheless submitted a request to Haci to allow Albanian to be used in churches; the Ottoman minister promised to review the request but never did.[52]

The metropolitanates of Durrës and Korça thus became fervent centres of the Albanian national movement in the period immediately prior to Albanian independence. The local Orthodox were largely in favour of the Albanian cause, with only a small number of Hellenists. The behaviour of the Greek government and the metropolitans had created friction between a considerable portion of Orthodox Albanians and the Greek state. Albanian demands were also very clear among the Orthodox in Berat and Gjirokastra, even though Hellenist metropolitans ruled over the church elderships. In Paramythia, Ioannina, Nicopolis, and Dibra, Orthodox Albanians were a minority alongside majorities of, respectively, Greeks, Vlachs, and Slavs, so the metropolitanates refused to consider their growing demands.

Nevertheless, the Albanian ecclesiastical movement was becoming a powerful wave in the period before independence – a wave that would eventually triumph.

Activity of the Orthodox hierarchs in the newly independent Albanian state

When the Balkan War began on 8 October 1912, a group of Albanian nationalist elite decided that Albania should declare independence. A handful of patriots, including Ismail Qemali bey Vlora (1844–1919; served as prime minister, 1912–1914), initially planned to take the first step towards independence in Durrës, but this proved impossible. The metropolitan of Durrës, Iakovos Gkigkilias (in office 1911–1919; as exarch of Korça, 1919–1921; as metropolitan of Mytilene, 1925–1958), born in Izmir in the Ottoman Empire, had been appointed to his position four years earlier. Iakovos had been deeply shaped by the concept of establishing a much stronger Greece that would span "five seas and two continents".[53] From the moment he arrived in Durrës, Iakovos attempted to set up a wide network of informants to facilitate his political role; he also supported the city's Greek consul. Moreover, he was a good friend of Greek Prime Minister Eleftherios Venizelos.[54] Metropolitan Iakovos met with Ismail Qemali and informed him that the Ottoman Empire was not yet dead and that Qemali would never raise the Albanian flag in Durrës.[55] Iakovos's stance was influenced by the Ottoman Empire's decline and a possible change in the ecclesiastical status quo. He expected that the arrival of forces from Serbia, the ally of Greece (and Venizelos) during the Balkan War, would alter the circumstances.[56] During the liturgy, the metropolitan preached that Ismail Qemali was an extremist Muslim who sought an Islamic independent Albania, and that this would destroy the harmony between religious communities.[57]

From 1908 to 1911, the Greek government had provided political and financial support to Ismail Qemali. This ended when it became apparent that the Albanian goal was to have an independent country comprising the vilayets of Kosovo, Shkodra, Manastir,[58] and Ioannina. Greece made no claims on Kosovo, Shkodra, or Manastir. The red line in Albanian–Greek relations was the Ioannina vilayet, a territory historically known as Epirus, or in modern times, Toskëria, where the two nationalities were interconnected as minorities and majorities in different areas. In June 1912, the Greek foreign minister, Lambros Koromilas, sent a memorandum to all consular agents in Albania with instructions regarding the government's stance on what constituted the *terra irredenta* of Greek Epirus: the Ottoman sanjaks of Preveza, Igoumenitsa, Ioannina, most of the sanjak of Gjirokastra, and half of the *kaza* (sub-district) of Vlora, part of the Berat sanjak. Koromilas stressed that Greece would not assist the Albanians if armed conflict against the Turks should arise. Athens was, however, willing to include Albanian as a foreign language in Greek schools, but it would oppose any attempt to conduct the liturgy in Albanian inasmuch as this was "forbidden by the rules of the Orthodox Church".[59] Metropolitans Vasil Papakristo (1858–1936; metropolitan of Dryinopolis, 1909–1916) and Germanos Anastasiadis (1870–1941; metropolitan of Korça, 1910–1915), who were in direct contact with Athens, rejected the request to send delegates to the National Assembly of Vlora, where the Albanians were about to declare independence. Some Orthodox priests, however, did take part in the process. Reverend Dhimitër Dhimitruka, the dean of Elbasan, made a significant contribution to the election of representatives to the Vlora Assembly; Reverend Jovan Plaku raised the Albanian flag over the ancient fortress of Berat; while Reverend Pano Çuçi, in Gjirokastra, Reverend Isaia in Vlora, Reverend Josif in Korça, and dozens of other priests continued to fight for the Albanian cause.[60]

On 28 November 1912, in Vlora, delegates from all the provinces and religious communities declared the independence of Albania and established the first independent Albanian government, which was led by Ismail Qemali. Three ministers – Pandeli Cale, the minister of agriculture; Lef Nosi, the minister of the post and telegraph; and Petro Poga, the minister of justice – represented Orthodox Albanians. The government, which was based in Vlora, ruled only a limited area around the city since, by this time, most of the Albanian territories were occupied by the various forces fighting in the First Balkan War.[61]

By the time its troops arrived in Durrës, Serbia had conquered all of central Albania – "the promised land" of Serbian lore. Metropolitan Iakovos and the Greek naval forces, positioned in the waters just opposite the city, were the first to welcome the Serbian army. Serbia was an ally of Greece, Bulgaria, and Montenegro in the war to expel the Ottomans from the Balkans. Thus, Iakovos had established cordial contacts with Serbia's political representatives, as well as with the patriarch of the Serbian Orthodox Church. The Serbian king awarded the metropolitan the Cross of St Sava, and Prime Minister Nikola Pašić presented him with a gold watch in which he had engraved his own initials.[62]

Meanwhile, Greece had conquered a portion of southern Albania with the aim of annexing it. The first province to expel the Turkish army and declare its incorporation into Greece was Himara, on 5 November, under the leadership of Spiro Spiromilo. As a strong Greek nationalist, Metropolitan Vasil praised the move and appointed Archimandrite Ierothe as his deputy in Himara.[63] The metropolitans and their entourages welcomed the invading troops when they marched into Korça (on 19 December 1912), Gjirokastra (16 March 1913), and Tepelena (19 March). In these towns, the soldiers were greeted not with the Greek national anthem, but with the paschal hymn "Christ is Risen" – despite it not being Easter.[64] Christians who proclaimed themselves Albanians suffered the same consequences as their Muslim compatriots. The same pattern can be seen a few weeks later when Greece invaded Chameria. Upon entering the region, Greece did its utmost to sow conflict between Orthodox and Muslim Albanians; they took full advantage of the fact that the Christians in the area were landless and lured their support by redistributing Muslim-owned lands – a reversal of the favouritism the Ottomans had shown the Muslims when it came to property issues. Many Orthodox Cham Albanians, however, rejected the Greek offer of properties owned by Albanian Muslims, and as a result, Greek forces did not spare the inhabitants in the Cham Orthodox villages of Stanova and Shenica in the Margëlliç district.[65]

On 2 December 1912, the countries involved in the First Balkan War declared a truce. The following day, a conference of ambassadors convened in London to resolve a number of issues, including that of Albanian independence. The fighting continued, however, and the Greek and Serbian occupations of Ioannina and Durrës signalled the collapse of the western reach of the Ottoman Empire. The Greek army had been in control of Thessaloniki since early November 1912, while the major cities of Ottoman Macedonia fell one by one into the hands of the Serbs, the Greeks, and the Bulgarians. Bulgaria captured Adrianople, not long after the Great Powers of Europe – the Great Britain, France, Germany, Russia, Austria–Hungary, and Italy – began negotiations in London. The newly established Albanian government sent a delegation comprised of Filip Noga, Rasih Dino, and Mehmet Konica to demand recognition of Albanian independence and lobby for their national goals. On 23 March 1913, the delegation told the Greek representatives that Albania would accept the rule of a Greek prince but only if the border between the two countries were drawn at the Lura River, thus leaving Ioannina, Preveza, and the entire Chameria region within Albania.[66] Greece rejected this proposal. Its army was already in central Albania, so it had no reason to withdraw.

The negotiations ended on 30 May 1913 with the signing of the Treaty of London. It was decided that, with the exception of Albania, the Balkan League – consisting of Greece, Bulgaria, Serbia, and Montenegro – would divide up most of the lands east of the Ottoman Empire in Europe. The Treaty of London recognized Albanian independence, placing the country under the guaranty of the six Great Powers; it would be led by a prince the Great Powers would choose, an event set to take place a few months later, on 29 July. Since Albanian independence would also affect the religious institutions in Albania, the autocephaly of the Albanian Orthodox Church was anticipated.[67] In Durrës, in June of that year, the Albanian minister of internal affairs, Myfit Libohova, declared that the goal of the Vlora government was to remove the Orthodox dependence on Constantinople. Metropolitan Iakovos expressed to Libohova his hope that the fledgling government would nevertheless preserve the Patriarchate's privileges, which "even barbarian governments like the Ottoman one" had so far respected. Libohova responded that the Patriarchate and the metropolitan should confine their concerns to their religious duties and put an end to the surge of anti-Albanian propaganda.[68]

In September, the government issued an order that foreign schools could operate only with its permission, which put it into conflict with the sole metropolitan whose jurisdiction overlapped with territories ruled by the Vlora government. Metropolitan Joakim Martishti (1875–1953; as metropolitan of Velegrad, 1911–1917), met with Luigj Gurakuqi, the minister of education, and requested that the schools operated by the metropolitanate remain open with the lessons being taught in Greek. When Gurakuqi refused, Martishti made an official request to open Greek-language schools, which caused even more friction with state officials.[69]

In October 1913, a former Ottoman military leader of Albanian origin, Esad Pasha Toptani, established a senate in central Albania that opposed the Vlora government. He was willing to award the Southern Albania to Greece, and his split from the Vlora government created a shift in the balance of power.[70] By now, Serbian troops had left Durrës after an ultimatum by the Great Powers. Metropolitan Iakovos then requested that Greek troops immediately invade the port city to ensure that "the Albanians" (the implication being that all Albanians were Muslim) did not jeopardize the lives of the 50,000 "Greek Orthodox" – who, in fact, were all ethnically Albanian. When it became clear that Greece could not intervene militarily, Athens began to utilize Esad for its own ends.[71] The talks between him and the Greek government attracted the attention of the Great Powers, the guarantors of Albanian independence. The Greek envoy in Podgorica, Montenegro, informed his government that Esad Pasha could be persuaded to act on their behalf, but only through bribery. Metropolitan Iakovos saw to the payment of the bribe. Along with being a priest of the Church, Iakovos was also a friend of Prime Minister Venizelos and a trusted agent of the Greek government, whom Athens employed for tasks they needed done in Albania. The metropolitan's clerical cassock did not prevent him from carrying out this particular sin of corruption.[72]

In January 1914, the British consul in Vlora notified his government in London that Iakovos had given 150,000 gold francs to Esad to pursue Greece's goals in Albania.[73] The conditions were clear: Esad should accept the annexation of southern Albania up to the town of Pogradec and recognize the same rights the Orthodox had enjoyed under the Ottoman *millet* system. Esad agreed to this proposal.[74] Greece's political intention was to annex Gjirokastra and Korça and, once this was done, they would set about establishing a Greek minority of Albanian-speaking Orthodox under the authority of the patriarch of Constantinople, whom the Greek Ministry of Foreign Affairs considered "the ruler of the Greek nation in the Ottoman Empire".[75]

The Great Powers had decided that an international commission should set the borders of Albania based on the ethnic composition of the settlements. They had previously stipulated that the land from the seacoast up to the bay of Ftelia, including the island of Sazan, across to the shore of Lake Ohrid at the Church of St Naum would remain in Albania. The commission would review the western border between Albania and Greece from Ioannina to Korça. They would then determine the nationality of the settlements there based on the language spoken at home.[76] In Korça, Greece maintained a small network of loyalists around Metropolitan Germanos, in addition to the occupying authorities under the command of General Alexandros Kontoulis, an Arvanite. In August 1914, the Korça church eldership, led by Germanos, made a formal request to Prime Minister Venizelos that Greece annex Korça,[77] which Venizelos agreed to.[78] Athens had a vastly superior military force ready to be used against the Albanians, and it was in charge throughout the region visited by the members of the border commission. This was the so-called Sacred Battalions – military units that together comprised 40,000 well-trained and well-equipped war veterans, mainly Cretans, whom the official Greek army had labelled "deserters", as it did not want to be held responsible by the Great Powers. The atrocities committed by these battalions forced many Albanians, most of them Muslims, to flee to the Vlora area governed by the independent Albanian state.[79]

The border commission began their work in Korça. The Greek officials there, led by Kontoulis and Metropolitan Germanos, had come up with a plan. They denied the commission's request to visit nearby villages and instead had them view a parade of schoolchildren. Hundreds of pupils from the metropolitanate marched with Greek flags in front of more than 4,000 armed members of the Sacred Battalions.[80] Hasan Qinami, an Albanian patriot from the village of Borova in the Kolonja region, managed to ruin the staged display. He took some coins from his pocket and threw them to the ground. When the children rushed to collect the coins, they began shouting in their mother tongue – Albanian – clearly disproving any claim that they were Greek.[81]

Having discovered that the parade was a hoax and that Korça was Albanian, they turned their focus to villages south of the city, in the region of Kolonja. There, in every village the commission passed through, Greek officials had contrived a scenario in which Albanian men, speaking Greek, would meet the international delegation. The commission soon became aware of this scheme and asked to meet men other than those brought to them by the Greek officials or to meet women, since women did not usually speak any foreign language. In the village of Borova, the Greek battalions expelled the commission members when they tried to enter a house where soldiers had besieged the residents, who did not speak Greek.[82] The Greek authorities also sent women to the Albanian villages from the Greek-speaking region of Pogoni, trying to pass them off as locals. But even local priests objected to the orders from Metropolitan Germanos. Shortly before the commission arrived in Vodica, the residents sent away the women who had been brought there by the Greek officials. All the Orthodox Albanians, including the village priest, Reverend Pashko Vodica (1881–1966; later, under the name Pais, he served as metropolitan of Korça, 1948–1949, and archbishop of Albania, 1949–1966), revealed the Greeks' plan to the commission.[83] On 31 October, Austria–Hungary and Italy announced that they would recognize as Albanian territory any village where Greeks were obstructing the commission's work.[84]

The Greeks' activity in Korça and Kolonja and the problems they created in Gjirokastra meant that the commission never had a chance to inquire about the wishes of the thousands of Albanians in Chameria. On 11 August, when further investigation proved impossible, the Great Powers established the frontier based on geographical criteria and the minimal requirements outlined by Austria–Hungary. On 17 December 1913, the commission signed the final agreement, the Florence Protocol, after which the Great Powers issued an ultimatum ordering Greece to withdraw behind the newly drawn Albanian border. Athens, however, delayed the withdrawal in hope of a more favourable outcome. That same month, King Constantine I of Greece announced that he was willing to abdicate his throne and lead voluntary military units himself in order to protect Northern Epirus.[85] The king backed down from his pledge only after the Great Powers informed him that Greece would be allowed to annex the islands in the Aegean the day after its armies departed Albanian territory.[86]

Athens then moved to "Plan B", setting up so-called National Protection Commissions in every city in southern Albania.[87] Greece appointed the metropolitans of Korça and Dryinopolis (based in Gjirokastra) as chairmen of their respective city commissions. In Përmet, Kolonja, Tepelena, and Delvina, the commissions were led by Greek army officers under the supervision of Georgios Zografos, the governor of Ioannina.[88] On 28 February 1914, Metropolitan Vasil of Dryinopolis convened an all-Epirote congress in Gjirokastra and declared the independence of "Northern Epirus". The metropolitan denounced the idea of awarding Epirus to "the unknowns of history, the Albanians, who are protected by the West", declaring: "Either free Greek Epirus, or death and destruction!"[89] The congress had no Muslim representatives, although Muslims constituted 50 per cent of the population, or anyone representing the Orthodox majority who desired union with Albania. The congress's outcome was, therefore, a foregone conclusion, and Vasil raised the flag of autonomy of the unilaterally proclaimed Epirote state, with the metropolitanate as its seat of government.[90] The congress elected a government led by Georgios Zografos and comprised the three metropolitans: Vasil of Dryinopolis, Germanos of Korça, and Spyridon of Vella and Konica.[91]

The Greek euphoria was short-lived. Two days later, after the Great Powers' ultimatum, Korça passed under the control of the Albanian government. Athens had nevertheless begun to implement its plan: on 24 February, the Greek army, led by Lieutenant Colonel Demetrios Doulis, entered Gjirokastra and was welcomed by Metropolitan Vasil.[92] The Greek army declared that Doulis was a deserter, and Zografos appointed him as war minister of Northern Epirus's interim government. A few days later, Zografos appointed his own son-in-law, Alexandros Karapanos, a Greek member of parliament from Arta, as foreign minister.

As the chaos grew, the Great Powers went ahead with their plan to choose a monarch for Albania. They selected the German Prince Wilhelm of Wied, who arrived on 7 March 1914 in Durrës, the newly declared capital. Prince Wied (as he was known) ruled Albania alongside the International Control Commission, composed of representatives from the Great Powers, which had been overseeing the management of the Albanian state since Ismail Qemali's resignation in January of that year. Clinging to the hope that Prince Wied could maintain a unified Albania, all the country's social classes welcomed him, including beys and petite bourgeoisie, Muslim and Christian leaders, foreign representatives, and the local population, from both south and north.[93]

On 8 March, just a day after Prince Wied's arrival, Metropolitan Iakovos became one of the first people to clash with him. The Orthodox of Durrës celebrated Orthodoxy Day with a special liturgy in the city's cathedral. Iakovos prayed for the Orthodox kings, whose representatives were present at the liturgy, but made no mention of the prince of Albania. At the end of his sermon, Iakovos announced that the official liturgy honouring the prince would take place the following Sunday.[94] Even so, most of the people attending the liturgy were furious at the metropolitan's failure to mention Prince Wied. Iakovos informed the Patriarchate that around 60 Albanians, led by Minister Mihal Turtulli, complained to the chairman of the International Control Commission. Turtulli and the other protesters requested a meeting with the prince regarding the incident, but Prince Wied denied their request.[95] The prince's secretary, a Briton named Duncan Armstrong, recalled that on 8 March, to honour the prince, a commemorative religious service took place in the Durrës mosque and in the city's Roman Catholic church, both attended by civil and military officials and foreign representatives. All of Albania's religious leaders except the Orthodox metropolitan had welcomed the new prince and pledged their allegiance.[96] Iakovos, meanwhile, argued that the rules of the Orthodox Church did not allow him to mention the new ruler because Prince Wied was a Protestant.[97]

Another development soon added to Iakovos's difficulties. The next day, Theofan Noli arrived in Durrës on 11 March 1914. That morning, voices echoed through the streets of the city calling on the Orthodox faithful to attend a liturgy held by Noli in honour of Prince Wied. As soon as Iakovos learned that a young Orthodox priest was challenging him, he sent the prince a letter saying that as the metropolitan of Durrës he alone could give permission for an Orthodox liturgy, and that Noli had received no such permission. But the letter requesting Noli to cease his activity did not arrive in the prince's hands until the liturgy was over. On 11 March 1914, Reverend Theofan and Reverend Damian, from Berat, held the liturgy in Albanian in front of the Royal Palace, with a pulpit set up especially for the occasion. Most of the city's elite and the Orthodox faithful stood before them, as well as Catholic and Muslim clerics and the Dutch garrison in the city. In his sermon, Reverend Theofan recalled that Iakovos in his liturgy had included the names of the Serbian and Greek kings, the enemies of the motherland who had slaughtered innocent Albanian women and children, but had omitted the name of the country's current ruler.[98] He invited all Albanians to unite behind the prince and fight for the sovereignty of the Albanian nation.[99] Iakovos had called on the Orthodox in Durrës to stay away from Noli's liturgy, but clearly the majority had not complied.[100]

In Korça, meanwhile, a Greek uprising disrupted the new Albanian state. On 4 April, the Dutch officer who commanded Korça's gendarmerie announced that there was evidence that Metropolitan Germanos was the main instigator behind the repeated uprisings. The Dutch then arrested Germanos and imprisoned him in Elbasan, along with the church eldership. The Greek press reported that Germanos had been wounded,[101] prompting Metropolitan Iakovos to request his release, but Prince Wied denied the request. After seeking instructions from the Greek government and the Patriarchate,[102] Iakovos asked Esad Pasha to intervene and threatened to start a general Orthodox uprising if the government did not release Germanos and the eldership.[103]

The departure of the Korça metropolitan changed the situation. Local officials, led by the Prefect Pandeli Evangjeli, appointed a new temporary eldership, headed by Reverend Josif Qirici. The new eldership and the city's Orthodox elite sent a telegram to the Great Powers requesting intervention; they hoped that this would make Greece abandon its claims on Korça. On 25 April, 323 Orthodox patriots from Korça demanded that the clergy either hold the liturgy in Albanian or be immediately dismissed, and that they remember Prince Wied in every religious service. The new eldership decided that Albanian would be the sole language of the Church and, for the first time in the Church's history, they began keeping records in Albanian.[104] This, however, lasted only until June, when Greek military forces again invaded Korça, under the guise of insurgents from Northern Epirus.[105] Still, it is important to note that this was the first time Albanian became the sole official language of a jurisdiction.[106]

The events in Korça accelerated Prince Wied's decision to intervene in the south, where, months earlier, Greek troops had declared the independence of Northern Epirus. Wied assigned the military intervention to Esad Pasha Toptani, his minister of war and interior affairs. Years later, Iakovos would recall that the productive secret network the Greeks had developed under his direction made it impossible for the Albanian government to launch military troops in the south.[107] Prince Wied later wrote that through this network Iakovos had informed Greece of Esad's intention to send 20,000 armed troops.[108] On 4 April, Greece's envoy in Albania reported to his country's Foreign Ministry that Esad was willing to comply with the Greek government's instructions in exchange for a 100,000 drachmas.[109] The Greek foreign minister, Georgios Streit, was confident that Esad Pasha was sincere, owing to his ambition to rule central Albania and create a future Albanian–Greek alliance. Even so, Streit, concerned that Esad might be a double agent for Italy, instructed the envoy to inform Esad that Greece had no territorial claims over Albania but was only requesting his help in obtaining an agreement for acceptable concessions in Epirus.[110]

The Principality's advance against the Northern Epirote insurgents was suspended after the intervention of Iakovos and the bribery of Esad from Greece. At the same time, Prince Wied faced another uprising, this time from Muslims in central Albania who still adhered to the precepts of the Ottoman Empire. These Turkish loyalists, supported by Esad Pasha Toptani, launched a coup d'état, which was led by the landowner Mustafa Ndroqi and the cleric Haxhi Qamili. The rebellion aimed to restore the Turkish *millet* system and, thus, on 8 June 1914, as soon as they gained control of Elbasan, the pious Muslim rebels released Metropolitan Germanos and the deposed Korça eldership from prison. Once freed, the metropolitan went to Athens, where he met with Prime Minister Venizelos and Foreign Minister Streit.[111]

It was not until late June that the connections between the Northern Epirus uprising, the uprising in central Albania, Metropolitan Iakovos, and Athens became clear. By then, the Muslim insurgents had surrounded Durrës and were calling for negotiations with the British Colonel George Phillips, who assisted Prince Wied. Phillips met the rebels on 27 June and informed the prince that they were insisting that Albania either rejoin Turkey or be assigned a Muslim prince as ruler. They also told Phillips that a Greek Orthodox priest had complained about Wied.[112] One of the rebels' demands was that Metropolitan Iakovos be allowed to visit their camps. The prince then convened his Crown Council, which was attended by representatives of the Great Powers.[113]

Prince Wied began the proceedings by stating that Metropolitan Iakovos had played a role in the uprising in central Albania. Russia's representative objected to this assertion, saying that Iakovos was simply a spiritual leader to whom Christians turned for advice. He later advised the hierarch to meet with the Albanian prime minister, Turhan Pasha, and deny any involvement. Turhan Pasha, aware of the metropolitan's relationship with Haxhi Qamili and Mustafa Ndroqi, told Iakovos that he would give him as much money as he wished to stop the uprising, but Iakovos replied that it was too late for him to assume such a responsibility.[114] Iakovos later recalled:

> By being in the Albanian prime minister's office, I understood that Prince Wilhelm's regime had declined. The Albanians themselves were internally ruining the Albanian Principality through the uprising of Mustafa bey. Any effort by me to save [the Albanian state] would be a colossal stupidity, an unforgivable mistake, almost a national crime. As a result, I left [the regime] to die.[115]

Iakovos's intentions are clear. The insurgents had urged the Albanian government not to attack Northern Epirus. The British representative in Durrës reported that the rebels in central Albania opposed the mobilization of troops to attack the south, arguing that since the Great Powers guaranteed Albania's impartiality, it was "Europe's" duty to secure the country's borders.[116] The Austro–Hungarian representative in Durrës informed his Foreign Ministry that far too many coins minted in Greece were turning up in the rebel provinces and that the Orthodox priests in Kavaja had incited the uprising due to the strong connections between the insurgents and Iakovos.[117]

This period coincides with the culmination of negotiations in Corfu regarding the Northern Epirus uprising. These talks concluded with the Corfu Protocol, which provided forms of autonomy for the prefectures of Gjirokastra and Korça. The Albanian representative, Mehdi Frashëri, considered this a violation of Albania's territorial integrity. On 3 June, the British representative, Harry Lamb, stated that the Corfu Protocol had paved the way for Greece to annex Epirus, which the Albanian government strongly opposed due to pressure from the populace of Korça. Lamb noted that the central Albanian uprising, which Greece had financed and supported, had changed the balance of power, making a war with Greece impossible.[118]

The Great Powers forced Albania to accept the Corfu Protocol. However, Georgios Zografos, the Northern Epirote prime minister, informed the International Control Commission that he would not sign the accord. The British believed that he wanted to benefit from Albania's weakness and would reject the entire agreement.[119] The outbreak of the First World War and his careful coordination with the central Albanian insurgents gave Zografos the hope that the time had come to invade Korça and annex it to Greece. On 22 June, the Greek Foreign Ministry ordered Zografos not to attack Korça and to avoid giving any indication that the Greek government was cooperating with either the Northern Epirus insurgents or those in central Albania.[120] But just a few days later, on 10 July, Greek Prime Minister Venizelos found another reason to invade Northern Epirus. He argued that an international army – or in its absence the Greek army – should occupy Epirus until Albanian troops were in place.[121] This about-face came after a one-on-one meeting between Zografos and Venizelos on 26 June. Zografos told the press that if he ceded Northern Epirus to Prince Wied, Muslim insurgents would attack Orthodox villages. The newspaper *Empros* (Forward) wrote that Zografos had no connections with the central Albanian uprising and that the insurgents knew he was impartial in this matter, but if Prince Wied were to take control of Northern Epirus, the central Albanian insurgents would immediately attack the Epirotes for violating the terms of the Corfu Protocol.[122] Greece used a clever reasoning in its approach towards the uprising it had incited and funded. Zografos and Venizelos said they were "obligated" to hold onto Northern Epirus, not because of any territorial claims, but because they had to defend the populace from possible attacks by the central Albanian insurgents who in fact were also financed by Greece.

Meanwhile, in those few days between Greece's two controversial stances, the important Albanian cities of Berat and Korça fell into rebel hands. The central Albanian insurgents took Berat, while the Northern Epirotes occupied Korça. In both cases, the two movements coordinated with each other. In his memoir, Prince Wied mentioned a letter he received from the central Albanian insurgents in Berat, who said they were undertaking a joint action with the advancing Greeks in the south, who had joined forces with the Triple Entente and Italy.[123] Korça's Prefect Pandeli Evangjeli announced that the Northern Epirotes seized Korça on 10 July due to the cooperation between the two movements.[124] Evangjeli had organized an army of 4,000–5,000 men, but finding themselves between the fires of two armies, they had been forced to withdraw from the Epirote front. Evangjeli reported that Iakovos had been the liaison between the two insurgencies. Immediately after arriving in Korça, the Northern Epirotes began setting fire to Muslim villages with the aim of driving the population out of the prefecture.[125] They also killed any Christian Albanians, including women and children, who refused to proclaim themselves as Greeks. The Epirote fighters massacred entire villages in Kolonja, forcing the survivors to flee to the remaining few square kilometres of free Albanian territory around Vlora. The Epirote assembly approved the Corfu Protocol on 5 August 1914, under the condition that Northern Epirus be given the right to unite with Greece.[126] Shortly afterward, in September, the central Albanian insurgents succeeded in occupying Durrës, only a few hours after Prince Wied fled his capital, never to return.

Prince Wied's rule was too short to put up any strong opposition to the secular and political role played by the Greek metropolitans in Albania. Faced with tremendous challenges, the prince had had neither time nor opportunity to deal directly with the ecclesiastical issue. Nevertheless, his government did succeed in laying the foundations of the Church's autocephaly when, on 10 April 1914, it approved the Organic Statute of Albania. Article 176 of this statute stipulated that the Albanian government would seek special agreements with the highest spiritual leaders of the religious communities in Albania.[127] The Northern Epirote insurgents knew that their power came from the metropolitans and the networks they ran; thus, the ecclesiastical issue became one of the most important topics in the Corfu talks. Zografos demanded that Albania recognize its Orthodox communities as juridical persons with full immunity from the state and insisted that the relationship between the Orthodox communities and their spiritual leaders could change only through an agreement between the Albanian government and the Ecumenical Patriarchate.[128] The Albanian government stressed that the Organic Statute had included many articles concerning the religious communities and that the Corfu Protocol went beyond them. All the same, Wied's short-lived government called on the International Control Commission to negotiate an agreement with the Patriarchate on the issue of the Orthodox Church in Albania, noting that it was confident the

Commission "would not act against the Albanian national interest".[129] The Albanization of the metropolitanate of Korça shows the prince's desire for a solution to the ecclesiastical issue, but his brief reign deprived him of any chance to develop an autocephalous church.

The Great War and the Albanization of the Church

The First World War broke out in July 1914 and the first battlefront was the border between Serbia and Austria–Hungary, within the Balkans. At the beginning of the conflict, Austria–Hungary was struggling to defeat the Serbian troops, while the other Balkan and Adriatic countries – Italy, Greece, Bulgaria, and the Ottoman Empire – were not yet involved in the war. Thus, when Prince Wied turned the governance of the country over to the International Control Commission, no nation other than Greece was threatening military intervention in Albania.[130]

Consequently, the two insurgent movements that had been spreading chaos throughout Albania – both financed by Greece and both inspired by the Ottoman *millet* system – were able to gain control of much of the country. The central Albanian uprising dominated the north and much of the country's southern half, including the important cities of Berat and Vlora. Greece, meanwhile, discarded its mask of neutrality and, on 27 October 1914, invaded Korça and Gjirokastra with the help of some of Zografos's autonomist troops. The local metropolitans chose not to subordinate themselves to the ecumenical patriarch, who had canonical jurisdiction over them, but in compliance with the political will of the Greek state, placed themselves instead under the authority of the Holy Synod in Athens.[131]

Metropolitan Germanos returned to Korça despite the Albanian courts having convicted him of the military uprising – a clear violation of the rules of the Orthodox Church. He ordered an immediate ban on the ecclesiastical use of Albanian, which by then had been flourishing for several months. He elected a new church eldership, which included no Albanians but only Greek émigrés even though Albanians constituted all of the native Orthodox in Korça, a fact that even the Greek state acknowledged. In Gjirokastra, Metropolitan Vasil thanked Venizelos and King Constantine for their support of the Northern Epirotes. He also asked that the male population be conscripted into military service alongside the Greek army.[132] Greek soldiers had killed hundreds of Albanians in Gjirokastra, but the metropolitan had failed to raise any complaint. The most shocking event was in Hormova, in the Tepelena district, where irregular troops forcibly assembled more than 200 villagers in a shrine and burned them alive. Vasil made no protest whatsoever, despite there being Orthodox among the victims.[133] Even such supporters of the Corfu Protocol as Vasil Dilo had expressed their outrage over the Hormova massacre and pleaded with Zografos and Doulis, the minister of war, to put a stop to the atrocities. The Northern Epirotes had a particular hatred of Muslims, but their rage did not spare

Orthodox Albanian patriots either. Doulis publicly announced that he had ordered the killing of anyone who fought against Greece.[134]

In Durrës, the rebel leaders Mustafa Ndroqi and Haxhi Qamili took power after the triumph of the central Albanian uprising. Three days after capturing the city, the insurgents set up a governing senate, which elected Iakovos as vice chairman, while Esad Pasha proclaimed himself the new prime minister of Albania. The insurgents, however, soon turned on Esad, who had been their primary supporter, ousting him in January 1915. Iakovos, who felt accepted by all sides, remained neutral, expressing his loyalty to both parties. Esad Pasha was Iakovos's friend, while Haxhi Qamili had given the metropolitan the same degree of power he had held under the Ottomans. In May 1915, Qamili pledged to punish anyone who did not attend church, did not honour the priests, or walked out on the liturgy, which of course would be held only in Greek.[135]

Other developments in the Balkans, of which Iakovos was regularly apprised by the Greek prime minister, further prompted the hierarch's neutrality. Bulgaria objected to the losses it had suffered in 1913, in the Second Balkan War, and wished to expand its territory to the regions now occupied by Serbia and Greece in Macedonia and Thrace. Greece, for its part, sought to conquer Ottoman lands in Asia Minor and Western Thrace. Italy, then still an ally of the Central Powers, had yet to be embroiled in the war. Thus, in early 1915, both the Triple Entente (Great Britain, France, and Russia) and the Central Powers (Germany and Austria–Hungary) sought alliances with Greece, Bulgaria, and Italy, urging them to enter the conflict. Venizelos was willing to accept the Entente's offer, but King Constantine objected, arguing that neutrality was the best course of action. The king believed that the Central Powers had larger military capabilities and would win the war. The conflict between the two men soon escalated when Greece's ally Great Britain declared war on the Ottoman Empire, which had sided with the Central Powers. Venizelos resigned on 21 February and called for early elections.[136]

Italy was the first of Albania's neighbours to abandon its neutrality. On 26 April 1915, it signed a secret treaty in London with France and Great Britain. The Entente pledged that Italy would be allowed to annex Austrian lands in the Tyrol and on the Adriatic coast, including the cities of Trieste, Zara (Zadar), and Ragusa (Dubrovnik). In addition, the treaty approved Italian sovereignty over Vlora and promised that what would remain out of Albania would become an Italian protectorate. Serbia, Montenegro, and Greece would each acquire part of the Albanian state, although they had yet to sign the treaty. In May 1915, Italy, Montenegro, and Serbia all invaded Albania, not with the immediate aim of territorial expansion but primarily to capture strategic positions for defeating their opponents. The exception was Greece, which officially annexed Northern Epirus. Bulgaria entered the war on the side of the Central Powers on 27 September 1915, attacking the

Serbian army, which capitulated in November and retreated to central Albania, along with the Serbian royal family, who were welcomed in Durrës by Metropolitan Iakovos at the metropolitanate. Their stay was brief; however, a few weeks later, Austria–Hungary and Bulgaria forced the Serbs to withdraw to Corfu. In the end, Austro–Hungarian forces controlled most of Albania.[137]

Bulgaria's alliance with the Central Powers led to a schism within the Greek state. Prime Minister Venizelos set up a parallel government in Thessaloniki and declared war on the Central Powers. This prompted Italy to invade southern Albania, including attacks on Gjirokastra, Saranda, and Delvina, which by then were controlled by the King Constantine's government in Athens, which supported the Central Powers. Concerned that Greek troops would surrender to Bulgaria or to armed Albanian guerrilla forces, France sent troops to Korça.[138] The Albanian guerrilla units of Sali Butka and Themistokli Gërmenji surrounded the Greek army in the city and demanded their immediate surrender. On 24 October 1916, Greek officials informed King Constantine that none of Korça's male population had enlisted in the army and that the Greek soldiers had lost all will to fight and wanted to return to their homeland. They also admitted that the Albanian national movement had grown significantly stronger, especially among the Orthodox.[139] On 28 November, three years to the day after Albania declared independence, French troops invaded Korça under the command of Colonel François Descoins (the commander of Korça, December 1916–May 1917). In the meantime, Great Britain and France were trying to persuade King Constantine to join the Entente. The king's refusal led to the Entente's recognition of the Venizelos government on 2 December 1916. Bulgaria had thus inadvertently accelerated Greece's internal division, the French expulsion of the Greek troops from Korça, and Italy's extension of power to Gjirokastra, Saranda, and Delvina.

The French envoys in Korça met with representatives of the population and concluded that both Muslim and Christian Albanians were ready to go to war if Greece again attempted to annex the region. The French army sought to maintain internal stability and prevent any rebellion, so their focus could be on fighting Bulgaria and Austria–Hungary. The various intentions of Greece, Italy, and Esad Pasha would have to wait. Negotiations between Korça's representatives and Colonel Descoins ended with the signing of the Protocol of Korça on 10 December 1916. The protocol stipulated that the Korça region would be self-governing, run by Albanian civil servants under French military protection. A council composed of 14 members, half Muslim and half Orthodox, would govern the region. The protocol also established two gendarmeries, both headed by Themistokli Gërmenji, who became the de facto leader of this entity, which was referred to locally as the Republic of Korça. The official language was Albanian, and the flag was similar to the Albanian flag, only with a French tricolour strip added. The governing council was composed entirely of Albanian nationalists, and the nationalist politician Koço Kota won the municipal elections.[140]

Metropolitan Germanos had left Korça prior to the departure of the Greek troops and arrived in Athens on 1 December 1916. Before leaving, he held a liturgy in which he mentioned both Venizelos and the king. The Greek military viewed this as part of a larger plot, with Germanos attempting to put Korça under the sway of the Thessaloniki government. Consequently, they had forced Germanos to go to Athens, where he apologized for his mistake and declared his allegiance to Constantine. Germanos had left Reverend Petro as the provisional vicar of the diocese of Korça, instructing him to ensure that the city's church eldership continued to be fully Hellenist.[141] Under the circumstances, however, the eldership was supported neither by the invading French army nor the local Orthodox community and so complied with the demands of the populace and restored Albanian as the official language of the Church.[142] From May 1917 to the end of the Korça Republic in 1920, the eldership kept all its records in Albanian.[143]

In Gjirokastra, the occupying Italian troops immediately announced their recognition of Albania's independence and territorial integrity. As a result, the Italians were enthusiastically welcomed by the local population. The expulsion of Metropolitan Vasil Papakristo on 22 September 1916 was one of the new governors' first moves: they justified their action on the grounds of the metropolitan having engendered the hatred of the populace by his support for the Republic of Northern Epirus and his complicity in the massacres committed under his supervision.[144] But the chief reason for Vasil's expulsion was his alignment with the royal government in Athens, which meant also with the Central Powers. Fourteen soldiers escorted Metropolitan Vasil out of Albania. In 1917,[145] the Italian authorities appointed Archimandrite Taras Koroni as vicar of the diocese of Gjirokastra, and for the first time in more than half a century, Reverend Pano Çuçi held the liturgy in Albanian in the fortress city.[146]

The southern Albanian city of Përmet was an exceptional case. Përmet, although under Italian occupation, was a deanery of the diocese of Korça. Albanian Orthodox patriots wished to rid themselves of the Hellenists running the deanery, but the Italians had done nothing about this because the local church leaders were not politically active against the Entente. The tense situation reached its peak at a meeting organized by the Italian army on 17 May 1917, when Vasil Dhaskali, the director of the metropolitanate's school, spoke in Greek. Reverend Stathi Melani left in protest, along with the Albanian nationalists Spiro Kosova, Koço Tasi, Dhimitër Kacimbra, and Viktor Plumbi. A decision was made to replace the dean of Përmet, Reverend Stavro, with Reverend Stathi. The next day, the four nationalists went to the deanery headquarters without Stathi Melani. Tasi told Reverend Stavro, his cousin, that they wanted to dismiss him because anyone who denied his mother tongue and his motherland did not deserve to be in charge of the city's Orthodox faithful. After exchanging harsh words with Reverend Stavro, they removed him from the building by force.[147] The eldership appointed Reverend Stathi as dean, who then formalized the use of Albanian in all churches under his supervision. Months later, on Christmas Day, Stathi was assassinated by a group of armed Greek irregulars. In March 1918, the journal *Albania* published the sentiment that there was no Albanian heart that did not grieve and no Albanian eye that did not weep for this great martyr of the nation.[148]

In Durrës, too, the situation had turned against the Greeks. In April 1916, an Albanian priest, supported by a choir of children and a group of local parishioners, began performing the liturgy in Albanian in the presence of Metropolitan Iakovos.[149] But the metropolitan's downfall was also politically motivated, though for the opposite reason to what had brought about the fall of Metropolitans Germanos and Vasil. Iakovos was one of the few Greek hierarchs who had supported Venizelos and the Entente; most had condemned the prime minister's activity and even excommunicated him because of his split with King Constantine.[150] Consequently, the rise of the Venizelos government in Thessaloniki had led to Iakovos's political revival, since in various ways it was obstructing the Central Powers troops in Durrës. Austro–Hungarian officials accused Iakovos of using his spy network to inform the Entente about their activities and to organize an armed rebellion in metropolitanate territories bordering on Entente-held lands. The occupying forces in Durrës expelled Iakovos, who ended up in Constantinople in April 1917.[151] The Austrian Military Court in Tirana sentenced him in absentia to seven years in prison as a collaborator with the Entente and a friend of Venizelos.[152]

In Berat, the centre of the Velegrad metropolitanate, things were remarkably different. Initially, when Albania declared its sovereignty, Metropolitan Joakim Martishti had taken a neutral and independent view, in sharp contrast to that of the Athens government. But after realizing that Albania would remain under the control of the Great Powers, Martishti renounced his neutral stance and supported his Albanian compatriots. Even the central Albanian insurgents, who had supported all the Greek metropolitans, did not behave kindly towards Martishti. When they invaded Berat, they forced him to flee to Vlora as revenge for his nationalist Albanian position.[153] Although at the outset the Italian forces had a positive partnership with the metropolitan, they eventually expelled him as a collaborator with the Central Powers.

Consequently, all the metropolitans left Albania: some were driven out by the Central Powers for cooperating with the Entente, while the Entente expelled the rest for collaborating with the Central Powers. In the end, thanks to the unforeseen circumstances of the First World War, the Albanian language was introduced into the Church throughout Albania without violence.

Figure 1.1 Albanian Pupil at the School of Negovani.

Figure 1.2 Fan Noli and the Albanian Diaspora in USA, 1908.

Figure 1.3 Father Stathi Melani and His Son.

Figure 1.4 The Head of the Orthodox League, the Albanian Renowned Poet, Publicist, and Revolutionary, Mihal Grameno.

Figure 1.5 Themistokli Gërmenji Raising the Albanian Flag and Establishing the Albanian Republic of Korça.

Notes

1 Nikolaidou, *Foreign Propaganda*, 308–309.
2 Pollo, *Footsteps*, 85.
3 At the time the region of Chameria, in north-western Greece and southern Albania, was inhabited by Albanians, Greeks, and Vlachs. In the ethnic cleansing at the end of the Second World War, however, Muslim Albanians were expelled from the region and Orthodox Albanians were assimilated.
4 A town in the Chameria region in north-western Greece, later renamed Margariti.
5 Blerina Sadiku: *Lindja e Çështjes Çame 1820–1943 [The Birth of the Cham Issue 1820 – 1943]* (Tirana: Naimi, 2011).
6 Pollo, *Footsteps*, 87.
7 Pollo, *Footsteps*, 89.
8 Nikolaidou, *Foreign Propaganda*, 342.
9 A town in north-western Greece, present-day Kastoria.
10 Petro Nini Luarasi, *Μαλκimi i Ckroŋavet Cqipe de çpεrfoja e Cqipεtarit [The Curse of Albanian Letters and the Slander of Albanian]* (Monastir: ITP, 1911), 3.
11 Luarasi, *The Curse*, 14–16.
12 Dhimitër Beduli, *Shënime për bashkësinë ortodokse të Tiranës [Notes on the Orthodox Community in Tirana]* (Tirana: Neraida, 2007).
13 Nikolaidou, *Foreign Propaganda*, 343.
14 Present-day Flampouro.
15 Visarion Xhuvani, *Vepra: Për Kishën Orthodhokse Shqiptare; Në Kuvendin e Shqipërisë; Për jetën dhe veprën [Works: On the Albanian Orthodox Church; at the Assembly of Albania; about his Life and Work]*, Nos Xhuvani dhe Pavli Haxhillazi ed. (Tirana: 55, 2007), 249.
16 Today, Edirne, Turkey, where there were once a number of villages inhabited by the Albanian diaspora. Noli was born on 6 January 1882. He served as a member of the Albanian parliament from 1921 to 1924 and as prime minister of Albania from 16 June to 23 December 1924. In 1919, he proclaimed himself the bishop of Boston and Kruja, the exarch of Illyria, a title he claimed until 1923, when he was canonically ordained and installed as the metropolitan of Durrës (1923–1924). He served as the archbishop of Boston of the Albanian Orthodox Church in America from 1924 to his death on 13 March 1965. Apart from his clerical and political career, Noli is noted as one of the most prominent Albanian poets, writers, and translators.
17 Fan Noli, *Autobiografia [Autobiography]* (Tirana: Elena Gjika, 1994).
18 Nasho Jorgaqi, *Jeta e Fan S. Nolit [Life of Fan. S. Noli] V. 1* (Tirana: Ombra GVG, 2006), 185–190.
19 Today, in Southern Albania.
20 Jorgaqi, *Noli I*, 185–190.
21 For an analysis on Noli's translations, see Beduli, *Albanian Language*.
22 AQSH, F. 14 "Fan Noli", f. 92, 1–3.
23 "Drita e Bukureshtit [Bucharest Light]", *Albania*, no. 5, 1900, 107.
24 Lasgush Poradeci, *Vepra 2 [Works 2]* (Tirana: Onufri 1999).
25 "Shqiptarët e Rumanisë [Albanians of Romania]", *Dituria [Knowledge]*, 1 January 1927, 87–89.
26 AQSH, F. 143 "Document Collection", Y. 1909, f. 1978, 1, Statute of the Albanian Orthodox Community.
27 Nikolaidou, *Foreign Propaganda*, 343–344. The dioceses were Nicopolis (Preveza), Paramythia, Ioannina, Konica and Vella, Kostur, Prespa, Dryinopolis, Velegrad, Durrës, Korça, Dibra, and Moglena, which were all part of Ottoman Albania, as well as Adrianople and Didymoteicho in Thrace, where there was a large Albanian community.

28 Ibid, 308–312.
29 *Lidhja Ortodokse [Orthodox League]*, 10 July 1909, 1.
30 "Orthodhoksët shqiptarë [Orthodox Albanians]", *Lidhja Ortodokse [Orthodox League]*, 10 July 1909, 1.
31 The newspaper *Korça* reported on 6 March 1909 that the Gospel was read in Albanian (*Korça*, 6 March 1909, 4). However, it seems this was an isolated case.
32 "Shoqërija kishëtare 'Lidhja Orthodhokse Shqiptare' ['Albanian Orthodox League' Church Association]", *Lidhja Ortodokse [Orthodox League]*, 31 July 1909, 2.
33 AQSH, F. 143 "Document Collection", Y. 1909, f. 7979, 1–3, Cale to Elbasan Church Eldership, 6 March 1909.
34 "Thirrje [Proclamation]", *Lidhja Ortodokse [Orthodox League]*, 31 July 1909, 1.
35 *Lidhja Ortodokse [Orthodox League]*, August 1909, 3.
36 "Zgjedhjet të Dhimogjerondis së Korçësë [Elections of Korça's Eldership]", *Lidhja Ortodokse [Orthodox League]*, 17 October 1909, 3.
37 *Lidhja Ortodokse [Orthodox League]*, 16 December 1909, 3.
38 "Të nalt Shenjtërisë Tij Patrikut Ikumenik Ioaqimit të 3-të [Of His Holiness Ecumenical Patriarch Ioakim III]", *Lidhja Ortodokse [Orthodox League]*, 2 October 1909, 1.
39 "Një dhespot gënjeshtar [One Lying Bishop]", *Lidhja Ortodokse [Orthodox League]*, 17 October 1909, 1.
40 Visarion Xhuvani, *Kujtim vepre dhe intrige [Memory of Work and Intrigue]* (Tirana: Tirana, 1926), 4–6.
41 "Komunitatea Shqipe 'Lidhja Orthodhokse' edhe hyqmet i Korçës' ['Orthodox League' Albanian Community also Korça's Fate]", *Lidhja Ortodokse [Orthodox League]*, 22 February 1910, 2.
42 "Παρασημοφορειται ο Μητροπολίτης της Κορυτσάς [Korça's Metropolitan Receives a Reward]", *Skrip*, 8 December 1900, 4.
43 Nikolaidou, *Foreign Propaganda*, 313–314.
44 Beduli, *Orthodox Community*, 12–28.
45 Ibid, 356–359.
46 Sadiku, *Cham Issue*, 13–25.
47 Alqi Jani, "Memorandumi i shqiptarëve ortodoksë dërguar Patrikanës së Stambollit [Orthodox Albanian Memorandum Sent to the Istanbul Patriarchate]", *55*, 6 June 1999, 11–12.
48 Nikolaidou, *Foreign Propaganda*, 366.
49 Kondis, *Elinismos I*, 187: Historical and Diplomatic Archives of the Greek Ministry of Foreign Affairs (IDAYE), f.A.A.K, no. 345, Istanbul Embassy to Greek MFA, 12 May 1910.
50 Kondis, *Elinismos I*, 202: IDAYE, f. B/52, no. 255, Gjirokastra Consulate to Greek MFA, 28 April 1911.
51 Kondis, *Elinismos I*, 205: IDAYE, f. B/52, no. 17007, Greek MFA to Consulates, 30 June 1911.
52 Kondis, *Elinismos I*, 244: IDAYE, f. B/52, no. 346, Bitola Consulate to Greek MFA, 8 May 1912.
53 Ioanis Em. Stratigakis, *Ο Μητροπολίτης Μυτιλήνης Ἰακωβος: ο άνθρωπος και η δράση του [Metropolitan of Mytilene Iakovos: The Man and His Action]* (Athens, 1956); Enosis Smyrneon, *Ο Μητροπολίτης Μυτηλήνης Ἰάκωβος, ο άπο Δυρραχίου [Metropolitan of Mytilene Iakovos, the One from Durrës]* (Athens: Enosis Smyrneon, 1965).
54 Glavinas, *The Orthodox Church*, 34. Venizelos was born in Crete in 1864 and died in Paris in 1936. He served as prime minister of Greece eight times, between 1910 and 1920 and then between 1928 and 1933.
55 Arben Puto, *Shqipëria politike 1912–1939 [Political Albania 1912–1939]* (Tirana: Toena, 2009), 36.

56 Jacob Gould Schurman, *Luftërat Ballkanike [The Balkan Wars]* (Tirana: Uegen, 2006).

57 Ledia Dushku, *Kur historia ndau dy popuj miq: Shqipëria dhe Greqia (1912–1914) [When History Divided Two Friendly Peoples: Albania and Greece (1912–1914)]* (Tirana: QSA, 2012), 140–141.

58 Centred in what is today Bitola, in the Republic of Northern Macedonia.

59 Kondis, *Albania and Greece,* 70–71.

60 Lef Nosi, *Dokumente historike 1912–1918 [Historical Documents 1912–1918]* (Tirana: Nënë Tereza, 2007), 80.

61 Dushku, *When History Divided,* 141.

62 Stratigakis, *Metropolitan of Mytilene,* 78–79.

63 Apostolos Katopodis, "Ο Μητροπολίτης Δρυινουπόλεως Βασίλειος Παπαχρήστου στο Βοριοηπειρώτικο Αγώνα, [Metropolitan of Dryinopolis Vasil Papakristo in the Northern Epirotan Struggle]", (PhD Dissertation, University of Thessaloniki, 2001), 36.

64 Vasilios Kondis, "The Northern Epirus Question (1881–1921)", in *Epirus, 4000 Years of Greek History and Civilization,* ed. Mixail B. Sakellariou (Athens: Ekdotike Athinon, 1997).

65 Pëllumb Xhufi and Hajredin Isufi, "Aneksimi i dhunshëm i Çamërisë nga Greqia dhe lufta e shqiptarëve për mbrojtjen e saj [The Violent Annexation of Chameria by Greece and the Albanian Battle for Its Protection]", *Studime historike [Historical Studies]* 1–4 (1996):13.

66 Kondis, *Elinismos I,* 269: IDAYE: D. 29, no. 9003, Sakturis to Koromilas, 11 March 1913.

67 Beduli, *Church and Culture.*

68 AQSH, F. 136 "Durrës Deanery", f. 11, 9, Iakovos to the Patriarch, 15 June 1913.

69 Dushku, *When History Divided,* 172–173.

70 Kastriot Dervishi, *Historia e Shtetit Shqiptar [History of the Albanian State] 1912–2005* (Tirana: 55, 2006), 54.

71 Xristina Pitouli-Kitsou, *Οι Ελληνοαλβανικές Σχέσεις και το Βορειοηπειρώτικο Ζήτημα κατα την Περίοδο 1907–1914 [Greek-Albanian Relations and Northern-Epirotes Issue during the Period 1907–1914]* (Athens: Olkos, 1997), 356.

72 Greek Logotechnical and Historical Archives (ELIA), F. "Eleftherios Venizelos", f. 1/7, f. 526, Evgeniadis to Greek MFA 15/28 October 1913.

73 Ledia Dushku, "Greqia midis qeverisë së Vlorës dhe Pleqësisë së Shqipërisë së Mesme [Greece between the Vlora Government and the Central Albania Senate]", *Studime historike [Historical Studies]* 3–4 (2008):80.

74 Kondis, *Albania and Greece,* 114–115.

75 AQSH, F. 136 "Durrës Deanery", f. 11, 22, Iakovos to the Patriarch, 1 December 1913.

76 Kaliopi Naska, *Dokumente për Çamërinë: 1912–1939 [Documents on Chameria: 1912–1939]* (Tirana: Dituria, 1999), 12–13.

77 Kondis, *Elinismos I,* 298: IDAYE, f. A/5, no. 204, Korça's Governor to Greek MFA, 2 August 1913.

78 "Ενθουσιώδης Υποδοχη του κ. Βενιζελου εν Θεσσαλονικη [Magnificent Reception for Mr Venizelos in Thessaloniki]", *Empros [Forward],* 1 February 1914, 4.

79 Joseph Swire, *Ngritja e një mbretërie [Albania: The Rise of a Kingdom]* (Tirana: Dituria, 2005), 146–147.

80 Eleftherios Karakitsios, "Ο Ελληνισμός στην Μητροπολιτική Περιφέρεια Κορυτσάς [Hellenism in the Metropolitanate of Korça]", (PhD Dissertation, Aristotle University of Thessaloniki, 2010), 253.

81 Vasil K. Thanasi, *Mëmëdhetari, luftëtar për paqe e progres, kleriku i shquar Paisi Vodica: 1882–1966 [The Patriot, a Warrior for Peace and Progress, the Outstanding Cleric Pais Vodica: 1882–1966]* (Tirana, 2004), 77.

82 Swire, *Albania*, 146–147.
83 Thanasi, *Pais Vodica*, 78–88.
84 "Το ηπειρωτικον ζητημα [Epirotes Issue]", *Empros [Forward]*, 26 January 1914, 2.
85 Swire, *Albania*, 147–148.
86 Garoufalia Anastasopoulou, *Αλβανοί Ορθόδοξοι και Έλληνες της Αλβανίας και ο ρόλος της Ορθόδοξης Εκκλησίας της Αλβανίας [Orthodox Albanians and the Greeks of Albania and the Role of the Orthodox Church of Albania]* (Athens: Vivliorama, 2013), 12–13.
87 Kosta Papa, who witnessed these events, explains in his memoirs that these commissions forced Orthodox Albanians to sign oaths that they would fight in favour of union with Greece. Kosta Papa, *Greek Atrocities in Albania* (Framingham: Journal Press, 1917).
88 Valentina Duka, *Historia e Shqipërisë 1912–2000 [History of Albania 1912–2000]* (Tirana: SHBLU, 2007), 64.
89 Katopodis, "Metropolitan of Dryinopolis", 51.
90 Kondis, *Elinismos I*, 324: IDAYE, f. A/5, no. 4599, Epirus Governor to Greek MFA, 18 February 1914.
91 "Η προκηρυξις της προσωρινης κυβερνησεως [The Declaration of the Interim Government]", *Skrip*, 18 February 1914, 4.
92 ELIA, F. "Eleftherios Venizelos", f. 113, 140, Forestis to Venizelos, 24 February 1914.
93 Duncan Heaton-Armstrong, *Gjashtë muaj mbretëri: Shqipëria 1914 [The Six Month Kingdom: Albania 1914]* (Tirana: Onufri, 2011), 34. Ferdinando Salleo, *Shqipëria: gjashtë muaj mbretëri [Albania: The Six Month Kingdom]* (Tiranë: SHLK, 2000), 74.
94 AQSH, F. 136 "Durrës Deanery", f. 34, 30–35, Iakovos to the Patriarchate, 13 March 1914.
95 Stratigakis, *Metropolitan of Mytilene*, 80.
96 Armstrong, *The Six Month Kingdom*, 40–44.
97 Stratigakis, *Metropolitan of Mytilene*, 80.
98 AQSH, Iakovos to the Patriarchate, quoted.
99 Jorgaqi, *Noli I*, 291–292.
100 AQSH, F. 70 "25th Anniversary of Self-Governance", f. 47, 11, Memoirs of Aleks Duka's biography.
101 "Τραυματίστηκε ο Μητροπολίτης Κορυτσάς [Metropolitan of *Korça* Wounded]", *Empros [Forward]*, 5 April 1914, 4.
102 ELIA, F. "Eleftherios Venizelos", f. 7, 28, Streit to Venizelos, no date.
103 Stratigakis, *Metropolitan of Mytilene*, 81–83.
104 AQSH, F. 141 "Metropolitanate of Korça", f. 410, 6, Eldership Meeting Decisions, April 27, 1914.
105 The last letter in Albanian dates back to May 29, 1914. AQSH, F. 141. "Metropolitanate of Korça", f. 390, 1, Eldership Proclamation, 27 May, 1914.
106 The church established in the United States by Theofan Noli was at first just a single parish; the Albanian jurisdiction did not become official until 1918.
107 Stratigakis, *Metropolitan of Mytilene*, 68–74.
108 Wilhelm Wied, *Promemorie mbi Shqipërinë [Memorandum on Albania]* (Tirana: Skanderbeg Books, 2010), 29.
109 ELIA, F. "Eleftherios Venizelos", f. 1/7, 542, Varatas to MFA, 22 March (4 April) 1914.
110 ELIA, F. "Eleftherios Venizelos", f. 1/4, 235, Streit to Venizelos, 31 March (13 April) 1914.
111 "Ο Μητροπολίτης Κορυτσάς, Γερμανός, συναντήθηκε με τον Πρόεδρο της Κυβερνήσεως και με τον Υπουργό κ. Στρείτ [Metropolitan of Korça, Germanos,

Meets with the Prime Minister and Minister Streit]", *Empros [Forward]*, 29 June 1914, 3.
112 Wied, *Memorandum on Albania*, 27.
113 Dushku, *When History Divided*, 306.
114 Stratigakis, *Metropolitan of Mytilene*, 90.
115 Ibid.
116 Duka, *Albania*, 440–441: NA, PRO. FO. 371. 1888, no. 23530, Lamb to Grey, 3 June, 1914.
117 Dushku, *When History Divided*, 330.
118 Duka, *Albania*, 463: NA, PRO. FO. 371. 1888, no. 24867, Lamb to Grey, 3 June 1914.
119 Duka, *Albania*, 495: NA, PRO. FO. 371. 1888, no. 26671, Lamb to Grey, 13 June 1914.
120 Kondis, *Elinismos I*, 333: IDAYE, f. A/5, no. 19969, Greek MFA to Epirus Governor, 22 June 1914.
121 Kondis, *Elinismos I*, 335: IDAYE, f. A/5, no. 20626, Prime Minister to Epirus Governor, 10 July 1914.
122 "Γιατί δεν δίνει την Βόρειο Ήπειρο στον Βηδ [Why He Is Not Giving Northern Epirus to Wied]", *Empros [Forward]*, 27 June 1914, 2.
123 Dushku, *When History Divided*, 288.
124 Romeo Gurakuqi, *Principata e Shqipërisë dhe Mbretëria e Greqisë 1913–1914 [The Principality of Albania and Kingdom of Greece 1913–1914]* (Tirana: UET Press, 2011), 207–208.
125 Mehdi Frashëri, *Kujtime [Memoirs] 1913–1933* (Tirana: OMSCA-1, 2005), 24.
126 Gurakuqi, *Principality*, 208–209.
127 Ibid, 114.
128 Duka, *Albania*, 425: NA, PRO. FO. 371. 1888, no. 23057, Lamb to Grey, 17 May 1914.
129 Ibid, 441: NA, PRO. FO. 371. 1888, no. 23291, Lamb to Grey, 30 May 1914.
130 Alan JP Taylor, *First World War* (London: Penguin Books, 1966).
131 The territories annexed by Greece – in Macedonia, Epirus, and Thrace – remained under the authority of the Ecumenical Patriarchate until 1928, when Greece and the Patriarchate signed an agreement transferring them to the Church of Greece. Theodoris Tsironis, *Εκκλησια Πολιτευομενη Ο Πολιτικός Λόγος και Ρόλος της Εκκλησίας της Ελλάδος (1913–1941) [Politicized Church: The Speech and Political Role of the Church of Greece (1913–1941)]* (Athens: Epikentro, 2011).
132 ELIA, F. "Eleftherios Venizelos", f. 7, 104, Vasil to the King and Venizelos, 18 October 1914.
133 Colonel De Weer, the Dutch officer in charge of the gendarmerie, documented the massacre and lodged a protest against the Greek government. The documents were later published in Owen Pearson, *Albania and King Zog: Independence, Republic and Monarchy, 1908–1939* (London and New York: Centre for Albanian Studies and I.B. Tauris, 2004).
134 Vasil Dilo, "Pushtimi italian dhe Shqipëria [The Italian Invasion and Albania]", *Gazeta Ndryshe [Different Newspaper]* 22 April 2007, 16–17.
135 Thanas Floqi, *Fytyra e vërtetë e Haxhi Qamilit: Kujtime për vitet e mbrapshta 1914–1915 [The True Face of Haxhi Qamili: Memories of the Evil Years 1914–1915]* (Tirana: 55, 2008), 55; Nosi, *Dokumente Historike*, 316.
136 Taylor, *First World War*, 122–138.
137 Ibid.
138 Muin Çami, *Shqipëria në rrjedhat e historisë 1912–1924 [Albania in the Course of History 1912–1924]* (Tirana: Onufri, 2007), 127–129. Edith Durham held

the same view; see Edith Durham, *Njëzetë vjet ngatërresa ballkanike* (Tirana: Argeta-LMG, 2001); originally published in English as *Twenty Years of Balkan Tangle* (London: Allen and Unwin, 1920).

139 Kondis, *Elinismos I*, 380–381: IDAYE, f. a/5/VII, no number, Argiropulos to Venizelos, 24 October 1916.

140 Çami, *Albania*, 127–151.

141 "Οι αποστάντες ιεράρχαι ζητούν να εκσηλεοθούν απέναντη του κράτους [Opponent Archpriests Want to Be Acquitted before the State]", *Skrip*, 16. 11. 1916, 2.

142 Kondis, *Elinismos I*, 394–395: IDAYE, f. B/33, no. 26, Florina District to MFA, 5 September 1917.

143 See the file of testaments, wills, and dowry agreements: AQSH, F. 141 "Metropolitanate of Korça", f. 393.

144 Kondis, *Elinismos I*, 410–421: IDAYE, f. A/5, no number, Bamiha to MFA, 28 February 1918.

145 Kondis, *Elinismos I*, 173: IDAYE, f. A/5, no. 4457, Epirus Governor to MFA, 28 March 1920.

146 "Personalitet i dyfishtë, Ikonom Papapano atdhetar shqiptar dhe prift shqiptar [Dual Personality, Ikonom Papapano, an Albanian Patriot and Albanian Priest]", *Autoqefalia Ortodokse Shqiptare [Albanian Orthodox Autocephaly]*, 10 September 1994, 3.

147 A detailed description of the incident is found in Spiro Kosova's memoirs: Mareglen Verli, ed., *Shqipëria e viteve 1912–1964 në kujtimet e Spiro Kosovës, Vëllimi 1 [Albania in the Years 1912–1964 in Spiro Kosova's Memoirs, Volume 1]* (Tirana: Klean, 2008), 152–153. See also: Apostol Kotnani, *Kapedan at Stath Melani me shokë [Captain Father Stathi Melani with Friends]* (Tirana, 2007).

148 "Vrasja e Atë Stath Melanit [Murder of Father Stathi Melani]", *Albania*, 16 March 1918, 4.

149 Petrit Bidoshi, "Një ngjarje e paharrueshme e vitit 1916 në Durrës [An Unforgettable Event of 1916 in Durrës]", *Autoqefalia Ortodokse Shqiptare [Albanian Orthodox Autocephaly]*, June 1994, 5.

150 Vasil and Germanos were among them. Tsironis, *The Politicized Church*, 82.

151 Glavinas, *The Orthodox Church*, 28; Llukani, *Orthodox Church*, 49; Tritos, *Church in Illyricum*.

152 Stratigakis, *Metropolitan of Mytilene*, 95–97.

153 AQSH, F. 152 "MIA", Y. 1928, f. 39, 116, Letter of Metropolitan Joakim, 21 November 1928.

2 Preparations for the establishment of the Albanian Church, 1918–1921

Establishment of the first Albanian Orthodox ecclesiastical jurisdictions

The efforts to establish an Albanian Orthodox jurisdiction could not have taken place in the midst of the armed struggle happening in the Balkans. Instead, Albanian patriots sought to carry out their plans in the United States. Reverend Theofan Noli, the movement's pioneer, returned to Boston at the beginning of the First World War, where, under his leadership, the Vatra Federation (*vatra* means "the hearth") became essentially an undeclared Albanian government in exile. Noli had achieved a diplomatic breakthrough during the war by personally submitting Albania's demands to the American president Woodrow Wilson. The priests under Noli's leadership all signed a joint memorandum to the president, requesting his support and rejecting any claim that Orthodox Albanians were Greek.[1]

Noli vowed that he would bring the archiepiscopal throne to the motherland, but that throne would first need to be created. To this end, he and Reverend Vangjel Çamçe attended the Congress of the Russian Metropolitanate, which was held in Ohio in March 1918.[2] Orthodox Albanians and Romanians, persecuted by other Churches, had taken refuge in the Patriarchate of Moscow and were requesting the creation of their own dioceses. The congress accepted the requests but postponed any final decision until it received the necessary permission from the patriarch of Moscow. Still, in spite of this obstacle, the congress made the important decision on 24 March 1918 to establish the Albanian Orthodox Mission in America under the leadership of Reverend Theofan Noli.[3]

In October, the Russian archbishop of North America, Alexander Nemolovsky (in office 1918–1921), elevated Noli to the rank of archimandrite. The Albanian mission then held an assembly in Boston on 25 March 1919 and officially elected Reverend Theofan as bishop. Archbishop Alexander had asked Patriarch Tikhon for permission to turn the Albanian Orthodox Mission into a diocese and ordain Theofan Noli, but the reply was endlessly delayed owing to the difficult circumstances caused by the Russian Revolution and the subsequent civil war. Twice, the mission called for meetings to ordain Noli as a bishop, but in both cases the Russian hierarchs failed to attend.[4] The Greek government instructed the Greek bishop of Rodostol to ask Alexander not to ordain Noli.[5] Indeed, the bishop slandered Noli, calling him an atheist and portraying him as someone who mocked the Orthodox faith. When the Russian bishops again failed to attend the mission's meeting on 26 July,[6] the Albanian faithful went forward anyway and appointed Noli as the ruling bishop of Boston, Kruja, and exarch of Illyria, in violation of ecclesiastical rules that required two attending hierarchs for the ordination of a bishop. Theofan Noli then declared the independence of the Albanian Orthodox Church,[7] which at the time consisted of no more than ten priests and seven parishes, with St George's Cathedral in Boston being the largest.[8]

Noli's actions infuriated a large segment of Orthodox Albanian priests. Reverends Naum Çere, Damian Angjeli, Nikolla Kristofor, and Vasil Marko, all nationalist activists residing in the United States, did not attend the opening meeting.[9] The first three joined forces with Archbishop Alexander against Noli, while Vasil Marko eventually sided with him. Nor did a number of other Albanian patriots support Noli's irregular action. Pandeli Evangjeli considered his move as potentially harming the national interest, saying that it gave a new weapon to the enemies of Albania.[10] On 3 April 1920, Archbishop Alexander issued a proclamation in which he described Noli's self-ordination as emanating from devilish and immature pride and threatened to excommunicate any priests and believers who continued to recognize Noli as a bishop.[11]

The establishment of the Albanian Church in the United States preceded similar efforts in Albania, where Prince Wied's former prime minister, Turhan Pasha Përmeti, had been leading a provisional government, based in Durrës, since December 1918. Working alongside Italian troops, this government extended its rule into central Albania. Iakovos, the former metropolitan of Durrës, meanwhile, was unable to reclaim the diocese since the Italians refused him entry to the city.[12]

In 1919, Archimandrite Visar Xhuvani (1890–1965; archbishop of Albania, 1929–1936; metropolitan of Berat, 1941–1945) arrived in Albania from Greece; born in Elbasan, he had recently obtained a doctorate in theology from the University of Athens.[13] After his arrival, Visar held a liturgy in Albanian in his birthplace, with the support of the local Orthodox clergy, most notably the dean of Elbasan, Reverend Dhimitër Dhimitruka.[14] The Elbasan eldership then stripped Iakovos of his metropolitan's title, citing his actions against the interests of the Orthodox of the region, and made Visar the head of the diocese, bestowing upon him the title "General Archimandrite and Preacher of Elbasan and Shpat".[15] Within a few days, the elderships of the other main towns in the diocese – Pogradec, Kavaja, Tirana, and Durrës – all supported the archimandrite, and petitioned the Durrës government to recognize his new position.[16] In January 1920, the government responded by recognizing Visar as the "Archimandrite of Orthodox Albanians". Visar was determined to lead the Albanian ecclesiastical struggle going forward; only he had not yet been ordained as a bishop. His only hope for ordination was to enlist the aid of one of the other national Orthodox Churches in the Balkans. Assisted by the Albanian diaspora in Romania, Xhuvani went to Bucharest and met with senior officials in the Romanian Foreign Ministry and the Romanian Orthodox Church. Visar told them that he had been elected as a religious leader in Albania with the ultimate goal of creating an autocephalous church. The representatives of the Romanian Church expressed their goodwill towards the Albanian effort, since Romanians had faced the same dilemma of non-recognition in the past.[17] Meanwhile, the Ministry of Foreign Affairs indicated that Romania would evaluate the request regarding the ordination of bishops only when Albanian sovereignty had been secured.[18]

Since these initial efforts had not been successful, Visar returned to Durrës, where he assumed the task of leading the diocese of Durrës.[19] He was wary of Iakovos's former associates and limited their activities to religious duties.[20] The archimandrite held the Orthodox liturgy in Albanian everywhere in the diocese, concluding with Christmas celebrations in the lakeside town of Pogradec, in front of hundreds of Orthodox from the town and the surrounding area.[21]

Metropolitan Iakovos and the Albanian–Greek battle for Korça

Albania had been unprepared for the new state of affairs when, on 11 November 1918, Germany's representative, Matthias Erzberger, signed the armistice of unconditional surrender, which marked the end of the First World War. In January 1919, attention turned to Paris, where the victors now gathered to determine the world's political future. Greece, Italy, and the Allies had signed the secret Treaty of London, which gave southern Albania to Greece, Vlora and the surrounding area to Italy, and the northern part of Albania to Serbia; what remained of the small state would become an Italian protectorate. Turhan Pasha, Albania's official representative in Paris, was no match for the sophisticated diplomacy of Greek Prime Minister Venizelos. Albania's only hope lay with the mercy of the Allies or the implementation of President Woodrow Wilson's *Fourteen Points* peace principles.[22]

Great Britain and France backed the territorial arguments Greece made at the Paris Peace Conference. Italy was the only country left that might hinder Greek territorial claims; it had no wish to empower either Athens or Belgrade, since either could assume the position once held by Austria–Hungary in the delicate Adriatic balance. Consequently, Italy supported the Albanian national movement in the areas invaded by Greece. Nevertheless, Italy and Greece found a mutual language in the secret London treaty. On 29 June 1919, the Greek prime minister and Italian Foreign Minister

Tommaso Tittoni signed the Venizelos–Tittoni agreement, by which Greece would annex the territories of Gjirokastra and Korça, while Italy would get Vlora, with the rest of Albania becoming its protectorate. Italy also pledged to withdraw from the Dodecanese Islands, which at a future date would be annexed by Greeks.[23]

The fate of Korça was at the centre of the Albanian–Greek controversy. The Great Powers were not entirely sure it would be best to surrender the region to Greece. The French, however, were inclined to support Athens and so dissolved Korça's autonomy and sentenced the Korça Republic's leader, Themistokli Gërmenji, to death.[24] The region, however, had no Greek-speaking population and the Albanian national movement was widespread, so Greece needed to create the proper preconditions for its annexation.[25] The change became evident on 3 November 1918, when the French authorities instructed Korça's priests to hold a liturgy in Greek in St George's Cathedral to commemorate the upcoming armistice. As the principal of the metropolitanate's school was lining up his pupils in the schoolyard to celebrate the return of Greek to Korça's Orthodox churches, the Albanian patriot Thanas Mano punched him in the head and threw him to the ground. This action served as a call to Albanian nationalists, who immediately started attacking the other émigré Greek teachers.[26] After this, no one had the courage to go back to using Greek in the liturgy until Iakovos returned to Albania.[27]

Venizelos saw Korça as an easy target. His main focus was on Asia Minor and Constantinople, which were the central goal of Greece's territorial aspirations. The Great Powers had authorized Greece to send military troops to oversee the outskirts of Izmir and the entire region of Thrace – but not Constantinople. Venizelos hoped to achieve a similar mandate in Albania with Korça and Gjirokastra. Meanwhile, the deputy prime minister, Emmanouil Repoulis, was running the government in Athens. On 11 August 1919, Venizelos instructed Repoulis to begin preparations for the occupation of Korça:

> I am sending a telegram to Constantinople asking the patriarch … to send as exarch to Korça [the metropolitan] of Durrës, who is a good choice. You will telegraph him immediately [to come] to Athens from Corfu, where he is staying, so he can go to Korça as soon as possible, before the arrival of our army. Instructions will be given to the military leader to be in close contact with the metropolitan in question, who is able to provide great services.[28]

The Patriarchate, obeying Venizelos's request, annulled the appointment of another hierarch, chosen just days before, and replaced him with Iakovos.[29] The Greek Foreign Ministry asked Metropolitan Iakovos to present himself to receive instructions for his new duty. In his autobiography, Iakovos admits that his mission was entirely political, "in violation" of the rules of the Eastern Orthodox Church. Since the Greek government was about to order its army to invade Korça, it was necessary to have a skilled representative there who understood Albanian affairs. In Venizelos's view, this person was his good friend Iakovos. The Greek Foreign Ministry appointed Achilleas Kalevras as the governor of Korça and instructed him to act in accord with the hierarch.[30]

The French authorities in Korça, however, fearing unrest in the local Albanian population, asked the Greeks to temporarily postpone the arrival of their troops – leaving Governor Kalevras stranded a few kilometres from the city in the town of Bilisht, in an area Greece had held since the start of the war. Not long afterwards, Iakovos arrived in Korça as the official representative of the Ecumenical Patriarchate.[31] His duty was to create the necessary conditions for an invasion that would result in the fewest Greek losses.[32] The metropolitan immediately met with Colonel Henri Reynard Lespinasse, the French commander of Korça (in office, June 1919–November 1919); he asked if it was true that Albanians were planning an armed uprising against the invading army. Lespinasse replied that he was certain the Albanians would resist.[33]

Iakovos began his work by meeting with several key figures in the city: the Serbian consul, a handful of Greeks who had remained in Korça since the first invasion, the Albanian officials who had been running the governing council and the municipality, although with little real authority, and the leaders of the Protestant American mission.[34] The metropolitan immediately informed his political superiors in Athens (but not his religious overseers in Constantinople) about the meetings. He described the preparedness of the Albanian paramilitary units under the command of Sali Butka, which included Themistokli Gërmenji's former guerrilla troops, now led by Leonidha Frashëri. Iakovos also apprised Athens that the Protestant school had introduced Greek into its curriculum in anticipation of the Greek invasion.[35]

Iakovos managed to convince the French officials that Greek should replace Albanian as the language used in Orthodox religious services.[36] He often went to Bilisht, where Kalevras relayed to him Venizelos's instructions. The Korça valley was located in what was geographically western Macedonia. Even in the part of Macedonia annexed by Greece, the Greeks were a minority. On 17 September 1919, Iliakis, the prefect of Kozani, reported that the majority of the population in Florina and Kastoria were not Greeks[37] – let alone Korça and Bilisht, which were populated by Albanians. The local governors in the Greek part of Macedonia admitted they were working hard to assimilate the population into the Greek nation. Meanwhile, on the Albanian side of the border, French officials did their best to assist Metropolitan Iakovos with his duties. Colonel Lespinasse's departure from Korça strengthened the Greek campaign. France was seriously considering the possibility of placing Korça under temporary Greek rule until a final decision was reached at the Paris Peace Conference,[38] and Lespinasse was not the right man for this: his emotional involvement with Korça's cause would make it difficult, if not impossible, for him to side with Greece. Iakovos later gave himself considerable credit for engineering the colonel's removal; he recalled that his insistence to Venizelos, who then intervened with French officials, caused Lespinasse to be replaced by the pro-Greek Lieutenant Colonel Emmanuel Cretin.[39]

The new French commander had clear instructions from Paris to support Greece's aims and listen to Iakovos. In early November 1919, Cretin reported that he had opened four Greek schools, in Ziçisht, Qytezë, Tërovë, and Boboshticë. He wrote that this decision had caused concern from the Albanians as it clearly proved his pro-Greek bias.[40] During this period, Iakovos did his best to exert his influence in occupied Korça. He allowed only two Albanian language classes per week, arguing that such classes were unimportant since "everybody already knew Albanian".[41] On 5 November 1919, the Greek military commander of Kozani and Florina, Kaklamanis, reported that the cooperation between Cretin and the metropolitan had altered the situation in Korça in Greece's favour.[42]

Nevertheless, as Cretin later recounted, Iakovos felt that his life was in danger, and that he was a target for Albanian patriots. While Cretin did not believe that Iakovos was under any serious threat, he suspected that opening the Greek schools had caught the attention of many who saw the hierarch as a pawn of Greece.[43] Cretin assigned three guards and several secret gendarmes – Greeks who were in his service – to provide security for the metropolitan.[44] The colonel noted that the presence of His Grace in Korça had become a serious obstacle, even to the pro-Greek policy he was following at the instructions of his superiors. On 1 December, Cretin reported that Iakovos had become the leader of a large propaganda organization, which was using the Greek schools for its political aims, albeit under the guise of humanitarian purposes.[45]

Everyone in Korça was expecting the Greek army to arrive at any moment. But the situation was not as it seemed. In early 1920, Greece had only one military division in the entire territory of Epirus and western Macedonia. On 7 March, General Orfanidis informed the Greek Ministry of War that this division would be unable to deal with any Albanian uprising.[46] The general's report was consistent with those the ministry had been receiving since the previous December. For the Greeks, the solution had to be more strategic than rapid, since their efforts in Thrace and Asia Minor were absorbing the lion's share of the army's capabilities. On 19 March, the ministry decided to send Greek soldiers of Albanian origin (Arvanites) to Korça, believing that by enlisting Albanian troops loyal to Athens the Greek army in the region would be stronger. Ultimately, however, the government abandoned the plan because it would be nearly impossible to move troops all the way from Thrace and Asia Minor and, more importantly, Athens feared that a division of Arvanites might end up fighting on behalf of the Albanian national cause.[47]

During the early months of 1920, Greece was bluffing. Athens announced that the Greek army would enter Korça as soon as the French left, although it was actually urging the French to delay their departure. To aid its plans, Greece put a military ploy into action. On 21 May 1920, Iakovos received a messenger from Florina who told him that Greece had reached an agreement with the French and its troops would soon be invading Korça. Iakovos met with Cretin and assured him that the Greek army would do its utmost not to upset the local population, that Greece accepted the state of affairs and would allow the Albanian schools to remain open. The colonel then instructed His Grace to keep the news to himself. But as soon as Iakovos left Cretin's office, he went to the metropolitanate, summoned his supporters, and asked them to inform the population of the invasion.[48] His failure to follow Cretin's instructions was a continuation of the Greek strategy to break the city's morale by making the population believe that an invasion was inevitable. Iakovos also took care to spread the news that those Greek troops would remain until the final decision of the Paris Peace Conference. The metropolitan was convinced that together these two rumours would forestall any rebellion.

Korça's Municipal Council Chairman Jorgji Raçi and Mayor Koço Kota demanded Iakovos's expulsion.[49] The council decided to hand the city over to the new government of Albania, which had been established by the Congress of Lushnja in January 1920. At the same time, the council began military preparations.[50] French officials reported that more than 7,000 soldiers from all over Albania were assembling to confront the Greek invasion.[51] Venizelos wanted to avoid armed clashes, but he too began military preparations. On 22 May, he ordered one army division to leave Izmir and head to Korça, reasoning that if the army did not immediately enter upon the French withdrawal, then Greece risked losing Korça forever.[52] But it was not possible for the troops stationed in Izmir to move in such a short time. The French had set 26 May as their date of departure and refused to postpone it yet again. Iliakis, the prefect of Kozani–Florina, estimated that the Greek army would have been able to invade Korça if the French had delayed their departure by just a single day.[53]

Prime Minister Venizelos told the governor general of Epirus that, although he was intent on invading Korça, the British had advised him not to proceed in order to avoid an Albanian revolt.[54] This rationale was also part of the explanation Venizelos presented to the Greek public. He informed the Ministry of Foreign Affairs, however, that it was impossible to invade Northern Epirus due to the lack of military personnel of the Greek military since the Greek army invasion of Eastern Thrace.[55]

On 26 May 1920, Eshref Frashëri, the vice prime minister of the government in Tirana, and Pandeli Cale, the prefect of Korça, took over the administration of region from the Municipal Council of Korça. But the Athens still had an ace up its sleeve. Venizelos's initial letter best sums up the plan: right after deciding not to invade Korça, the prime minister asked the deputy prefect of Florina to send additional instructions to the metro-politan of Durrës and send him further instructions. He said that Iakovos should give the Albanians the impression that he had convinced the Greek government to stop the invasion on the condition that the Albanians keep the Hellenists safe and preserve their institutions in Korça.[56]

Iakovos met with representatives of the Albanian government and told them there was little doubt that the Greek army would invade Korça. As a priest, he said, he hated bloodshed, so he offered to mediate a settlement and would arrange a meeting with the Greek general Nikolaos Trikoupis.[57] The Albanians accepted his offer and met with General Trikoupis in the vil-lage of Smardes[58]; they asked the general to call off the military intervention since the people of Korça were ready to fight the Greeks, if necessary. The general replied that he had strict orders to invade Korça and was obliged to carry out the command of his superiors. He then sent the Albanian delega-tion to Florina, where they met with Prefect Iliakis for further talks.[59] Ili-akis confirmed the imminent invasion but pledged to ask the prime minister to stop the attack, since he was moved by the pleas of the metropolitan of Durrës.[60] The Albanians had gone to the meeting feeling hopeless, but they were determined not to waste this last opportunity to prevent the Greek takeover of Korça. None of them believed that the intervention of a priest, even one with Iakovos's political credentials, could prevent the imminent war. Prime Minister Venizelos's sudden reversal caught them by surprise, which Reverend Petro witnessed when Iliakis told them that the Greek in-vasion had been called off.[61] The next day, it was decided that delegations of the two governments would meet in Kapshtica. Iliakis told the Albanians that it was Iakovos who made the agreement possible and that both sides should be grateful to His Grace.[62]

Metropolitan Iakovos drafted a protocol, which the two delegations signed in Kapshtica on 28 May. Eshref Frashëri, Jorgji Raçi, Pandeli Cale, Nikollaq Zoi, and Selaudin Blloshmi represented the Albanian side, while General Trikoupis and Prefect Iliakis represented the Greeks. The Protocol of Kapshtica stipulated that the Greek army would not enter Korça, that the Albanian authorities would protect the Greeks living in the city and main-tain the status quo in Greek schools and churches, and that until the Paris Peace Conference determined the final Albanian–Greek frontier, the Alba-nian gendarmerie would not go beyond the present borders. Some Albanian villages around Bilisht would temporarily remain under Greek control.[63] It seems likely that the Albanians would not have made such concessions to Greece if they had known that a Greek invasion was impossible due to the lack of a significant Greek military presence in the region. Given that a mil-itary intervention could not have been successful in Korça, Athens had won a diplomatic victory. Nonetheless, the Albanians were able to profit from the Kapshtica Protocol, since it allowed Tirana to focus on the armed conflict it faced with the Italians in Vlora, a war won by the Albanians. Ultimately, the success of Greece's ploy was nullified, as Greece's resurgence would soon be followed by a tremendous military defeat. Italy ended up renouncing the Venizelos–Tittoni agreement after its military defeat in Albania, an indirect consequence of the protocol that backfired on Greece.[64]

The Albanian government thus extended its authority to Korça and appointed Nikollaq Zoi as prefect of the region. Zoi stripped Iakovos of all the political privileges he had enjoyed under the French and limited him only to religious duties.[65] But Iakovos still had a very powerful tool in the network of spies he had created around the metropolitanate. Although not large, it was efficient. The intelligence ring consisted of Greek schoolteachers and a small number of priests. Serving as a de facto consul, the metropolitan kept his superiors in Athens abreast of new developments, despite the prefect having banned him from all political activities.[66] Iakovos's network operated as a coherent unit, spying systematically on particular individuals as requested by the Greek government.[67] In March 1921, the metropolitan met with an Albanian minister and told him there would be constant misunderstanding between Albania and Greece until the issue of Northern Epirus was settled once and for all. The minister replied that there was no such issue, since Albania's 1913 frontier had been recognized and Greece had given up all territorial claims.[68]

Albanian–Greek relations began to change in late November 1920. Elections in Greece brought the defeat of Venizelos's liberals and Venizelos himself failed to win his seat in parliament. A new government, led by Demetrios Gounaris, took the reins of power in Athens. Greece's national minorities, including the Albanians, had voted overwhelmingly in favour of Gounaris, who had promised to end the war with Turkey and repatriate the Greek soldiers. With Venizelos's defeat, Metropolitan Iakovos lost his political guide, while Gounaris's victory gave impetus to the nationalist movements in the territories occupied by Greece and those lands threatened by a Greek invasion.[69]

Albania's first parliamentary elections took place under these new political circumstances. Greece demanded that the elections be cancelled, and threatened invasion if they proceeded as planned.[70] Although Albania knew that the Greek military was unable to intervene and so rejected such intimidations, Athens nevertheless won a surprising victory. Since Metropolitan Iakovos had no other tools, he spread the word that the Greek army was expected to enter Korça at any moment. These rumours caused a handful of Korça's citizens to draft a memorandum on 13 February 1921,[71] in which they announced that they would not participate in the elections for the parliament without clear provisions for the decentralized administration of Korça and Gjirokastra. The Korça Memorandum stated that, while Albania was a homogeneous nation, its progress and unification would not be possible if Muslims were allowed to rule southern Albania, since, as the memorandum noticed, Muslims were less educated than Christians in Albania. In the opinion of the Korça group, if the government in Tirana were to approve a decentralized administration for Gjirokastra and Korça regions, the Albanian nation would be safe from the hostile intentions on the part of Greece.[72]

Many Albanian patriots believed that the memorandum would put an end to Greek threats of invasion because, if its conditions were at least temporarily accepted, no one could say that Albania was mistreating the "Greeks" in Korça. Governance by Orthodox Albanians could not be represented as "Ottoman Islamic", a charge Greece often levelled against the Albanian state. As a result, the Korça Memorandum found support among prominent Albanian patriots who reasoned that it was far better if the Hellenists were part of the Albanian political opposition than if they were aligned with Greece and the metropolitanate. This turned out to be an unlikely victory for Iakovos, who used the opportunity to re-enter the political battlefield by presenting the memorandum as proof of the religious divide among the Albanians.[73] Rallies were organized throughout the country, as many Albanians, including such prominent Korça citizens as Mihal Grameno, Pandeli Cale, and Eshref Frashëri, fiercely objected to the memorandum.[74] The Tirana government replied that it could not address the issues raised by the memorandum, since these were questions the parliament would have to decide. Tirana's only instruction was that local officials should take whatever measures they saw fit.[75] On 21 March, Nikollaq Zoi reported that the authors of the memorandum were a small minority and that many of Korça's citizens accused them as pawns of Greece.[76] On 24 March, the government requested the arrest of those who initiated the memorandum – Rodhe, Kota, Bimbli, and Milto Gura[77] – but Zoi objected, saying he would ask Reverends Vasil Marko and Theofan Noli to intervene with the Korça group so they retracted the memorandum, as the Korça group was composed mainly of Albanian nationalists, whom Noli could impact.

Parliamentary elections took place on 21 April 1921. A significant portion of the Orthodox population in the city of Korça did not participate in the voting, but the election campaign was successful in the region's Orthodox villages, where most of its Christian population resided.[78] Governor Eshref Frashëri blamed the low turnout on the meddling of Iakovos, Greek funding, and the intervention of Italy. He argued that, although the entire population supported the Albanian cause, people were afraid to say this, since almost everyone feared a Greek invasion and a recurrence of the atrocities they had suffered from the Greek army in the First World War.[79]

The votes from the Orthodox in the villages combined with those of a minority in the city were enough for Korça to elect a slate of nationalist Albanian MPs: Pandeli Evangjeli, Loni Kristo, Pandeli Cale, Sotir Peçi, and Kristo Kirka were supported by Orthodox voters, while the Muslim community elected Banush Hamdiu, Eshref Frashëri, Sejfi Vllamasi, Tefik Mborja, and Tefik Panariti, in the first and only elections of Albania where the voting system was based on religious affiliation.[80] On 26 April, the Ministry of the Interior instructed Prefect Zoi to investigate Metropolitan Iakovos's behaviour during the election campaign.[81] The director of the police, Nik Dishnica, reported that Iakovos had been meeting continually with opponents of the Albanian state and had indirectly participated in the elections by advising his followers not to vote. Dishnica wrote that Iakovos, through his spies, was keeping Greece up to date on every development, and he concluded that the metropolitan was working against the interests of the Albanian state.[82] This was the first time an official of the Albanian government had requested Iakovos's expulsion.[83]

Greece also did what it could to undermine the elections in Gjirokastra. Although Athens was initially unable to win the removal of Archimandrite Taras Koroni – the dean who had brought Albanian language into the Church[84] – after the signing of the Venizelos–Tittoni agreement, the Italians replaced him with Reverend Thanas Duka, a confidant of Metropolitan Vasil Papakristo.[85] In the opinion of Greek officials, the Albanian national movement had gained tremendous strength, winning the support of such prominent Gjirokastra citizens as Vasil Dilo, Apostol Dhima, and Athanas Noti. Albanians constituted about two-thirds of the Orthodox population in the districts of Gjirokastra and Delvina, and the vast majority of them supported the Albanian national movement, while the other third were ethnic Greeks.[86] The new dean tried in vain to persuade the Orthodox to boycott the elections, and the Korça Memorandum found no support in Gjirokastra.[87] The meetings organized by the metropolitanate had very low attendance.[88] Gjirokastra Prefecture, led by Kol Tromara, carefully monitored the Church's activities, and when Tromara was presented with evidence that the metropolitanate had been organizing political meetings, he threatened to prosecute the dean.[89] Reverend Thanas responded that the metropolitanate had the right to organize Christian meetings on ecclesiastical issues and that he would continue to hold such gatherings whenever he deemed it necessary.[90]

But even under Reverend Thanas, the ecclesiastical movement in Gjirokastra was still gaining momentum. Reverend Pano Gjirokastra continued to hold the liturgy in Albanian and led the Albanization movement forward. He reported that anti-national activity was taking place in the Metropolitanate of Dryinopolis and that the church eldership, composed mainly of Greeks, was misusing the Church money. On 8 June, the Gjirokastra faithful attended an Albanian-language service led by Reverend Pano,[91] who held another liturgy in Albanian in Tërbuq on 11 October[92] and, again, at St Michael's Church in Nivan to honour the nation's martyrs on 26 November. Although Reverend Thanas also attended this last service, he did not co-officiate with Reverend Pano.[93]

Main Orthodox groups engaged in the ecclesiastical issue

The Albanian Church of America had sent Reverends Vasil Marko and Vangjel Çamçe to Albania under the leadership of their elected bishop, Theofan Noli.[94] The three men landed in Vlora on 28 October 1920, to the cheers of hundreds of supporters. The following day, they left for Durrës. Upon their arrival, the prefect informed Noli that he could not enter Albania, so he returned to Italy. For a short while, the "Noli issue" caused a degree of instability in the Tirana government, with Interior Minister Ahmet Zog and Foreign Minister Mehmet Konica threatening to resign if Noli was not permitted to return.[95] Faced with such pressure, Prime Minister Sulejman Delvina reversed the decision, but Noli decided not to return anyway.[96] During this time, the Tirana government appointed Noli to lead the delegation to the League of Nations to make the case for Albanian membership in that organization. A few months later, Noli returned to Albania in triumph.

The overwhelming majority of Albania's Orthodox elite were fully in favour of autocephaly for the Albanian Church, with the only exception the elite in the ethnic Greek minority. But this opposition constituted a tiny minority, who ultimately were unable to shape the future. The historian Joseph Swire points out that, while most southern Albanians were Hellenophiles with a strong affinity for Greek culture, only a small minority were truly Hellenists, who sought the political advantage of Greece at Albania's expense. Most Albanian Hellenophiles were nationalists who opposed Greece's territorial claims and its attempt to obstruct the political freedoms of Albanians.[97]

Albania was, in fact, among the countries with the most homogeneous Orthodox population: almost 90 per cent of its Orthodox were ethnic Albanians. In the first decades of the twentieth century, before the population exchanges of the early 1920s, Romania and Bulgaria each had large minorities of the other's nationality. The Serbian Orthodox Church included a large minority population in Macedonia as well as several thousand Orthodox Romanians, Greeks, and Albanians. In Greece, ethnic Albanians, Vlachs, and Bulgarians constituted more than 30 per cent of the Orthodox under the authority of the Church of Greece. Yet despite the ethnically homogeneous make-up of its Orthodox believers, Albania remained the only example of a country where the Church forbade holding the liturgy in the national language.

The vast majority of Orthodox Albanians were convinced that autocephaly was necessary for three main reasons. First, the activities of Iakovos, Vasil, and Germanos had highlighted the Patriarchate's anti-Albanian intentions. Second, ecclesiastical rules stipulated that an independent nation with a native Orthodox population had the right to an autocephalous Church. Third, if the Orthodox Church continued to be led by foreigners, this could lead to political turmoil and divisions among Albanians. Therefore, the three elite groups in Albanian Orthodoxy, from the most liberal to the most conservative, all saw autocephaly as the only solution, even if they were divided over who should lead the Church and supervise the ecclesiastical movement. These groups were the liberal nationalists, the supporters of Fan Noli, and Orthodox Albanian conservatives.[98]

The largest group was the liberal nationalists, who demanded an autocephalous, internationally recognized Orthodox Church with Albanian as its sole official language. They strongly opposed Noli's self-ordination as a bishop, although they were willing to support him if he were properly ordained in the future. Archimandrite Visar Xhuvani was the religious leader of the group, to which belonged almost all the most prominent Orthodox politicians and the majority of Korça's citizens. The liberal nationalists managed to spread their influence to other regions and eventually won the full support of the Albanian government.[99]

The second group consisted mainly of the ardent supporters of Fan Noli and the Vatra Federation. Just as Noli had boldly ordained himself a bishop, this faction felt that a radical solution was required for the ecclesiastical issue too. They believed that the autocephalous Church established in the United States in 1919 need only move its seat from Boston to Tirana – a formal proclamation of autocephaly was worthless and talks with the Patriarchate unnecessary. Noli was the group's political and religious leader, and he was assisted by the priests Vasil Marko and Vangjel Çamçe and such prominent Vatra supporters as Mihal Grameno. The movement found little support, however, in the political sphere, apart from, initially, the short-lived backing of Noli's fellow party members Ahmet Zog, Mehmet Konica, and Terenc Toçi, who later sided with the liberals.

The third group was made up of a diverse blend of conservative Orthodox Albanian patriots. It included those wary of Muslim and Catholic rule over Orthodox Albanians. They fiercely opposed every action by Noli and sought the Church's independence through negotiations between local elderships and the Patriarchate with no government interference. They sought friendly relations with Greece as a means to ensure that Muslim Albanians did not gain total control over their Orthodox compatriots, but at the same time they did not want such ties to encroach on Albania's independence. It was no coincidence that this group came mainly from Gjirokastra, where the Orthodox feared Muslim rule – a fear that was prompted by the lingering local Muslims' feeling that the Orthodox in that region were less supportive of the Albanian cause due to the Greek minority among them. There were, certainly, many Albanian nationalists, both Muslim and Orthodox, throughout the southernmost part of the country, who made no religious distinctions among Albanians. But some did perceive danger from other creeds and tried to define their own code of national unity. Meanwhile, in other regions of the country, where there was no Greek minority, most Orthodox felt no such threat from Muslims or Catholics. Outside of the Gjirokastra region, then, Orthodox believers generally supported the liberal nationalists.

When Noli returned to Albania from the League of Nations in Geneva, both the liberal nationalists and the conservatives made it clear that he should not be involved with the ecclesiastical issue. The self-ordained bishop remained in constant communication with Çamçe and Marko, who had settled in Korça, but he did not act as a hierarch; instead, he confined himself to his new political role as a member of the parliament, to which he had been elected by Vatra in March 1921.[100] Sotir Peçi, now the minister of education, warned Noli that, as long as the Protocol of Kapshtica was in force, any religious service he might hold as a bishop could put the Albanian nation at risk. Peçi warned that the current situation was fragile, as the Patriarchate was looking for any plausible reason to deny autocephaly, especially in a country with a Muslim majority. He was concerned that the Patriarchate could use Noli's claim to episcopal status as a pretext for taking action against the Albanians and suggested that he wait for the establishment of the autocephalous Church, an agreement with the Patriarchate, and proper ordination by two other bishops. Only after these steps had been taken could Noli lead the ecclesiastical movement.[101]

Matter of St George's Cathedral and the expulsion of the last Greek hierarch

Although all Korça's citizens were in favour of holding the liturgy in their native language, the Easter celebrations of 1921 were not expected to be in Albanian, as those of the previous year had been. Thanks to orders issued by the French troops, Metropolitan Iakovos had succeeded in returning the liturgy to the Greek language. Moreover, even under Albanian rule, he had preserved the status quo through the provisions of the Protocol of Kapshtica. On 26 November 1920, Reverends Vangjel Çamçe and Vasil Marko arrived in Korça without Noli. Iakovos refused to allow them to perform the liturgy in Albanian.[102] They met with Noli after his return from Geneva[103] and held an Albanian liturgy in Tirana on 3 April 1921, alongside a local priest,[104] and, again, several days later, in the southern lakeside town of Pogradec, assisted by two local priests.[105]

Korça, once in the vanguard of the Albanization movement, had suddenly become one of the only remaining places in Albania where church services were performed solely in Greek. On 24 April, the city's Orthodox elite made plans to hold the liturgy in Albanian at St George's Cathedral during Easter. They sent their request to Sotir Peçi and other MPs from the region. They stressed that they considered it a tremendous disgrace to hold the liturgy in a foreign language, since Orthodox Albanians in America and even in Romania could hold their church services in Albanian. The Korça Orthodox elite had tried to get permission for this from Prefect Zoi, but he threatened to imprison them if they so much as entered the church premises. They said that just as they had not cowered before either Greek or French bayonets, nor would they cower before their fellow Albanians. They declared their intention to hold religious services in Albanian and would kill anyone who tried to stop them, and then kill themselves. They demanded the removal of Iakovos and threatened to do him harm if their demands were not met.[106]

The provocation that ultimately changed the status quo came from an unexpected quarter: the army. The initiator was a man named Spiro Kosova, from the village of Kosova in the Përmet district; a supporter of the Vatra Federation, he had returned from the United States in 1914 to enlist in the

Albanian army as a lieutenant. He led Company III of the First Army Battalion, which was stationed in Korça, and most of his soldiers were also Orthodox. On 28 April 1921, he asked his battalion commander, Colonel Mustafa Aranitas, if he could find a suitable location to perform a religious service in their native language. The lieutenant suggested holding the service at another sacred site, as it was impossible to do this in a church. Kosova, hoping to provoke a suitable reaction from the commander, then asked if they could use a mosque for the Orthodox liturgy. Aranitas replied sharply that there were plenty of Muslims in the mosques already, and the Orthodox faithful could go to any church they wanted and perform their services in Albanian if they wished. Kosova knew that Aranitas had not given much thought to this decision, but the battalion commander's permission was enough for him. Joined by sub-lieutenant Kol Gjoni, Kosova went straightaway to St George's Cathedral, and, as soon as the doorkeeper opened the church, he took his keys. Leaving Kol Gjoni alone in the church, he then went to get Reverend Vasil Marko.[107]

Reverend Vasil entered the church and, after the ringing of the bells, donned his vestments. Orthodox faithful from all over the city began making their way towards the cathedral, where they were met by the head of the Korça police force, Nik Dishnica. He and his force had been ordered by the prefect to stop parishioners from entering. As the police lined up outside the cathedral, Reverend Vasil, Spiro Kosova, and Kol Gjoni, waiting inside, called the first Albanian Army Battalion to keep order and had them line up in front of the police force. Thus, if any clash took place, it would be between the Korça police and the Albanian army. Kosova came out of the cathedral and told Dishnica not to argue with the soldiers. Then he and Dishnica went to meet with Prefect Nikollaq Zoi, who described the action as "a coup". Kosova, rejecting the charges, responded that it was his duty to suppress any uprising against the homeland and the government. He told Zoi and Dishnica that he was determined to pray to God in Albanian since he did not speak Greek.[108]

The prefect immediately telephoned the interior minister in the Albanian capital and asked that the Ministry of Defence intervene to stop any confrontation between the army and the local police. While the prefect was speaking with the minister, Dishnica's men were unable to prevent people from entering St George's Cathedral. Reverend Vangjel Çamçe also arrived, and a congregation of more than a thousand believers attended the city's first Albanian liturgy in over a year.[109] The army had brazenly disobeyed the law, and the Ministry of Defence summoned Spiro Kosova and Kol Gjoni to Tirana face the consequences, but Colonel Aranitas responded that if he was forced to send Kosova and Gjoni to the capital, he would order all of Company III to go with them.[110] As a result, Zoi was unable to obey the government's orders and take the cathedral by force. The prefect protested that there was nothing he could do so long as the army was involved in the matter; the officers had taken the keys to the cathedral and called anybody who tried to close it a traitor.[111]

Two days later, on 30 April, Zoi apologized to Metropolitan Iakovos for what had occurred, expressing his regret at not being able to prevent this "coup". He assured him that Iakovos would regain the church after Easter.[112] In Athens, meanwhile, the reaction to the news nearly caused war.[113] On 3 May 1921, the Greek Foreign Ministry falsely reported that four people had died, nine were injured, and there was uncertainty about the personal safety of Metropolitan Iakovos, although there were no injured or casualties.[114] Prefect Iliakis of Kozani met with Prefect Zoi and informed him of Greece's main condition: the immediate delivery of the St George's Cathedral to Iakovos and the expulsion of all Korça Orthodox from the Albanian army because "they are Greeks".[115] Iliakis noted that the Kapshtica Protocol gave him the right to interfere in ecclesiastical issues and threatened that Greece was ready to use all its power to do what the Albanian government could not do, as it was its national duty to defend Greek dignity.[116] The matter of St George's Cathedral soon became the casus belli that Tirana had feared it would be. In retaliation, Greece imprisoned a large number of Albanians in Ioannina for several weeks, including the Elbasan prefect and Hysni Vrioni, a member of the Albanian parliament.[117] Tirana accepted the Greek demands in part, agreeing to preserve the status of the Church as defined by the Kapshtica Protocol until Orthodox Albanians established better relations with the Patriarchate. The Ministry of Interior ordered Zoi to take back the keys to the cathedral, by force if necessary. As for Greece's other demands, the government told Athens that these were Albanian internal affairs and not covered by the protocol.[118]

St George's Cathedral remained closed after the Easter Sunday celebration, which had raised the expectations of the people of Korça. To hamper the government's effort to seize control of the cathedral, a group of women had taken the keys. Reverends Vasil Marko and Vangjel Çamçe were placed under an unofficial house arrest, and Tirana ordered the Korça authorities to take the keys from the women by force since the law applied equally to both sexes.[119] But the local officials, fearing the outrage this would cause, were reluctant to execute the order. Mihal Grameno wrote in *Koha* (Time) that the cathedral belonged to Korça's Orthodox faithful and criticized Tirana for taking the side of the enemy and forcing Albanians to live under Greek intimidations.[120] It took the Albanian government two weeks to convince the women to hand over the church keys, but first it had to promise that they would not be given to Iakovos.[121]

The Albanian government then held on to the keys, certain that the people of Korça would rebel if Iakovos had them. Also, as tensions continued to rise, with Greece very likely considering military action, keeping St George's Cathedral closed seemed the wisest course. Although this left the Orthodox of Korça unhappy, because the Albanian liturgy was again banned from local churches, Greece was appeased, since closing the cathedral did not affect the supremacy of the Greek language in the metropolitanate.

On 15 June, Interior Minister Fuat Dibra ordered the prefecture of Korça to encourage local citizens to draft a memorandum asking the government for permission to hold the liturgy in Albanian. This was both a diplomatic strategy and a way to soften the bitter feelings of Korça's citizenry.[122] The memorandum stated that being forbidden to pray in Albanian was an injustice to the mothers, women, sisters, and children of Korça, while performing religious services in Greek seemed like a continuation of their churches' subjugation during the time of their ancestors. The memorandum noted that Albania was the only nation that enjoyed political freedom yet was ruled by foreign bishops who banned the use of the native language in religious services. It noted that religious books were available in Albanian and that priests could fulfil their duty in other countries where Albanian was allowed. So, the ban in Albania made no sense. The memorandum concluded with the saying "The voice of the people is the voice of God" and appealed to the government to find a solution to this issue, which so vitally affected Orthodox Albanians. More than 7,000 Korça citizens signed the memorandum, including all the most prominent people in the city and surrounding areas.[123] The newspaper *Posta e Korçës* (Korça Post) wrote that Korça's citizens had demonstrated their eagerness to enjoy their natural rights and that the government must now fearlessly intervene.[124] The newspaper added that the Orthodox of Korça were demanding the expulsion of the foreign agents who led the churches and named Iakovos specifically.[125] On 8 June, Pandeli Evangjeli, the chairman of the Albanian parliament and a Korça native, declared that St George's Cathedral would open within 15 days,[126] a decision later postponed by Prime Minister Iljaz Vrioni due to political developments.[127]

By August 1921, the situation in the Balkans had changed completely. King Constantine I, in exile since the last months of the First World War, had been reinstated by the new Greek government, creating a rift with the Great Powers, especially France, which resulted in the reduction of economic and military aid to Greece. A second factor was the launch of a final Greek offensive in the war with Turkey, with more than 200,000 Greek soldiers sent to Asia Minor.[128] Finally, press reports indicated that Great Britain was going to support the Albanian frontier set by the Protocol of Florence in 1913. Thus, the Tirana government no longer saw Greece as a military threat. On 22 August, Prefect Zoi asked for permission to hand the keys to St George's Cathedral to the people of Korça,[129] but Minister Sulejman Delvina refused.[130] Zoi then informed the minister that the citizenry had managed to open the cathedral anyway, and since he had been unable to stop them, he had simply handed over the keys.[131] Clearly, the government had lost control over the situation. The Council of Ministers resolved to dismiss Nikollaq Zoi and the local gendarmerie leaders for failing to obey the government's orders, but they did not do this straightaway; they felt it best to wait until a suitable replacement could be found for Zoi, since this was not the time for a void in the Korça government.[132]

Why Zoi did not follow Tirana's orders is unclear. Certainly, he was aware that Albania would not be invaded any time soon – an experienced patriot like Zoi, after all, would not have taken such a risk. There were, however, multiple reasons for Zoi to oppose his superiors, starting with a series of articles in the local press that for six months had claimed he was harbouring a pro-Greek bias on the ecclesiastical issue. And if this was not enough, a four-member commission composed of supporters of Iakovos was requesting his dismissal. Zoi himself reported to Prime Minister Vrioni that the metropolitan was leading a movement to instil confusion in the Albanian government.[133] Vrioni, who did not support Zoi, met with the commission, claiming this was a routine matter.[134] All these reasons might have prompted Zoi to hand over the keys to St George's Cathedral, confident that Greece was unlikely to invade – a confidence borne out by the lack of reaction from the Greek military. Iakovos's days as a power broker were numbered once the Albanian frontiers were finalized. Although some state officials, including the prefects of Korça and Gjirokastra, had previously called for the metropolitan's expulsion,[135] the Albanian government had chosen not to take the risk, preferring to keep things as they were until the question of the frontier was settled.[136]

Zoi again asked for Iakovos's expulsion[137] when the local press confirmed that the metropolitan had been conducting consular affairs for Greece.[138] By now, Iakovos's position had grown weaker, as enrolment in Korça's Greek schools fell sharply[139] and most local priests began siding with Reverends Vasil Marko and Vangjel Çamçe. Zoi informed the government that many citizens were demanding he take action against the metropolitan, and that he was trying to prevent them from removing him on their own.[140] A group of local Orthodox had threatened to expel Iakovos by force,[141] which led to the prefecture increasing the security around Iakovos.[142]

The Tirana government waited until 9 November 1921, when the Peace Conference recognized the borders outlined in the Florence Protocol. On the morning of 19 November, the *Posta e Korçës* headline read: "The Last Straw – Bishop Iakovos Must be Expelled by Any Means".[143] That same day, the government unanimously approved Iakovos's expulsion.[144] Korça Police Director Nik Dishnica went to the metropolitanate, where he found Iakovos sleeping.[145] The ministry had instructed Dishnica to take special care not to offend the religious dignity of the hierarch.[146] Iakovos's protests were useless. He asked permission to go to St George's Cathedral one last time, before departing via Kapshtica, but Dishnica denied his request.[147] A few Orthodox officers and gendarmes accompanied Iakovos until he left Albania the following day, never to return.[148]

A delegation from the League of Nations, visiting the country a few months later, noted that the metropolitan's expulsion was the natural consequence of Iakovos's actions. They observed that only a very small minority of the population wished to live under Greek rule, while Iakovos's sustained anti-Albanian efforts had made the Albanians eager to be rid of him.[149] The day Iakovos left Albania, the Orthodox faithful of Korça filled the churches as never before. The metropolitanate's priests led a requiem for the martyrs of the national movement, which was attended by all local civil and military officials, as well as a sizable segment of the population.[150] The priests of Korça elected a new eldership, with Llambro Mbroja as chairman and Foqion Postoli as secretary. The priests declared their obedience to the new eldership and agreed to use only Albanian in their religious services.[151] The new eldership charged Iakovos in absentia with having stolen church money to fund his anti-Albanian activities.[152] The metropolitan's departure marked the end of Greek education in Korça.[153] The Greek newspaper, *To Fos* (The Light), reported on 23 November that Albanians had occupied the schools and churches. *Posta e Korçës* responded that nobody but Albanians could occupy the churches since there were no Greeks in Korça.[154] Meanwhile, once Iakovos had been removed, the Council of Ministers acted on their earlier decision, and Nikollaq Zoi was finally dismissed.[155]

Religion and Albanian-Greek diplomatic relations, 1919–1921

The Paris Peace Conference officially concluded its mission on 16 January 1920, passing the baton to a newly established permanent organization, the League of Nations, based in Geneva. Albania now had a central government and an emerging political elite, as established by the Congress of Lushnja. On 12 October 1920, the new government submitted an official request to join the League and sent a delegation to Geneva led by Fan Noli and composed of three other Christians. The positive impression created in Paris by the Albanian foreign minister, Mihal Turtulli, had influenced this decision. Greece had attempted to portray Albania as a nation divided by religion. Thus, having an Orthodox present Albania's request for admission to the League of Nations seemed the best rebuttal to Greek claims. On 17 December 1920, the League accepted Albania as a full member, with 35 votes in favour, 7 abstentions, and none opposing. Several reasons can explain Albania's admission, including the fact that it was no longer possible for any member nation to characterize Albania as "Little Turkey" or a "Muslim country", where Christians lived under threat. On the contrary, the League praised Albania as a multi-religious nation in which nationality was more important than religious affiliation, a rare example of Muslim–Christian unity. It was Fan Noli, the eloquent Orthodox priest, who made the case for his homeland in front of the representatives in Geneva. His presence alone was enough to refute Greece's claims. Noli recalled how he was overcome with emotion when he saw the neighbouring nations vote in favour of the Albanian request. He said that Albania's admission did great honour to the League of Nations.[156]

Nevertheless, Albania faced many formal complaints in Geneva related to religion. The first complaint was lodged on 25 November 1920, just a month before the League approved its membership, by the Pan-Epirotic Union in the United States, led by Ioannis Kasavetis. The Union, asserting that the true will of the people of Northern Epirus was to unite with Greece, said it felt obliged to submit a letter of protest now that the Greek state had officially withdrawn its territorial claims on Korça and Gjirokastra. The Union rebutted the Albanian argument that language was proof of nationality, citing the fact that French was spoken in both Belgium and France, just as English was in both the United States and Great Britain. Kasavetis asserted that, despite their mother tongue, Albanian-speaking Orthodox were, in fact, Greeks.[157] A few months later, the Union went on to deny even the existence of the Albanian language, claiming that it was merely a dialect spoken alongside Greek, even by Muslims. The group concluded that Albania's "Muslim government" was persecuting the Northern Epirotes by closing their schools and expelling Greek priests.[158]

On 9 February 1921, Prime Minister Iljaz Vrioni responded to the Union's charges by explaining that all Albanians were part of four religious communities, none of which formed a majority. He insisted that freedom of conscience and creed prevailed in his country, and that all Albanian citizens freely enjoyed the same political and social rights regardless of religion. Vrioni further outlined the composition of the main state institutions. The Regency (formed after Prince Wied had not been allowed to return to power) was composed of one Catholic Christian bishop, one Orthodox Christian, one Sunni Muslim, and one Bektashi Muslim. The parliament, the army, the gendarmerie, the police, the administration, and the local councils all had a similar composition.[159]

After the Korça Memorandum was signed on 13 February 1921, the Pan-Epirotic Union argued that the memorandum was proof that the Christians of Northern Epirus were opposed to being part of Albania. Kasavetis stressed that Korça's Orthodox, who constituted a majority of the city's intellectual and commercial elite, were demanding full independence from Albania, whose government was trying to create a "little Turkey" in the western Balkans. He noted that the Korça Memorandum contradicted Noli's claims that the Christians of Northern Epirus wanted to join Albania and said that if the people of Korça had the choice, they would join Greece. He claimed that the Albanian government had ordered anyone who refused to participate in the parliamentary elections to be killed. Kasavetis also asserted that the parliament had approved an old Turkish law to prosecute any Christian the government considered dangerous.[160] The Union, however, had misread the recent developments surrounding the Korça Memorandum. The memorandum's initiators immediately responded that their original missive "was addressed to our national government in Tirana" and accused Kasavetis of "deviously" attempting to portray them as Hellenists.[161] On June 21, Prime Minister Vrioni wrote that the memorandum was the result of the actions of several pious people, who were nevertheless true Albanian patriots, and that they had been trying to prevent the temporary invasion of Korça by Greece.[162]

The matter of St George's Cathedral provoked the harshest attacks in the League of Nations. On 10 May 1921, the Northern Epirotic League of Athens and Piraeus lodged its own complaint against Albania. The Northern Epirotes lamented that Muslim soldiers, accompanied by several fanatics, had staged an ecclesiastical coup, which had resulted in the deaths of 12 people. In fact, there had been no casualties and the instigators were Orthodox soldiers led by the Vatra supporter Spiro Kosova.[163] On 18 May, the Albanian delegation rejected these charges; they noted that the situation in Korça was calm and there was no build-up of Albanian troops at the border. On the contrary, the Albanians accused Greece of moving its army close to the border and assaulting and murdering the innocent citizens of Chameria.[164] A few days later, the Albanian delegation added that there had been no rioting, no opposition, no resistance, and consequently no victims in southern Albania.[165] The Albanian diaspora in Romania backed these statements.[166]

At the League of Nations, Greece itself made the assertion that Albania had a "Muslim nature" that was obvious to anyone who visited the country and evident in the composition of its parliament and the Regency, governing bodies in which Muslims occupied half the seats, as many as Catholics and Orthodox combined. The Greek representative, Dendramis, reached this conclusion after Prime Minister Vrioni's letter stressed that the religious map of Albania comprised three important parts: Catholics, Orthodox, and Muslims.[167] Dendramis's argument was based on the Albanian prime minister's words that the Muslim population encompassed two separate *sects*, while the Christians were two separate *religions*. Dendramis chose to use the word "religion" in its narrowest sense, despite Vrioni having explained that all four groups were religious communities. For Dendramis, the Muslims were represented by both the Sunni and the Bektashi members in the Regency, making them equal to all Christians.

Dendramis therefore accused the Albanian government of being Albanian-Turkish and hating the Orthodox. He asked that the Albanian constitution be amended to ensure the fair representation of the religious minorities in the parliament, government, and civil service. He also requested that any Muslim who wished to convert to Christianity be able to do so without fear of persecution. In addition, he asked that Albania provide special status to the religious communities, recognize the right of minorities to freely use the language of their choice, and restore all the rights that Christians had enjoyed under the Ottoman Empire. Lastly, he asked that any state have the right to supervise the implementation of these provisions and inform the League of Nations if Albania violated any of them.[168]

On 21 June 1921, Prime Minister Vrioni responded that there was no persecution of either the Orthodox population or the Greek minority. He objected to Dendramis's conclusion that Muslims had greater representation in the government than Christians, as each faith comprised two different groups, so basic statistics invalidated that argument. He emphasized that the members of these two faiths were brothers with one language, united forever by their love for the motherland, and that there had been Orthodox elected to parliament even in areas without any Christians. Albania had implemented most of Dendramis's requests by default, since neither the Albanian state nor the Albanian nation had a religious nature. Vrioni noted that Albania had already guaranteed governmental representation of religious communities, lack of punishment for conversion, and the rights of the Greek minority whose population numbered no more than 16,000. He concluded that Albania would follow the same principle as other independent Balkan countries and pursue the establishment of an autocephalous Orthodox Church.[169]

The conflict between the two countries peaked when the Korça police put Metropolitan Iakovos under surveillance. On 1 September 1921, Dendramis blamed the Albanian government for forcing the Greek minority to flee into exile.[170] Archimandrite Visar Xhuvani, writing on behalf of Albania's Orthodox priests and believers, replied in a telegram to the League of Nations that Albanians were united despite their different religions. Metropolitan Vasil of Dryinopolis refuted Xhuvani's claim and accused him as being a pawn of a "Muslim government".[171]

All aspiring members of the League of Nations were requested to create a legal framework for the protection of the minorities within their borders through bilateral agreements with neighbouring nations. Albania and a few other League aspirants were offered the alternative of signing a unilateral declaration by which they undertook specific obligations towards their minorities. On 21 October 1921, Fan Noli submitted the *Declaration Concerning the Protection of Minorities in Albania.* It included full protection of religion for all Albanian citizens regardless of birthplace, nationality, language, race, or creed and the right of citizenship to anyone who was born or lived in Albania before the First World War. By signing the declaration, Albania agreed to the possibility of bilateral voluntary migration for the country's national minorities under the supervision of the League of Nations.[172]

Albania recognized the rights of all its religious minorities – although, as Vrioni had stressed only a few weeks earlier, no religious community constituted a majority. The declaration acknowledged the right of minorities to speak any language they chose, including in their religious services. Lastly, the declaration recognized Greece's right to inform the League of any violation of the declaration, a concession that paved the way for the two countries' later diplomatic conflict over the ecclesiastical issue. Citing the declaration, Greece would insist that Albania must accept the right of every Orthodox community, even Albanian communities, to hold the liturgy and establish schools in Greek. While the government proposed the establishment of a religious quota in the parliamentary elections of 1923, parliament fiercely opposed this proposal. The Vlora MP, Qazim Koculi, called the declaration "a stupid mistake".[173]

After the settlement of Albania's borders and Metropolitan Iakovos's subsequent expulsion on 19 November 1921, Greece condemned the introduction of Albanian into schools and the forced exile of "the spiritual leader of the Greeks in Korça". The new Albanian prime minister, Xhafer Ypi, replied that Iakovos had been a danger to both the Albanian state and the Albanian people, and that Christian believers had freely elected the church eldership in Korça. He explained that the Tirana government could not intervene and that the eldership had closed the Greek schools due to economic difficulties created by Iakovos having transferred two million gold francs into Greek bank accounts from church funds, money which the Bank of Athens refused to repatriate.[174]

Figure 2.1 Fan Noli Entering the League of Nations.

Figure 2.2 Liturgy at St George's Cathedral.

Figure 2.3 Metropolitan Iakovos of Durrës.

Figure 2.4 Noli at the League of Nations General Assembly.

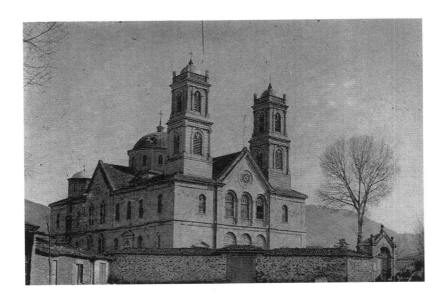

Figure 2.5 St George's Cathedral.

Notes

1 Avni Spahiu, *Noli: Jeta në Amerikë [Noli: Life in America]* (Tirana: Toena, 2007), 41.
2 Jorgaqi, *Noli I*, 346–351.
3 The establishment of an ecclesiastical jurisdiction refers to the creation of a diocese, mission, or vicariate. This was undoubtedly the most important event in Albanian church history before the declaration of autocephaly. Ultimately, it helped ensure that Albanians had their own ecclesiastical structure, even though it was only a mission under the jurisdiction of the Russian Metropolitanate in the United Sates.
4 Jorgaqi, *Noli I*, 349; Duka, "Veprimtaria", 36–40.
5 Glavinas, *The Orthodox Church*, 44.
6 Andrea Llukani, *Kanonet dhe statutet e kishës ortodokse [Canons and Statutes of the Orthodox Church]* (Tiranë: Trifon Xhagjika, 2011), 18.
7 Mihal Grameno, "Pishkopata Autoqefale Orthodhokse Kombëtare [National Orthodox Autocephalous Diocese]", *Koha [Time]*, 11 September 1919, 1.
8 Fan Noli, *Pesëdhjetëvjetori i Kishës Ortodokse Shqiptare 1908–1958 [The Albanian Orthodox Church's Fiftieth Anniversary 1908–1958]* (Boston: AOC, 1959), 138–140.
9 Xhuvani, *Visarion Xhuvani*, 139.
10 Çami, *The War I*, 300–306.
11 AMFA, Y. 1920, f. 1, 1, Memorandum to Albanian Believers, 21 March/3 April 1920.
12 Stratigakis, *Metropolitan of Mytilene*, 96.
13 Xhuvani, *Works*, 14.
14 AQSH, F. 155 "MJ", Y. 1931, f. VIII-175, 1–10, OACA to MJ "Mbi Pikëpamjen Kanonike të gjendjes së sotshme të KOASH [On the Canonical View of the Actual AOAC Situation]", 14 December 1931.
15 AQSH, F. 152 "MIA", Y. 1919, f. 286, 1, Dhimitruka to MIA, 30 October 1919.
16 Visarion Xhuvani, *Çashtje politiko-religjoze Kostandinopoli-Tiranë (Botohet me rastin e bisedimeve përkatëse që janë tyke u bamë kto dit në Tiranë) [Political and Religious Issues between Constantinople and Tirana (Published on the Occasion of the Relevant Talks Currently Being Held in Tirana)]* (Tirana: Tirana, 1926), 18; All relevant decisions are in AQSH, F. 152 "MIA", Y. 1921, f. 1011.
17 AQSH, 2 "ASDRENI", f. 75, 77–78, Asdreni to Sotir Gjika, 28 September 1920.
18 AQSH, F. 99 "The Albanian Colony in Romania", f. 267, 1, no author, no date.
19 AQSH, F. 152 "MIA", Y. 1921, f. 1011, 16, Archimandrite to MIA, no date.
20 AQSH, F. 152 "MIA", Y. 1921, f. 104, 1, Xhuvani to MIA, 15 September 1921.
21 Religious services in Durrës had been held in Albanian since 1916. AQSH, F. 152 "MIA", Y. 1921, f. 111, 2, Korça Prefecture to MIA, 16 January 1921.
22 Puto, *Political Albania*, 160.
23 Thanos Veremis, *Balkan Expansion of Greece* (Athens: Hellenic Foundation for Foreign and European Policy, 1995), 14–33.
24 Muin Çami, "Ushtarakët francezë në Korçë, mbështetës të aspiratave kombëtare të popullsisë (1916–1920) [The French Military in Korça, Supporter of the People's National Aspirations]", *Studime historike [Historical Studies]* 1–2 (2002):61–77.
25 GAK, F. "PMO", f. 229, 3, Efrem Gjini to MFA, 14 February 1918.
26 Kondis, *Elinismos II*, 55: IDAYE, f. A/5, no number, The Prefect of Florina to MFA, 3 November 1918.
27 ELIA, F. "Eleftherios Venizelos", f. 7/1, 3, Paraskevopoulos to Venizelos, 28 September 1919.

28 Kondis, *Elinismos II, 98–99:* IDAYE, f. A/5/VII (1), no. 7944, Venizelos to Repoulis, 11 August 1919.
29 Fotios G. Ikonomou, *Η Ορθόδοξος Εκκλησία της Αλβανίας και η συμβολή της εις την διατήρησιν του ελληνισμού της Βορείου Ηπείρου [The Orthodox Church in Albania and Its Contribution to Safeguarding the Hellenism of Northern Epirus]* (Athens: Nees Thesis, 1988), 17.
30 Stratigakis: *Metropolitan of Mytilene*, 100–101.
31 Kondis, *Elinismos II*, 128: IDAYE, f. A/5/ VII (1), no. 8807, Diomidis to Venizelos, 30 August 1919.
32 Stratigakis, *Metropolitan of Mytilene*, 101.
33 Kondis, *Elinismos II*, 111: IDAYE, f. A/5/II, no. 8255, Kalevras to MFA, 21 August/3 September 1919.
34 Stratigakis, *Metropolitan of Mytilene*, 102.
35 Kondis, *Elinismos II*, 135: IDAYE, f. A/5/VIIc (1), no. 8985, Paraskevopoulos to Venizelos, 9 September 1919.
36 Stratigakis, *Metropolitan of Mytilene*, 105.
37 GAK, F. "PMO", f. 228, 1, Florina Prefect to Greek MFA, 17 September 1919.
38 Çami, "Kleri i Lartë", 47–48.
39 Stratigakis, *Metropolitan of Mytilene*, 103.
40 Çami, *The War I*, 379.
41 Kondis, *Elinismos II*, 148–149: IDAYE, f. A/5/II (9), no. 15681, General Headquarters to MFA, 3 November 1919.
42 GAK, F. "PMO", f. 228, 44, no. 1060, Kozani-Florina Command to the Ministry of War, 16 November 1919.
43 Çami, *The War I*, 380.
44 Kondis, *Elinismos II*, 148–149: General Headquarters to MFA, quoted.
45 Çami, *The War I*, 381–388.
46 Kondis, *Elinismos II*, 165–167: IDAYE, f. A/5, no. 5415, Orfanidis to the Ministry of War, 7 March 1920.
47 Kondis, *Elinismos II*, 170–173: IDAYE, f. A/5, no 3753, Ministry of War Report, 19 March 1920.
48 Çami, *The War II*, 177–192.
49 Ibid.
50 Duka, *History of Albania* 155.
51 Çami, *Albania*, 205–206.
52 Kondis, *Elinismos II*, 208: IDAYE, f. A/5, no. 6095, Venizelos to the Ministry of War, 9 May 1920.
53 Kondis, *Elinismos II*, 232–235: IDAYE, f. A/5, no. 7261, Iliakis to MFA, 30 May/12 June 1920.
54 Kondis, *Elinismos II*, 216: IDAYE, f. A/5, no. 6446, Venizelos to Kalevras, 15/28 May 1920.
55 Kondis, *Elinismos II*, 248: IDAYE, f. a/5, no. 7535, Venizelos to MFA, 6/19 June 1920.
56 Kondis, *Elinismos II*, 216: IDAYE, f. a/5, no number, Venizelos to Florina Deputy Prefect, 28 May 1920.
57 Stratigakis, *Metropolitan of Mytilene*, 113.
58 Nowadays the village is situated in Greece called Krystallopigi.
59 Kondis, *Elinismos II*, 225: IDAYE, f. A/5, no. 938, Thessaloniki Military Command to MFA, 10 June 1920.
60 Kondis, *Elinismos II*, 232–235: Kozani-Florina Prefect to MFA, 30 May/12 June 1920.
61 Kondis, *Elinismos II*, 225: Thessaloniki Military Command to MFA, quoted.
62 Kondis, *Elinismos II*, 232–235: Kozani-Florina Prefect to MFA, 30 May/12 June 1920.

63 Stratigakis, *Metropolitan of Mytilene*, 113–114.

64 On 28 June 1920, the Greek government was informed that Italy supported the territorial integrity of Albania. Kondis, *Elinismos II*, 255: IDAYE, f. A/4, no. 8519, Rome Embassy to MFA, 28 June 1920.

65 Stratigakis, *Metropolitan of Mytilene*, 116.

66 Iakovos's diplomatic correspondence is preserved in AMFA, Y. 1925, f. B/35. A portion of these papers are published in Apostolos Glavinas, "Ο Μητροπολίτης Δυρραχίου Ιάκοβως και οι δραστηριότητες του για το εκκλησιαστικό ζήτημα της Αλβανίας [The Metropolitan of Durrës Iakovos and His Activity for the Ecclesiastical Issue in Albania]", *Ηπειρότηκο Ημερολόγιο [Epirotan Calendar]* 2 (1986):56–58.

67 Such a case occurred in April 1921 when a Turkish Colonel Qamili from Ohrid appeared in Korça. Kondis, Elinismos II, 336: IDAYE, f. A/5/10, no. 5446, Florina Deputy Prefect to MFA, 12/25 May 1920.

68 Kondis, *Elinismos II*, 318–319: IDAYE, f. A/5, no. 3611, Metropolitan Iakovos to MFA, 22 March 1921.

69 Stratigakis, *Metropolitan of Mytilene*, 107–108.

70 Kondis, *Elinismos II*, 293: IDAYE, f. A/5, no. 61/115, MFA to Epirus Governor, 3 January 1921.

71 AQSH, F. 152 "MIA", Y. 1921, f. 111, 5, Korça Prefecture to MIA, 13 February 1921.

72 AQSH, F. 152 "MIA", Y. 1921, f. 45, 3, Korça Memorandum, 13 February 1921.

73 AQSH, F. 152 "MIA", Y. 1921, f. 45, 3, Korça Prefecture to MIA, 16 February 1921.

74 AQSH, F. 152 "MIA", Y. 1921, f. 45, 9, Berat Prefecture to MIA, 24 February 1921. AQSH, F. 152 "MIA", Y. 1921, f. 45, 31, Elbasan Prefecture to MIA, 26 February 1921; AQSH, F. 152 "MIA", Y. 1921, f. 45, 36, Lushnja sub-prefecture to MIA, 26 February 1921; AQSH, F. 152 "MIA", Y. 1921, f. 45, 37, Tirana Municipality to MIA, 26 February 1921; AQSH, F. 152 "MIA", Y. 1921, f. 45, 38, Durrës Prefecture to MIA, 26 February 1921; AQSH, F. 152 "MIA", Y. 1921, f. 45, 44, Fier Sub-prefecture to MIA, 26 February 1921; AQSH, F. 152 "MIA", Y. 1921, f. 45, 47, Vlora Prefecture to MIA, 26 February 1921; AQSH, F. 152 "MIA", Y. 1921, f. 45, 22, Mallakastra sub-prefecture to MIA, 26 February 1921. AQSH, F. 152 "MIA", Y. 1921, f. 45, 55, MIA to Mihal Grameno, 5 March 1921.

75 AQSH, F. 152 "MIA", Y. 1921, f. 45, 33, MIA to Korça Prefecture, 17 February 1921.

76 AQSH, F. 152 "MIA", Y. 1921, f. 45, 15, Korça Prefecture to MIA, 21 March 1921.

77 AQSH, F. 152 "MIA", Y. 1921, f. 45, 80, MIA to Korça Prefecture, 24 March 1921.

78 AMFA, Y. 1920, f. 3, 10, Dr Turtulli to Mid'hat Frashëri, no date.

79 AMFA, Y. 1920, f. 3, 20, Eshref Frashëri to Mid'hat Frashëri, no date.

80 Dervishi, *History*, 128.

81 AQSH, F. 152 "MIA", Y. 1921, f. 111, 10, MIA to Korça Prefecture, 26 April 1921.

82 AQSH, F. 149 "PMO", Y. 1921, f. VI-61, 2, Korça Police to the Prefect, 28 April 1921.

83 Stratigakis, *Metropolitan of Mytilene*, 107–108.

84 Kondis, *Elinismos II*, 423: IDAYE, A/5I I3, no. 2360, Epirus Governor to MFA, 9 March 1918.

85 AQSH, F. 156 "The Dictation Court", Y. 1923, f. 4, 143, Report on Thanas Duka, no date.

86 Kondis, *Elinismos II*, 150–153: IDAYE, f. A/5/II (9), no. 12431, Orfanidis to Ministry of War, 27 November 1919.

87 Vasil Dilo, "Psikoza e 'Vorio Epirit' dhe marrëveshjet mbi protokollin e Korfuzit [The Psychosis of 'Northern Epirus' and Agreements on the Corfu Protocol]", *Ndryshe [Different]*, 26 April 2007, 16–17.

88 AMFA, Y. 1921, f. 88, 14, Letter from Pan-Epirotic Union in the USA, 18 April 1921.

89 AQSH, F. 152 "MIA", Y. 1921, f. 96, 15, Gjirokastra Prefecture to MIA, 21 February 1921.

90 AQSH, F. 152 "MIA", Y. 1921, f. 96, 7, Metropolitanate to Prefecture, 24/31 January 1921.

91 Jani, "Papa Pano", 88–92.

92 *Posta e Korçës [Korça Post]*, 11 October 1921, 2.

93 *Posta e Korçës [Korça Post]*, 26 November 1921, 1.

94 Sejfi Vllamasi, *Ballafaqime politike në Shqipëri [Political Confrontations in Albania]* (Tirana: Vllamasi, 2012), 235–236.

95 Jorgaqi, *Noli I*, 391.

96 AQSH, F. 152 "MIA", Y. 1920, f. 69, 4, Durrës Prefecture to MIA, 29 October 1920.

97 Swire, *Albania*, 23.

98 These are the author's own designations for these groups, which were not organized in any formal way and therefore were multipolar and leaderless. Nevertheless, they represented very distinct positions with regard to the autocephaly effort.

99 AQSH, F. 55 "Sotir Peçi", f. 77.

100 The Vatra Federation was given the right to elect an MP in the first Albanian parliament as a reward for their patriotic work. Thus, Vatra elected Noli. The omnipotence of the elected Bishop Theofan was recognized by a government decision, on 1 February 1921. AQSH, F. 152 "MIA", Y. 1920, f. 3, 6, Council of Ministers Decision no. 109, 1 February 1921.

101 AQSH, F. 55 "Sotir Peçi", f. 77, 14, Sotir Peçi's Letter, no date.

102 "Andej-Këndej [Here and There]", *Koha [Time]*, 27 November 1920, 3.

103 "Andej-Këndej [Here and There]", *Koha [Time]*, 5 March 1921, 3.

104 Rako Katundi, "Nga Tirana: Meshë shqipe [From Tirana: Albanian Liturgy]", *Koha [Time]*, 23 April 1921, 1.

105 "E para meshë në gjuhën amtare në Kishën e Pogradecit! [The First Liturgy of the Mother Tongue in the Pogradec Church!]", *Koha [Time]*, 30 April 1921, 1.

106 AQSH, F. 55 "Sotir Peçi", f. 72, 12, Submission to Korça MPs, 24 April 1921.

107 Verli, ed., *Spiro Kosova I*, 188–202.

108 Ibid.

109 AQSH, F. 152 "MIA", Y. 1921, f. 111, 12, Korça Prefecture to MIA, 28 April 1921.

110 Verli, ed., *Spiro Kosova I*, 188–202.

111 AQSH, F. 152 "MIA", Y. 1921, f. 111, 20, MIA to Korça Prefecture, 1 May 1921.

112 Kondis, *Elinismos II*, 333: IDAYE, f. A/5/10, no. 4640, Florina Sub-Prefecture to MFA, 24/7 May 1921.

113 Beqir Meta, "Vështrim rreth kombëtarizimit dhe pavarësimit të Kishës Ortodokse [Overview of the Nationalization and Independence of the Orthodox Church]", *Studime historike [Historical Studies]* 1–2 (2006):74.

114 Kondis, *Elinismos II*, 324–325: IDAYE, f. A/5/10, no. 4538, Ministry of War to MFA, 21 April 1921.

115 AQSH, F. 152 "MIA", Y. 1921, f. 60, 4, Korça Prefecture to MIA, 6 May 1921.

116 Kondis, *Elinismos II*, 327: IDAYE, f. A/5/10, no number, Kozani Prefecture to MFA, 23 April 1921.

117 Meta, "Overview of the Nationalization", 79–80.

118 AQSH, F. 152 "MIA", Y. 1921, f. 60, 9, MIA to Korça Prefecture, 6 May 1921.
119 AQSH, F. 152 "MIA", Y. 1921, f. 111, 27, MIA to Korça Prefecture, 11 May 1921.
120 Mihal Grameno, "Armiku u dërrmua [The Enemy Was Crushed]", *Koha [Time]* 21 May 1921, 1.
121 *Koha [Time]*, 21 May 1921, 2.
122 AQSH, F. 152 "MIA", Y. 1921, f. 111, 28, MIA to Korça Prefecture, 12 June 1921.
123 The telegram along with the signatures is found in the AQSH: AQSH, F. 152 "MIA", Y. 1921, f. 111, 29, Citizens Request to MIA, 16 June 1921.
124 *Posta e Korçës [Korça Post]*, 18 June 1921, 2.
125 *Posta e Korçës [Korça Post]*, 21 June 1921, 2.
126 AQSH, F. 152 "MIA", Y. 1921, f. 111, 43, Korça Prefecture to MIA, 23 June 1921.
127 AQSH, F. 152 "MIA", Y. 1921, f. 111, 44, MIA to Korça Prefecture, 4 July 1921.
128 Ioanis Daskarolis, *Στρατιωτικά κινήματα στην Ελλάδα του Μεσοπολέμου (1922–1935) [Military Movement in Mid-War Greece (1922–1935)]* (Athens: Gnomon, 2012), 15.
129 AQSH, F. 152 "MIA", Y. 1921, f. 111, 57, Korça Prefecture to MIA, 22 August 1921.
130 AQSH, F. 152 "MIA", Y. 1921, f. 111, 58, MIA to Korça Prefecture, 22 August 1921.
131 AQSH, F. 152 "MIA", Y. 1921, f. 111, 63, Korça Prefecture to MIA, 22 August 1921.
132 AQSH, F. 152 "MIA", Y. 1921, f. 97, 1, Council of Ministers Decision no. 709, 23 August 1921.
133 AQSH, F. 152 "MIA", Y. 1921, f. 45, 136, Korça Prefecture to MIA, 10 August 1921.
134 AQSH, F. 152 "MIA", Y. 1921, f. 45, 137, MIA to Korça Prefecture, 10 August 1921.
135 AQSH, F. 149 "PMO", Y. 1921, f. VI-66, 2, Gjirokastra Prefecture to MIA, 18 August 1921.
136 AQSH, F. 152 "MIA", Y. 1921, f. 111, 68, Council of Ministers Decision no. 726, 30 August 1921.
137 AMFA, Y. 1921, f. 159, 26, Korça Prefecture to MIA, 27 August 1921.
138 *Posta e Korçës [Korça Post]*, 10 August 1921, 1.
139 Glavinas, "Metropolitan of Durrës", 59–60.
140 AQSH, F. 152 "MIA", Y. 1921, f. 111, 77, Korça Prefecture to MIA, September 1921.
141 AQSH, F. 152 "MIA", Y. 1921, f. 111, 105, Korça District to Gendarmerie General Command, 27 October 1921.
142 *Posta e Korçës [Korça Post]*, 27 October 1921, 2.
143 "Kupa u mbush – Dhespot Jakovi duhet dëbuar medoemos [The Last Straw – Bishop Iakovos Must Be Exiled by All Means]", *Posta e Korçës [Korça Post]*, 19 November 1921, 2.
144 AQSH, F. 152 "MIA", Y. 1921, f. 111, 196, Council of Ministers Decision no. 910, 19 November 1921.
145 Stratigakis, *Metropolitan of Mytilene*, 199.
146 AQSH, F. 152 "MIA", Y. 1921, f. 111, 60, MIA to Korça Prefecture, 20 November 1921.
147 Stratigakis, *Metropolitan of Mytilene*, 201.
148 "Qeveria largoj nga Korça Dhes. Jakovë [Government Removes Bishop Iakovos from Korça]", *Posta e Korçës [Korça Post]*, 22 November 1921, 1.
149 Swire, *Albania*, 304.
150 *Posta e Korçës [Korça Post]*, 22 November 1921, 4.
151 *Posta e Korçës [Korça Post]*, 26 November 1921, 2.

152 *Posta e Korçës [Korça Post]*, 3 December 1921, 2.
153 Stratigakis, *Metropolitan of Mytilene*, 107–108.
154 "Shpifjet e gazetave greke mbi dëbuarjen e Dhespot Jakovit [Greek Newspapers Slanders Over the Expulsion of Bishop Iakovos]", *Posta e Korçës [Korça Post]*, 3 December 1921, 1.
155 "Përgjigje Z-Tij N. Zoit, ish-prefektit të Korçës [Reply of Mr N. Zoi, former Prefect of Korça]", *Posta e Korçës [Korça Post]*, 26 November 1921, 2.
156 Puto, *Political Albania*, 241–289; Turhan Pashë Përmeti, *Shqipëria përballë Konferencës së Paqes Paris 1919 [Albania in Front of the Paris Peace Conference 1919]* (Tirana: Eugen, 2007).
157 AMFA, Y. 1921, f. 88, 1, Letter from Pan-Epirotic Union in the USA, 27 January 1921.
158 AMFA, Y. 1921, f. 88, 30, Letter from Pan-Epirotic Union in the USA, 19 April 1921.
159 AMFA, Y. 1921, f. 87, 12–14, Vrioni to the League of Nations, 9 February 1921.
160 AMFA, Y. 1921, f. 88, 4, Letter from Pan-Epirotic Union in the USA, 19 May 1921.
161 AMFA, Y. 1921, f. 88, 63, Bimbli etc. to the Nations League, no date.
162 AMFA, Y. 1921, f. 88, 16, Letter from the Chairman of the Council of Ministers of Albania, 4 July 1921.
163 AMFA, Y. 1921, f. 88, 3, Athens and Piraeus Northern Epirotic League to the Nations League.
164 AMFA, Y. 1921, f. 88, 39, Letter from Albanian Delegation, 23 May 1921.
165 AMFA, Y. 1921, f. 88, 17, Frashëri to the League of Nations.
166 AMFA, Y. 1921, f. 88, 12, Albanian Colony in Bucharest to the Nations League. 105; The Pan Albanian Federation of America Vatra, *Statement of the Christian Orthodox Albanians Natives of the Districts of Koritza and Kolonia in Reply to the Declaration of the Pan-Epirotic Union in America, of May, 1919* (Boston: Vatra, 1919).
167 AMFA, Y. 1921, f. 88, 5, Letter from Greek Delegation, 21 May 1921.
168 Ibid.
169 AMFA, Y. 1921, f. 88, 20, Vrioni to the League of Nations, 21 June 1921.
170 Ledia Dushku, "Debatet shqiptaro-greke dhe Lidhja e Kombeve (1920–1922) [Albanian-Greek Debates in the League of Nations (1920–1922)]", *Studime Historike [Historical Studies]* 3–4 (2006):79.
171 AMFA, Y. 1921, f. 171, 8, Xhuvani to Albanian League of Nations Delegation, 8 September 1921.
172 "Declaration Concerning the Protection of Minorities in Albania", *League of Nations Treaty Series 51* (Geneva: League of Nations, 1922).
173 Beqir Meta, "Autoqefalia e Kishës Ortodokse Shqiptare në procesin e formimit të institucioneve kombëtare në vitet 1920–1924 [The Autocephaly of the Albanian Orthodox Church in the Process of Establishing National Institutions during 1920–1924]", *Studime Albanologjike [Albanological Studies]* 11:1 (2011):84–85.
174 AMFA, Y. 1921, f. 87, 88, Ypi to the League of Nations, no date.

3   Declaration of autocephaly and its consequences, 1921–1924

Preparations for autocephaly

All the leaders of the Albanian ecclesiastical movement were prominent national politicians. Visar Xhuvani was elected as a member of the first Albanian National Assembly representing Durrës, while Theofan Noli would join him one year later, after being elected as a representative of the Albanian diaspora in the United States.[1] The Orthodox believers of central Albania began addressing Archimandrite Visar as "His Grace", a title used only for bishops. On 28 November 1921, Visar Xhuvani laid the cornerstone for an autocephalous Church, after a liturgy held on the ninth anniversary of Albanian independence, attended by the highest officials of the country and Orthodox faithful. On behalf of the priests and members of Tirana's church eldership, Archimandrite Visar announced the decision to establish a self-governing National Orthodox Church of Albania. This decision called for an all-Orthodox meeting as soon as possible, to be assembled in a city determined by the Ministry of Interior. Orthodox elderships throughout Albania would send one to three representatives, who would vote on the final decisions. However, the main issue was already predetermined, as the congress would establish a council that would temporarily lead the Church, maintaining full dogmatic unity with all other Churches. All Orthodox faithful attending the liturgy supported the resolution. The following day, the Albanian government released a declaration recognizing the autocephaly of the Albanian Orthodox Church.[2]

The elected bishop, Theofan Noli, was not present for the declaration of autocephaly in Tirana's main Orthodox cathedral, as he was celebrating the ninth anniversary of independence in Vlora. Reverends Vangjel Çamçe and Vasil Marko had managed to rise to the top of Korça's church eldership, and Vatra supporter Koço Grameno became Korça's new mayor. As a result, circumstances were ripe to fulfil Noli's aim of remaining full time in Albania.[3] On 9 December 1921, he arrived in Korça, where he was greeted by thousands of people, including the church eldership, all the priests, the members of the Municipal Council and the Muslim clergy.[4] Noli congratulated his flock and announced that he would continue his path for the consolidation of the Orthodox Church.[5]

Noli's presence in Korça convinced him that he must undertake the final action: to hold the liturgy as hierarch, contrary to the promises he had made to the Tirana government. On 21 December 1921, Noli held this liturgy in front of thousands of believers at the city's cathedral. His action brought expressions of tremendous support from all over Albania. However, his bold move had put at risk the efforts initiated in Tirana on 28 November.[6] On 22 December 1921, the Orthodox MPs Agathokli Xhitoni, Koço Tasi, and Sotir Peçi objected fiercely to Noli's liturgy, calling it a sacrilege from a religious perspective, an unconscious betrayal in the political realm, and a violation of religious freedoms from a legal standpoint. Sotir Peçi, who had been among Noli's first supporters to become a priest, and then a bishop, was particularly furious. Peçi wanted Noli to wait until he reached an agreement with the Orthodox MPs as the legal representatives of the Orthodox community. Once this had been carried out, an Orthodox congress should take place and select and install two Albanian bishops. After this, the two hierarchs could duly ordain Noli, thus clearing his path to the archbishop's throne.[7]

Back in the Albanian capital, there were rapid political developments: five governments in succession had been sworn in and resigned within December 1921 alone. Noli held the position of minister of foreign affairs from the sixth to the twelfth of December in two consecutive governments, all while being in Korça. Only at the end of December 1921 Albania managed to achieve stability under the leadership of Xhafer Ypi, whose government included Noli's friend and ally, Ahmet Zog, the future king of Albania, as the interior minister. Zog informed Noli about the uncertain political situation in Tirana and the fierce objections to his actions from the three MPs: Xhitoni, Peçi, and Tasi. On 24 December, Zog suggested that Noli return immediately to Tirana. Noli expressed his willingness to return, but only on the condition that Zog appoint Terenc Toçi as the prefect of Korça and grant him full power to remove the few opponents of the national Church.[8] The government managed to convince the self-ordained Bishop Noli not to actively engage in the ecclesiastical matter, because even Noli's adopted bastion of support, Korça, did not agree with the bishop's judgement that the Church had been autocephalous from the time he had declared it in Boston, Massachusetts.[9]

Two simultaneous developments would prevent the Albanian state from swiftly following the road to autocephaly as laid out by Visar Xhuvani in Tirana. The Investigation Commission, set up by the Ambassadors Conference, was reviewing the issue of 26 villages in southern Albania and the final settlement of the country's northern frontier. Under these circumstances, the Albanian authorities did not want to make it possible for Greece to complain that the government in Tirana was interfering in religious matters.[10] A date for organizing the Orthodox congress would be set in mid-August of 1922, in the aftermath of a meeting between Kalamaras, the Greek representative of the Investigative Commission, and Albanian Prime Minister Xhafer Ypi.

Kalamaras expressed his concern about the banning of the Greek language in religious services. Ypi responded that the Albanian government was not religious and had left the matter up to the will of the faithful.[11] The prime minister stated that the government would abide by any decision made in the upcoming all-Orthodox congress, which would convene in early September. The setting of a mid-September date for the congress appears to have been a last-minute decision. As soon as the meeting with Kalamaras was over, Ypi rushed to ask Ahmet Zog that the Council of Ministers decide on the date of the Orthodox congress in its next session.[12]

The prime minister shared his concern with the prefect of Korça, who called a meeting of the city's church eldership. The prefecture of Korça reported to Zog that it was working on the matter; thus it would not seem as if the government had initiated the congress, but that it came as a suggestion from the local church.[13] Initially, the Tirana government planned that the mayor of Durrës, Kosta Paftali, representing the city's Orthodox, would convene a gathering of church officials there. However, after due consideration, the Albanian government decided there would be a congress after all and that it would take place in the central city of Berat.[14]

Asked by Ahmet Zog for its official opinion, the Foreign Ministry replied on 14 August 1922 that any Albanian issue that dealt with Greece should be resolved before the end of the Greco-Turkish War in Anatolia. The Foreign Ministry noted that this period would be the most appropriate time to organize the Orthodox congress, which would send a delegation to negotiate with the Patriarchate. The ministry emphasized that the language issue was secondary to the independence of the Albanian Orthodox Church.[15]

Such calculations by the Albanian Ministry of Foreign Affairs proved to be a perfect reading of international developments. There had been no conflict between Greece and Turkey in nearly a year, ever since Greek troops had arrived in the area near Ankara. However, the stalemate helped Turkey to reorganize and prepare for a final battle for its independence. Turkey would launch its counter-attack 12 days after the Albanian Foreign Ministry instructed Orthodox leaders to hold the congress as soon as possible, and, after 16 days of fighting, the Turkish army pushed the Greek troops into retreat to the Aegean Sea. On the very day that the Albanian Church Congress commenced in Berat, Greece signed the treaty of surrender, its largest contemporary military disaster.[16]

Zog ordered Mayor Kosta Paftali of Durrës to send out the congressional invitations as soon as he received the go-ahead from the Foreign Ministry. Theofan Noli did not attend the congress and remained side-lined, by agreement with the government, so as not to provoke discord between the factions within the Orthodox Church. The primary purpose of the congress was to convince the Patriarchate to grant independence to the Albanian Church, and the presence of a self-proclaimed bishop might undermine this effort. This did not, however, mean that the selection of the representatives was not a competition between Noli and Xhuvani. Noli was represented by

Reverend Vasil Marko, Reverend Vangjel Çamçe, and dozens of other supporters who wanted to force the congress to elect him as the first archbishop of Albania.[17] Visar Xhuvani led the church eldership meetings of the prefectures and sub-prefectures that were within the diocese of Durrës, where he tried to influence the selection of representatives.[18] However, the situation soon swung in Theofan Noli's favour as the sub-prefectures in the Korça metropolitanate elected representatives who fiercely supported him. Noli's singular strength was that the reach of his influence could spread beyond the metropolitanate's borders.[19] A few days before the congress opened, Archimandrite Visar received a final blow as the representatives from Elbasan, his own birthplace and the starting point of his ecclesiastical struggle, abandoned him and supported Noli.[20]

All elderships chose their representatives without any controversy.[21] The only exception was Gjirokastra, which did not hold an election until the end of August. On 28 August 1922, the Gjirokastra church eldership convened under Vicar Thanas Duka and decided to refuse Paftali's request, claiming that the eldership represented only the city of Gjirokastra and not the entire diocese. The eldership members argued that the Albanian state and the Patriarchate should resolve this matter through a bilateral agreement, as each of the newly independent nations had done. The Gjirokastra church eldership was composed mostly of ethnic Greek clergy and laymen, and Albanian patriots were in the minority.[22] Given the refusal of the Gjirokastra church eldership to represent the entire district, four of the ten eldership members along with the elders of the Orthodox villages in the prefecture gathered under the leadership of Reverend Pano Çuçi to elect their delegates to the Congress of Berat.[23]

Congress of Berat

On the morning of Monday, 10 September 1922, representatives from all over Albania made their way through the narrow alleys of Berat's Mangalem quarter, under the shadow of the centuries-old fortress that dominated the hill above the city. Sessions commenced in the city's central two-story school building.[24] The Albanian government was concerned about how the rival factions would behave towards each other. Noli had triumphed in Korça, Bilisht, Leskovik, and Përmet,[25] while Visar Xhuvani had managed to influence the representatives from Durrës, Dibra, and Shkodra. The other members, from Kavaja, Tirana, Berat, Fier, Lushnja, Libohova, and Delvina, had yet to take sides.[26]

The Albanian government openly supported Visar Xhuvani, a candidate viewed as a loyal clergyman capable of achieving autocephaly. Zog's friendship with Theofan Noli had changed since Noli resigned from Xhafer Ypi's government. However, the Vatra supporters had the overwhelming majority in the Congress of Berat and requested that the congress appoint Noli as the new archbishop. Despite this move, the government officials managed to convince the representatives that achieving autocephaly was more important and so were able to temporarily side-line Noli.[27]

As a result, on 11 September, the congress unanimously elected Josif Qirici as its chairperson. In both 1914 and 1921, Qirici had been instrumental in Albanizing the church in Korça, while managing to keep his position in Korça's metropolitanate without being expelled by Germanos or Iakovos. In his opening address to the congress, Reverend Vasil Marko saw the ecclesiastical battle as a national imperative. The government's representative considered Marko's speech "so sweet and full of skill and logic" that it appeared to persuade all the representatives, other than the ones from Durrës and Dibra, and Tol Arapi from Vlora.[28] Archimandrite Visar Xhuvani then took the floor and declared the Church's autocephaly.[29]

Even without the attendance of any official representatives from the metropolitanate of Dryinopolis, based in Gjirokastra, the validity of the autocephaly declaration was irrefutable. The representatives from the other regions represented seven times more Orthodox believers than the members of the diocese based in Gjirokastra. As a noted theologian, Visar Xhuvani had written the legal basis of the autocephaly decision, arguing that, based on the principle of "an independent Church in an independent country", the Orthodox Church in Albania had been autocephalous ever since 1912, the year Albania proclaimed its independence.[30] The Congress of Berat merely *declared* the existence of the status of autocephaly in 1922, while the Ecumenical Patriarchate would *recognize* it at the opportune moment. The main difficulty in achieving recognition was the fact that there was no officially appointed bishop in Albania. The Ecumenical Patriarchate of Constantinople had to choose, ordain, and appoint the hierarchs if the Church in Albania was under its authority. However, the approach taken by the Congress of Berat was that the Albanian Church had been autocephalous even prior to its declaration. Consequently, no foreign Church, including that of Constantinople, had the right to choose its bishops. The argument made clear the need to establish a Church High Council, whose purpose would be to elect four regular bishops, who would then constitute the Holy Synod, and run the Church until recognition was received.[31]

During a break between sessions, Visar Xhuvani told Reverend Vasil Marko that he had prepared an alternative plan if the Patriarchate did not recognize the Church's autocephaly. Xhuvani had met with representatives of the Serbian Orthodox Church, who had promised to ordain Albanian hierarchs.[32] However, the Patriarchate had sent Metropolitan Iakovos to Belgrade to persuade the Yugoslav government and Serbian Church leaders not to support the Albanian cause.[33] Reaching an agreement on the seat of the Albanian Autocephalous Church caused much controversy. Different representatives suggested Albanian cities as varied as Berat, Tirana, Gjirokastra, and Korça. Finally, the congress decided that the seat of the Church should be Korça, citing its venerable ecclesiastical history.[34]

The majority of representatives eventually turned against Visar Xhuvani, accusing him of exhibiting a megalomaniac attitude during the first session of the congress. Xhuvani had assumed control of the Berat proceedings to declare the Church's autocephaly, telling everyone that he had the government's support to lead the Church. Thus, the Tirana government and Noli's supporters agreed to elect Reverend Vasil Marko as the chair of the Church High Council, which would be composed of eight other members as well: one clergyman and one layman from each diocese. The clergymen would act as vicar for each of the respective dioceses until bishops arrived. The congress elected Archimandrite Visar as vicar of the diocese of Durrës. Following instructions from the government, Reverend Vasil Marko requested that Xhuvani be elected as the metropolitan for Durrës, and be ordained as soon as two other bishops could be found.[35] The congress elected Reverend Josif Qirici as vicar for the diocese of Korça, Reverend Anastas for Berat, and Reverend Pano for Gjirokastra. A teacher, Dhosi Havjari, was elected as the layman representative for Korça, Stathi Kondi for Gjirokastra, Simon Shuteriqi for Durrës, and Tol Arapi for Berat.[36]

On 17 September, the congress compiled the statute and regulations of the Albanian Orthodox Church, based on the draft presented by Archimandrite Visar. The statute stipulated that the National Orthodox Autocephalous Church of Albania (OACA) was inseparable from the Universal Apostolic Orthodox Church. This Church consisted of the Orthodox believers of Albania, ruled over by the official-appointed bishops and the Holy Canons. A metropolitan would lead the Church, which would comprise five dioceses, four of which would be demoted from metropolitanates to bishoprics, with the exception of the newly created metropolitanate of Tirana. The head of each diocese constituted the Holy Synod, which would govern the Church. Until the formation of the Holy Synod, the statute established that the Church High Council would perform the synod's duties, except on occasions needing the authority of ordained bishops. The main aim of the Church High Council was to find at least two Albanian bishops from the Ecumenical Patriarchate, or other Churches, within two years and secure the recognition of the Albanian Autocephalous Church. Finally, an assembly would convene after three months, following the establishment of the Synod, to approve a revised statute and regulations.[37]

The Albanian Foreign Ministry had ably gauged the finale of the Greco–Turkish conflict one month earlier, sharing the satisfaction of that judgment with the interior minister, Ahmet Zog. On 14 September, the foreign minister wrote that the national annals would record the importance of this event and thanked Zog for his contribution.[38] On 18 September, the Council of Ministers ratified the decisions of the Berat Congress,[39] immediately briefing the prefectures about the changes in the church issue.[40]

The Albanian Church informed the patriarchates, the autocephalous Churches, and the Albanian diaspora about the events in Berat. Reverend Josif signed the telegram, which informed all concerned that the Albanian

Church Congress had unanimously and jubilantly declared the creation of the National Orthodox Autocephalous Church of Albania.[41] The telegram briefly stated that the Albanian Church was independent, but remained spiritually connected with all the autocephalous Churches, including the Ecumenical Patriarchate.[42] At that point, the Albanian state was so poor that it was unable to make the notification sooner. On 25 September, since telegram costs were so high, the Foreign Ministry stated that it was constrained to make the notification of autocephaly in just a few words, mentioning only the declaration of the independence of the Albanian Church. This was followed by Reverend Josif sending letters via ordinary mail with further clarifications. However, the letter detailing the reasons behind the decisions of the Berat Congress would not reach the other autocephalous Churches and the Albanian diaspora until a month later.[43]

The fragility of a state that could barely send a telegram underscores the tremendous victory in declaring the autocephaly, favoured by the shifting terrain of international circumstances. A few years later, Metropolitan Chrysanthos of Trebizond, who was later the archbishop of Athens, reasoned that the Ecumenical Patriarchate was facing an anxious battle for its survival. The military disaster in Asia Minor had devastated Greece, leaving it without the power or dignity to influence either politics or matters of faith.[44] This opportune moment gave the Albanian state the upper hand in declaring autocephaly. The battle, however, had just begun.

From the start of the twentieth century, the dioceses of the Orthodox Church in Albania had been unstable. For much of the time, the metropolitanates were left without a ruling bishop, and when one was present, the metropolitans dealt with matters of the Greek state rather than ecclesiastical affairs. As a result, the Church High Council was faced with the challenge of establishing the functional institutions that for two decades had been missing. The fear that a portion of the priests would oppose the decisions of the Berat Congress was unfounded. Korça's metropolitanate, which became the first diocese where all the priests aligned with the Albanian Autocephalous Church, held a liturgy on 8 October 1922 to commemorate the event.[45]

Theofan Noli's supporters wasted no opportunity in displaying their superiority over those who had opposed them.[46] Soon, the grudge his supporters held against Visar Xhuvani became obvious. The Church High Council had elected Archimandrite Visar as the vicar of the Durrës diocese, but the layman representative of that diocese, Simon Shuteriqi, was the first person to object to Visar's appointment. He orchestrated a meeting of the elderships of the main cities of the district, who then replaced Xhuvani with the dean of Elbasan, Dhimitër Dhimitruka. Xhuvani blamed Shuteriqi and Reverend Vasil Marko for forging a secret agreement to bring about his dismissal and opposed his ousting as illegal.[47]

In mid-November 1922, Xhuvani travelled to Korça to participate in the sessions of the Church High Council. He was ridiculed in the press in articles written by Noli's supporters,[48] while Reverend Vasil Marko refused to allow him into the Council session. Visar expected the government to intervene on his behalf, but the Tirana officials did not want to create a conflict with Noli's supporters. Finally, the Church High Council decided not to appoint any vicar for the Durrës metropolitanate until the dispute was resolved.[49]

The situation was similarly tense in the diocese of Dryinopolis. In order to strengthen the patriotic elite of the diocese, the Council had appointed Reverend Pano Çuçi as vicar. Members of Albania's Greek minority disputed Çuçi's election, especially after he met with members of an investigation commission of the League of Nations. Çuçi had said that the Albanian liturgy would be mandatory for all Christians, including Greeks,[50] which created an outcry from the Greek minority for his removal.[51] Reverend Vasil Marko refused to consider this request as he blamed the commission's translator for misinterpreting Pano's remarks. Marko pointed out that Reverend Pano was among the first to take part in the national ecclesiastical movement in Gjirokastra, even before Albania's independence.[52] At the beginning of March 1923, Marko asked for Çuçi's resignation, replacing him with a priest from Pogradec, Reverend Thanas Nikolla. The decision came after local officials assessed that Çuçi's presence was causing disruption among the Greek minority in the villages around Gjirokastra.[53] The swift solution of these two issues enabled the internal consolidation of the Church, allowing it to focus on the two foremost matters: recognition of autocephaly and the establishment of the Holy Synod.

Shkodra ecclesiastical dispute – a Serbian–Albanian conflict

Alongside the majority of Muslims and Catholics in northern Albania, the Orthodox constituted a small minority, divided into two large dioceses of the Ecumenical Patriarchate. The majority of Albania's north, including Shkodra, Kukës, Mirdita, and Lezhë, were under the jurisdiction of the metropolitanate of Prizren. The north-eastern region of Dibra formed a separate diocese, composed primarily of Bulgarians with a small Orthodox Albanian minority in the Reka region, which Serbia had annexed during the First World War. Very few Orthodox lived in the eastern Golloborda area, located in the Albanian part of Dibra. On the other hand, the Orthodox population in Shkodra, while small, had considerable influence. There were 170 households in the city, numbering 705 Orthodox followers, of whom 649 were Albanian and 45 were of Slavic origin. The village of Vraka, to the north of Shkodra, consisted of 151 Orthodox households, made up of 1,855 Montenegrins.[54]

The Balkan Wars in the early 1910s brought both Dibra and Shkodra under Serbian and Montenegrin occupation, but Albania regained Shkodra after the temporary Montenegrin invasion. Due to its distance, the metropolitanate of Prizren could not lead the ecclesiastical life in this lakeside urban centre. For this reason, the adjacent metropolitanate of Cetinje incorporated Shkodra's churches, arguing that the Ottoman Empire's defeat also meant the end of jurisdiction by the Ecumenical Patriarchate.[55] Metropolitan Gavrilo of Cetinje reorganized northern Albania's Orthodox churches by establishing the vicariate of Shkodra, Vraka, and Kamenica. He appointed the newly ordained 39-year-old Archimandrite Viktor Mihajlović as its vicar.[56] After the union of the Montenegrin and Serbian Churches in November 1918, the vicariate of Shkodra recognized the jurisdiction of the Serbian Church.[57]

The Ecumenical Patriarchate handed over the metropolitanates of Prizren and Dibra to the Serbian Church, which extended that Church's authority over northern Albania. The creation of the Albanian Orthodox Church altered this equation, however, because the principle "an independent Church in an independent state" implied that the whole territory of a state should be under the jurisdiction of its respective autocephalous Church.[58] At the beginning of 1922, the Holy Synod of the Serbian Church elected Viktor Mihajlović as the assistant bishop for Shkodra, Vraka, and Kamenica. This hasty move, which preceded the declaration of Albanian Church's autocephaly, was carried out by the Serbian Patriarchate and the newly established Kingdom of the Serbs, Croats, and Slovenes, later known as Yugoslavia, with the intention of creating a permanent presence in Albania. This fait accompli was cemented when the metropolitans of Montenegro and Krajina ordained Viktor in Karlovci on 22 June 1922.[59]

The Serbian Patriarchate and the Yugoslav government were willing to support the Albanians in their cause for autocephaly due to their past differences with the Ecumenical Patriarchate, which was now in a weakened position after the Greco-Turkish War. The Yugoslavs and the Serbian Patriarchate managed to reach an agreement with Archimandrite Visar Xhuvani. The Serbian Church promised to ordain Visar as bishop if no agreement could be reached with the Ecumenical Patriarchate.[60] A month before the Berat Congress, Visar had secured the Tirana government's acceptance of Viktor, a concession to the Serbians for future help.[61] The Yugoslav foreign minister, Momčilo Ninčić, had encouraged the League of Nations representatives to intervene with the Ecumenical Patriarchate in recognizing the Albanian Church. Ninčić added that the Serbian bishop would stay in Shkodra until autocephaly was recognized.[62]

In December 1922, Viktor set off from Belgrade, accompanied by a Shkodra-born Serbian priest, Lazar Matijević. As he was an Albanian citizen, His Grace Viktor had received his passport from the Albanian embassy in Belgrade, promising to obey all Albanian laws and not interfere in politics.[63] As soon as he arrived, however, Viktor informed the Orthodox faithful in Shkodra, and the Church High Council in Korça, that he was the ruling bishop of Shkodra. Reverend Vasil Marko objected, stating that the Church's statute forbade the enthronement of a foreign bishop without the Council's consent.[64] Marko and the Tirana government feared that the Serbians were in agreement with the Ecumenical Patriarchate to force Albania accept ruling bishops for ethnic minorities, thus undermining the

Autocephalous Church.[65] Marko informed the Tirana government that it could grant a temporary, limited acceptance of Viktor's status, but only on the condition that the Serbian Church would officially recognize the Albanian Orthodox Autocephalous Church, a development which did not occur.[66]

The press heavily criticized the Albanian government. Mihal Grameno wrote in the *Koha* newspaper that Viktor's presence in Shkodra would compel the Autocephalous Church to ordain dozens of bishops and send them to Serbia, or elsewhere, to perform religious services for Orthodox Albanians living outside the motherland.[67] On 22 January 1923, Interior Minister Ahmet Zog ordered the local authorities of Shkodra to put an end to the dispute.[68] The deputy prefect of Shkodra ordered Viktor not to officiate in any liturgy until he received permission from the Albanian Orthodox Autocephalous Church.[69]

In late 1923, the Albanian government informed Yugoslav officials that it could not accept Viktor's appointment as the ruling bishop of Shkodra. The Albanian Ministry of Foreign Affairs argued that Shkodra had never been a diocese and, given its small and poor Orthodox community, it could not financially support a diocese. The government underlined that the Orthodox in Shkodra were Albanians and that no foreign Church could appoint a hierarch, who, according to the Statute of the Albanian Church, had to be Albanian for at least two generations. Albania pledged to defend its minorities and allow religious services in their native language.[70]

On 7 February, the Yugoslav embassy replied that it considered any measure taken against Viktor to be illegal. The embassy argued that autocephaly would indeed bring Shkodra under the jurisdiction of the Albanian Orthodox Autocephalous Church, but it did not consider the Albanian Church independent until the Serbian and the Ecumenical Patriarchate recognized it as such. The Yugoslav government requested an amicable solution that would allow Viktor to perform his religious responsibilities in Shkodra without hindrance, promising that the Serbian Patriarchate would press the Ecumenical Patriarchate to recognize the Albanian Church as soon as possible.[71]

His Grace Viktor ordained new priests and transferred Reverend Mihal Strikić to Serbia, since the priest had participated in the election of representatives to the Berat Congress. The Albanian Ministry of Interior ordered the prefecture to ban the entry of any other priests into Albania and to close the Orthodox Church in Shkodra.[72] The Albanian government asked European governments and the League of Nations to intervene with the Yugoslav government to prevent the Serbian Church from violating church rules.[73] As a solution to the dispute, the Yugoslav government suggested on 15 March that Viktor ask the Church High Council in Korça to recognize him as being under its jurisdiction, but Albania rejected the proposal.[74]

On 6 April, the Albanian government reopened the church in Shkodra with Mihal Strikić holding the Easter liturgy. His Grace Viktor did not participate in the Easter service, while Lazar Matijević attended only as a parishioner, because both men were still banned from officiating at religious services.[75] That same day the Yugoslav government informed its Albanian counterpart that it was obliged to suspend diplomatic relations and withdraw its embassy from Tirana.[76] The Albanian minister of foreign affairs, Pandeli Evangjeli, asked the Albanian embassies in Rome and Paris, as well as the consulate in Geneva, to inform their respective host governments and the League of Nations about this diplomatic crisis. The Tirana government called the suspension of diplomatic relations an insult to the state and interference in Albania's internal affairs.[77] In addition, Evangjeli expressed to the Yugoslav government its willingness to send a delegation to Belgrade to discuss Shkodra's ecclesiastical situation.[78] International intervention reduced tensions between Yugoslavia and Albania. Italy pledged to urge the British and French governments to suggest to Yugoslavia that it alter its position.[79] On 12 June, the Yugoslav government reversed its decision to break ties, stating that it would now leave the resolution of the matter to the Serbian Orthodox Church and the Albanian Church High Council.[80] The Albanian government continued to ban Viktor's religious activities until October 1923, when through Visar's mediation a modus vivendi was reached. Albania would allow Viktor to continue to reside in Shkodra, but only as a guest of the Church High Council and not as ruling bishop. This temporary compromise would last until the Ecumenical Patriarchate decided to recognize the Albanian Church's autocephaly.[81]

With the church conflict thus suspended, Viktor remained in Shkodra and was allowed to hold the liturgy as a guest bishop; he would refer to the Serbian patriarch when the Albanian government's attention was elsewhere, and to the Church High Council when he was under the scrutiny of Albanian officials. The Yugoslav government had backed down from the diplomatic confrontation, thanks to the intervention of Italy and France. Yet Belgrade had nevertheless managed to achieve a special status quo, with a bishop of their choice having settled in Shkodra and leading its church life. Viktor was waiting for the right moment to formalize his appointment. On its part, Albania had stopped the expansion of the Serbian Church, paving the way for the Albanization of the deanery of Shkodra, although this final goal would not be achieved for several years.

Inconsistency of the Patriarchate – initial blessing followed by non-recognition

Iakovos, the former metropolitan of Durrës, initially hailed the decisions of the Berat Congress and offered to mediate between the Albanian Church and the Patriarchate.[82] The national press reported that Iakovos had even written a letter supporting the Albanian Church's autocephaly, although this proved false.[83] Metropolitan Vasil of Dryinopolis complained to the League of Nations that Muslim mayors, egged on by the Tirana government, had organized a congress of Orthodox laymen with the aim of establishing an autocephalous Church.[84] The Albanian government responded that it was Kosta Paftali, the Orthodox mayor of Durrës, who had personally taken the initiative to call the congress. The Albanian authorities claimed that they had never meddled in ecclesiastical matters and quoted a memorandum from Ahmet Zog declaring the government's non-interference in religious affairs. The government stated that its only intervention was in Gjirokastra, where they had been obliged to dismiss Vicar Thanas Duka, as an internal quarrel in the local church could provoke rioting.[85] The Albanian Foreign Ministry instructed the Church High Council to respond to Vasil's complaint.[86] Shortly after, in a letter addressed to the League of Nations, Reverend Vasil Marko defended the legitimacy and the eligibility of the declaration of autocephaly.[87]

Italy supported the declaration of autocephaly,[88] although it suspected that the ecclesiastical question could push Albania closer to the Kingdom of the Serbs, Croats, and Slovenes.[89] Greece, however, was strongly opposed. The Ecumenical Patriarchate's envoy in Geneva assured the Greek representative that the Church of Constantinople would not recognize Albanian autocephaly.[90] On 11 September, the Ecumenical Patriarchate established a commission, led by the metropolitan of Rhodes, to review the Albanian question; it was made up of former hierarchs from the four Albanian dioceses, including[91] the former metropolitan of Berat, Joakim Martishti, who was an Albanian from Voskopoja.[92] Joakim informed the Albanian government that, with the exception of Iakovos, the commission was in favour of the recognition of autocephaly.[93] Three weeks later, the former metropolitan of Berat, accompanied by another Albanian bishop, Metropolitan Ierothe of Mylitoupoli (born Janaq Jaho in Përmet, he would later serve as the metropolitan of Korça from 1923 to 1929), met with the Albanian consul in Istanbul. Joakim informed Consul Nezir Leskoviku that the Patriarchate had assigned Ierothe to visit Albania to negotiate on its behalf with the government and the Orthodox MPs as the sole legal representatives of the Orthodox in the country. Leskoviku replied that Albania had a secular government which did not interfere in religious issues. Joakim assured Leskoviku that the Patriarchate was in favour of the Church's autocephaly.[94]

On 30 November 1922, His Grace Ierothe arrived in Korça and met with local officials, the Church High Council, and Orthodox MPs, who enthusiastically welcomed him. Before taking the final decision, His Grace also met with the Greek consul.[95] The prefect of Korça was convinced that the bishop would not object to the Church's autocephaly after the meetings he had, the city's display of popular enthusiasm, and the insistence of Reverend Vasil Marko.[96] On 22 December 1922, Ierothe declared his recognition of the Albanian Autocephalous Orthodox Church at St George's Cathedral. Ierothe stated that the Patriarchate had sent him to Albania to observe and fulfil the wishes of its Orthodox faithful, which, in his view, were clear after the decisions of the Berat Congress and the OACA Statute. His Grace hailed the devotion, love, and honour towards the Ecumenical Patriarchate, praising the respect Albania had shown for the Holy Canons of the Church. Ierothe concluded by stating his belief that the Ecumenical Patriarchate would recognize and bestow its blessing on its daughter, the Orthodox Church of Albania. A few days later, Metropolitan Ierothe sent an official request to the ecumenical patriarch that he recognize the Autocephalous Church and send in Albania another Constantinople-based bishop, His Grace Kristofor Kisi, to help him establish the Holy Synod.[97] Kristofor responded that he was ready to come to Albania and join the effort of establishing the country's Orthodox Church, but requested a postponement until after February 1923, as he still had some unfinished matters to deal with. In any case, His Grace Kristofor said he would be willing to leave Constantinople at any time if the Albanian state was in a hurry to resolve the ecclesiastical issue.[98]

On 15 December, only two days after he arrived in Korça, His Grace Ierothe elevated Reverend Çamçe to the rank of archimandrite.[99] His actions convinced the Albanian government that the matter would have a quick and final settlement.[100] On 3 February 1923, the Ecumenical Patriarch Meletios asked Ierothe to return to Constantinople as soon as possible, accompanied by one representative from each of the dioceses for negotiations.[101] Following instructions from the Albanian authorities, Ierothe replied to the patriarch that as Reverend Vasil Marko and the Church High Council were the leaders of the Church in Albania, the only solution was to send a full Albanian representation of the Autocephalous Church to Istanbul. Ierothe added that not only must he remain in Korça on important matters, but he also requested that Kristofor Kisi come to Albania as soon as he was able.[102] The Patriarchate accepted the composition of the delegation, but insisted that Orthodox MPs be included in addition to the Church High Council. The patriarch stressed that Ierothe must come to Istanbul at the earliest opportunity or, if that was impossible, instead send him a detailed report with the delegation.[103] On 24 February, the Holy Synod of the Ecumenical Patriarchate discussed the Albanian issue, where Joakim, as a member of the Synod, spoke at length in favour of recognizing the Church's autocephaly. On the same day, Joakim told Ierothe that the ecclesiastical issue would be resolved successfully in accord with the wishes of their long-suffering motherland and suggested that he send the delegation to Istanbul at their earliest convenience.[104] Kristofor Kisi was of the same feeling, suggesting to Ierothe that the delegation leave immediately for Istanbul.[105]

By this time, however, the political situation had radically changed in both Greece and Turkey. In an unprecedented case in modern Greek history, key members of the Gounaris government and those of his immediate successors were overthrown in a coup d'état, arrested, tried, and sentenced to death. High-ranking, pro-Venizelos military officers, veterans from the war in Asia Minor, established a new government until Venizelos himself could officially take power. The Greco-Turkish War would soon come to end in Lausanne, Switzerland. Turkey had risen from the ashes of the Ottoman Empire and now set about negotiating an end to the foreign presence in its land. In a bold move, these two former enemies signed a treaty on 30 January 1923, agreeing to exchange 1.5 million Orthodox in Turkey with 500,000 Muslims in Greece.[106]

The population exchange was not only a momentous event for both Greece and Turkey but also had a tremendous impact on the Ecumenical Patriarchate. The Patriarchate's power would almost disappear as the Orthodox Church of Greece extended its borders to include Crete, the Aegean Islands, and the lands of Macedonia, Thrace, and Epirus that had newly been incorporated into Greece. With the Church in Albania declaring its autocephaly, now only Turkey would remain under the jurisdiction of the Ecumenical Patriarchate. This development meant that the expulsion of Orthodox from Turkey practically would abolish the Patriarchate. Thus, Greece took steps in order to secure the existence of the Ecumenical Patriarchate, first of all by not transferring the lands it had annexed in 1913 to the Church of Greece. Furthermore, the Holy Synod in Athens transferred the control of its missions in the diaspora – mainly in the United States of America – to the Ecumenical Patriarchate, a move that would be followed by the Churches of Alexandria and Jerusalem. These decisions were explained by the reasoning that only the Ecumenical Patriarchate had the right to establish dioceses in lands where no such jurisdictions existed. The non-Greek Churches, however, would not recognize this as a valid principle.[107]

Greece's political shift also brought a policy change in Athens. The need to influence the Orthodox Church in Albania again made the ecclesiastical issue a priority for the Greek government. Greece had an additional reason to return to the Albanian issue, as its huge loss in Asia Minor made it more determined to preserve a Greek community outside its formal borders.[108] The Albanian envoy to Lausanne, Mehdi Frashëri, informed the Greek and Turkish delegations that the Patriarchate had recognized the Albanian Church based on Metropolitan Ierothe's recommendation. The Ecumenical Patriarchate, however, through its envoy in Geneva, Archbishop Germanos, issued a harsh response to this, stating that the patriarch had instructed Ierothe to reinstate the unlawfully expelled Greek metropolitans in Albania and that no autocephalous Church could be established in a Muslim-majority country. The Patriarchate said that it would allow the Albanian language only in those communities which officially requested its use, but on the condition that the Greek language was also used among Albanian communities. Lastly, the Patriarchate said it would be willing to only offer autonomy, but only if the expelled metropolitans returned to Albania.[109]

The Albanian delegation made the trip to Constantinople to request autocephaly, even though the Patriarchate had announced beforehand that, at most, it would accept only autonomy. The Albanian delegation arrived in Constantinople in mid-April to negotiate with the Patriarchate and to persuade Kristofor Kisi to return home. On 7 May 1923, Patriarch Meletios (Emmanuel Metaxakis, 1920–1923) received the Albanian representatives. Reverend Vasil Marko presented the decisions of the Berat Congress, along with the wish of the Albanian government to have an autocephalous Church, just as Greece, Serbia, and Romania had. The patriarch objected to the comparison with the other countries in the region, emphasizing that Albania did not have an Orthodox majority to ensure that the country's laws were in line with religious dogma. Meletios offered his belief that Orthodoxy had only survived in Albania owing to the connection between the local churches and the Ecumenical Patriarchate, thus he announced that the Holy Synod would not grant the tomos of autocephaly. However, considering that Albania had become independent, the Ecumenical Patriarchate was willing to instate autonomy, and the patriarch presented the delegation with a prepared statute titled "Statute of the Orthodox Archdiocese in Albania".[110]

The Albanian delegation rejected the argument that there were no autocephalous Churches in countries without an Orthodox majority. In fact, only a few months later, the Patriarchate would recognize the Church in Poland, where Orthodox believers constituted only 1 per cent of the population, much less than Albania's 20 per cent. For the Albanians, the special statute presented by Patriarch Meletios was unacceptable. First, this statute entrusted the patriarch with approval of the bishops of the Albanian Church, a prerogative he did not possess even in the Greek autonomous archdioceses, such as those of Crete or the USA. Second, the statute retained Greek as the official language of the Church in Albania, despite the fact that the chief request of Orthodox Albanians was to hold the liturgy in their native language. Lastly, the Patriarchate had to approve every regulation of the Church of Albania. The only difference from the current status was that one of the metropolitans would be raised to the rank of archbishop, but he would be an archbishop who led a Synod with no real powers. The draft was not a surprise to the Albanian government, as its ambassador in Geneva had forwarded the document to Tirana three days prior to the delegation's meeting with the patriarch. The Patriarchate's envoy in Geneva, Archbishop Germanos, had met with the Albanian representative, Benedikt Blinishti, requesting that the Albanian government intervene with the delegation by asking it not to insist on autocephaly. Blinishti replied that the Tirana government was not involved in the ecclesiastical issue, but it respected the requests and wishes of Albania's Orthodox.[111] The patriarch also sent a telegram to Ahmet Zog, who was now prime minister, explaining that the Church in Albania would be autonomous and that the Patriarchate would only retain those competencies which were indispensable for the preservation of the Church Canons and Orthodoxy.[112]

The Albanian delegation refused the patriarch's proposal as it ignored the decisions of the Congress of Berat.[113] Therefore, the only solution was to convince Bishop Kristofor Kisi to return to Albania and, together with Metropolitan Ierothe Jaho and two other hierarchs ordained by them, fill the vacant dioceses of the Church. Reverend Vasil Marko asked Ierothe, as a theologian, if he believed that the Patriarchate had the right to interfere in matters of the Albanian Church after the declaration of autocephaly. Ierothe replied that the Patriarchate had no right to excommunicate him or denounce the Autocephalous Church and that everything should proceed according to the plan outlined in the statute that had been agreed to at the Berat Congress.[114] The Albanian government had prepared other contingency plans, securing the willingness of the Bulgarian Church to ordain any bishop that was acceptable to both the Albanian state and the Albanian Church.[115]

Albanian diplomacy had thus achieved a partial victory. The Tirana government had successfully determined the right moment to declare autocephaly, an achievement confirmed by the patriarch's envoy who recognized the legitimacy of the decisions reached by the Berat Congress. The Patriarchate, however, had refused to officially recognize the Church's autocephaly. The population exchange agreement between Greece and Turkey had significantly influenced the non-recognition of Albanian autocephaly, an issue that would remain unresolved for several years.

Unilateral actions towards establishing the Holy Synod, 1923–1924

Greece's Northern Epirotic associations had lost their influence during the tenure of Greek Prime Minister Demetrios Gounaris. However, these nationalist groups revived when the Venizelists returned to power. Rumours about Greek expansion at the expense of Albania increased after the disappointment in Asia Minor, but Greek officials remained cautious in their meetings with their Albanian counterparts. Greek Foreign Minister Apostolos Alexandris declared to Mid'hat Frashëri, the Albanian ambassador in Athens, that Greece considered its main challenges to be Slavic encroachment, Italian imperialism, Bolshevik communism, and the Turkish threat. The Greek minister pledged that Greece and Albania would soon reach some kind of agreement.[116]

Frashëri had personally experienced the complicated situation in Greece. When Frashëri met King George II, the king had surprised the ambassador by saying that he himself felt half-Albanian and wished to learn the language. The Greek monarch had been born in Tatoi, a suburb of Athens where all the surrounding villages spoke the Arvanitic dialect of Albanian.[117] On the other hand, the state officials in Athens kept a close watch on the Greek schools and churches in Korça, despite the pleas, even from the few remaining Hellenists in Korça, for Greece to stop interfering in Albania.[118] In June 1923, Foreign Minister Alexandris admitted to the Albanian ambassador in Rome, Mehmet Konica, that he had summoned all the Greek-paid spies of "Epirus and Albania" and fired them. Alexandris told Konica that Greece did not want to interfere in Albania's internal affairs, but sought good relations with its northern neighbour. Alexandris had instructed these spies to become good Albanian citizens and to follow the example of the Albanians who lived in Greece.[119] However, one month later, in a conversation with Frashëri, Alexandris pretended that he was in a difficult position, having to deal with the requests of various Northern Epirotic associations, who were pressing him about the re-opening of Greek schools in Albania. Frashëri noticed that the Greek foreign minister continued to confuse secular minority schools with the religious ones that the Patriarchate had supported for Orthodox Albanians. Frashëri replied to Alexandris that, while Albania financially backed 40 Greek schools, Greece had not supported any Albanian schools on its territory, either for Cham Albanians or for the Arvanites.[120]

This was the background of the changing nature of Albanian–Greek relations. The Albanian government encouraged the Albanian Orthodox clergy – and especially bishops Ierothe and Kisi, who had left Constantinople to fulfil their patriotic duty – with the assurance that the Patriarchate would quickly recognize the Albanian Church.[121] The Albanian parliament decided to adopt a law on religious communities, which stipulated that religious leaders should be of Albanian origin going back at least three generations, and be able to speak and write in Albanian. This stipulation excluded foreign-born citizens but not the ethnic minorities in Albania, who the government explained had been living within Albanian territory for more than 100 years.[122]

By the end of 1923, the country was ready to hold elections. During this time, Theofan Noli had become a key politician and led the opposition against Ahmet Zog's government. The Greek ambassador in Durrës, Panourgias, noted that the number of Hellenists was negligible since the overwhelming majority of Orthodox were Albanian patriots. As a result, Greece instructed its supporters to participate in the elections and vote for Ahmet Zog, whom it considered a strong and honest politician and, above all, the toughest opponent of the Italians.[123] It was not surprising that Greece chose Zog and the Muslim landowners who ruled the government majority rather than the Orthodox elite who had gathered around Noli, inasmuch as the Greek government sought to subdue the fierce nationalistic Orthodox rhetoric of Noli. On 18 August, Noli arrived in Korça, where he was greeted with cheers by numerous supporters, and then went on to hold meetings in Vlora, Fier, and Berat, presenting his party's platform.[124] Noli led an active campaign, marked by enthusiastic political rallies such as Albania had never seen before. Noli, however, succeeded in winning a majority only in Korça during the December 1923 elections, while losing in the rest of the nation.[125]

Despite this loss, Noli was ready to conclude his ecclesiastical destiny. In October 1923, the Church High Council appointed Metropolitan Ierothe as metropolitan of Korça and Bishop Kristofor as metropolitan of Berat. On 3 December, the two new metropolitans convened and ordained Noli as a bishop, this time in accordance with canon law.[126] Noli's supporters declared the ordination as the best solution to settle hostilities and bring peace among all Orthodox Albanians. The ordination took place in Korça's St George's Cathedral, only a day after Noli was elected bishop by the Church High Council, in the presence of Foreign Minister Pandeli Evangjeli, Mayor Vasil Avrami of Korça, the Municipal Council, the prefect, officers from the army and the gendarmerie, numerous local civil officials, and an enormous crowd of onlookers. The Church High Council decided to install Noli as the new metropolitan of Durrës at the beginning of January. After this, only the metropolitanate of Gjirokastra would still be vacant.[127]

The disobedience of bishops Ierothe and Kristofor was a serious blow to the Greeks. The Ecumenical Patriarchate could not challenge the ecclesiastical leadership established by the Church of Albania. The Greek embassy made the assessment that Noli had gone to Italy, some days after his ordination, "to receive instructions" since it considered the bishop merely a tool of the Vatican.[128] But, in reality, Noli was a threat to the Italians, as the Italian embassy feared that the metropolitan wanted to achieve autocephaly for the Albanian Orthodox Church, to spread Bektashism among the Muslims, and Protestant Methodism among the Catholics. The Greek embassy considered the situation dire, but it could do very little given the collapse of relations between Metropolitan Ierothe and the Ecumenical Patriarchate. His Grace Ierothe viewed the decision by his superiors not to recognize Albanian Church's autocephaly as a betrayal and even refused to congratulate the new ecumenical patriarch, let alone resume negotiations with the Patriarchate. The Greek embassy thought that any negotiations would result in an Albanian Orthodox Church entirely independent of the Patriarchate. They believed that, prior to any decision regarding the Albanian Church, the best course would be to coordinate their actions with the governments of Belgrade and Bucharest.[129] Greek Ambassador Panourgias asked Mid'hat Frashëri, the Albanian ambassador to Greece, to send a delegation to Istanbul[130] since the Patriarchate was ready to recognize the Church's autocephaly.[131] Panourgias's statement was false, and the Albanian consulate in Istanbul denied that the Patriarchate had taken any such decision.[132] The Greek intention was simply to avert any unilateral solution by Albania.

The assassination of the chairperson of the Albanian-Greek Frontier Commission, General Enrico Tellini of Italy, marked a turning point in Greek policy. At the beginning of March 1924, the Greek embassy in Durrës informed Athens that Greek influence in Albania had disappeared after the defeat in Asia Minor and the assassination of General Tellini. Therefore, it advised that the immediate solution of the ecclesiastical question was a conditional recognition of the Albanian autocephaly.[133]

However, the political developments in Albania again altered the dynamics, as a major political division within Albania began in April 1924. In

February of that year, Ahmet Zog had survived an armed attack within the parliament building. To calm the situation, Zog resigned and appointed a close associate, the landowner Shefqet Vërlaci, as acting prime minister. Beqir Valteri, the would-be assassin, named MP Avni Rustemi, the celebrated activist who shot Esad Pasha Toptani dead in Paris, as the person behind the attack on Zog. Rustemi was then assassinated on 22 April 1924, which created an uproar. The opposition attended Rustemi's funeral in Vlora and called for the establishment of a new government, composed only of opposition members. Although he had a majority in the parliament, Vërlaci resigned, and, in order to reduce tensions, Iljaz Vrioni was sworn in as the new prime minister. The government was no longer able to keep order, and two of the country's military divisions, from Përmet in the south and Shkodra in the north, marched towards Tirana. These two units, along with opposition MPs, entered Tirana on 10 June, and Theofan (Fan) Noli, the metropolitan of Durrës, was sworn in Albania's new prime minister.[134]

In July 1924, the Greek ambassador returned to Durrës, but he neither recognized nor challenged the new Noli government. On 12 October, the Greek ambassador reported that some of the most prominent Christians in Durrës would be requesting Noli to resign from politics and concentrate instead on his religious duties.[135] During the brief period Noli was prime minister, he appointed Archimandrite Vangjel Çamçe as vicar of the diocese of Durrës and delegated all his authority to Çamçe. During Noli's tenure as metropolitan of Durrës, Orthodox priests officiated at the liturgy only in Albanian; the Greek language was banned from religious services. The religious books that Noli had translated in the United States spread throughout Albania, while the government closed the Vlach church in Elbasan in order to show that the metropolitanate of Durrës would not tolerate any non-Albanian churches.[136] In March 1924, the Church High Council decided to adopt the new Orthodox liturgical calendar.[137]

Minister of Justice Stavro Vinjau and the head of state, Sotir Peçi, tried to establish an Orthodox seminary that would educate younger generations to serve in the Albanian Orthodox Autocephalous Church. Vinjau and Peçi met the Greek ambassador in Durrës to demand that the inheritance of Jovan Banga, a native of Korça, be distributed according to the deceased's will. The Greek state had frozen his inheritance after the expulsion of Iakovos to Greece. The eldership of Korça was the executor of Banga's will, but Greece would not allow funds from the inheritance to be withdrawn from the Bank of Athens. The first question that Ambassador Panourgias asked Sotir Peçi was whether the Orthodox seminary would teach the Greek language. Peçi replied that Greek was the language of the Holy Scripture and therefore the curricula would include it, but only for that purpose. Panourgias expressed his consent for this school to the Greek Foreign Ministry, as its opening would reinstate the Greek language in the Albanian educational system.[138] The Greek government declared that it would accept the Albanian request, if Greek were the only language used in the classes, based on the same curricula as was taught at the Athens Rosario School, and taught by teachers of Greek origin.[139] If these conditions were not met, the Greek state would not allow the metropolitanate of Korça to withdraw the funds allotted in Banga's will. Swift political developments, however, prevented any further negotiations on this issue.

Prime Minister Noli faced his strongest criticism from within the Church. On 17 May 1924, his long-standing opponent, Archimandrite Visar Xhuvani, had begun to publish a pro-Zog, anti-Noli newspaper titled *Gjergj Kastrioti*.[140] After Noli seized power, the periodical became a monthly religious gazette.[141] Even though it was an ecclesiastical newspaper, *Gjergj Kastrioti* became a strong opposition voice against Noli. In the paper, Xhuvani blamed the metropolitan for denying communion to some parishioners in Tirana's Orthodox cathedral, which was within the diocese of Durrës.[142] Xhuvani also openly criticized Noli's newly founded church choir in Tirana dedicated to Russian religious music, arguing that Orthodox Albanians were more accustomed to Byzantine music.[143] In September, Visar Xhuvani wrote that the Albanian people wanted bread more than politics, alluding to the poor harvest that year.[144] Visar Xhuvani took an even more openly anti-government stand after a speech Noli gave at the League of Nations, where he expressed the opinion that for the time being Albania did not need a new parliament. Visar wrote that the Great Powers were angry enough at Albania and there was no reason for the prime minister to upset them further. Visar demanded free elections, saying there was no time to wait: the people wanted to express their will through their parliament.[145] In the last edition of the paper, Visar mocked the prime minister, claiming that he had brought only "bubbles" from the League of Nations.[146] On 1 November 1924, the government exiled Visar to Vlora, far from the ecclesiastical developments that were then occurring in Tirana and Korça.

The Church High Council was preparing for the election and future ordination of Vangjel Çamçe as metropolitan of Gjirokastra.[147] Thus, all was ready for the creation of the Holy Synod of four bishops and the election of Prime Minister Theofan Noli as the first archbishop of Albania.[148] However, just days before this decision could be finalized, political developments once again took a dramatic turn. On Christmas Day in 1924, Noli was overthrown and Zog's troops returned. After a year of running the metropolitanate of Durrës and six months of governmental rule, and just a few days before his election as archbishop, Metropolitan Theofan Noli left Albania never to return. Ahmet Zog returned to Albania from Yugoslavia triumphant.

Figure 3.1 Fan Noli, Albanian Metropolitan, Prime Minister, Writer, Poet, Publicist, Translator, and Revolutionary.

Figure 3.2 Father Josif Qirici, the Head of the Congress of Berat.

Figure 3.3 Noli and Notable Albanian Politicians.

Figure 3.4 Noli's Ordination as Metropolitan of Durrës.

Figure 3.5 Delegates at the Congress of Berat.

Notes

1 Dervishi, *History*; Academy of Sciences, ed., *Historia e Popullit Shqiptar, Vëllimi III [History of the Albanian People, Volume III]* (Tirana: Toena, 2007); Diana Estrefi, *Ligjvënësit shqiptarë 1920–2005 [Albanian Lawmakers 1920–2005]* (Tirana: Albanian Parliament, 2005).
2 Xhuvani, *Memory*, 27–29.
3 *Posta e Korçës [Korça Post]*, 3 December 1921, 2.
4 "Episkop Theofani në Korçë [Bishop Theofan in Korça]", *Posta e Korçës [Korça Post]*, 10 December 1921, 1.
5 "Buletin Zyrtar nga e Sh. Mitropoli e Korçës [Official Bulletin from St Metropolitanate of Korça]", *Posta e Korçës [Korça Post]*, 13 December 1921, 2.
6 AQSH, F. 149 "PMO", Y. 1921, f. VI-56, 1, Korça Prefecture to MIA, 21 December 1921.
7 AQSH, F. 14 "Fan Noli", Y. 1921, f. 130, 1, Protest from MPs.
8 AQSH, F. 152 "MIA", Y. 1922, f. 247, 1, Fan Noli to MIA, no date.
9 AQSH, F. 152 "MIA", Y. 1922, f. 52, 7, Gjirokastra Prefecture to MIA, 30 May 1922.
10 AQSH, F. 152 "MIA", Y. 1922, f. 64, 3, Korça's Prefecture to MIA, 6 January 1922; AQSH, F. 152 "MIA", Y. 1922, f. 64, 8, Korça's Prefecture to MIA, 26 January 1922.
11 GAK, F. "PMO", f. 702, 1, Kalamaras to Ministry of War, 25 July/8 August 1922.
12 AQSH, F. 152 "MIA", Y. 1922, f. 52, 9, Ypi to MIA, 8 August 1922.

13 AQSH, F. 152 "MIA", Y. 1922, f. 49, 1, Korça Prefecture to MIA, 9 August 1922.
14 A first draft of the 13 August 1922 letter read, "the Orthodox from Durrës with their insistence want to have a meeting in Durrës". In the final draft, the word "meeting" was replaced with the word "congress", while "Durrës" was replaced with "Berat". AQSH, F. 152 "MIA", f. 49, 3, Concept-Letter, 13 August 1922.
15 AMFA, f. 186, 7, MFA to MIA, 14 August 1922.
16 The timing and speedy reaction of the Albanian government came as a direct result of Greece's wartime vulnerability, but the separation of Albania's religious communities from foreign influence was one of the main goals of the Albanian nationalist movement. On 12 March 1922, Albania's Sunni Muslim community led the way by splitting from the Islamic religious centre in Istanbul. The Bektashi denomination would soon follow this same path. Beqir Meta, *Tensioni greko-shqiptar 1939–1949 [Albanian-Greek Tensions 1939–1949]* (Tirana: Geer, 2002), 37.
17 AQSH, F. 152 "MIA", Y. 1922, f. 49, 8, Shkodra Prefecture to MIA, 16 August 1922.
18 Xhuvani, *Memory*, 122.
19 "Andej-Këndej [Here and There]", *Koha [Time]*, 2 September 1922, 2.
20 *Koha [Time]*, 10 September 1922, 2.
21 AQSH, F. 152 "MIA", Y. 1922, f. 49, 31 MIA to Berat Prefecture, 21 August 1921.
22 AQSH, F. 156 "The Dictation Court", Y. 1922, f. 4, 37, Church Eldership Decision, 28 August 1922.
23 AQSH, F. 156 "The Dictation Court", Y. 1922, f. 4, 39, Minutes, 29 August/11 September 1922.
24 AQSH, F. 152 "MIA", f. 53, 11, Prodani to MIA, 13 September 1922.
25 "Andej-Këndej [Here and There]", *Koha [Time]*, 2 September 1922, 2.
26 These representatives included Pal Xhumari and Andre Ikonomi from Kavaja; Reverend Simon and Mark Hobdari from Tirana; Lon Xoxa and Mit Qilica from Fier; Tun Gjergji and Llaz Boxhja from Lushnja; Spiro Kati from Libohova; and Kosta Thomaj from Delvina.
27 AQSH, Prodani to MIA, quoted.
28 AQSH, F. 152 "MIA", f. 53, 122, Theodhos to MJ, 23 September 1922.
29 Xhuvani, *Memory*, 186.
30 The nineteenth-century theologian Archimandrite Theoklitos Farmakidis, who led the movement for the autocephaly of the Church of Greece, originally defined this principle, which was later elaborated by Patriarch Joachim III of Constantinople. Reverend Jivko Panev, "Some Remarks on the Notion of Autocephaly", *Sourozh* 63 (1996):25–32.
31 This reasoning is a novelty in canon law. Subsequent scholars of the Albanian ecclesiastical issue were mostly Greeks and thus referred to the Berat Congress as "non-canonical". However, the reason behind this conclusion has never been widely elaborated. The theologian Pirro Kondili emphasizes that the lack of a formal request from a Holy Synod makes the Congress of Berat at odds with canon law (Pirro Kondili, "Η Ορθόδοξη Εκκλησία της Αλβανίας κατά τη διάρκεια της κομμουνιστικής δικτατορίας [The Orthodox Church of Albania during the Communist Dictatorship]", (MA Thesis, Athens University, 2002), 21). However, this reasoning is faulty, since the canons do not address the issue of autocephaly. They belong to a period when the very notion of autocephaly for new Churches did not exist. Apart from the Church of Cyprus, all other Orthodox Churches came into existence at a later period, without a clear definition regarding the canonical right to a tomos of autocephaly. Xhuvani's reasoning, that the Albanian Church was autocephalous since 1912 even though the declaration would take place ten years later, was based on the ecclesiastical principle of "an independent Church in an independent state". There was no case

in which the establishment of an autocephalous Church was the result of an official request from a local synod. Although there were dozens of Orthodox bishops throughout Greece, the autocephaly of the Church of Greece was declared at a meeting of Greek archimandrites. Twenty years later, the Ecumenical Patriarchate granted the tomos, but Greece's Orthodox Church referred to this as "recognition", not "declaration". (Only a few historians consider the declaration of 1833 as not canonical, such as Emmanuel Kostandinides, *Η ανακηρυξις του αυτοκεφαλου της εν Ελλαδι Εκκλησιας (1850) και η θεσις των μητροπολεων των Νεων Χωρων (1928)* [*Declaration of the Church's Autocephaly in Greece (1850) and the Place of Metropolitanates in New Countries (1928)*] (Athens: Parrhsea, 1974), 13–45. Even the Orthodox Autocephalous Church of Albania (OACA) stressed, until 1967, that its autocephaly had been "declared" in 1922 and "recognized" in 1937, a narrative that changed after 1991, when the new Orthodox Church leaders marked 1937 as the year of gaining autocephaly). In the absence of bishops and to avoid misunderstandings (since the Orthodox were not a majority in Albania), the Berat Congress was convened as a clerical–secular congress (unlike the Greek case, in which bishops existed but were not summoned and autocephaly was decreed by the king, who was a Roman Catholic). The autocephaly of the Albanian Church is perhaps the only case in which full canonical reasoning led to the convening of a congress. This does not make that reasoning necessarily correct, but it does make it a unique interpretation of canon law. The legal scholar Aurela Anastasi argues that the temporary nature of the statute adopted by the Congress of Berat and the provision that the Holy Synod had the exclusive right for a number of acts and decisions is evidence of the legality of Albanian autocephaly (Anastasi, "Statute of the Church", 54–55).

32 AQSH, Theodhos to the MJ, quoted.
33 Glavinas, "Metropolitan of Durrës", 70.
34 Naska, "Kongresi", 16.
35 AQSH, Theodhos to MJ, quoted.
36 Xhuvani, *Memory*, 192.
37 OACA, *Statuti i Kishës Orthodhokse Autoqefale Kombëtare të Shqipërisë [The Statute of the National Orthodox Autocephalous Church of Albania]* (Korça: Dhori Koti, 1923).
38 AMFA, f. 186, 15, MFA to MIA, 14 September 1922.
39 AQSH, F. 155 "MJ", Y. 1922, f. 5, 1, Council of Ministers Decision no. 809, 18 September 1922.
40 AQSH, F. 141 "Metropolitanate of Korça", f. 436, 9, Memorandum from MIA, 24 September 1922.
41 AMFA, Y. 1922, f. 186, 25–32, Telegram from Berat Congress, 24 September 1922.
42 AMFA, Y. 1922, f. 186, 18, Telegram from Berat Congress, 18 September 1922.
43 AMFA, Y. 1922, f. 186, 21, MFA to MIA, 25 September 1922.
44 Georgios Tasoudis, *Βιογραφικαί αναμνήσεις του Αρχιεπισκόπου Αθηνών Χρύσανθου του από Τραπεζούντος: 1881–1949 [The Biographical Memoirs of the Archbishop of Athens, Chrysanthos from Trebizond: 1881–1949]* (Athens: Kostandinidi & Mihala, 1970), 29.
45 AQSH, F. 152 "MIA", Y. 1922, f. 538, 48, Korça Prefecture to MIA, 18 October 1922.
46 "Kisha Autoqefale dhe Pishkop Theofan Noli [The Autocephalous Church and Bishop Theofan Noli]", *Koha [Time]*, December 1922, 2.
47 Xhuvani, *Memory*, 23.
48 *Koha [Time]*, 18 November 1922, 2.
49 Xhuvani, *Memory*, 36.

50 AQSH, F. 152 "MIA", Y. 1923, f. 26, 70, MIA to Korça Prefecture, 14 February 1923.
51 AQSH, F. 152 "MIA", Y. 1923, f. 26, 26, Vasil Dilo to MIA, 3 February 1923.
52 AQSH, F. 152 "MIA", Y. 1923, f. 26, 71, Korça Prefecture to MIA, 15 February 1923.
53 AQSH, F. 152 "MIA", Y. 1923, f. 26, 28–29, Gjirokastra Prefecture to MIA, 28 February 1923.
54 Beqir Meta, "Qëndrimi i shtetit shqiptar ndaj pakicës etno-kulturore vllehe dhe asaj malazeze në vitet 1920–1924 [The Albanian State Position towards the Vlach Ethno-Cultural Minority and the Montenegrins in 1920–1924]", *Studime historike [Historical Studies]* 3–4 (2009):45–66. Regarding the Orthodox of Golloborda, see Kristofor Beduli, *Ortodoksët e Gollobordës [The Orthodox of Golloborda]* (Tirana: Neraida, 2008).
55 Aleksandar Stamatovic, *Kratka istorija Mitropolije Crnogorsko-primorske (1219–1999) [A History of Montenegro's Metropolitanate (1219–1999)]* (Cetinje: Svetigora, 2000).
56 Dimso Peric, *Srpska pravoslavna crkva i njena dijaspora [The Serbian Orthodox Church and Its Diaspora]* (Toronto: Serbian Orthodox Diocese of Canada, 1996).
57 AQSH, F. 142 "Shkodra Orthodox Community", f. 123, 1, Cetinje Metropolitanate to Shkodra Vicariate.
58 Mirko Avakumovic, "Pravoslavna Crkva u Albaniji [The Orthodox Church in Albania]", *Arhiv za pravno i drustvene nauke [Archive of Social and Judicial Studies]* 4 (1936):41–67; found in AMFA, Y. 1935, f. 305, 17.
59 AMFA, Y. 1937, f. 308, 4, Biography of His Grace Viktor, no date.
60 AQSH, Theodhos to MJ, quoted.
61 Roberto M. Della Rocca, *Kombësia dhe feja në Shqipëri 1920–1944 [Nationality and Religion in Albania 1920–1944]* (Tirana: Elena Gjika, 1994), 56–57.
62 AMFA, Y. 1922, f. 186, 50, Belgrade Embassy to MFA, 5 November 1922.
63 AMFA, Y. 1922, f. 332, 4, Belgrade Embassy to MFA, 30 December 1922.
64 Meta, "The Position of the Albanian State", 52–64.
65 AQSH, F. 152 "MIA", Y. 1923, f. 27, 2, Korça Prefecture to MIA, 21 January 1923.
66 AQSH, F. 152 "MIA", Y. 1923, f. 27, 7, Korça Prefecture to MIA, 18 January 1923.
67 "Një skandull në Korçë [A Scandal in Korça]", *Koha [Time]*, 27 January 1923, 2.
68 AMFA, Y. 1923, f. 186, 61, MIA to Shkodra Prefecture, 22 January 1923.
69 AMFA, Y. 1923, f. 186, 67, Shkodra Prefecture to His Grace Viktor, 28 January 1923.
70 AMFA, Y. 1923, f. 186, 58, MFA to Serbian-Croatian-Slovenian Embassy, 30 January 1923.
71 AMFA, Y. 1923, f. 331, 10–12, Serbian-Croatian-Slovenian Embassy to MFA, 7 February 1923.
72 Meta, "The Position of the Albanian State", 61–62.
73 AMFA, Y. 1923, f. 332, 28–29, Report, 24 February 1923.
74 AMFA, Y. 1923, f. 332, 108–110, Belgrade Embassy to MFA, 15 March 1923.
75 AQSH, F. 152 "MIA", Y. 1923, f. 27, 67, Shkodra Prefecture to MIA, 6 April 1923.
76 AMFA, Y. 1923, f. 331, 70, Belgrade Embassy to MFA, 7 April 1923; Lambros Psomas, "Το πρόβλημα της άρνησης των Σέρβων για υποστήριξη των πρώτων προσπαθειών των Ορθοδόξων Αλβανών για αυτοκέφαλη Εκκλησία [The Problem of Serbian Refusal of the First Efforts of Albanian Orthodox for an Autocephalous Church]", *Theologia [Theology]* 77:2 (2006): 645–655.
77 AMFA, Y. 1923, f. 331, 71, MFA to Albanian Embassies, 7 April 1923.

78 AMFA, Y. 1923, f. 331, 72, MFA to Serbian-Croatian-Slovenian Embassy, 7 April 1923.
79 AMFA, Y. 1923, f. 331. 73–75, Blinishti to MFA, 14 April 1923.
80 AMFA, f. 332, 120, MFA to MIA, 12 June 1923.
81 AQSH, F. 155 "MJ", Y. 1923, f. 21, 1, MJ to MIA, 13 October 1923.
82 AQSH, F. 152 "MIA", Y. 1922, f. 53, Metropolitan Iakovos to Durrës Municipality.
83 *Koha [Time]*, 7 October 1922, 2.
84 Della Rocca, *Nationality and Religion*, 53–54.
85 AMFA, Y. 1922, f. 102 38–39, MIA to MFA, 12 November 1922.
86 AMFA, Y. 1922, f. 102, 37, MFA to MIA, 6 November 1922.
87 AQSH, F. 152 "MIA", Y. 1922, f. 181 23, Church High Council to the League of Nations Secretary, 14 November 1922.
88 Della Rocca, *Nationality and Religion*, 53–54.
89 The Albanian ecclesiastical issue draw the attention of the Italian government. See: AQSH, F. 163 "Italian Embassy", Y. 1922, f. 13.
90 Tritos, *Church in Illyricum*, 64.
91 AQSH, F. 55 "Sotir Peçi", f. 92, 12, Patriarch Meletios to Metropolitan Joakim, 15 September 1922.
92 Apostolos Glavinas, "Ιωακείμ Μαρτίστης η Μαρτινιανός [Joakim Martishti or Martiniani]", *Ηπειρωτικό Ημερολόγιο [Epirotes Diary]* 3 (1981):44–53; Dr Dion Tushi, "Joakim Martiniani", *Kërkim [Research]* 6 (2010):81–93.
93 AMFA, Y. 1922, f. 186, 48, Istanbul Consulate to MFA, 6 October 1922.
94 AMFA, Y. 1922, f. 186, 53, Istanbul Consulate to MFA, 4 November 1922.
95 *Koha [Time]*, 2 December 1922, 3.
96 AQSH, F. 152 "MIA", Y. 1922, f. 53, Korça Prefecture to MIA, 30 November 1922.
97 AQSH, F. 152 "MIA", Y. 1922, f. 53, Korça Prefecture to MIA, 12 December 1922. "Personalitet madhor i Kishës sonë Orthodhokse: Imzot Kristofor Kisi [Great Personality of Our Orthodox Church: Bishop Kristofor Kisi]", *Ngjallja [Resurrection]*, July 1996, 9. Born Sotir Kisi in Berat in 1882, died in Tirana in 1950; metropolitan of Berat 1922–1929, metropolitan of Korça 1933–1937; archbishop of Albania 1937–1949.
98 Apostolos Glavinas, "Ο Συναδών Χριστόφορος και οι δραστηριότητες του για το εκκλησιαστικό ζήτημα της Αλβανίας [Kristofor of Synadon and His Activity for the Ecclesiastical Issue in Albania]", *Ηπειρότηκο Ημερολόγιο [Epirotan Calendar]* 2 (1984):71–72.
99 *Koha [Time]*, 16 December 1922, 2.
100 AMFA, Y. 1922, f. 186, 56, MIA to MFA, 28 December 1922.
101 AQSH, F. 152 "MIA", Y. 1923, f. 26, 96, Patriarch Meletios to Exarch Ierothe, 3 February 1923.
102 AQSH, F. 152 "MIA", Y. 1923, f. 26, 96, Exarch Ierothe to Patriarch Meletios, 6 February 1923.
103 AQSH, F. 152 "MIA", Y. 1923, f. 26, 97, Patriarch Meletios to Exarch Ierothe, 9 February 1923.
104 AQSH, F. 152 "MIA", Y. 1923, f. 26, 98, His Grace Joakim to Exarch Ierothe, 24 February 1923.
105 AMFA, Y. 1923, f. 331, 32, Korça Prefecture to MIA, 27 February 1923.
106 Daskarolis, *Military movement*, 31–37.
107 The Albanian Orthodox Church is an exception as the only non-Greek Church that, since 1991, does not have ecclesiastical districts in the diaspora.
108 Meta, "Autocephaly", 82.

109 AMFA, Y. 1923, f. 331 10, Sofia Consulate to MFA, 25 February 1923.
110 *Zëri i Gjirokastrës [Gjirokastra's Voice]*, 7 July 1923, 2.
111 AMFA, Y. 1923, f. 331, 60–64, Geneva Consulate to MFA, 4 May 1923.
112 AMFA, Y. 1923, f. 331, 65–66, Patriarch Meletios to Ahmet Zog, no date.
113 AMFA, Y. 1923, f. 331, 56, Church High Council to MFA, 7 May 1923.
114 AQSH, F. 152 "MIA", Y. 1923, f. 26, 4, Korça Prefecture to MIA, 20 May 1923.
115 AMFA, Y. 1923, f. 331, 90, Passport Office in Bulgaria to MFA, 28 June 1923.
116 AMFA, Y. 1923, f. 142, 4–9, Athens Embassy to MFA, 28 February 1923.
117 AMFA, Y. 1923, f. 142, 22, Athens Embassy to MFA, 23 March 1923.
118 AMFA, Y. 1923, f. 142, 23, Athens Embassy to MFA, 23 March 1923.
119 AMFA, Y. 1923, f. 141, 1, London Embassy to MFA, 13 June 1923.
120 AMFA, Y. 1923, f. 142, 27, Athens Embassy to MFA, 24 July 1923.
121 AQSH, F. 152 "MIA", Y. 1923, f. 26, 117, MIA to Korça Prefecture, 8 August 1923.
122 AMFA, Y. 1923, f. 210, 39, Geneva Consulate to the League of Nations, 1 September 1923.
123 Kondis, *Elinismos III*, 104: IDAYE, f. A/5 (2), no. 7237, Durrës Embassy to Greek MFA, 20 July 1923.
124 "Pishkop Noli në Korçë [Bishop Noli in Korça]", *Koha [Time]*, 18 August 1923, 2.
125 GAK, F. "PMO", f. 725/2, 1, Military Troops V to Venizelos, 14/27 December 1923.
126 Glavinas, "Kristofor of Synadon", 85–86.
127 "Ceremonia e Imzot Nolit në Shën Gjergj [Ceremony of Bishop Noli in Saint Gjergj]", *Koha [Time]*, 8 December 1923, 1.
128 Kondis, *Elinismos III*, 125: IDAYE, f. B/35, no. 1707, Durrës Embassy to Greek MFA, 7 January 1924.
129 AQSH, F. 163 "Italian Embassy", Y. 1922, f. 13, 6, Italian Embassy to Italian MFA, 22 December 1922.
130 Constantinople was officially renamed Istanbul at the end of October 1923.
131 AMFA, Y. 1924, f. 501, 1–2, Athens Embassy to MFA, 18 January 1924.
132 AMFA, Y. 1924, f. 501, 7, Istanbul Consulate to MFA, 19 February 1924.
133 Kondis, *Elinismos III*, 137: IDAYE, f. a/5, no. 139, Durrës Embassy to Greek MFA, 5 March 1924.
134 Dervishi, *History*, 74.
135 Kondis, *Elinismos III*, 181: IDAYE, f. A/5, no. 9018, Durrës Embassy to Greek MFA, 12 October 1924.
136 AMFA, Y. 1924, f. 292, 5–6, Bucharest General Consulate to MFA, 8 October 1924.
137 *Gazeta e Korçës [Korça Gazette]*, 1 April 1924, 1.
138 Kondis, *Elinismos III*, 184–185: IDAYE, f. B/33, no. 44754, Durrës Embassy to Greek MFA, 1 November 1924.
139 Kondis, *Elinismos III*, 189–190: IDAYE, f. B/33, no. 44754, Greek MFA to Durrës Embassy, 17 November 1924.
140 Archimandrite Dr Visar Xhuvani, *Gjergj Kastrioti*, 17 May 1924, 1.
141 Archimandrite Dr Visar Xhuvani, *Gjergj Kastrioti*, 7 July 1924, 1.
142 Archimandrite Dr Visar Xhuvani, "Një vepër andikanonike me rëndësi [An Important Anti-Canonical Work]", *Gjergj Kastrioti*, 28 August 1924, 1.
143 Archimandrite Dr Visar Xhuvani, "Populli do dritë shpirtënore ma parë dhe pastaj muzika [The People Want Spiritual Light First and then Music]", *Gjergj Kastrioti*, 28 August 1924, 1–2.
144 Archimandrite Dr Visar Xhuvani, "Populli do ma shumë bukë se politikë [The People Want More Bread than Politics]", *Gjergj Kastrioti*, 9 September 1924, 1.

145 Archimandrite Dr Visar Xhuvani, "Shqipnia në Këshillën e L. Kombevet – Kryeministri ynë zemëron Evropën [Albania in the League of Nations Council – Our Prime Minister Angers Europe]", *Gjergj Kastrioti*, 10 October 1924, 1.
146 Archimandrite Dr Visar Xhuvani, *Gjergj Kastrioti*, 19 October 1924, 1.
147 Fotios G. Ikonomou, *Η Ιστορια των τοπικων εκκλησιων της Ηπειρου Τομος Β' [History of the Churches of Epirus, Volume 2]* (Athens, 1969), 32.
148 *Gazeta e Korçës [Korça Gazette]*, 1 November 1924, 1; *Liria [Freedom]*, 8 November 1924, 3.

4 Efforts towards the recognition of autocephaly, 1924–1928

Zog's secret deal with Greece in Belgrade, Ierothe's alternative plan, and Xhuvani's ordination

During his exile in Belgrade and prior to his arrival in Albania, Ahmet Zog had reached several agreements with the Yugoslav and Greek governments. In order to overthrow Theofan Noli, loyal troops would have to enter from Yugoslavia and Greece, the only countries that shared land frontiers with Albania. Zog reached his agreement with Yugoslavia in exchange for several concessions that Albania would carry out in the future. Some scholars claim that this agreement would force Albania to put its Orthodox Church under the influence of the Serbian Patriarchate. Nevertheless, the agreement of August 1924 focused primarily on territorial concessions and only indirectly affected the ecclesiastical issue.[1]

Greek support, however, was also necessary, not only to ensure that troops could enter Albania from the south to demolish any resistance from Noli's government, but also to avoid any Greek interference that might occur during this period of political instability. The Greek embassy in Belgrade used Mihal Kaso as a liaison to Zog. Kaso, an MP for Gjirokastra who was loyal to Zog, had fled Albania with the parliamentary majority when Noli's supporters seized power. On 3 September 1924, Kaso listed the terms of Greece's assistance to Zog.[2] The first condition was that Christians living in Albania would have equal rights with the rest of the population and that the government would not oppress them. Greece intended to use the same formula to protect the Orthodox in Albania, just as the Russian Empire had done during the Ottoman period.[3] Kaso told Zog that Greece sought non-intervention on the ecclesiastical affairs of the Orthodox, free schools in Northern Epirus, and the teaching of the Greek language in Albanian schools if requested by the local communities.[4] This implied that Ahmet Zog would not interfere in the negotiations for the recognition of autocephaly. The ecclesiastical question had political implications for Zog, considering that Metropolitan Theofan Noli, the leader of the Albanian Orthodox Church, had thrown him out of power. Zog took on the responsibility of ensuring that Christians would be able to practice their religion in their chosen language with no interference from the government.[5] The third commitment – to open Greek schools in Albania without governmental interference – was the same promise undertaken through the Declaration for the Protection of Minorities. The fourth condition, however, was a significant one, as Zog pledged to allow the Greek language to be taught in Orthodox Albanian schools if requested by the local population. This concession copied a legal sanction from the Ottoman period, ensuring that the Greek language would be taught in the Orthodox educational system alongside the country's official language. The final concession regarded the southern Albanian city of Himara. Greece demanded the return of the special privileges this region had enjoyed during the Ottoman Empire. Zog deemed the requests admissible and reasonable and authorized Kaso to convey Zog's acceptance to the Greek embassy, thus reaching a deal with Greece.[6]

Ahmet Zog's return to power in January 1925, this time as president of the Albanian Republic, had deep reverberations with regard to the ecclesiastical issue, for as long as Metropolitan Theofan Noli remained both the overthrown prime minister and the leader of the autocephaly movement. In January 1925, nobody knew if Zog's new government would retaliate against Noli's supporters Marko and Çamçe, who together constituted the remaining core of the Albanian Orthodox Church leadership. Under such conditions, the metropolitan of Korça, Ierothe Jaho, crossed over to the Greeks. Just a few months earlier, Ierothe had refused to send a letter of congratulations to the Ecumenical Patriarch. Now, immediately realizing that the balance of power had passed to Greece, he drew up an alternative plan. Ierothe sent Pandeli Kotoko, a former teacher from the Greek school in Korça and a prominent Hellenist, to Athens to seek the support of the Greek government on the ecclesiastical issue.[7] On 2 February 1925, Kotoko delivered to the Greek Foreign Ministry Ierothe's secret, 13-point plan. Through Kotoko, Ierothe requested the Patriarchate to send Metropolitan of Dryinopolis Vasil to Albania, arguing that he was the only old metropolitan the Albanian government could accept, since he was a friend of Zog's main supporter, Myfit Libohova. Ierothe reasoned that the return of Metropolitan Iakovos was unacceptable after his Greek nationalist activity, while Joakim was rejected as an Italophile. Ierothe was trying to prepare the ground for the Patriarchate to assign him the archbishop's throne. Thus, Kotoko wrote, on Ierothe's behalf, that cooperation with Vasil, or any other pro-Greek hierarch, was a necessity, as Noli and Kisi, the other two bishops in Albania, were Albanian nationalists.[8]

Ierothe sought to dissolve the Church High Council of the Albanian Orthodox Church and, along with the mayor of Korça, Vasil Avrami, to call a new ecclesiastical congress. The new congress would again declare the autocephaly of the Albanian Church, as the majority of Orthodox Albanians would reject autonomy.[9] The difference between the new congress and the Berat Congress was that this time it would be led by Ierothe and the other bishops installed by the Patriarchate. Ierothe expressed his desire to meet with Noli in Greece in order to reach common ground for all

Orthodox Albanians. He also called for the repatriation of a number of notable Albanian Hellenists residing in Greece, such as Bishop Polikarp and the professors Harallamb Dhonato, Vasil Joanidhi, and Mihal Kriqi. Ierothe requested that the Patriarchate officially appoint him metropolitan of Korça, a title that had been bestowed on him in Albania by the Church High Council. Lastly, Ierothe pleaded with the Greek government to allow the Albanian Church to receive the bequests of notable Albanian benefactors that were being blocked by the Bank of Athens.[10]

Ierothe's plan marks a key moment in the Albanian ecclesiastical movement, as it was drafted immediately after the Belgrade deal between Greece and Zog. Ierothe presented this plan while posing as a Hellenist, but his suggestions were entirely in line with the Albanian national ideology. It is obvious on several points that the Hellenist vernacular he used was simply an attempt to make amends with Greece. First, the premise that the nationalist Vasil Avrami would call the new congress shows that Ierothe's plan had been coordinated with Albanian patriots. Second, the dissolution of the Church High Council and its replacement with a Synod was in accordance with the statute approved by the Berat Congress, but again Ierothe left open no option but autocephaly. Ierothe's argument that the Hellenists had to return to fill the vacancies in the Albanian Orthodox Church was the same reasoning he had used when he called for the return of Kristofor Kisi a year earlier. The controversies regarding Metropolitan Theofan Noli are obvious. On one hand, Ierothe calls him "the most dangerous" proponent of autocephaly, while, on the other, Ierothe asks for the Greek state's opinion as to whether he should meet with Noli to reach a mutual position. Such moves show that Ierothe's aim was recognition of autocephaly by the Patriarchate and the lessening of the Albanian Orthodox Church's economic dependence on Greece. However, in light of the political developments after the Belgrade deal, this was possible only with the help of Greece itself. In the first months after his return to power, Ahmet Zog was under pressure from different sides, while Noli's supporters saw themselves at risk. The Hellenists, openly supported by the Greek embassy in Albania, were trying to sabotage the Albanian Autocephalous Church. Thus, a third group gathered around Ierothe, seeking a flexible tactic with the Hellenists to ensure the recognition of the Albanian Church.

Under such circumstances, the liberal patriots rallied once more around Archimandrite Visar Xhuvani, who had been excluded from the Church since 1923. After the fall of Noli's government and his ensuing flight, Zog had freed Xhuvani from his exile in Vlora. He again started publishing the newspaper *Gjergj Kastrioti*, which restated the need for an autocephalous Orthodox Albanian Church. This move reconciled him with some of Noli's supporters, such as Mihal Grameno, who wrote in *Koha* on 21 February 1925, that there were no doubts that the Albanian theologian supported the National Church.[11] After the unprecedented attack *Gjergj Kastrioti* had launched against Noli's government, it was no surprise that Visar Xhuvani had the full support of state officials. Thus, for the newly elected President

Ahmet Zog, the archimandrite was the right choice. Visar Xhuvani was a well-known theologian with a PhD from the University of Athens and a patriot who was loyal to the new president. On 24 March 1925, the Albanian Ministry of Interior asked the Church High Council, under official secrecy, to appoint Archimandrite Visar Xhuvani as vicar of the metropolitanate of Durrës now that His Grace Theofan Noli was in exile.[12]

Following this request, on 8 April 1925, Visar Xhuvani took over the Durrës diocese; however, his full ordainment was still missing. In a missive to believers, Xhuvani asked them for their full support and cooperation.[13] This missive clearly displayed the archimandrite's belief that he would soon be elected the future metropolitan of Durrës. Such a swift appointment would have saved President Zog from Greek pressure to fill the clerical vacancies with hierarchs favoured by Athens. Although the Church High Council, still being run by Noli's supporters, was ready to put Xhuvani's opposition to Noli behind them and elect him as a ruling bishop, Visar's ordination by Bishops Kristofor and Ierothe was almost impossible. Kristofor had an ongoing feud with Xhuvani, while Ierothe was trying to lure Athens once again. A possible solution was for foreign bishops to conduct his ordination, as Xhuvani himself had been pondering ever since the Berat Congress. However, this was an undesirable scenario as it would reveal the government's influence on such a decision, at a time when Ahmet Zog was pretending to be willing to apply the Belgrade deal. Moreover, this would sow discord between the two metropolitans and the rest of the Church, which could possibly develop into a dispute with the government.

Xhuvani called it a national necessity that he be ordained as soon as possible, because Bishops Kristofor and Ierothe had violated the statute of the Albanian Orthodox Church, thus putting its very existence at risk. In April 1925, Archimandrite Xhuvani asked Kristofor Kisi and Ierothe Jaho if they would be willing to ordain him. Ierothe refused to act without the Patriarchate's order, while, although His Grace Kristofor was willing, he could not ordain Xhuvani without the participation of a second regular bishop. Archimandrite Xhuvani was angry at Ierothe's refusal, especially because the two bishops had rebelled against the Patriarchate by ordaining Theofan Noli just two years before.[14]

Archimandrite Visar Xhuvani decided to follow the path of Fan Noli and asked bishops of the Russian Church in Exile to ordain him. Ahmet Zog and other prominent state leaders were informed of these developments and provided full governmental support to Xhuvani. Xhuvani had also asked for official permission from Reverend Vasil Marko, who responded that he would go to Tirana to talk to Xhuvani in person. Xhuvani did not wait to meet with Marko, as the lack of any immediate refusal by the Church High Council was enough for him to go ahead with his plan. In June 1925, in Montenegro, at the request of the church elderships of Durrës, Elbasan, and Tirana, two Russian hierarchs ordained Visar Xhuvani as bishop with the name Visarion.[15]

The Church High Council did not react immediately and Xhuvani, considering the two-week silence from the Albanian Orthodox Church as consent, continued to lead the diocese of Durrës.[16] The Albanian press was surprised; Mihal Grameno swiftly called the ordination "suspicious" and implied that Xhuvani would be serving a foreign Church since the Church High Council had not elected him.[17] *Gazeta e Korçës* (Korça Gazette) was even tougher, calling Visarion "a Serbian bishop" and predicting that the Council would soon dismiss him as vicar of Durrës.[18] In an effort to maintain the fragile balances created between the metropolitans and the Church High Council, Reverend Vasil Marko did not recognize the ordination and banned Xhuvani from officiating at any religious services. Marko informed Justice Minister Petro Poga that the ordination was unlawful and not in the best interest of the Church and the country.[19] On 16 May 1925, Minister Poga replied that the Church was free not to recognize Visarion and to ban him from holding liturgy as a bishop.[20]

Although the Albanian government agreed to Xhuvani's ban, it now had an ace up its sleeve that could be used at the first opportunity. Ierothe had warned Athens about the possibility that Albania would fill the vacancies in its dioceses quickly. Hence, Visarion's ordination softened the Greek pressure to Zog.

Greek pressure on Ahmet Zog to implement the Belgrade deal

The Albanian government was under pressure owing to the Belgrade deal and could not yet use the services of Visarion Xhuvani. Vasil Dilo's newspaper *Liria* (Freedom) launched the first attack against the Church High Council. On 11 January 1925, two weeks after Zog's return to power, the paper wrote that Reverend Vasil Marko, a priest from Korça and the self-proclaimed chairperson of the Church Council, wanted to interfere in the affairs of Gjirokastra's churches. Dilo argued that the Church Council had ceased to exist after the arrival of the bishops in Albania and called for a new congress, which, he said, was also the wish of the government.[21] Dilo's request was quite similar to Ierothe's secret plan.

The Greek ambassador in Durrës, Panourgias, met President Zog at the beginning of February 1925. Zog stated that he would resolve the ecclesiastical and educational issues as agreed in Belgrade, even if he had to use violence against his own citizens. However, he insisted that before the government could act, the inhabitants of Albania's Orthodox villages needed to request the teaching of Greek in their schools.[22] Those MPs from Gjirokastra that represented the Greek minority, at the urging of Ambassador Panourgias, with whom they were regularly in touch, raised the issue of the Belgrade promises in a meeting with Zog as soon as the parliament elected him president of the Albanian Republic. The Greek ambassador told these MPs to gather signatures from Gjirokastra asking the government to convene an Orthodox congress regarding these ecclesiastical and linguistic matters.[23] Accordingly, on 4 April 1925, 120 elders from the district's Christian villages signed a petition and presented it to the Albanian Ministry of Justice. The signatories requested the establishment of a religious seminary in Gjirokastra and the teaching of the "religious language" in Orthodox schools.[24] Vasil Dilo argued in *Liria* that for the Orthodox, the Greek language was as important as Arabic and Turkish were for the Muslims or Latin for the Catholics. He added that a ban on the Greek language in the Orthodox Church constituted a war against religion,[25] unless the Holy Synod defined in the future Albanian as the only language in the Church.[26]

From Dilo's point of view, the temporary need to use Greek in religious services was, in fact, an attempt to offset Greek pressure. Autocephaly was undoubtedly the essence of the Albanian demands, and all other concessions could be repealed once the Church gained independence. However, the articles in *Liria* were mocked in newspapers such as *Koha* or *Gazeta e Korçës*. MP Rauf Fico attacked Vasil Dilo by recalling his suspicious past and asked for measures to be taken against such betrayal.[27]

The Greeks' only success was Albania's acceptance of the opening of an Orthodox seminary in Korça that included the teaching of Greek. This was seen as a double victory, as the school would operate in line with the requests made by Sotir Peçi and Stavro Vinjau during Noli's rule. This decision enabled the release of Jovan Banga's bequest, which the Greek government had frozen for many years. The school request became official at the first meeting between Ahmet Zog and Metropolitan Ierothe of Korça, who was received by the president on 8 March 1925. Zog praised the importance of having an autocephalous Albanian Church, vowed to support its formation and existence, and wished for the progress of all Orthodox Albanians.[28]

Although there is no record of this meeting between Zog and Ierothe, it is probably the most important event regarding the Albanian reaction to Greek diplomatic pressure during this period. In a letter dated several months after the meeting, Ierothe stated that he and Zog had reached an agreement to send a new delegation to Istanbul to resolve the ecclesiastical issue.[29] This shows that either Ierothe did not mention at all the alternative plan he had sent to Athens, or that, unbeknownst to the Greeks, he drafted a new agreement with President Zog to make possible the Albanian Church's autocephaly. Following this meeting, on 23 March, the Albanian government approved the opening of the Orthodox seminary.[30] Its birth meant that future generations of priests would be educated in Albania, thus enabling the continuity necessary to an autocephalous Church.[31] Ierothe left Tirana on 23 March, expressing his satisfaction regarding the meeting with President Zog and believing they had reached full agreement on the Church's road to autocephaly.[32] Ahmet Zog then received His Grace Kristofor, the metropolitan of Berat, on 28 March[33] and Reverend Vasil Marko, the chairman of the Church High Council, on 23 May. The latter meeting was important as it confirmed the Albanian government's support for the Church High Council and for Reverend Vasil Marko. Zog pledged to provide help in empowering the Church and praised its leader as a tireless worker who had battled fearlessly for an autocephalous national Church.[34] Immediately afterwards, Marko called a High Council meeting to discuss important religious matters.[35] The supporters of both Zog and Noli, including Mihal Grameno, expected the Council to appoint Bishop Visarion as a ruling metropolitan during the meeting.[36] Kristofor Kisi announced that resolution of the ecclesiastical problem was only a matter of time and that establishing the Holy Synod was essential. He also said that the Church had a duty to inspire patriotism among Orthodox Albanians and to strive for the nation's progress. But this could be achieved only through actions, not empty speeches.[37]

Turmoil in Istanbul, however, was delaying recognition of autocephaly: the Patriarchate had no leader since Patriarch Gregory VII died on 17 November 1924. The Holy Synod elected his successor, Constantine VI, in early December, but he led the Church for only 43 days before being expelled by the Turkish army on 30 January 1925. The disputes between Turkey and Greece left the Patriarchate leaderless for an extended period and it was not until 13 July 1925 that the Synod managed to elect a new patriarch, Basil III (Vasileios Georgiadis, 1925–1929). Ierothe considered this the right moment to implement the agreement reached with President Zog and wrote to him that the time had come to resolve the issue. He asked that the Church High Council be excluded from the delegation sent to the Patriarchate, which, in his view, should be composed of Orthodox MPs as the true representatives of Orthodox Albanians.[38] Nezir Leskoviku, the Albanian consul in Istanbul, met the new patriarch and expressed the wish of the Albanian government to send a delegation to discuss the details of the recognition of the Albanian Church. Basil stated that he was looking forward to such an agreement but could not determine its outcome alone, as this was a matter for the Holy Synod.[39] The Patriarchate explained in a letter, delivered on 8 August, that it was willing to receive a delegation to decide what was best for the Orthodox Christians of Albania, as long as it was in line with the Holy Cannons.[40] Unsatisfied, Leskoviku asked for further explanation as to the Patriarchate's position on Albanian autocephaly, to which the patriarch refused to reply.[41] After this, the consul concluded that the Patriarchate would not grant the tomos of autocephaly and opposed the departure of any delegation to Istanbul.[42] Consequently, the Albanian government advised the Church High Council to extend the implementation of the statute approved by the Berat Congress as long as it was needed.[43]

In 1925, Ahmet Zog had managed to avoid Greek pressure for nine months. At the end of August, Ambassador Panourgias met with Zog to resolve these matters, down to the smallest detail, and requested that the Church's delegation to Istanbul soon depart.[44] Zog replied that he had given Greece a free hand regarding the ecclesiastical issue, and proof of this was his expressed support for Ierothe, whom Zog called a Greek and Greece's pawn, becoming the archbishop of Albania. Zog said he was only willing to send the delegation on the condition that it did not return empty-handed, without the Patriarchate's recognition of autocephaly. Panourgias reminded

Zog that, in Belgrade, he had said that declaring autocephaly was a mistake. The president responded by saying that the way Theofan Noli had declared the Albanian Church independent was a mistake, but autocephaly itself was a necessity. Zog also said he had ordered that no Albanian metropolitanate should be assigned to Visarion, thus delivering the Orthodox Church into Ierothe's hands, even though most believers wanted Visarion to be appointed archbishop. Panourgias wondered if perhaps Albania had no clear opinions; it insisted on the word *autocephaly* but disregarded every other ecclesiastical issue, including the use of language.[45] From Zog's point of view, however, autocephaly was the key issue: if the Church was independent, then the government could change the language in the religious services, remove hierarchs, and thwart any potential threat to the Albanian nation. Zog managed to avoid the school issue during the meeting with Panourgias by saying it was up to Vasil Bamiha and Mihal Kaso, the Gjirokastra MPs. In fact, the Education Inspectorate in Gjirokastra had rejected any efforts by the MPs to open Greek schools in the area. Jani Minga, the supervisor, had called such a request a direct implementation of Greek policy and the "resurrection of a two-headed viper" similar to the Protocol of Corfu.[46] Moreover, the Albanian government had forbidden the opening of a Greek school in the southern city of Saranda, arguing that it could not allow instruction in Greek in a town inhabited exclusively by Orthodox Albanians.[47] Zog told Panourgias that he was not aware of these developments. He added he was in a difficult position due to the concessions he had made to Yugoslavia, which had left him looking weak in front of his citizens. He, therefore, asked for more time and flexibility regarding the pledges made in Belgrade.[48]

But Greece had no time to waste. The Greek consulate in Korça informed its Foreign Ministry that the city's Orthodox population had not requested the inclusion of Greek in their schools, arguing that they were threatened by Albanian nationalists. According to the consulate, within two years these people had been losing their Greek identity and were becoming Albanians, having lost hope for a Greek military presence. This rapid "de-Hellenization" of Orthodox Albanians suggested that the fear of invasion was the only reason why a Greek movement existed at all in Albania. It was a national imperative for Greece to preserve this psychological effect of a military incursion; without an immediate threat no Orthodox Albanian declared as Greek.[49]

From January to September 1925, Ahmet Zog faced constant criticism in regard to the promises he had made to the Greeks while residing in Belgrade. Vasil Dilo's newspapers and a number of Gjirokastra's MPs pressured the president to implement his promises, but Ierothe, the metropolitan of Korça, eased Zog's burden. Their meeting made it clear that they both opposed accepting anything less than the recognition of autocephaly. His Grace Kristofor and Reverend Vasil Marko supported this stance. The use of Ierothe as the common ground between Albania and Greece kept the Greeks from appointing a new exarch, who in all probability would have been Greek. This enabled the deferral of the Greek demands to the point where Greece ended up shifting its stance regarding Albanian matters. The change of balance, however, was mostly due to events in Athens.

Second Albanian–Greek rapprochement and the Church Protocol of Tirana

Greece had recovered slowly from its disaster in Asia Minor. The military government that seized power in 1922 and executed the main members of the Gounaris government as traitors managed to rule for two years until January 1924. Eleftherios Venizelos then formed a new cabinet, which lasted only a few days, until 6 February 1924. That same year, Venizelos's allies established four other governments, which dethroned the king and declared Greece a republic. Andreas Michalakopoulos, sworn in on 7 October, led the last government of 1924. In accordance with the Belgrade deal, Michalakopoulos allowed Zog's troops to enter Albania from Greece and overthrow the government of Fan Noli.[50]

Within a short period, however, Greek policy would completely change. One of the country's most prominent generals, Theodoros Pangalos, was dissatisfied with the recent political developments. He had been among the key generals who overthrew Demetrios Gounaris and had served as a minister in nearly all the governments of 1924. Aided by his good reputation as a courageous warrior in the Balkan Wars of the early 1910s, Pangalos had gained tremendous power by training army units that were loyal to him alone. When the Michalakopoulos government tried to curtail his power, Pangalos staged a coup d'état, set up a new government, and asked for a vote of confidence by the Greek Assembly.[51]

During the summer of 1925, Pangalos strengthened his overall political and military position and in September ordered the dissolution of the Greek Assembly, arguing that it had lost the trust of the nation. Pangalos himself was of Albanian descent, as both his parents came from an area near Athens that was mainly inhabited by Albanians. His mother, a native of the village of Elefsina, had married Demetrios Pangalos, a former Greek MP from Salamina Island. Thus, the Pangalos government was willing to take a sincere approach towards Albanian–Greek relations, and, as a first step, set aside the Belgrade deal. In December 1925, the Greek foreign minister, Loukas Roufos, told the Albanian ambassador in Athens, Mid'hat Frashëri, that Greece was ready to open a new chapter in relations between the two countries. Greece withdrew all land claims against its northern neighbour and recognized the Muslims of Chameria as an Albanian national minority, a move that stopped their expulsion in the population exchange with Turkey.[52] In an interview with *Gazeta e Korçës* in February 1926, Pangalos declared that the Greek minority in Albania consisted only of the Greek-speaking Orthodox in the south. He stressed that the Greek government rejected "the wrong opinion that every Orthodox was Greek" and announced that he had ordered the closing of the Northern Epirotic associations.[53]

For Albania, even before the official announcements, the change of course was evident. The appointment of Colonel Alexandros Kontoulis as the Greek ambassador to Albania was a clear sign of the new relations. The newspaper *Koha* welcomed Kontoulis with enthusiasm, recalling his positive attitude when he ruled Korça during the Greek invasion of southern Albania in 1914. During this chaotic time, Kontoulis had duly delivered Korça to Prince Wied. For the Albanian press, the appointment of Kontoulis was a sure sign of an Albanian–Greek rapprochement.[54] The Albanian government, for its part, tried to make the most of this favourable situation, with its first "victims" being Vasil Dilo's newspapers *Liria* and *Tirana*, which were shut down for their stance towards the Albanian Church.[55] Given the Greek government's new position, the Church High Council sought to restore a sense of Albanian national spirit in the country's Orthodox churches. On 10 September, a renewed patriotic effort began in Korça, when the local church, led by Reverend Vasil Marko, celebrated the third anniversary of the Berat Congress.[56]

The beginning of the year 1925 had been depressing for Albania, as Greece seemed to be gaining momentum, but the new governmental changes in Athens had brought fresh hope. On 21 November 1925, the Albanian government summoned Reverend Vasil Marko to Tirana to discuss the ecclesiastical issue. The press, for some time now, had been circulating many names about the possible composition of the Holy Synod of the Albanian Church,[57] all of whom were Albanian patriots. That year's municipal elections showed this to be an accurate barometer of events: the winners in Korça were all nationalist Orthodox Albanians.[58] The Albanian government passed a law placing all monasteries under the jurisdiction of the Church High Council, an effort that had been impossible just a few months earlier, when Greek pressure was at its peak.[59] The High Council managed to spread its authority even to Himara, which until then had been a troublesome and rebellious region: at the end of 1925, 40 leading citizens from the town of Himara signed a letter addressed to the Church leadership recognizing its authority.[60]

During this time, the Albanian ecclesiastical movement was able to regain the momentum it had had in June 1924. In February 1926, a group of prominent Orthodox Albanians, led by Vasil Avrami, the mayor of Korça, decided to establish the Holy Synod, which would be composed of Ierothe, Kristofor, Visarion, Archimandrite Vangjel Çamçe, and Reverend Vasil Marko. Both Ierothe, the metropolitan of Korça, and Kristofor, the metropolitan of Berat, had condoned the plan.[61] It did not go ahead, however, as the Patriarchate, after the intervention of the Greek government, had agreed to grant the tomos of autocephaly and had assigned Metropolitan Chrysanthos of Trebizond to work out the details.[62] On 13 April 1926, Patriarch Basil III wrote a letter to President Zog, emphasizing the Patriarchate's fatherly care to all Orthodox Albanians and promising to provide a quick and final settlement of the matter. The patriarch informed Zog that he would be sending an exarch to draft a memorandum on the resolution of the ecclesiastical issue.[63]

Metropolitan Chrysanthos was not a random choice. He served as the Ecumenical Patriarchate's liaison with the Greek government, while, at the same time, helping to maintain its diplomatic relations with other countries. The Greek press often referred to Chrysanthos as the foreign minister of the Patriarchate,[64] although his office was located inside the building of the Greek Foreign Ministry.[65] Thus, the selection of Chrysanthos as the new envoy was important for Greece, as he was loyal to both the Greek government and the Holy Synod of the Ecumenical Patriarchate, preventing any new "betrayal" such as had occurred with Metropolitans Ierothe Jaho and Kristofor Kisi.

Before setting off for Albania, Chrysanthos reviewed the history of the Church in Albania and the relations between Orthodox Albanians and Orthodox Greeks. Among the documents he reviewed was a Greek memorandum which noted that Albania could request equal rights for the 300,000 Orthodox Albanians living in central Greece. The memorandum also claimed that southern Albania was home to 40,000 Greek-speakers and tens of thousands of Albanian Orthodox who still affiliated themselves with the Greek nation. Nonetheless, Chrysanthos discovered no reciprocal request from Albania concerning the use of the Albanian language in the liturgy for the Orthodox Albanians of central Greece.[66]

Greek Prime Minister Theodoros Pangalos had instructed Chrysanthos to accept the Albanian demands because he wanted to end the stagnation in relations between the two countries. His brief to Chrysanthos was precise and clear, to the point that the metropolitan considered his own personal ideas on the matter as non-essential. Sometime later, Chrysanthos wrote that recognition of autocephaly was predetermined, and there was no need to deal with the essence of the matter but only with the formalities. Prior to his travel to Tirana, Chrysanthos had met in Athens the Albanian MP Vasil Bamiha.[67] Bamiha, who represented the Greek minority in the villages around Delvina, was the liaison between the Albanian government and Chrysanthos in February and March 1926, to ensure that the solution regarding the Albanian Church would not be taken unilaterally. Bamiha told Chrysanthos that Albania would accept nothing less than autocephaly.[68] This opinion was outlined after Bamiha had met with the highest Greek state leaders, including General Pangalos, Minister Roufos, and the diplomats Tsamantos and Panourgias.[69] His Grace Chrysanthos arrived in Tirana in early May 1926, confident that the Albanian distrust of Greece was a result of Greece's previous policy mistakes and its wrongful and persistent stance that all Orthodox Albanians were Greeks.[70] Chrysanthos stayed at the Greek embassy in Durrës, where he was constantly in touch with Athens as well as with the patriarch of Constantinople. He began his work by visiting other foreign embassies in Albania, assuring them of his intention to achieve a quick solution in the matter of autocephaly.[71]

The Albanian government set up an ad hoc commission to negotiate with Chrysanthos. This commission included only Orthodox senators and MPs, under the leadership of Senate Chairman Pandeli Evangjeli and

Assembly Chairman Koço Kota. Neither representatives of the Church High Council nor the two Albanian metropolitans, Ierothe and Kisi took part in this body. The other commission members were Senators Pilo Papa and Andon Beça, and the MPs Mihal Kaso, Dr Simon Simonidhi, Vasil Rusi, and Vasil Bamiha.[72] On 24 May, negotiations officially began, and the national press immediately informed the reading public that the parties had resolved the ecclesiastical issue. *Gazeta e Korçës* published an article titled "The Patriarchate Recognizes the Autocephaly of the Church", in which it was noted that Evlogji Kurilla had been selected to serve as archbishop.[73] According to Chrysanthos, these talks lasted 40 days and were often in danger of being suspended. Only the support of Simonidhi, Bamiha, and Kaso made it possible for Chrysanthos to reach a mutual understanding with their fellow Albanian negotiators.[74] Chrysanthos realized that the instructions from Pangalos and Roufos were the only way forward. From the initial meeting, President Zog made it perfectly clear that he would accept nothing but autocephaly. Even the Greek minority MPs in the Albanian parliament expressed the opinion that there was no other solution in such a situation. The representatives of the Orthodox communities, which Chrysanthos had visited in cities all over Albania – Lushnja, Berat, Narta, Vlora, Përmet, Gjirokastra, Delvina, and Saranda – shared the same view. The Orthodox in Korça, moreover, had not welcomed Chrysanthos at all.[75]

On 6 June 1926, the Albanian Commission and Metropolitan Chrysanthos signed the final agreement, which was titled the "Church Protocol of Tirana". The Albanian foreign minister, Hysni Vrioni, immediately sent the protocol to Patriarch Basil III in Istanbul. The agreement stated that the Albanian Orthodox Church would be composed of five dioceses, based in Tirana, Korça, Gjirokastra, Berat, and Durrës, and the metropolitan of Tirana would serve as archbishop. According to the agreement, to fill the three vacant dioceses, the Patriarchate would appoint bishops chosen by the Albanian Orthodox Commission, while Ierothe and Kristofor would be appointed to the dioceses they already led. The protocol maintained the status quo by allowing the Albanian language in those Albanian Orthodox communities that had used it before the signing of the protocol. The Holy Synod would see to the translation of the services that would be used by the rest of the Albanian communities, provided that the Albanian Church had approved these works. The Albanian state undertook an oath to ensure independence and full freedom for the development of the religious life of all Orthodox believers. The Protocol also stated that Albania pledged to fulfil the rights of its ethnic minorities, based on the Declaration for the Protection of Minorities submitted to the League of Nations. Article 7 stipulated that Albania would compensate the Ecumenical Patriarchate for the monasteries, which would pass under the jurisdiction of the Albanian Orthodox Church. Finally, as soon as both parties signed the agreement, the Ecumenical Patriarchate promised to deliver the tomos. The Annex to the Protocol named possible candidates for the bishops who would fill the three vacant dioceses. They were the Polikarp, the metropolitan of Trikki, who was from Përmet; Joakim, the metropolitan of New Pelagonia; Pandeli Kotoko; and Evlogji Kurilla, the secretary of the Lavra Monastery on Mount Athos.[76]

The Protocol not only recognized the independence of the Church but also acknowledged it as national, calling it the "Albanian Orthodox Church", not the "Church of Albania". Chrysanthos informed the Patriarchate that the language used in religious services would soon change because Orthodox Albanians preferred to use their native tongue in Church; therefore, he advised that it would be proper to assist with the translation of services into Albanian. Additionally, His Grace highlighted the fact that Albanian Orthodox youth were all nationalists and not influenced by Greece.[77]

The new candidates for the three bishopric seats were from different lobbying groups. Ierothe had proposed Metropolitan Polikarp in his secret plan in Athens a year earlier. Metropolitan Joakim had good relations with the Albanian government, not only because he was the former metropolitan of Berat, but also because of his proactive effort during the Albanian delegation's journey to Istanbul in 1923. Evlogji Kurilla, meanwhile, had contributed to the Albanian National Renaissance through his nationalist activity even before Albania achieved independence in 1912, but he was also a genuine Hellenophile. The proposal of Kurilla as the future archbishop of Tirana shows a compromise on a prominent figure to whom neither Albanians nor Greeks could object. The Greeks also viewed one more candidate, the theologian Pandeli Kotoko, as one of the most prominent Hellenists in Korça. They did not, however, trust at all Ierothe and Kristofor. Chrysanthos assured the Patriarchate that he had worked tirelessly to ensure that the three new bishops be elected from among the Hellenists in order to overcome the influence of Ierothe and Kristofor. Chrysanthos had strongly insisted on increasing the number of bishops to five in order to add more "healthy Greek elements" to the Albanian Church's Holy Synod.[78] In the newspaper *Dajti*, Visarion Xhuvani wrote that Kotoko would be the last possible choice as a bishop, and then only if one of the other three candidates refused to take up the post.[79] Ierothe proposed that the Albanian Orthodox Commission add Vasil Joanidhi to the list of potential bishops, but he was excluded because he was a Vlach.[80] On the other hand, as was expected, Chrysanthos had explicitly ruled out Bishop Visarion Xhuvani and Archimandrite Vangjel Çamçe as candidates.[81]

In late July, Vasil Bamiha set off again to Athens, aiming to conclude the necessary formalities.[82] On 26 July, the Greek embassy showed its goodwill towards the autocephaly cause by announcing to the Albanian government that the Corfu seminary would start teaching in Albanian. This would continue until the Bank of Athens distributed the funds from Jovan Banga's bequest, which would enable the establishment of the Albanian seminary.[83] This move was in sharp contrast with previous requirements that even the classes in the Korça seminary be taught in Greek. At the same time, the government in Athens was dealing with Northern Epirotic rallies that were protesting the recognition of Orthodox Albanians as non-Greeks and label-ling the Greek government as "betrayers to the nation".[84]

But even some Albanians were dissatisfied, as the Protocol had side-lined Bishop Visarion and Noli's supporters. President Zog received Çamçe and Reverend Josif Qirici on 14 August, assuring them that they would have a central role in the Albanian Orthodox Church in the future.[85] However, as Albanians waited for the formalities to be dealt with so the tomos of auto-cephaly could be granted, political developments in Athens once again led to a stalemate.

Venizelos returns of Venizelos to power – and stalemate

His Grace Chrysanthos left Albania with an agreement accepted by both Albania and Greece. Imminent political developments in Athens, however, were about to change this newfound rapport considerably. The summer of 1926 was as hot as the previous summer, meteorologically as well as polit-ically. The dispute between Greek Prime Minister Pangalos and Venizelos reached its peak, and a coup organized by the same army battalions that had helped Pangalos seize power now turned against him. His fellow Arvanite, Pavlos Kountouriotis, was chosen as president on 24 August, while Colonel Georgios Kondylis was sworn in as prime minister. The new regime arrested and imprisoned Pangalos on the same day that Kondylis took the oath of office. Pangalos was in prison for two years, until 13 July 1928.[86] The Venizelists' return to power changed Greece's position towards Albania. The new government of Colonel Kondylis allowed Northern Epirotic associations to reappear everywhere in Greece. These associations, led by Themistokli Bamiha, the brother of Gjirokastra MP Vasil Bamiha, again proclaimed that all Orthodox Albanians were Greeks.[87]

The hot August of Greek politics did not initially concern Tirana, as the Albanian government hoped that the Patriarchate would honour the Tirana Church Protocol. Sure of the outcome of autocephaly, the Church High Council organized extensive celebrations in Korça to mark the fourth anni-versary of the Berat Congress. Even in Gjirokastra, it only gradually became noticeable that the political changes in Athens had led to increased Greek nationalism. The prefect reported that the Gjirokastra district's Orthodox MPs and senators, with the exception of Petro Poga, had begun to sow dis-cord and hate against the Albanian Church.[88] Italian envoys in Albania also referred to the diocese of Gjirokastra as a political hub for Greece.[89]

Waiting for the political situation in Athens to become clearer, the Ecumenical Patriarchate thought best not to grant the tomos of autoceph-aly as promised. On 3 October, the patriarch assured the Albanian consul in Istanbul that the tomos would be granted, although he linked the decision on Albanian autocephaly with the issue of the Orthodox Church in the Do-decanese Islands. After the Italians annexed these islands in the Aegean Sea, they immediately requested the establishment of an autocephalous Church, even though the population was entirely Greek. The patriarch informed the Albanian consul that at that moment the Patriarchate was unable to grant autocephaly to the Albanian Church. If they did, they would also have to grant it to the Church in the Dodecanese Islands, a move that could only be done after the confirmation of Greece.[90] A month later, Consul Nezir Leskoviku informed the Tirana government that Greece had instructed the Patriarchate to grant autocephaly to the Dodecanese Church. Leskoviku believed this development would clear the way for Albanian autocephaly.[91]

The consul had not fully comprehended what was going on behind the scenes or how radically the political changes in Athens had altered Greece's attitude towards Albania. The Patriarchate never acted without the approval of the Greek government. During the turbulent transition period in Athens, the lack of instruction from the Greek government surprised the Patriarchate, leaving the hierarchs uncertain how to proceed.[92] The Italians had always believed that the Patriarchate sought to maintain its status and survival by relying heavily on its traditional backer, Greece. Mancuso Pietro, the interpreter of the governor of the Dodecanese Islands, the key figure in the battle for the islands' ecclesiastical issue, was of the opinion that the Patriarchate was fully dependent on the income it received from Greece and was unable to carry out any moves without prior consent from Athens.[93]

The Patriarchate had truly been prepared to grant Albania autocephaly during the government of Pangalos. But the linkage between the Albanian and Dodecanese issues was not due to the Patriarchate's supposed fear of Italian influence, as Leskoviku had informed Tirana. On 30 August 1926, the Greek Foreign Ministry noted that the Albanian ecclesiastical issue was the only reason that the Patriarchate did not recognize the autocephaly of the Dodecanese Church.[94] This shows that the Orthodox Church in Albania was far more important for Greek policy than any other ecclesiastical issues. The Orthodox in the Dodecanese were Greek and, as such, an autocephalous Church; they would not affect matters since it would still be Greek clergymen who would lead the islands' believers. An independent Orthodox Church in Albania, however, would be fully Albanian, as 90 per cent of the faithful were of Albanian ethnicity, which meant that Greek influence would diminish. The Patriarchate's avowal to the Albanian government was deeply untrue. The Greeks delayed responding to the Dodecanese question in order to delay Albanian autocephaly. In November 1926, these developments ran counter to the articles in the Albanian press, which considered the autocephaly issue resolved for good after Evlogji Kurilla accepted the proposal to be ordained as the new archbishop of Albania, in accordance with the Tirana Church Protocol.[95]

The radical changes in Balkan geopolitics had nonetheless affected relations between Albania and Greece. The Venizelos government could no longer make use of the Belgrade deal, which Prime Minister Pangalos had declared diplomatically void. Meanwhile, on 27 November 1926, the Albanian government signed a pact with Italy, later known as the First Pact of Tirana, which enabled Zog to overcome Greek and Yugoslav pressures. Italy, as the new protector of Albania, ensured Ahmet Zog's personal power as well as Albania's territorial integrity.[96] Thus, the threats and pressures that had accompanied all of Zog's discussions with Greek representatives since coming to power in early 1925 now evaporated.

On 11 January 1927, Consul Leskoviku informed the Tirana government that the Patriarchate would deliver, through the Greek embassy, an affirmative response regarding the tomos of autocephaly. The Albanian press immediately spread the news that the Patriarchate would grant the tomos.[97] Foreign Minister Vrioni was certain that the tomos had been delivered into the hands of His Grace Chrysanthos and asked the Albanian embassy in Greece to meet with the Greek hierarch. "The good news", however, soon proved false. The hierarch told the Albanian ambassador in Athens, Stavro Stavri, that the issue was not yet concluded and that the Patriarchate would present the tomos when both parties signed a new protocol.[98] The Patriarchate had instructed Chrysanthos to return to Tirana to discuss a new, special, protocol that would redefine the conditions for the recognition of autocephaly.[99] A few days later, Patriarch Basil III sent a letter to Zog informing him of Chrysanthos's new mission.[100]

His Grace Chrysanthos arrived in Tirana at the beginning of February 1927. He proposed to Zog that the president appoint the archbishop of the Church, but the choice he suggested was not included on the list that had been agreed to. Chrysanthos asked Zog to choose Metropolitan Athenagoras of Corfu as archbishop, a man who was from the Albanian village of Vasiliko in the Chameria region. Zog refused, insisting that to avoid further conflict, the ad hoc Albanian Orthodox Commission must first review and accept the candidates. Chrysanthos handed Zog a new protocol, which the Patriarchate had drafted specifically for this trip.[101] Zog replied that the Albanian government had entrusted the matter to the ad hoc Commission and that, once they reviewed the draft, they would decide what to do with the new protocol. On 15 February, the members of the Commission, led by Pandeli Evangjeli, gathered in Tirana and contemplated a very different protocol from the one they had agreed to a year earlier.

The new draft protocol consisted of ten parts. The first part differed greatly from the Tirana Protocol of 1926 in that it referred to the Church as "the Orthodox Autocephalous Church of Albania" and not, as previously agreed, "The Albanian Orthodox Church", which implied a national institution. The third part stated that a bishops' court made up of 12 bishops would be able to assess and judge a bishop, but so long as Albania had only 5 hierarchs, the other 7 bishops would be summoned from the Patriarchate. The new protocol stipulated that ecclesiastical courts would be established in each diocese and entrusted with resolving cases such as marriages, separations, custody, and so on. A mixed court would arbitrate in civil cases such as dowry, inheritance, adoption, and paternity, which could be appealed to the archdiocese. The fourth part altered the language provisions, stating that the Church could use Albanian only in communities that had used it up to then. According to the eighth part, the Albanian state was given four more obligations regarding the Church, including execution of the decisions of the new ecclesiastical courts. Among other things, the draft protocol declared null and void the decisions of the Berat Congress, named the Patriarchate as the arbitrator of any future disputes, and stipulated that the Patriarchate could revoke the tomos if Albania failed to honour its commitments. Lastly, Albania had to approve the tomos by law, and the parties would register the protocol at the League of Nations and ask the League to supervise its implementation.[102]

The differences from the 1926 protocol were obvious and significant. The Albanian government asked the Patriarchate to clarify why His Grace Chrysanthos had come with a protocol that was completely different from the one it had agreed to only six months before.[103] The Patriarchate replied that it had merely filled out the details in the writing of the articles and agreements of the first protocol.[104] Chrysanthos met with Simonidhi and Kaso, the only two MPs on the Commission who supported him, but he was unable to persuade the others. Kaso and Simonidhi viewed the new protocol as a detailed account of the previous agreement and suggested the Commission to accept it in principle and discuss later which articles should be changed, rejected, or accepted. The majority, consisting of Evangjeli, Kota, Beça, Rusi, and Papa, called the new protocol an unacceptable attempt to create a religious deep state within the state, which sought to rule over Orthodox Albanians. The Commission was outraged at the provision that the parties had to submit the protocol and tomos to the League of Nations for ratification. The Commission members wrote that this article implied that Orthodox Albanians were an oppressed ethnic minority, whom the Patriarchate needed to protect with the help of the League's powers. The majority of the Commission also opposed the call for seven bishops to come from the Patriarchate to make up the number required to establish the bishops' court. The Commission argued that the independence of the Albanian Church meant that it had full rights to assign the additional foreign bishops required to achieve the number of hierarchs needed for trial.[105]

The Commission also objected to the request that the Albanian Holy Synod be the only body to oversee and distribute the Albanian Church's budget; it underlined the fact that all believers had the right to make their own decisions regarding their local church's prosperity. In addition, the adjudication of civil cases by religious courts was a shameless intrusion into state affairs. The Commission regarded as shocking the articles in Part Ten which stated that the Patriarchate had reserved for itself veto rights, as if it were a state within the state. Thus, the Commission rejected the new protocol, calling it a direct threat to Albanian sovereignty. The Commission instructed the Albanian government to take all the necessary measures to ensure that autocephaly was accepted, but only on the basis of the 1926 protocol.[106]

In several meetings led by Ahmet Zog, the Albanian Council of Ministers read the opinions of both the majority and the minority of the ad hoc Albanian Orthodox Commission. On 24 February, the Council decided to reject the new protocol as incompatible with the state interests of Albania.[107] Zog received His Grace Chrysanthos the following day and notified him that the new protocol went too far and constituted an attempt to offer special treatment to the Orthodox clergy over the country's Muslims and Catholics. Zog emphasized that Albania was a democratic country and, contrary to many articles of the new protocol, had implemented civil laws and codes inspired by the French system. Zog described the idea of submitting the new protocol to the League of Nations as unprecedented and noted that only fully recognized states had the right to submit agreements to this body and not religious non-sovereign institutions such as the Patriarchate. President Zog therefore objected to any revised agreement; only the 1926 protocol was acceptable.[108]

His Grace Chrysanthos understood that it was impossible for Albania to accept the new protocol. On 7 March, in his final submission to the Patriarch, Chrysanthos wrote that the Patriarchate should consider the 1926 protocol a victory. After Albania's pact with Italy in 1926, Albania was in a stronger position and could create the Holy Synod without the Patriarchate. In addition, because of the improved relationship between Albania and Italy, Chrysanthos believed that Orthodoxy in Albania was under the constant threat of Uniatism. He therefore advised the Patriarchate to accept the terms of the 1926 protocol.[109]

The Patriarchate responded that it did not understand which points in the new protocol were incompatible with the 1926 Church Protocol of Tirana. The Albanian consul in Istanbul suspected that this response was an effort to delay the negotiations and had been initiated by Greece[110] since the same draft protocol was submitted to the Italians for the Dodecanese Orthodox Church. The records of the Greek Interior Ministry show clearly that this move was an attempt to delay any resolution to the question of Albanian autocephaly and enable Athens to backtrack from the policy of the Pangalos government.[111] Ahmet Zog responded that until a new decision was received on the matter, the Church High Council and the statute approved by the Berat Congress would remain the cornerstones of the Albanian Orthodox Church. Reverend Vasil Marko continued to be the official head of the Church.[112]

None of these developments had any impact on the internal stability of the Albanian Church. Albanian nationalists triumphed in the first elections for Korça's church eldership that were held in March 1927. An overwhelming majority of the city's Orthodox took part and all the winning candidates belonged to the nationalist side,[113] proving that the Hellenists constituted only a small minority among Korça's Orthodox. Meanwhile, internal skirmishes began to concern the metropolitanate of Durrës. Vangjel Çamçe had led the diocese since 9 November 1926, in an attempt to put an end to Bishop Visarion's actions.[114] On 16 January 1927, the dean of Elbasan, Veniamin Haxhijakovi, invited Visarion to officiate at the liturgy as a bishop.[115] In his power as vicar, Çamçe turned against Haxhijakovi, dismissed the "rebellious Elbasan dean", and appointed in his place a loyal nationalist, Reverend Dhimitër Dhimitruka.[116] Haxhijakovi, defying this order, refused to hand over the church archives to his successor, saying that Archimandrite Çamçe's move was inspired by political motives.[117] The conflict between the two clergymen continued for months, with the saga finally ending on 7 May, when Interior Minister Abdurrahman Dibra ordered the prefectures to halt any liturgy Visarion Xhuvani might try to hold.[118] In October 1927, the Albanian police placed Xhuvani under surveillance in an effort to prevent him from participating in ecclesiastical duties.[119] In the south, meanwhile, His Grace Kristofor faced economic difficulties in Berat,[120] even though he and the eldership in the district were fully nationalist Albanians.

With the overall situation under its control, the Albanian government decided to wait – rather comfortably, too – on the decisions of the Patriarchate. Following Chrysanthos's report, the Patriarchate felt it had lost ground in Albania, so all it could do was delay the resolution without challenging the Albanian demands any further. On 19 May 1927, the Patriarchate officially replied to the Albanian government that the Holy Synod had decided to grant the tomos of autocephaly to the Albanian Church, as envisaged in the Tirana Church Protocol of 1926. Patriarch Basil III explained that it was necessary to preserve the spirit of the Protocol's fifth article, which demanded the full independence of the Orthodox Church. After the selection of the five bishops, they would be sent to Istanbul to receive the tomos.[121] In Athens, the newspaper *Aggelioforos* (Messenger) wrote that the Patriarchate had recognized the Church, and an Albanian delegation would soon be leaving for Istanbul.[122] Following this news, Ierothe asked permission from the Patriarchate to carry out certain political moves in Albania to secure himself the archbishop's seat.[123]

The new Greek position towards Albania was manifested in the Greek consul's unprecedented participation in the anniversary celebrations of the Berat Congress.[124] In October 1927, the Albanian government's press office secretly spread the news that if the Patriarchate did not send the tomos soon, the stand-off would end swiftly as the government would proceed unilaterally.[125] The Albanian press, meanwhile, published the names of the expected bishops: Ierothe in Korça, Kristofor in Berat, Pandeli Kotoko in Gjirokastra, Vasil Joanidhi in Durrës, and Evlogji Kurilla in Tirana as archbishop of Albania.[126]

Despite the Patriarchate's assurance in May, the resolution remained at a standstill another six months because Albania was negotiating a new agreement with Italy after the initial pact of 1926. After intense negotiations, the two parties signed the Second Pact of Tirana in November 1927. The new pact stated that Italy would intervene militarily on behalf of Albania if its territorial integrity was in danger. The reason for hurrying the new negotiations was the cold relationship between Italy and Yugoslavia. Greece and Yugoslavia had helped bring Zog to power and expected their respective agreements with him to be implemented. But Zog had played a double game, avoiding both Greek and Yugoslav pressure largely by relying on Italy's geopolitical fears. The Second Pact of Tirana was, then, an important achievement in protecting Albania from the territorial threat posed by its two neighbours.[127]

This was the chief reason behind the Albanian government's inattention to religious matters in 1927. Once the second pact was signed, the ad hoc Albanian Orthodox Commission unanimously approved a reply to the Patriarchate on 23 November. The Commission thanked the Patriarchate for accepting the 1926 protocol and expressed the gratitude of Orthodox Albanians for the conclusion of the long negotiations. The Albanian Commission asked the patriarch to fill the vacant episcopal thrones, recognize the Church, and grant the tomos.[128] On 3 April 1928, the ecumenical patriarch conveyed to Consul Leskoviku in Istanbul that the Patriarchate had not yet decided on the matter, stressing that Albanian autocephaly was a small and unimportant problem and the Patriarchate was overwhelmed with work and had few people to carry out such tasks. The patriarch announced that the Holy Synod would review the issue after Easter. Leskoviku learned via other channels that Greece had ordered the members of the Holy Synod to delay the resolution, even though Patriarch Basil III was in favour of granting the tomos. The same strategy of delay was used simultaneously with the Italians regarding the Dodecanese Church. The Albanian government was in no mood to wait indefinitely for a final decision and found the Patriarchate's attitude offensive. Even the Hellenist Pandeli Kotoko expressed the view that Albania should establish its Orthodox Church through an ecclesiastical coup.[129] On 13 April 1928, the Albanian foreign minister, Xhafer Vila, sent final instructions to Leskoviku, ordering him to make it abundantly clear to the Patriarchate that it must decide as soon as possible, since it had already delayed the question a considerable amount of time.[130]

Meanwhile, the Albanian government began implementing its alternative plan: the unilateral establishment of the Holy Synod.[131] On 5 May 1928, His Grace Kristofor arrived in Tirana and delivered a patriotic speech, having first jointly held the liturgy with Archimandrite Çamçe in both Albanian and Greek.[132] The Tirana government also summoned Reverend Vasil Marko and Pandeli Kotoko, who arrived in the capital two days later.[133] On 8 May, His Grace Chrysanthos informed the Albanian government of the Patriarchate's displeasure with any unilateral action.[134] Attempting a further delay, Patriarch Basil III sent another letter to the government asking for clarification of certain articles in the Tirana Church Protocol of 1926. The Patriarchate wanted Chrysanthos to return to Tirana for further negotiations before it proceeded with the canonical establishment of the Albanian Orthodox Autocephalous Church. The Patriarchate also said that Vasil Joanidhi must be one of the five bishops, leaving out either Joakim, Kotoko, or Kurilla.[135] His Grace Chrysanthos informed Metropolitans Ierothe and Kristofor that the patriarch would hold them responsible for violating the Holy Canons if they continued with a unilateral solution.[136]

The Albanian government had two choices. The first was the official route: to accept the new requests presented by Chrysanthos, which the ad hoc Albanian Orthodox Commission would then review. The next step would be the approval of the Albanian Council of Ministers, with its verdict sent to the Patriarchate through Chrysanthos. The Holy Synod of the Patriarchate would then convene, would accept the reply from Tirana and send back the protocol with any changes and comments to yet another ad hoc commission, whose opinion the Synod would again have to review. The Patriarchate would then make its final decision, which Chrysanthos and Leskoviku would convey to the Albanian government. Ultimately, the Patriarchate would grant the tomos of autocephaly only if each of these steps was successfully completed and if the Patriarchate had the will to do so. The second choice was the unilateral establishment of the Albanian Holy Synod, which, as His Grace Chrysanthos noted in his memoirs, would have presented the Patriarchate with a fait accompli that would eventually compel it to accept autocephaly.

The Albanian Orthodox Commission and the Church leaders Vasil Marko, Ierothe, Kristofor, and Kotoko had been in Tirana since 7 May,[137] but an unrelated administrative conflict forced the clergymen to wait two weeks before holding any meetings.[138] The leaders were able to convene only at the end of the month. Initially, the Commission and the hierarchs could not reach agreement on several points.[139] The Church leaders requested that the Tirana Church Protocol of 1926 be viewed as the only possible solution, but governmental representatives Kota and Evangjeli objected.[140] However, by the end of their meetings, it was decided unanimously to establish the Holy Synod with four bishops: Ierothe Jaho, Kristofor Kisi, Pandeli Kotoko, and Vasil Joanidhi. According to this decision, an ecclesiastical assembly would convene to draft and approve the new statute of the Albanian Church; it would then confirm the Holy Synod, after which the new bishops would be ordained. The agreement stipulated that Reverend Vasil Marko would continue to lead the Church in the meantime.[141] These steps coincided with the secret alternative plan delivered in Athens by Ierothe and Kotoko at the beginning of 1925. The only difference was that the Holy Synod would not be established by the Patriarchate, but would be the result of a unilateral action by the Albanians. His Grace Ierothe, Kotoko, and Reverend Vasil Marko returned immediately to Korça, where they waited for Joanidhi to arrive from Greece so they could implement the plan.[142]

The government's decision not to wait was proved correct by events in the summer of 1928. Although the Ecumenical Patriarchate was erecting a number of obstacles to the resolution of the Albanian issue, it did not hesitate to approve the handover of all areas annexed by Greece in 1913 to the sole jurisdiction of the Church of Greece. In July, the Greek parliament passed a special law that ordered that the New Lands be made part of the Church of Greece; the Patriarchate accepted this with no objection in August and relinquished its authority over the New Lands to Greece.[143] Albania perceived this sudden political manoeuvring as a provocation. The Patriarchate had agreed to follow a law of the Greek state, but did not yet recognize the independence of the Albanian Church, despite the fact that an all-Orthodox congress had declared it. The Patriarchate's double standards thus hastened the Albanian government's refusal to enter into new negotiations, convincing it that there was only one possible solution: the unilateral establishment of the Synod.

Figure 4.1 Bishop Ierothe Jaho.

Figure 4.2 Bishop Kristofor Kisi.

Figure 4.3 Father Vasil Marko, the Head of the Albanian Church Prior to the Establishment of the Holy Synod.

Figure 4.4 Metropolitan Chrysanthos, the Patriarchate's Envoy Entrusted to Negotiate with the Albanian Orthodox Commission.

Figure 4.5 Pandeli Evangjeli, the Head of the Albanian Orthodox Commission during the Negotiations with the Patriarchate.

Notes

1 Ksenofon Krisafi, *Për tokën dhe detin e Shqipërisë [On Albania's Land and Sea]* (Tirana: UET Press, 2014).
2 The telegram in the Greek MFA Archives which contains the Greek terms is not complete. The surviving fragment of the telegram states:

Mr Kaso met with Zog. He would ask to help Greece with its expansion into Northern Epirus, non-interference in Orthodox Church issues, free schools in Northern Epirus, and the teaching of the Greek language in Albanian schools if requested by the communities. Zog accepted the terms, finding them acceptable and logical, but I expect to meet Zog myself.

(Kondis, *Elinismos III*, 160: IDAYE, Y. 1924–1925, f. Γ/62/α, no number, Belgrade Embassy to Greek MFA, 3 September 1924). A reconstruction of the Greek demands was made based on a September 1925 meeting between the Greek ambassador in Durrës, Panourgias and Ahmet Zog, in which Panourgias reminded Zog of his "pledges" to Belgrade. (Kondis, *Elinismos III*, 233: IDAYE, Y. 1924–1925, f. Γ/62, no. 12655, Durrës Embassy to Greek MFA, 5 September 1925).

3 Albanian ambassador in Athens, Mid'hat Frashëri, reported this predominant tendency in Greek politics in 1926. AMFA, Y. 1926, f. 239, 20, Frashëri to MFA, 19 April 1926.
4 Kondis, *Elinismos III*, 160: IDAYE, Embassy of Belgrade to MFA of Greece.
5 Kondis, *Elinismos III*, 233: IDAYE, Embassy of Durrës to Greek MFA.
6 Kondis, *Elinismos III*, 160: IDAYE, Belgrade Embassy to Greek MFA.
7 Kotoko, later the metropolitan of Gjirokastra, was one of the most prominent Hellenists in Korça. In 1915, he served in the Greek army and was later recruited, at the Greek consulate's instructions, to act against Albania. See also: Maria Gianakou, "Ο Μητροπολίτης Αργυροκάστρου Παντελεήμων και το Βορειοηπειρωτικό Ζήτημα [Metropolitan of Gjirokastra Pandelejmon and the Northern Epirotic Issue]", (MA Thesis, Thessaloniki University, 2009); Sifi Kola, *Ο Αργυροκάστρου Παντελεήμων: Ο Αγωνιστής Ιεράρχης της Β. Ηπείρου [Pandelejmon of Gjirokastra: The Archpriest Fighter of Northern Epirus]* (Athens, 1970).
8 Kondis, *Elinismos III*, 196–207: IDAYE, Y. 1924–1925, D. Γ/62, no. 2470, Greek MFA Third Political Office to Greek MFA First Political Office, 16 February 1925.
9 His Grace Kristofor Kisi made a similar request in a letter he sent to Ierothe on 25 January 1925. Glavinas, "Kristofor of Synadon", 91.
10 Kondis, *Elinismos III*, 196–207.
11 "Lavdërim [Praise]", *Koha [Time]*, 21 February 1925, 2.
12 AQSH, F. 152 "MIA", Y. 1925, f. 58, 3, MIA to Korça Prefecture, 24 March 1925.
13 "Mitropoli e Durrësit [Metropolitanate of Durrës]", *Liria [Freedom]*, 7 April 1925, 2.
14 Xhuvani, *Memory*, 23–28.
15 AMFA, Y. 1925, f. 260, 2, Belgrade Embassy to MFA, 15 May 1925.
16 AQSH, F. 155 "MJ", Y. 1931, f. 170, 1–3, OACA to MJ, 14 December 1931.
17 "Arqimandrit Xhuvani Episkop [Archimandrite Xhuvani Bishop]", *Koha [Time]*, 16 May 1925, 1.
18 "Arqimandrit Xhuvani [Archimandrite Xhuvani]", *Gazeta e Korçës [Korça Gazette]*, 16 May 1925, 2.
19 AQSH, F. 155 "MJ", Y. 1925, f. VIII-31, 34, Church High Council to MJ, 14 May 1925.
20 AQSH, F. 155 "MJ", Y. 1925, f. VIII-31, 33, MJ to Church High Council, 16 May 1925.
21 Vasil Dilo, "Tribun'e Lirë [Free Tribune]", *Liria [Freedom]*, 24 January 1925, 2.
22 Kondis, *Elinismos III*, 195: IDAYE, f. Γ/62/a, no. 2215, Durrës Embassy to Greek MFA, 13 February 1925.
23 Kondis, *Elinismos III*, 208: IDAYE, f. Γ/62/a, no. 3803, Durrës Embassy to Greek MFA, 6 March 1925.

24 "Një nevojë e ngutshme [An Urgent Need]", *Liria [Freedom]*, 7 April 1925, 1.
25 "Gjuha Greke [The Greek Language]", *Liria [Freedom]*, 10 April 1925, 1.
26 "Gjuha Greke [The Greek Language]", *Liria [Freedom]*, 14 April 1925, 1.
27 *Liria [Freedom]*, 25 April 1925, 2.
28 "Rëndësia e Kishës Autoqefale [The Importance of the Autocephalous Church]", *Koha [Time]*, 14 March 1925, 1.
29 AQSH, F. 152 "MIA", Y. 1925, f. 271, 1, His Grace Ierothe to President Zog, 22 July 1925.
30 *Liria [Freedom]* 3 April 1925, 2.
31 Ierothe's pro-Albanian attitude was apparent following the complete Albanization of the churches in Korça. In 1925, the newly appointed Greek consul, Tsormpatzi, informed the Greek Ministry of Foreign Affairs that the children of Korça did not know the Greek language and that the entire population of the city spoke only Albanian due to the lack of Greek schools. The Greek consul added that, with very few exceptions, the Orthodox liturgy in Korça was held in Albanian and that the Gospel was also read in Albanian. The consul emphasized that only Korça used the Albanian language in the liturgy. (Kondis, *Elinismos III*, 273: IDAYE, f. Γ/62, no. 6094, Korça Consulate to Greek MFA, 23 April 1925).
32 *Liria [Freedom]*, 24 March 1925, 2.
33 "Audiencë [Audience]", *Liria [Freedom]*, 3 April 1925, 1.
34 "Kryetari i Kishës Autoqefale, i Përndershmi Atë Vasil Marko u prit me nderime të posaçme në sallën e Kryetarit të Republikës [Chairman of the Autocephalous Church, Reverend Vasil Marko Was Received with Special Honors in the Hall of the President of the Republic]", *Koha [Time]*, 30 May 1925, 1.
35 *Koha [Time]*, 20 June 1925, 3.
36 "Mbledhja e Këshillës të Kishës Autoqefale Orthodhokse [The Meeting of the Autocephalous Orthodox Church Council]", *Koha [Time]*, 27 June 1925, 2.
37 "Çështja Kishëtare [The Ecclesiastical Matter]", *Gazeta e Korçës [Korça Gazette]*, 11 July 1925, 2.
38 AQSH, His Grace Ierothe to President Zog, 22 July 1925, quoted.
39 AMFA, Y. 1925, f. 261, 3, Istanbul Consulate to MFA, 15 August 1925.
40 AMFA, Y. 1925, f. 261, 7, Verbal Note from the Ecumenical Patriarch, 8 August 1925.
41 AMFA, Y. 1925, f. 261, 8, Verbal Note from the Ecumenical Patriarch, 15 August 1925.
42 AMFA, Y. 1925, f. 261, 4, Istanbul Consulate to MFA, 15 August 1925.
43 *Koha [Time]*, 22 August 1925, 3.
44 AMFA, Y. 1925, f. 137, 4, Note, no date.
45 Kondis, *Elinismos III*, 233: Durrës Embassy to Greek MFA, 5 September 1925, quoted.
46 Beqir Meta, "Përpjekjet për konsolidimin e institucioneve kombëtare (1925–1935) [Efforts on Consolidation of National Institutions (1925–1935)]", *Studime historike [Historical Studies]*, 3–4 (2008):88.
47 AMFA, Note, quoted.
48 Kondis, *Elinismos III*, 233: Durrës Embassy to Greek MFA, 5 September 1925, quoted.
49 Kondis, *Elinismos III*, 271: IDAYE, f. B/33, no. 16224, Thessaloniki Command to Greek MFA, 4 November 1925.
50 Regarding political developments in Greece, see also: Alkis Rigos, *H B΄ Ελληνική Δημοκρατία 1924–1935 [The Second Greek Republic 1924–1935]* (Athens: Themelio, 1988), 30–80.
51 Ibid; Theodoros Pangalos, *Τα απομνημονεύματά μου 1897–1947 [My Memoirs 1897–1947]* (Athens: Aetos, 1959).

52 Luan Malltezi and Sherif Delvina, ed. *Mid'hat Frashëri Ministër fuqiplotë: Athinë (1923–1926) [Mid'hat Frashëri Plenipotentiary Minister: Athens (1923–1926)]* (Tiranë: Lumo Skëndo, 2002), 259–261.
53 "Intervistë me Pangallosin [Interview with Pangalos]", *Zëri i Korçës [Voice of Korça]*, 27 February 1926, 2.
54 *Koha [Time]*, 26 September 1925, 2.
55 *Zëri i Korçës [Voice of Korça]*, 14 September 1925, 1.
56 "Kisha Autoqefale Orthodhokse [Orthodox Autocephalous Church]", *Koha [Time]*, 10 September 1925, 1; *Zëri i Korçës [Voice of Korça]*, 15 September 1925, 4.
57 Among others: Bishop Visarion Xhuvani, Archimandrite Vangjel Çamçe, Bishop Joakim Martishti, monk Evlogji Kurilla, Kostë Çekrezi, etc. "Çështja kishtare [Ecclesiastical Issue]", *Gazeta e Korçës [Korça Gazette]*, 21 November 1925, 2.
58 *Zëri i Korçës [Voice of Korça]*, 12 December 1925, 1.
59 AQSH, F. 155 "MJ", Y. 1925, f. 32, 1, Council of Ministers Decision no. 585, 26 November 1925.
60 Meta, "Efforts to Consolidate", 92–93.
61 AQSH, F. 155 "MJ", Y. 1925, f. 50, 1, Korça Prefecture to MIA, 17 February 1926; AQSH, F. 152 "MIA", f. 119/2, 5, Metropolitan Kristofor to Kota, 15 March 1929.
62 AMFA, Y. 1926, f. 239, 20, Mid'hat Frashëri to MFA, 19 April 1926. Metropolitan Chrysanthos, Charilaos Filippidis was metropolitan of Trebizond (1913–1938) and later archbishop of Athens (1938–1941).
63 AMFA, Y. 1926, f. 239, 26, Patriarch Basil III to President Zog, 13 April 1926.
64 AMFA, Y. 1929, f. 851, 79, Article from "Politia", 13 March 1929; Τραπεζούντος Χρύσανθος: Επίσημα έγγραφα περι της Εκκλησιαστικής και Εθνικής δράσεως του [Chrysanthos of Trebizond: Official Documents on His Ecclesiastical and National Activity] (Alexandria, 1925); Ioustinios Marmarinos, "Η συμβολή του Μητροπολίτη Τραπεζούντος Χρύσανθου στην ανακήρυξη του αυτοκεφάλου της εν Αλβανία Ορθοδόξου Εκκλησίας [The Contribution of the Metropolitan of Trebizond, Chrysanthos in the Declaration of Autocephaly of the Orthodox Church in Albania]", (MA Thesis, National and Kapodistrian University of Athens, 2003).
65 AMFA, Y. 1932, f. 99, 141, Athens Embassy to MFA, 20 June 1932.
66 ELIA, F. "Chrysanthos, Athens Archbishop", f. 3/1, 7–67, Submission on Greek-Albanian Relations.
67 The archives of Chrysanthos also includes Bamiha's letters that were most likely delivered to His Grace during their meetings. ELIA, F. "Chrysanthos, Athens Archbishop", f. 3/1, 1, MJ to Vasil Bamiha, 19 May 1926.
68 Tasoudis, *Biographical Memoirs*, 33–34.
69 Meta, "Efforts to Consolidate", 41–65.
70 Tasoudis, *Biographical Memoirs*, 20–25.
71 AQSH, F. 163 "Italian Embassy", Y. 1926, f. 115, 6. Italian Embassy to Italian MFA, 5 May 1926.
72 AQSH, F. 149 "PMO", Y. 1926, f. VI-220, 2, Council of Ministers Decision no. 141, 8 May 1926.
73 "Patriarkana e Njeh Autoqefalin e Kishës [The Patriarchate Recognizes the Autocephaly of the Church]", *Gazeta e Korçës [Korça Gazette]*, 25 May 1926, 1.
74 Tasoudis, *Biographical Memoirs*, 36.
75 Ibid, 20–34.
76 AMFA, Y. 1926, f. 239, 1–5, President and MFA to the Patriarch, 7 June 1926. See also: Fatmira Rama, "Shteti dhe njohja e Kishës Autoqefale Shqiptare (1922–1929) [The State and the Recognition of the Albanian Autocephalous

Church (1922–1939)]", *Studime Albanologjike [Albanological Studies]* 11:1 (2011):69–70.
77 Tasoudis, *Biographical Memoirs*, 34–44.
78 Ibid, 42.
79 Bishop Visarion, "Përfundime Orthodhokse [Orthodox Conclusions]", *Dajti*, no. 122, 9 June 1926, 1.
80 AQSH, F. 152 "MIA", Y. 1926, f. 103, 11, Korça Prefecture to MIA, 1 June 1926; and AMFA, Y. 1926, f. 239, 37.
81 Tasoudis, *Biographical Memoirs*, 31.
82 GAK, F. "PMO", f. 959, 1, Kontoulis to PMO, 29 July 1926.
83 AMFA, Y. 1926, f. 138, 7, Greek Embassy in Durrës to MFA, 26 July 1926.
84 GAK, F. "PMO", f. 959, 4, Janaqi Spiro to Greek MFA, 12 August 1926.
85 "U pranuan n'audiencë Arhimandriti V. Çamçe dhe Ikonom Atë Josifi, prej Shkëlqesës së tij Kryetarit Republikës [Archimandrite V. Çamçe and Ikonom Reverend Josif Accepted in an Audience by His Excellency the President of the Republic]", *Koha [Time]*, 21 August 1926, 1.
86 *Koha [Time]*, 28 August 1926, 2.
87 Vasilios Kondis and Eleftheria Manda, ed., *The Greek Minority in Albania: A Documentary Record (1921–1993)* (Thessaloniki: Institute of Balkan Studies 1994), 52.
88 AQSH, F. 152 "MIA", Y. 1926, f. 34, 18, Gjirokastra Prefecture to MIA, 7 November 1926.
89 Kondis and Manda, The Greek Minority in Albania, 53: Italian Foreign Ministry Archive (ASMAE), f. 738/489, no. 243/75, Italian MFA to Italian Embassy in Durrës, 24 January 1927.
90 AMFA, Y. 1926, f. 239, 47, Istanbul Consulate to MFA, 3 October 1926.
91 AMFA, Y. 1926, f. 239, 48, Istanbul Consulate to MFA, 3 November 1926.
92 Kostas Tsalaxouris, *Το Αυτοκέφαλο της Εκκλησίας της Δωδεκανήσου: από τα αρχεία του Υπουργείου των Εξωτερικών της Ελλάδος [Autocephaly of the Dodecanesean Church: From the Archives of the Greek Foreign Ministry]* (Athens, 1992), 95.
93 GAK, F. "PMO", f. 545, no. κ. 103. α, Mancuso's Secret Report, no date.
94 Tsalaxouris, *Dodecanese*, 146.
95 "Çështja Kishëtare merr fund E. Korilla pranoj të dorëzohet Episkop [The Ecclesiastical Matter Reaches Its Conclusion. E. Korilla Accepts to Be Ordained a Bishop]", *Koha [Time]*, 30 November 1926, 2.
96 Puto, *Political Albania*, 350–450.
97 *Zëri i Korçës [Voice of Korça]*, 15 January 1927, 2.
98 OACA, *L'Eglise Autocephale Orthodoxe d'Albanie [Orthodox Autocephalous Church of Albania]* (Geneve: Imprimerie Albert Kundig, 1929), 28.
99 ELIA, F. "Chrysanthos, Athens Archbishop", f. 3/1, 5, Chrysanthos to the Patriarch, no date.
100 AMFA, Y. 1927, f. 238, 10, Patriarch Basil to the President of the Republic, 22 January 1927.
101 Tasoudis, *Biographical Memoirs*, 48–52.
102 OACA, *The Church*, 18–25; the official translation of the protocol in Albanian is available in AMFA, Y. 1928, f. 333, 29–34, Ecumenical Patriarchate's Protocol.
103 AMFA, Y. 1927, f. 238, 19, MFA to Istanbul Consulate, 14 February 1927.
104 AMFA, Y. 1927, f. 238, 20, Istanbul Consulate to MFA, 17 February 1927.
105 AMFA, Y. 1927, f. 238, 38–40, Dissenting Report from the Commission, 17 February 1927.
106 Ibid.

107 AMFA, Y. 1927, f. 238 28, Council of Ministers Decision no. 72, 24 February 1927.
108 Tasoudis, *Biographical Memoirs*, 49–50.
109 Ibid, 52–55.
110 AMFA, Y. 1927, f. 28, 28, Istanbul Consulate to MFA, 23 February 1927.
111 GAK, F. "PMO", f. 545, no. κ. 103. α, Mancuso's Secret Submission, no date.
112 AQSH, F. 155 "MJ", Y. 1927, f. 66, President of the Republic to MIA, 13 April 1927.
113 "Dhimogjerondia e Re [New Eldership Council]", *Zëri i Korçës [Voice of Korça]*, 5 April 1927, 4.
114 *Zëri i Korçës [Voice of Korça]*, 9 November 1926, 4.
115 AQSH, F. 152 "MIA", Y. 1927, f. 210, 3, Haxhijakovi to Elbasan Prefecture, 21 February 1927.
116 AQSH, F. 152 "MIA", Y. 1927, f. 210, 1, Durrës Metropolitanate to MIA, 22 January 1927.
117 AQSH, Haxhijakovi to Elbasan Prefecture, 21 February 1927, quoted.
118 AQSH, F. 152 "MIA", Y. 1927, f. 210, 24, MIA to all Prefectures, 7 May 1927.
119 "Visar Xhuvani nën vërejtje [Visar Xhuvani Placed under Surveillance]", *Zëri i Korçës [Voice of Korça]*, 18 October 1927, 2.
120 The metropolitan complained that his metropolitanate had not received any state funds since the declaration of autocephaly – even though he had continuously requested help from the government for needs he deemed urgent. (AQSH, F. 155 "MJ", Y. 1927, f. VIII-64, 1, Berat Metropolitanate to MJ, 10 October 1927). However, this complaint was not taken into account, as the Albanian government was of the opinion that it was the Church High Council's responsibility to resolve the matter. (AQSH, F. 155 "MJ", Y. 1927, f. VIII-64, 2, MJ to Berat Metropolitanate, 12 October 1927).
121 AMFA, Y. 1927, f. 238, 48–49, Patriarchate to Istanbul Consulate, 19 May 1927.
122 *Zëri i Korçës [Voice of Korça]*, 2 August 1927, 2.
123 Apostolos Glavinas, Εγγραφα περί της πραξικοπηματικής συγκροτήσεως της συνόδου της Ορθοδόξου Εκκλησίας της Αλβανίας (1929) [Documents on the Coup d'État Organization of the Orthodox Church Synod of Albania (1929)] (Ioannina: The Foundation of Ionian and Adriatic Space, 1981), 11–12.
124 *Zëri i Korçës [Voice of Korça]*, 13 September 1927, 4.
125 "Çështja e Kishës [The Ecclesiastical Issue]", *Zëri i Korçës [Voice of Korça]*, 4 October 1927, 2.
126 *Zëri i Korçës [Voice of Korça]*, 8 October 1927, 4.
127 Puto, *Political Albania*, 350–450.
128 AMFA, Y. 1927, f. 238, 56, Ad-Hoc Commission for the Albanian Orthodox Autocephalous Church Issue to the Ecumenical Patriarch, 22 November 1927.
129 Glavinas, *Documents 1929*, 12.
130 OACA, *The Church*, 44.
131 AMFA, Y. 1928, f. 333, 88, Article from the newspaper *Patridos*, 21 April 1928.
132 *Zëri i Korçës [Voice of Korça]*, 5 May 1928, 2.
133 *Zëri i Korçës [Voice of Korça]*, 8 May 1928, 4.
134 AMFA, Y. 1928, f. 333, 83–84, Metropolitan Chrysanthos to MFA, 8 May 1928.
135 AMFA, Y. 1928, f. 333, 84–87, Patriarch Basil to MFA, 5 May 1928.
136 Glavinas, *Documents 1929*, 43: IBE, F. "Metropolitan Ierothe", Ierothe to the Patriarch, 13 March 1929.
137 "Çështja e kishës orthodhokse së çpejti mer funt [The Orthodox Church Issue to Be Concluded Soon]", *Zëri i Korçës [Voice of Korça]*, 12 May 1928, 2.
138 *Zëri i Korçës [Voice of Korça]*, 19 May 1928, 4.

139 "Çështja e Kishës Autoqefale [The Autocephalous Church Issue]", *Zëri i Korçës [Voice of Korça]*, 29 May 1928, 2.
140 Glavinas, *Documents 1929*, 43.
141 "Çështja e Kishës Orthodhokse mori funt [The Orthodox Church Issue Is Over]", *Zëri i Korçës [Voice of Korça]*, 16 June 1928, 2.
142 *Zëri i Korçës [Voice of Korça]*, 16 June, 1928, 4.
143 Kostandinides, *The Declaration of Autocephaly*, 65–105.

5 Establishment of the Holy Synod and the Congress of Korça, 1928–1929

Establishment of the Holy Synod and the enthronement of the bishops

Ahmet Zog had become the undisputed leader of Albania. Zog had been a key politician ever since the re-establishment of the Albanian state through the Lushnja Congress in 1920, and finally, after returning from exile in 1924, he became the country's first president in 1925. After the pacts he signed with Italy in the Albanian capital, Yugoslavia and Greece were no longer seen as a threat, at least for the time being. In the summer of 1928, the streets of Tirana were buzzing with rumours about the country's future. The Albanian Assembly and Senate had amended the Constitution on 7 June, allowing it to be changed through a Constitutional Assembly. Numerous supporters, organized throughout the country, were calling Zog to be named king. The speaker of the Constitutional Assembly read these requests at its third meeting on 29 August. The Assembly unanimously declared Albania a kingdom and, at 9 o'clock in the morning on 1 September 1928, named Ahmet Zog as Zog I, Skanderbeg III, king of Albanians. Zog accepted the crown an hour later and took the oath before parliament at 4:40 that afternoon in a ceremony which was followed by three days of celebration throughout the country.

The autocephaly of the Albanian Orthodox Church was a long-time goal of the newly named monarch, especially since, as interior minister, Zog had run the Berat Congress from behind the scenes. The appointment of Koço Kota, the former mayor of Korça, as prime minister, was one of the king's first acts. Like the majority of Korça's citizens, Kota was an ardent supporter of the Church's autocephaly. He considered the Albanian Church's independence a matter of national dignity and, in particular, the dignity of Orthodox Albanians, who did not want to be dependent on the Ecumenical Patriarchate and, consequently, on the Greek state.[1]

The Church celebrated the anniversary of the Berat Congress in both Tirana and Korça, where the liturgy was led by Reverend Vasil Marko. However, only half an hour before the service began, His Grace Ierothe set off for Përmet, which caused outrage in the press. Over the years, Ierothe had deliberately missed the celebrations of the Berat declaration of autocephaly, but he had always justified his absence in advance. The reason for Ierothe's behaviour this time may have been the internal developments regarding the ecclesiastical issue. Vasil Joanidhi had recently arrived in Korça. Joanidhi claimed that both Ierothe and Vasil Marko had intentionally sabotaged the implementation of the agreement reached just days before in Tirana on the establishment of the Holy Synod. The behaviour of the two Church leaders had so saddened him that he expressed his wish to leave the country as soon as possible.[2] Pandeli Kotoko and Joanidhi had had some kind of disagreement with Church leaders in Korça, but the actual reasons behind the clash remain unclear. On 3 October 1928, Prefect Rexhep Jella summoned the two episcopal candidates to his office and asked them to pledge their willingness to be ordained. Both Kotoko and Joanidhi said they were willing.[3] The Albanian government then asked His Grace Kristofor to go to Korça to oversee the establishment of the Holy Synod.[4] On 10 October, however, Joanidhi again announced to the prefect that he was leaving for Thessaloniki because of his despair over the behaviour of the hierarchs. Prefect Jella asked Joanidhi to go to Tirana as part of a delegation to congratulate the king on his coronation; his hope was that Prime Minister Kota would persuade Joanidhi to remain in Albania and be ordained.[5] Joanidhi left for Tirana with His Grace Ierothe, Reverend Vasil Marko, and Reverend Josif Qirici.[6] The delegation expressed their congratulations to the king,[7] while Patriarch Basil III congratulated Zog a few days later.[8] Earlier, before offering these good wishes, Metropolitan Ierothe had promised the Patriarchate that he and his colleagues would not settle the Albanian ecclesiastical issue in the manner desired by the Albanian government, and Consul Nezir Leskoviku had relayed this news to Tirana.[9]

Ierothe asked the government for new negotiations with the Patriarchate, which it refused, since it believed that "the Ecumenical Patriarchate would humiliate Albania again".[10] The government announced that it intended to establish the Holy Synod, so the two metropolitans must ordain Joanidhi and Kotoko as soon as possible, draft the statute, and call a new congress, which would confirm the Synod.[11] According to the government plan, Joanidhi and Kotoko would be ordained first as deacons and then, a month later, as bishops.[12] On 4 November 1928, His Grace Kristofor Kisi returned to Korça and Prime Minister Kota ordered Jella to summon the bishops and ask for their official decision.[13] Speaking on behalf of the four clergymen, Kristofor demanded that the government officially request, through a decree, that the High Church Council establish the Holy Synod.[14] The prime minister refused and instead drafted a letter to the two metropolitans asking them to ordain Joanidhi and Kotoko and convene the Synod according to the agreement reached in Tirana. As an additional assurance to Kristofor, the letter was published in the press.[15]

Prime Minister Kota immediately summoned Reverend Vasil Marko, Joanidhi, and Kotoko to the capital.[16] After this meeting, however, the government gave up the plan to ordain Joanidhi and Kotoko, even if it meant losing the support of Ierothe and Kristofor. *Gazeta e Korçës*, comparing the ecclesiastical issue to "gangrene", asked the bishops to stop defending the Ecumenical Patriarchate and consider the welfare of the Albanian Church. The Korça newspaper hinted darkly that the Albanians knew of other ways to resolve the ecclesiastical dispute, noting that, in the past, they had generated churches, priests, and bishops from scratch.[17]

October and November were marked by back-and-forth recriminations between the different sides. Joanidhi and Kotoko continued to impede any resolution to the ecclesiastical question, charging Ierothe and Kristofor with being the leaders of an "anti-Albanian plot". The letter Ierothe had sent to the Patriarchate, with the promise that he would work to settle the issue in accordance with the Patriarchate's demands, led the Albanian government to believe that he was working on behalf of Greece. In retrospect, however, this does not seem to be the case. Ierothe did not want to risk a patriarchal anathema if Albania went ahead with the unilateral establishment of the Holy Synod – as had happened on similar occasions in the past – and was instead trying to find a solution based on the plan delivered in Athens three years earlier. This would mean that the Church received the tomos of autocephaly in a way that was fully to the national benefit of Albania, with only Albanian bishops performing their duties with the patriarchal blessing and with the full dignity of their position. At the same time, Greece, and therefore the Patriarchate, would not object to this plan. The Greek state could hardly attack Ierothe if it believed that what the hierarchs implemented was the same plan that Pandeli Kotoko had presented years before as being in the best interests of Greece. The Ecumenical Patriarchate could be deceived into thinking that Ierothe, its sympathetic son, had implemented a plan for which he had no other choice after his assurances that nothing would be done to the Patriarchate's detriment. This was the reason behind the first request His Grace Kristofor delivered to Prime Minister Kota. After the developments of June, July, and August, the hierarchs had expected that the Albanian government would object to any new negotiations with the Patriarchate, but they needed this objection in writing in order to present to the Patriarchate the Holy Synod's establishment as an unavoidable obligation. The hierarchs' second request, claiming that they "were obligated" to complete the Synod by a governmental decree, supports this hypothesis. Moreover, Kristofor, Ierothe, and Reverend Vasil Marko demanded the dissolution of the Church High Council and the convening of a congress, as had been agreed to in Tirana in June 1928. This strategy would remove the final obstacle to the full implementation of Ierothe and Kotoko's secret plan, which had been presented in Athens in January 1925. Vasil Joanidhi saw Ierothe's action as treason against the state. It is clear, however, that Bishop Kristofor, Reverend Vasil Marko, and other Noli's supporters, whose patriotism the Albanian government did not question, were also involved in the plan. Finally, in mid-November 1928, Prime Minister Kota abandoned the plan to ordain Pandeli Kotoko and Vasil Joanidhi. This move suggests that

Kotoko and Joanidhi had been the main obstacle for the establishment of the Holy Synod. The Greek consul in Korça later recounted that Kotoko had always operated under his instructions. The Greek diplomat wrote that during this period he was the one who had pressed Kotoko not to accept the bishopric seat and that Kotoko had asked that, for his obedience, Greece reward him monetarily.[18]

The failure of this effort forced Prime Minister Kota to seek an alternative plan. He sent a Korça-based journalist to Florina, Greece, to mediate with Metropolitan Joakim Martishti and ask him to be the first archbishop of the Albanian Orthodox Church. At the same time, the Albanian government proposed that Bishop Visarion Xhuvani fill the other vacant diocese in order to avoid any new obstacles by Ierothe and Kristofor. Through this mediator, Kota asked Joakim if he would be willing to cooperate with Bishop Visarion in the ordination of two other bishops and requested that Joakim leave immediately for Tirana.[19]

On 22 November, Joakim accepted all the government's terms and expressed his willingness to travel to Albania. Joakim asked for a loan, which he promised to pay back in two years, to settle his debts and to purchase new robes. He said he would go to Albania, but first he had to visit Athens to hand in his resignation. Joakim affirmed that the Church would be under the paternal protection of the government in every area except issues of dogma and pledged to ordain any cleric the government requested. A congress would convene after the ordinations and declare the wish of the people in the name of patriotism. According to Joakim, no one had the right to stop him from returning to Albania after he paid off his debts and resigned his position; in his view, the Albanian Church had been independent from the moment Albania itself declared independence, regardless of when the Church declared autocephaly.[20]

The Albanian government at once sent its envoy back with the loan, on the condition that Joakim leave Greece immediately. Kota proposed that Joakim hand in his resignation once he arrived in Albania. In other words, Joakim's failure to return with the envoy would be considered a rejection of the government's demands.[21] The envoy instructed the metropolitan to set off from Florina or Bitola with his Albanian passport and claim urgent family needs, possibly a personal matter with a cousin in Korça, if the border officials did not allow him to cross with his Greek passport.[22] On 7 December, two days before the deadline set by the government,[23] Joakim left Florina for Korça. However, the Greek gendarmerie did not allow him to cross into Albania – along with his 27 boxes and 6 suitcases filled with personal belongings. Upset, His Grace returned to Thessaloniki and informed the Greek authorities that he would then be going to Athens to resign, with the intention of returning to Albania.[24] The Tirana government did not question Joakim's will to travel, as he had expressed his firm intention to return to Albania in a secret letter sent to a cousin in Korça.[25] On 8 December, the Albanian Foreign Ministry instructed Joakim to find an excuse to go to the

Greek island of Corfu, where he was to board an Italian boat and from there sail to the southern Albanian port of Saranda.[26]

Zog invited Bishops Visarion Xhuvani and Kristofor Kisi separately to the royal palace in late November 1928. The king informed them that he had asked Joakim to come to Albania as he firmly intended to find a solution to the issue; they pledged to help him achieve this goal.[27]

It was not until 29 December that His Grace Ierothe found out about the recent events regarding the Orthodox Church. Prefect Jella informed Ierothe that the government was going to solve the ecclesiastical issue in line with the decisions approved by the Berat Congress by establishing a Holy Synod composed of Joakim, Kristofor, Visarion, and Ierothe. The three other bishops had accepted the terms, and the Albanian government was expecting Joakim's arrival in order to resolve the situation. If Joakim was unable to come to Albania, Kisi and Xhuvani agreed to ordain new bishops.[28] His Grace Ierothe replied that, while he accepted Joakim, he was not willing to continue with the plan if only Kristofor Kisi and the so-called Xhuvani took part. Ierothe stated that he was a soldier of the Church and a servant of Albania, but he estimated that the Orthodox Church would not attain the high and honourable status Zog desired for it with only Kisi and Xhuvani being part of it.[29]

In Ierothe's view, Metropolitan Joakim's arrival in Albania implied that a Synod composed of four bishops with long experience would ultimately increase the dignity of the Church. Joakim's absence, however, was not an obstacle to the Albanian government's plan, but it meant that the Synod's composition would be limited to Bishops Kristofor and Visarion and two other bishops they would ordain. On 18 December, the Albanian government instructed its embassy in Athens to aid His Grace Joakim in any remaining duties he needed to perform in the Greek capital and to meet any request he might have.[30]

At the end of December, His Grace Joakim was informed that everything was arranged for him to go to Albania. Joakim would hand in his resignation and after that, he was convinced, there would be no other obstacle from the Greek government.[31] Prime Minister Kota instructed the Albanian envoy, Lec Kurti, to assess the lay of the land by contacting the Greek leadership.[32] Kurti met with the Greek Foreign Ministry's political director, who told him that no bishop could move without the permission of the Holy Synod of the Greek Church, so Kurti would have to ask the archbishop of Athens if this was possible.[33] In early January, the Albanian embassy informed Tirana that the Greek Synod had received no request from His Grace Joakim for the necessary permission required to go to Albania.[34] On 14 January, Prime Minister Kota informed the metropolitan that talks would continue only if he delivered his request for permission to leave Greece.[35]

This was the last interaction between Kota and Metropolitan Joakim. The exposure of Albania's official intentions must have motivated Greece to block Joakim's resignation, thus putting him under immense pressure.

Joakim had asked Tirana to provide its support during his stay in Athens, but the Albanian government's public actions revealed the true reason behind the metropolitan's request to resign and led to the Greek Synod's refusal to accept it. The government thus lost Joakim and, with him, Ierothe, who had linked his own participation in the government's plan with Joakim's presence. Consequently, the eagerly sought plan to establish a Synod led by Joakim crumbled within a month.

The newly appointed Greek ambassador to the Albanian capital, Leon Melas, warned that what he viewed as Albania's rebellious solution to the ecclesiastical issue would result in Greece not compensating Albanians for the properties it had appropriated from them. At the time, there were thousands of acres owned by Albanians in Chameria, along with vast landholdings held by numerous beys from Korça and Berat, especially in Preveza, Trikalla, and Ioannina. In response, Prime Minister Kota approved a request by his friend Zoi Xoxa, the publisher of the newspaper *Gazeta e Re* (New Gazette), to reply to this open Greek threat. Owing to Kota's influence over the paper, *Gazeta e Re* was followed closely by Albanian readers who wanted to know the government's opinion. On 10 January 1929, Xoxa wrote in a front-page article that the Albanians had succeeded in gaining a highly elevated national conscience. He went on to praise King Zog, saying that the king truly deserved Skanderbeg's crown owing to his fearless and firm protection of the country's national interests. Xoxa noted that autocephaly was not simply a religious issue for the Albanian state but also a national one, rooted in the spirit of all Albanians, and any foreign interference in this matter was unacceptable.[36]

After the failed efforts to establish a Synod led, respectively, by Evlogji Kurilla, Ierothe, and Joakim, a fourth name in less than four months was proposed to lead the incorporation of the Albanian Church. On 20 January 1929, King Zog summoned the metropolitan of Berat, Kristofor Kisi, to the Albanian capital. Kristofor believed that Albania should solve the ecclesiastical problem on its own and as soon as possible establish a Synod composed of nationalist clerics who were already in Albania. Kristofor asked Zog's permission to draft a Church statute, which would then be approved by the Council of Ministers and a Church congress.[37]

On 25 January, His Grace Kristofor submitted an initial draft to Prime Minister Kota, who did not object to any point in the draft. Three days later, however, King Zog and his government submitted an alternative proposal, in which several articles of Kristofor's original draft had been amended. The metropolitan reviewed Zog's revisions and, finding many of the changes reasonable, submitted a final version to the king at the end of January. The articles the government had objected to related to the election of bishops, the management of Church property, and the legal status of the archbishop. In his initial draft, Kristofor had defined the Synod as consisting of the archbishop and the bishops, which was in accord with the statute approved by the Berat Congress, which stipulated that the Synod consist only of bishops.

The government suggested adding a chief secretary as a member, delegating this position to Reverend Vasil Marko, the chairman of the Church High Council. Kristofor had proposed that the bishops be ethnically Albanian with a theological degree or with some other university degree. The government added a line to the draft, stating that an archimandrite in the service of the Autocephalous Church should be ordained as bishop, but just this once, since Archimandrite Vangjel Çamçe had no degree. The government also requested that if the king did not approve a bishop appointed by the Church, then the Synod must elect another. Both Kristofor and the government agreed that the Synod would elect the bishops but that they would not start exercising their duties until they received the king's approval. Two meetings, which took place at the end of January and the beginning of February, bore no fruit and the state officials told Kristofor that he must agree with the revisions drafted by the government.[38]

According to His Grace Kristofor, his only disagreement with the government related to one name in particular. He had accepted the three clerics who would compose the Synod: His Grace Visarion, Archimandrite Vangjel Çamçe, and Reverend Efthim Hoshteva. A few days after announcing this, Kristofor informed Reverend Josif Qirici that the remaining deadlock was over Reverend Vasil Marko, whom the government had predetermined as a member of the Synod even though he was not a hierarch. Kristofor believed that this choice conflicted with Article II of the statute approved by the Berat Congress, which stated that the Synod must consist only of bishops. He stated that, while he had no personal objection to Reverend Vasil, his opposition to the proposal was based on principle. The metropolitan suggested convening a congress within a week to amend the pertinent article of the statute so that any further action would conform to ecclesiastical law.[39]

The Tirana government sensed that Kristofor was trying to delay the creation of the Synod and abandoned any further attempt to work with him. Visarion Xhuvani took on the challenge and asked the king for full freedom of action, explaining that he would go to Yugoslavia and return with another bishop. Based on the prime minister's recommendation, the king gave Visarion *carte blanche* to do what he thought necessary. Zoi Xoxa later recalled that King Zog and Prime Minister Kota were fully aware of Visarion's shortcomings and would have preferred a well-known tested patriot with high moral standards, like His Grace Kristofor. However, Bishop Visarion was the only remaining choice and had proved in the past that he could accomplish any task he was assigned without causing unexpected problems.[40]

In his capacity as chairman of the Church High Council,[41] Reverend Vasil Marko officially appointed Visarion Xhuvani as the metropolitan of Durrës and Tirana, and the bishop received permission to travel to Belgrade.[42] The Albanian government, after their earlier failed attempts to find a solution to the Synod quandary, ordered the press not to report on anything regarding these developments so as not to undermine their efforts.[43] On 3 February,

Visarion arrived in Belgrade and met with Patriarch Dimitri and senior officials of the Yugoslav Ministry of Foreign Affairs, with whom he had always kept in touch. In less than a week, he returned to Albania with the support of the Yugoslav officials,[44] but contrary to what he had promised, he came back alone. Instead, he brought with him a permit that would allow him to perform his task without the need of a bishop from abroad. Visarion stopped in Shkodra to meet his old friend, His Grace Viktor Mihajlović, who had been living in the city for the past seven years thanks to the intervention of Visarion. Visarion requested Viktor to ordain three other bishops. This would mean that the Church of Albania would have four Albanian bishops, without the need of including Viktor in the Holy Synod. For his actions, Albania would reward the Serbian bishop by allowing him to stay on in Shkodra as an assistant to the archbishop. Prime Minister Koço Kota, who was in his office when he learned that Visarion had succeeded, called his friend Zoi Xoxa and asked him to accompany him to the Orthodox cathedral.[45]

Reverend Vasil Marko and the Church High Council, then, elected Archimandrite Vangjel Çamçe as bishop under the name Agathangjel. The next day, at 10 o'clock in the morning, the ordination liturgy began in the Tirana cathedral attended by Prime Minister Kota, other ministers, MPs, a representative of the king, and a crowd of Orthodox believers.[46] The next day, 13 February, Bishops Visarion, Viktor, and Agathangjel led the liturgy for the ordination of Reverend Efthim Hoshteva, who took the name Eugjen.[47] The government had hoped that either Kristofor or Ierothe or Joakim would agree to participate in their plan, but they all refused. Thus, once Visarion assumed control of the mission, only Çamçe and Reverend Efthim were destined to become bishops. That same day, after these first two bishops had been ordained, the government urgently summoned to Tirana the vicar of the diocese of Gjirokastra, Reverend Thanas Nikolla,[48] who was ordained on Sunday, 17 February, taking the name Ambroz.[49] Then, on the following day, the Church High Council appointed Visarion Xhuvani as the metropolitan of Tirana, Durrës, and Elbasan; Agathangjel Çamçe as the bishop of Berat and Vlora; and Ambroz Nikolla as the bishop of Gjirokastra, Delvina, and Himara, a jurisdiction he had already been leading for several years as vicar. The Council left the metropolitanate of Korça vacant, while it appointed His Grace Eugjen as assistant to the metropolitan, as the titular bishop of Peshkopia.[50] Reverend Vasil Marko signed the decision to form the Holy Synod and then promptly resigned, thus suspending the Church High Council.[51] With the backing of Mayor Vasil Avrami, Korça's church eldership decided that His Grace Visarion would serve as the ad interim bishop of Korça.[52] Reverend Vasil Marko was included in the Synod as the great mitrophore iconom. Meanwhile, Zoi Xoxa, Kota's best friend and the publisher of *Gazeta e Re*, was named the Synod's lay secretary.[53]

The Law on Religious Communities and the statute approved by the Berat Congress stipulated that the head of the Albanian state had to approve the Holy Synod and swear in its members. On the morning of 26 February 1929, six automobiles lined up in front of the Tirana International Hotel to accompany the five members of the Holy Synod and Secretary Xoxa to the royal palace. They entered the king's residence, where they were welcomed by a musical band and honoured with a military salute. Around 400 people, including the capital's most prominent intellectuals, attended the reception and Zog I personally welcomed each of the members of the Synod. Archbishop Visarion was the first to be sworn in, as the bishops pledged loyalty to Orthodox dogma and the ecclesiastical canons, as well as to the king and their Albanian homeland. The king expressed his pleasure at the proceedings and declared that an Albanian considered freedom as necessary and as precious as life. Zog declared that, although his government was secular, it honoured all the religions the Albanian people adhered to and promised his support to the Orthodox Church.[54]

The members of the Holy Synod planned to convene for the first time at the end of March, in order to prepare for the upcoming congress, which would coincide with the Day of Orthodoxy and the first anniversary of the liturgy that Theofan Noli had held in America.[55] The main reason, however, for the month-long delay in meeting was that the bishops first needed to be enthroned in their respective dioceses. On 27 February, the Albanian Interior Ministry informed the prefectures about the bishops' elections. Although the ministry expressed its respect for Kristofor and Ierothe as clerics and citizens, it requested that the local authorities ban them from acting as ruling metropolitans. The ministry also ordered the prefects to organize magnificent receptions, fully befitting religious celebrations, and in line with the rules of the bishops' enthronements.[56]

Ever since the government had removed Metropolitan Kristofor Kisi from its ecclesiastical plans, he had been residing in the monastery of Ardenica. On 6 March, right before the new bishop arrived in Berat, he moved to the St Jovan Vladimir Monastery in Elbasan.[57] His successor, His Grace Agathangjel, was welcomed with great enthusiasm in all the cities in the diocese.[58] Archbishop Visarion encountered similar popular receptions during his trip to the main centres of his diocese, namely, Tirana, Durrës, and Elbasan. On 13 March, Visarion travelled to Shkodra, where he was welcomed by local officials, believers, and the newly elected dean, His Grace Viktor, who would now remain in the northern city under the jurisdiction of the Albanian Church without being a member of the Holy Synod.[59] Visarion left Shkodra and went to Durrës, the metropolitanate's traditional centre, where he was received with the highest honours on 16 March. The secretary of the Synod, Zoi Xoxa, read the decree of appointment of the archbishop, and the former church eldership member Dr Ilia Lavda emphasized the spiritual support given to the ecclesiastical question by the king and the prime minister.[60] The archbishop then led the first liturgy as the head of the Church, which was followed by similar liturgies in Kavaja, Pogradec, and his birthplace, Elbasan, the central Albanian city that was also the birthplace of His Grace Ambroz.[61]

The enthusiasm expressed in the other regions was not reflected in the diocese of Gjirokastra, which comprised Albania's entire Greek minority. The Greek consulates in Gjirokastra and Saranda tried to influence not just the Greek minority against the Holy Synod but also the region's Orthodox Albanians. The Greek minority inhabited 53 out of the 65 Orthodox villages in the districts of Saranda and Delvina, and formed the majority in the Orthodox neighbourhood in the town of Delvina. Albanians, however, were the clear majority in these areas: Orthodox Albanians constituted the entire population of 12 villages[62] and the town of Saranda, while Muslim Albanians made up almost half the population in the region. Orthodox Albanians were also the majority in the coastal region of Himara. In the prefecture of Gjirokastra, meanwhile, they formed the entire population in areas such as Lunxhëria, Zagoria, as well as in the Orthodox villages of Libohova and the Orthodox neighbourhoods of Gjirokastra. The Dropulli and Pogoni regions, however, had a Greek population. Nonetheless, a census taken in 1923 shows that not only did Albanians, both Muslim and Orthodox, form the lion's share of the population of the region, but Orthodox Albanians alone outnumbered the Greeks in the diocese by two-thirds. That left the Greeks who populated the Dropulli, Vurgu, and Pogoni regions and the Orthodox neighbourhood of Delvina as a minority, even among the total Orthodox population in the area.[63]

His Grace Ambroz was faced with the difficult task of co-operating with two opposing sides: on the one hand, Albanian nationalists such as Petro Poga, Reverend Pano Çuçi, and Thoma Papapano, and, on the other, Greek nationalists, backed by the Greek consulate. On 1 March, an Albanian priest from Gjirokastra, Reverend Jani, visited the Greek consulate for the traditional blessing with Holy Water. The consul said that this was the last time he would receive Reverend Jani, since the Patriarchate had declared the Albanian Church to be heretical.[64] In the beginning of March, the Greek subconsulate in Saranda informed Athens that most of the priests in this southern port city and the surrounding villages were supporting Greece. The Saranda priests requested instructions on what to do, as they were concerned that mentioning His Grace Ambroz in the liturgy might legitimize what they called "a state coup carried out against their will". For the pro-Greek priests, a rejection of the bishop would have serious consequences they could ill afford owing to the poor conditions in which they lived.[65]

On 10 March, Ambroz held a liturgy in Tirana and the next day sailed from Durrës to Saranda.[66] Arriving in the town's port, Ambroz was welcomed by local officials at the pier, along with pupils of the Chameria School, who hailed him with flowers. Ambroz and the group of well-wishers then proceeded to the town hall where the former MP Ilia Muzina gave a patriotic speech on behalf of the town's citizenry. Ambroz led a service in Saranda's Orthodox church and then made his way to the only hotel in town, the Piro Palace.[67] As the town was made up almost entirely of Orthodox Albanians, the Saranda reception welcoming the new hierarch was impressive. In an equally festive environment, around 700 people in the nearby town of Delvina, led by Subprefect Dhimitër Jovani, welcomed His Grace Ambroz and cheered for the Church and the king.[68] They included not only the town's most prominent Orthodox Albanians but also leading members of the Greek minority, such as Timo Bamiha, Oresti Anastasiadhi, and Dr Marto, who thanked Prime Minister Kota for resolving the ecclesiastical issue.[69] However, Delvina's priest, Reverend Nikolla, pretended to be ill and missed the reception.[70] Ambroz then went to Gjirokastra, where he again found a festive spirit, after passing through some villages of the Greek minority, such as Jergucati and Derviçani, which did not welcome him. As vicar, Ambroz had run the diocese for six years by performing a clever balancing act, and by faithfully serving both the Autocephalous Church and the Albanian state. During this time, he had even managed to persuade the Hellenist secretary of the diocese, Jani Dado, that the ecclesiastical resolution had to be unilateral. All the priests of the city of Gjirokastra, along with the Albanian Orthodox elite, sent letters expressing their gratitude to the king and prime minister. On Sunday, 17 March, Ambroz held the first episcopal liturgy in the city's packed Orthodox cathedral, praying for Albania and the king. He proclaimed that Albanians were the great-grandchildren of Skanderbeg, their national hero, and so the Albanian nation had earned the right to proudly say that it had saved European civilization during the Middle Ages.[71]

Orthodox Albanians, who made up the majority of Orthodox believers, as well as part of the Greek minority, now obeyed the dictums of the Autocephalous Church, thus creating a very different set of circumstances from the situation six years earlier.[72] But there were few exceptions in some areas of the Greek minority. In Delvina, Reverend Nikolla claimed that Ambroz was not truly a bishop and, along with other priests in the subprefecture of Delvina, refused to mention His Grace's name in their liturgies.[73] This was in contrast with Albanian villages, where Ambroz was referred to as the new bishop. The subprefecture of Delvina requested the expulsion of Reverend Nikolla, but the prefect of Gjirokastra replied that this would make a bad impression and suggested that the Orthodox Church instead move Nikolla to a monastery.[74] On 2 April, the government asked the archdiocese to send Nikolla to either Berat or Elbasan.[75] His Beatitude Visarion chose to send Reverend Nikolla to Tepelena, but the priest replied that it would be best if the Church just dismissed him altogether.[76] In September 1929, when Nikolla went to Greece for a short visit, the Church suspended him from performing his religious duties and the Albanian government banned him from returning to Albania, a decision that was reversed a few months later.[77]

Korça Church Congress

In March 1929, the members of the Holy Synod arrived in Korça, welcomed by around 10,000 people, in a grand reception that had been planned in detail by the local authorities.[78] The sessions of the Holy Synod began with the extended participation of the eldership members, priests, and Orthodox officials, who served as representatives for all Orthodox Albanians.[79] On 9 April, the Synod reconvened and unanimously approved the new statute of the Church, as well as a budget that included the establishment of a seminary, a commission for translating and publishing ecclesiastical texts, and scholarships to send students overseas.[80] The Synod's sessions concluded on 14 April, and, with the exception of Archbishop Visarion and Reverend Vasil Marko, the bishops left for their respective dioceses.[81] Visarion then chaired a Korça church eldership meeting, where it was decided that a new cathedral should be built in the city.[82] Visarion was concerned with building a power base for himself in the diocese of Korça, a city where his many opponents had not forgotten his old, all-consuming feuds with Theofan Noli. The archbishop held the liturgy in a number of the city's churches, including the Easter service, which Korça celebrated with the largest turnout of believers the city had ever recorded.[83] On 13 May, Visarion returned to Tirana to oversee the elections of elderships in Kavaja and Durrës, securing the victory of those who supported him,[84] before returning again to Korça on 4 June.[85]

On 21 April, His Grace Ambroz, the only bishop who faced any difficulty, arrived in Gjirokastra.[86] He then travelled to Himara, the last centre of the diocese he had yet to visit. The reception was enthusiastic and well-attended even though the dean, Reverend Spiro, had only been informed of the bishop's visit three hours before his arrival.[87] However, clashes with the Greek minority continued and, within days, the most serious incident took place in Delvina. On Good Friday, a number of men in the church started stamping their feet as soon as the liturgy began, while women threw boiling water from the roof, injuring the parishioners below, and screamed curses against the Albanian language and Albania, while cheering in favour of Greece and the Greek language. With the help of several Orthodox believers, including members of the Greek minority, the police arrested the organizers of the incident who were sent to stand trial in Tirana. Saranda faced the possibility of a similar effort by the Greek minority, but the town was inhabited exclusively by Orthodox Albanians, who easily prevented any incident from occurring.[88] Following the trial of the five accused in the Delvina incident, the situation returned to normal. According to local officials, there was tremendous dissatisfaction with the ecclesiastical solution among the Greek minority,[89] but the fervour behind the anti-Church campaign had dissipated by early June, when members of the Greek minority in Gjirokastra, Delvina, and Saranda, seeing no other way but to accept the new situation, took part in elections for delegates to a new ecclesiastical congress.[90]

Thus, alongside the Albanians, the Greek minority of the Gjirokastra diocese finally joined the Albanian Orthodox Church. This was a marked change from seven years earlier, during the days of the Berat Congress, when a minority of Albanians had selected the diocese's representatives to the congress. At the end of May 1929, His Beatitude Visarion sent two memos to all prefectures, calling for a congress to be held in Korça on 16 June[91] to affirm the consent of Orthodox priests and believers for the reorganization of the Church. The election of delegates was set to take place in two rounds, on 9 and 11 June.[92] Unlike during the Berat Congress, the Tirana government this time restrained its role in the proceedings, leaving the archbishop to lead the organization of the elections.[93] Visarion announced that the Church had ensured quick and fruitful progress for the future, such that even the most loyal patriot had never imagined.[94]

The representatives arrived in Korça on 15 June 1929[95] with the chief purpose to approve the Church's statute and regulation.[96] On 16 June, the congress began its sessions in St George's Cathedral, and Archbishop Visarion presented the statute he had drafted, emphasizing that it fully embraced the Holy Gospel, the Canons of the Ecumenical Synod, and the experience of the other autocephalous Churches. In addition, the statute had the national interest at its core, in line with the principle of a "free Church in a free state". The archbishop noted that the statute saw to the Church's economic welfare and also attempted to establish a strong ecclesiastical order. On 30 June, all but one of the representatives approved the final statute,[97] signing it during a reception at the diocesan headquarters.[98]

The proceedings of the Korça sessions echoed throughout Albania, as churches held religious services to celebrate the congress. On 18 June, King Zog sent a letter to Prime Minister Koço Kota that was published the next day in the national and international press. The king recalled the struggles stemming from the country's centuries-old backward traditions and the confusion brought about by ecclesiastical leaders when confronted by the Albanian people's unwavering desire for freedom. Zog made reference to the declaration of autocephaly at the Berat Congress in 1922, when he was the interior minister and Kota was the prefect of Berat, and recalled the years from 1922 to 1929, which, he said, had been wasted in fruitless negotiations, despite the willingness, suffering, and efforts of the Albanian state. Zog justified the unilateral action as the only choice Albania had to preserve its rights. The king wrote that the Albanian people could not remain hostage to hostile foreign forces, and went on to observe that state leaders were the servants of the people and could not avoid their responsibility to resolve this issue. Zog expressed his satisfaction that the leader carrying out this task was one of his oldest and most energetic associates, Prime Minister Koço Kota, and concluded by thanking the priests and the press who had protected the national interest. In his letter, Zog wrote:

> The Albanian state is not divided into Orthodox, Catholic, and Muslim, but is undivided. A free country, with no majority or minority, it has no official religion, but it protects and honours all religions. Despite this, it does not allow anyone to use religion as a tool to infringe on this brotherhood of one blood and one language. Well-wishers and those

who have relations with this State should know that the State's domestic affairs belong exclusively to the sovereign people, who cannot tolerate any interference from anywhere or anyone.[99]

It was the only letter Ahmet Zog published during his 11-year reign as king. It demonstrates the unlimited support Prime Minister Kota had been given in his attempt to resolve the ecclesiastical issue. The king attributed the success to Kota, one of the most prominent members of the Orthodox elite and a figure whose religious devotion and patriotism were beyond question. This refuted any rumours that Muslims had led the effort. The next day, *Gazeta e Re* wrote that the letter was significant in showing that other nations could no longer use the religious make-up of Albania for their own purposes. The newspaper article emphasized that the king's letter made it clear that Albania had taken protective measures that resembled those taken by any civilized state.[100]

The statute adopted by the Congress of Korça consisted of 8 chapters and 64 articles. It stipulated that the Orthodox Autocephalous Church of Albania (OACA) remained dogmatically and spiritually united with all other patriarchates and Churches, preserving unchanged the Holy Scriptures, the Gracious Traditions, and the Canons. The Holy Synod, composed of the archbishop, the bishops, and the great mitrophore iconom, would lead the Church, whose sole official language would be Albanian. The Albanian Church was comprised of four dioceses, with the borders they had thus far, which could be changed only by a decision of the Synod, the approval of the government, and a royal decree. The bishops, once ordained, were permanent, but they could be removed by the Holy Synod and a royal decree for serious offences and exceptional reasons, while only a bishops' court composed of 12 bishops and priests could dismiss them for dogmatic reasons. The liturgy would include prayers for the king, the nation, the Albanian army, and the Church could not accept gifts from a foreign power.[101]

On 16 July 1929, the Albanian parliament approved a new law on religious communities that aimed to reduce foreign interference in Albania's four religious communities.[102] This law provided that the religious communities were legal persons that enjoyed all rights with the exception of meddling in political affairs. The Council of Ministers would approve their statutes, which would then be officially decreed by the king. The new law also stated that all religious leaders, assistants, and their deputies must be at least 25 years old, Albanian by citizenship and origin, and able to speak and write in Albanian. The religious communities could not accept money from abroad and had to receive governmental approval for expenses made for humanitarian purposes. Given the passage of this law, the king decreed as binding the statute adopted by the Congress of Korça.[103]

Albania had thus succeeded in officially incorporating its Orthodox Church. With a Holy Synod approved by an all-Orthodox congress, along with the blessing of the state and the government, the Albanian Church was ready to continue on its independent path. For once, Greek influence had played no decisive role in Albania's ecclesiastical affairs.

Position of Yugoslavia during the Albanian–Greek OACA controversy

The momentum begun in Shkodra in 1923 after Visarion Xhuvani's intervention had enabled the establishment of the Holy Synod seven years later. Ever since early January 1924, the Greek embassy had felt that Viktor Mihajlović's presence in Albania could be a hindrance to Athens' goals.[104] In late January 1925, Metropolitan Ierothe claimed that on his arrival in Albania he had discovered the existence of an agreement between the leaders of the Berat Congress and the Serbian Church for the recognition of the Albanian Church's autocephaly. He attributed the acceptance of His Grace Viktor in Shkodra to this agreement. Ierothe had informed Athens that, in line with the pledges Zog had made to the Yugoslav authorities, the plan was to appoint Viktor as the new metropolitan of Durrës.[105]

The only request to have His Grace Viktor removed from Shkodra came from the vicar of the diocese of Durrës, Archimandrite Vangjel Çamçe, on 26 January 1927, but the government did not act upon it.[106] The situation changed, however, when in 1928 the state and the Albanian Church hierarchs decided to unilaterally establish the Holy Synod with Joanidhi and Kotoko as members. As this solution meant that the OACA would extend its authority to also include all of Albania, Reverend Vasil Marko appointed Archimandrite Sofron Borova as dean of Shkodra in August of that year. Borova began his duties, but only after the intervention of the state authorities, as His Grace Viktor initially declined to hand over the deanery.[107] Contrary to the agreement reached in 1923, His Grace Viktor refused to vacate his office and started to act as the local bishop. At the same time, the archbishop of Ohrid appointed a priest in Golloborda, a rural area inside Albanian borders that had a sizeable Slavic minority. The Albanian government did not allow the priest to enter Golloborda and placed Viktor's activity in Shkodra under surveillance.[108]

However, Greece's fears at the beginning of 1925 proved to be true, and His Grace Viktor suddenly became an important figure in the Albanian Church issue. After their initial miscalculations, Bishops Visarion and Viktor were seen as providing the only possible way to establish the Holy Synod in Albania.[109] On 23 February 1929, the Serbian patriarch informed the Albanian ambassador in Belgrade, Rauf Fico, that the Serbian Church would soon recognize the independence of the Albanian Church.[110]

Yugoslavia and Greece were no longer the closest of allies, as the Serbs and the Greeks had been during the Balkan Wars, when their two nations had doubled their territory at the expense of their neighbours. Belgrade took advantage of Greece's sudden decline after the loss of its war with Turkey, aiming for concessions that in other circumstances would have been unimaginable. The Yugoslavs sought access to the Aegean Sea as well as a special regime in Greek Macedonia, where, until the Greco-Turkish population exchange of 1923, Slavs outnumbered Greeks. During this time, Greece was attempting to assimilate the Slavs who had been under the jurisdiction of the Ecumenical Patriarchate. Consequently, Yugoslavia requested that the Slavs in Greek Macedonia, including those in the port of Thessaloniki, be allowed to attend school in the Serbian language, elect their own priests, and to use Old Church Slavonic in their liturgy. Belgrade claimed that one of the main churches in Thessaloniki, St George's Church, should specifically serve the city's Slavic population. It also demanded that a section of the port of Thessaloniki, as well as a railway line connecting the city to the Yugoslav–Greek border, come under Yugoslav sovereignty.[111]

Just as with the Albanian ecclesiastical issue, Theodoros Pangalos had been the only Greek prime minister to give the Serbian demands serious consideration. Because he viewed Turkey as the only genuine threat to Greece, Pangalos sought to resolve whatever issues Greece had with its other neighbours; thus, he believed that an agreement with Yugoslavia was essential. He instructed the Greek Ministry of Education to allow the liturgy to be performed in Slavic in Greek Macedonia and to recognize the right of ethnic Slavs to elect their own priests. Both countries signed an agreement on 17 August 1926 that recognized Yugoslavia as the sole protector of the Slav minority in Greece and gave special status to the port of Thessaloniki. This pact brought Pangalos's downfall, as General Kondylis and his troops used it as the main reason to overthrow the regime. The new Greek government quickly revoked the agreements with Yugoslavia and denied any national or religious rights to Greece's Slavic population, while Venizelos's victory in the 1928 elections again changed the balance of power in the region.[112]

Belgrade initially backed the Albanian Church not only because of the special rights given to Bishop Viktor in Shkodra but also as a way of putting pressure on Greece.[113] In March 1929, after the enthronement of the new bishops, the Holy Synod of the Albanian Church appointed Viktor as the new dean of Shkodra. His Beatitude Visarion said that the Serbian bishop would now be part of the Albanian Church, as he had severed all ties with the Serbian patriarch and was as a loyal soldier to the Albanian king and Church.[114] On 3 March, the deputy chairman of the Serbian Patriarchate's Holy Synod, Metropolitan Gabriel, congratulated His Grace Viktor on the appointment and described the new Holy Synod of the Albanian Church as a great achievement not only for Albania but for all of Orthodoxy. Gabriel also promised that the Serbian Church would co-operate and help the OACA in the future.[115]

It proved fortunate, however, that all the Albanian bishops had been ordained in February of that year. At the end of February, the Yugoslav and Greek delegations convened again in Lausanne, Switzerland, to discuss the issue regarding the port of Thessaloniki. On the same day, His Grace Chrysanthos arrived in Belgrade as the envoy of the Ecumenical Patriarchate. He met with Patriarch Dimitri, who confirmed that he had permitted Viktor to aid the Albanian Church so as to put an end to the Church Protocol of Tirana, which was hampering Yugoslav influence in Albania. The actions of the Serbian Church were aimed at positioning trusted hierarchs, such as His Beatitude Visarion, who would enable His Grace Viktor to stay on in Shkodra. On 16 March, the Yugoslav king, Alexander, received Chrysanthos and assured the envoy that he would do his best to repair relations between the Churches of Constantinople and Serbia. Metropolitan Gabriel also assured Chrysanthos that the Church of Serbia would not recognize the Albanian Church and would request that Viktor no longer co-officiate with the other bishops, criticizing him for his irregular actions.[116]

The reason for the withdrawal of Yugoslav support had nothing to do with either Albania or the ecclesiastical state of affairs. During the first days of Chrysanthos's presence in Belgrade, the Yugoslav government and the Serbian Church were ready to recognize the Albanian Church.[117] The sudden reversal came neither from the threat of Viktor's excommunication, nor from Chrysanthos's visit to Yugoslavia. Rather, it was the result of Chrysanthos's political role as a go-between: he informed Belgrade that Greece was threatening to postpone any solution to the Thessaloniki issue if the Serbian Church recognized the Albanian Holy Synod. The Yugoslav king and his foreign minister got the message and tactfully withdrew their support for the Albanian Church, even though the Yugoslav prime minister favoured its recognition.[118] The talks between Yugoslavia and Greece concluded with an agreement the day after Chrysanthos's meeting with Alexander. Greece and Yugoslavia signed a treaty of friendship in Belgrade on 27 March. The agreement granted Belgrade special rights over both the port of Thessaloniki and the railway line connecting the port to the town of Gevgelija in southern Yugoslavia.[119]

This agreement blocked the only official recognition that the Albanian Church had thought to be certain and caused Albania to reconsider the ecclesiastical question of Shkodra. The Albanian government had no wish to provide special rights to Yugoslavia, especially since the Orthodox in Shkodra were mainly Albanians. In April 1929, the Albanian government was informed that the Serbian Patriarchate had promised not to recognize the Albanian Church.[120] The announcement prompted Albania to alter its conduct towards His Grace Viktor, who had just appeared in the sessions of the Korça Congress, surprising Archbishop Visarion. Viktor claimed that he had come to Korça because he had been the one who initiated the solution to the ecclesiastical issue and wished to personally congratulate the Albanian bishops on their triumph.[121] The Albanian government, however, did not want Viktor to stay in Korça and ordered Prefect Hil Mosi to prevent Viktor from participating in the sessions or the liturgy. On 16 June, Viktor left Korça and returned to Shkodra.[122] The Albanian government's concern proved well-founded: Shkodra's representatives at the Korça Church Congress, who had been elected under Viktor's influence only from among the Slavic minority, submitted a complaint regarding Viktor's ban. They requested that Bishop Viktor become a member of the Synod, that local priests in Shkodra be Slavs, and that the deanery of Shkodra celebrate the holidays according to the old calendar, as was the case in all Slavic churches.[123] The Albanian government's representative, Vasil Bidoshi, forbade the Shkodra delegates from reading their complaints.[124] One of the main articles in the statute directly affected His Grace Viktor. Article 16 stipulated that all bishops and deans, as well as the archbishop, must be Albanian by origin and citizenship and able to speak and write in Albanian. This meant that Bishop Viktor could no longer be a dean, since he was of Montenegrin origin. One of the participants, Reverend Veliša, tried to raise this issue on the last day of the sessions, but Bidoshi refused to allow him to do so. In the end, Veliša, a priest from Vraka, a village near the Montenegrin border, refused to sign the statute.[125]

His Grace Viktor and Reverend Miho Strikić co-officiated at a liturgy held in Shkodra to celebrate the approval of the new statute. Strikić read the official declaration proclaiming the establishment of the Holy Synod, which at the same time signalled Viktor's dismissal, as he was not of Albanian origin. To replace Viktor as dean of Shkodra, the Holy Synod appointed Reverend Josif Qirici, who yet again was assuming a challenging duty within the Church.[126] Archbishop Visarion appointed His Grace Viktor as the abbot of St Blaise's Monastery in Durrës, but eight days later, on 10 September 1929, Viktor requested a passport in order to travel to Yugoslavia.[127] Nor did Reverend Josif last very long in Shkodra. In October 1929, he was replaced by His Grace Eugjen, the titular bishop of Peshkopia, in an effort to bolster the Orthodox spirit in Shkodra by appointing another bishop to lead the faithful.[128]

The Albanization of the deanery of Shkodra followed the example of the north-eastern Dibra region, where the priests had started holding the liturgy in Albanian since July 1929.[129] The last stronghold of Slavic nationalism was Vraka, a small village near Shkodra that was inhabited by Orthodox Montenegrins. At the end of 1929, the Albanian police detained Reverend Veliša Popović and eight others in Vraka, accusing them of activities against the state.[130] The archbishop had Reverend Veliša transferred to the famous St Jovan Vladimir's Monastery in Elbasan, in central Albania, while the Serbian patriarch, at the request of His Grace Viktor, asked for his release from detention.[131] The Albanian Church appointed Reverend Erazmi Jorgo as priest for the parish of Vraka, but the local population rejected him because he did not perform the services in Slavic. After eight months of detention in Elbasan, Reverend Veliša returned to Vraka in May 1930.[132]

His Grace Viktor returned to Shkodra for the last time in mid-September 1930, but by now many of his former allies had turned against him. Pressure from the press made the government claim that Viktor was visiting Shkodra for personal reasons, while His Beatitude Visarion stated that he had done everything possible to see that the Serbian bishop left Albania once and for all. On 15 October, Viktor departed from Shkodra never to return. He passed away at the Deçani Monastery in Kosovo on 8 September 1938.[133]

The Serbian–Albanian conflict over the deaneries of Shkodra and Dibra had come to an end, and from then on the liturgy would be held in Albanian.[134] Now only one matter was left unresolved: the recognition of the Albanian Church by the Ecumenical Patriarchate.

Reaction from the Patriarchate, Greece, and the Albanian diaspora

The establishment of the Holy Synod brought the Albanian government under fire. Although Greece had declared its impartiality on the matter, it had promised the Ecumenical Patriarchate that it would hinder Albania politically. The Patriarchate set up a commission to review the issue; it was composed of Bishops Germanos, Polikarp, and Fotios, as well as representatives of the Greek minority in Albania.[135] In February 1929, the patriarch and the Holy Synod of Constantinople sent an open memorandum to the Albanian people that blamed the Albanian government for not implementing the Church Protocol of Tirana.[136] The Patriarchate sent a copy of the memo to His Grace Ierothe, requesting that he present it to the public. As he was unable to do it himself, the dethroned metropolitan of Korça assigned the task to Pandeli Kotoko,[137] while the Greek consulates in Albania distributed the memo with the relevant instructions.[138]

The Ecumenical Patriarchate denounced the new bishops of the Albanian Church as "a bunch of pathetic opportunists" who were backed by a Muslim government but lacked any support from their own flock.[139] The Patriarchate was certain that its position would be fully supported by the Churches of Jerusalem, Greece, Cyprus, Antioch, and Alexandria, since the Greek hierarchs who led them fully obeyed the guidelines of the Greek Foreign Ministry. Chrysostomos, the archbishop of Greece, called the developments in Albania a coup d'état and dismissed the Albanian bishops as wicked. He alleged that there had been accusations against Visarion since the early 1910s, when he was serving in the Greek church in Sofia.[140] The archbishop of Cyprus and the patriarch of Alexandria similarly hailed the position of the Ecumenical Patriarchate, with the latter lodging a complaint with the League of Nations.[141]

To prevent any recognition from the Churches that were not under the influence of Greece, the Patriarchate sent His Grace Chrysanthos to Belgrade, Bucharest, and Warsaw.[142] Meanwhile, the Russian Patriarchate, the last non-Greek Church, was impossible to reach due to its total isolation by the Soviet regime. Initially, the Russian Patriarchal Holy Synod stated that the Albanian Church was legitimate based on the principle that each state should have its own Church. The Russian Church alluded to the example of the Church of Poland, which the Ecumenical Patriarchate had recognized swiftly on this principle in an effort to remove it from the jurisdiction of the Russian Patriarchate. After succeeding in his mission to the Serbian Patriarchate, Chrysanthos met with Patriarch Miron of all Romanians. The Romanian patriarch promised not to be the first to recognize the Albanian Church, despite the warm feelings that the Romanians had openly expressed in support of the Albanian cause.[143] The Romanian consul in Istanbul believed that the Ecumenical Patriarchate, being merely a tool of the Greek state, would not recognize the Albanian Church, regardless of the fact that the Albanian request was right and sound.[144]

In Albania, His Grace Kristofor Kisi chose to withdraw to a monastery within the country, while His Grace Ierothe left for Greece via the Kapshtica border crossing on 5 March 1929.[145] Before he left, Ierothe handed a telegram to the deacon accompanying him, with instructions to send it immediately to King Zog.[146] In the telegram, Ierothe told the king that he was leaving his beloved homeland with great sadness as a result of the illegal order issued by the government. He thanked the king for consolidating the state and expressed his wish for the nation's continuing progress.[147] Ierothe, however, faced no better welcome in Greece. The Greek government ordered him to remain in Florina, where the local metropolitan welcomed him for only two weeks, then forced him to move to a hotel in mid-March.[148] It was clear that Athens and the Ecumenical Patriarchate no longer had any need for the bishop since his pro-Albanian activities had made him suspect to the Greeks. The difference from His Grace Kristofor Kisi was obvious. The former metropolitan of Berat, cloistered in an Albanian monastery, would a few years later be given the leadership of the Albanian Church as a reward for his nationalistic endeavours. Ierothe, however, had left Albania convinced that the Patriarchate would appoint him as a ruling bishop in a vacant diocese, but instead he ended up secluded on Mount Athos for more than 35 years – the only bishop living among the Orthodox monks in this monastic state – until he passed away in 1965.[149]

The Greek state would continue to abuse Ierothe's name in its ongoing diplomatic attack against Albania, when it presented the League of Nations with forged complaints supposedly written by the bishop. According to Ierothe, Athens had pressured him to sign and seal a 100 blank letters which the Greek government could complete and use as it wished.[150] Greece delivered the first of these complaints, allegedly from Ierothe, to the League of Nations on 6 March. The letter claimed that Albania had exiled Ierothe from its territory and asked for the League's immediate intervention.[151] Albania's deputy foreign minister, Mihal Turtulli, responded that the metropolitan had left for Greece on his own free will, and asserted that the claim that the government had exiled him was untrue.[152] On 17 April, another letter signed by Ierothe but written by the Greek government accused Albania of forbidding a number of priests from officiating at religious services.[153]Albania denied all charges that it had interfered in any of these religious matters. The Albanian foreign minister replied that all Orthodox Albanians had used their lawful right, in the best interest of the nation, to declare the independence of the Albanian Church as a true expression of their patriotic

feelings. Minister Rauf Fico, unaware that the complaints signed by Ierothe had been forged, went on to say that Ierothe had been in the service of
foreign governments and waged campaigns from foreign lands in order to
slander the Albanian nation.[154]

The Greek government relied on His Grace Ierothe's forged missives
twice more, sending two more letters on 20 and 27 May. These counterfeit
documents included the hierarch's signature and listed Florina, Greece, as
the sender's address, although Ierothe had moved to the sanctuary of Mount
Athos weeks earlier. The complaints stated that the Albanian border city of
Delvina was a "Greek town" and alleged that Muslims had been conducting
the liturgy there, while the people of Delvina wanted the liturgy to be held
in Greek.[155] On 5 and 8 June, Minister Fico replied that Delvina had witnessed an unseemly criminal action (the disruption of the service and boiling water poured on church patrons), which had been opposed by the town's
inhabitants, including the Greek minority.[156] On 28 October, the secretary
of the League of Nations put an end to the series of telegrams by rejecting
the complaints that were supposedly emanating from His Grace Ierothe.
The League refused to pass judgement on the ecclesiastical law and legitimacy of the Albanian Church and considered the assurances presented
by the Albanian government as sufficient.[157] Also decisive here was a letter
signed by representatives of the Greek minority in Albania, who insisted
that they had not been persecuted by the Albanian state.[158]

In this fight, the Greek government made use of other means as well. On
2 March 1929, Albania's envoy to Athens, Lec Kurti, was informed that
the pro-Albanian General Kontoulis had expressed his objections regarding
the government's solution to the ecclesiastical issue.[159] The Chairman of the
Albanian-Greek League, Admiral Nikolaos Votsis, delivered a letter to
Kurti on behalf of its members, who were all of Albanian origin, condemn-
ing the unilateral action. The members of the Albanian-Greek League were
opposed to His Beatitude Visarion, whom they considered unworthy, as well
as a Serbian pawn. They were afraid that the tense situation could lead to
Uniatism.[160] The Northern Epirotic organizations in Athens held a meeting
in which they asserted again that all the Orthodox in Albania were Greek.[161]
Led by Konstandin Skënderi and Metropolitan Vasil of Dryinopolis, these
groups held a protest rally in front of the Albanian embassy in the Greek
capital.[162]

From February 1929 on, the Greek press intensified its attacks on the Albanian Church with a surge of articles.[163] *Elinikos Tahidromos* (The Greek
Courier) wrote that the principles of autocephaly could not apply in the
Albanian case given that the Muslim majority was attempting to control
the country's Orthodox minority.[164] *Ethnos* (Nation) wrote that Ahmet Zog
was trying to control the Orthodox Albanians using the same methods as
the Turkish leader Mustafa Kemal Atatürk.[165] On 14 March, the widely
read morning paper *Kathimerini* (The Daily) published what perhaps was
the only truthful article: it reported that autocephaly was not the idea of
the Muslims in Albania. The article noted that the establishment of an

independent Church was the main goal of most Orthodox Albanians, led by such prominent Orthodox as Prime Minister Koço Kota and Assembly Speaker Pandeli Evangjeli.[166]

His Beatitude Visarion was at the centre of the attacks; another Greek newspaper characterized him as "a false hierarch" and "adventurous".[167] Reverend Vasil Marko was described as "an uneducated priest without any value", while His Grace Agathangjel was "without knowledge", His Grace Eugjen was "meaningless", His Grace Viktor was "in violation of the canon law", and His Grace Ambroz was "merely a chemistry and math teacher".[168] The Greek press underlined that the faithful had not welcomed the new bishops into their dioceses, especially His Grace Ambroz.[169] During this time, the Greek papers were filled with reports of widespread detentions, beatings, and violence against the Orthodox, reports that were immediately refuted by the Albanian press.[170]

Not only were such charges groundless, the attacks in the Greek press resorted even to outright fabrication, with false accounts that often shocked Greek readers. On 25 February 1929, for example, *Kairon* (The Times) maintained that the Albanian Church had accepted Uniatism by facilitating the marriage of the Albanian king with an Italian princess,[171] although neither of them was either Uniate or Orthodox. On 8 March, *Proia* (Morning) maintained that Albania had expelled Ierothe, claiming that the bishop had said he would speak Albanian in the church only when the imam had done the same in the call to prayer from the top of the minaret.[172] Ironically, during the seven years he served in Korça, Ierothe had conducted the liturgy solely in Albanian.

The frontal attack by the Greek press was intended to make it clear to the Albanians that there would be no solution to the ecclesiastical issue without the approval of Athens. At the beginning of March, the Albanian government's press office published a long article in response to the Greek allegations. The article underlined that the Patriarchate's tactics had forced the Orthodox Albanians to pursue a path consistent with the nation's interests.[173] On 5 March 1929, the Greek newspaper *Elefthero Vima* (The Free Tribune) retorted that Albania had established the Autocephalous Church with unworthy, suspicious priests, who had been carelessly ordained by the pseudo-bishop Visarion with the aid of a foreign bishop. The Greek article went on to accuse Koço Kota's government as opposing the religious principles of thousands of Orthodox believers in southern Albania. The Greek periodical also denounced the Tirana government as fiery nationalists possessed by an oppressive Muslim mentality.[174]

In *Gazeta e Re*, Zoi Xoxa replied that, while Albania expected no applause from Athens, the Greek press was deceiving its readers. His Grace Viktor's intervention had been nothing more than spiritual guidance given by the Serbian Patriarchate and, consequently, the ordination of the bishops and the establishment of the Holy Synod had been lawful. Xoxa blamed the Greeks for using lies to conceal their long-time territorial aspirations, and concluded by saying that the Albanians would not allow anyone to infringe upon the sovereignty of their country.[175] Offering statistics, Xoxa underlined that there was only a very small minority of Greek speakers in Albania, much smaller than the Albanian minority in Chameria.[176] *Gazeta e Re* argued that the establishment of the Holy Synod had been in accordance with canon law and quoted the Greek writer Adamantios Korais, who had stressed that local priests must lead the Orthodox Church. Archbishop Visarion had used these same arguments two days earlier in reply to an article in the British press by the London-based archbishop of Thyatira, Germanos, who had written that the Church in Albania was under the jurisdiction of the Ecumenical Patriarchate. His Beatitude Visarion strenuously argued that there was no canonical rule which gave the ecumenical patriarch the right to interfere in the ecclesiastical issues of independent countries.[177]

The Ecumenical Patriarchate had paid a considerable amount of money to place articles about the Albanian Church in Turkish, French, and English newspapers. The Albanian consul in Istanbul similarly requested financial support from Tirana in order to mount Albania's own publicity campaign.[178] The important French daily *Le Temps* supported the Patriarchate, while its counterpart, *Journal des débats*, took the Albanian side.[179] The Albanian Church received support from the Bulgarian and Romanian press, as well as from the British journal *The Near East and India*.[180] The London *Times* published opposing articles by the Albanian ambassador, Eqrem Vlora, and Archbishop Germanos, repeating the arguments already presented, respectively, in the Albanian and Greek press.[181]

The Albanian government did not wish to further aggravate the public dispute. The matter was officially closed in June 1929, after the intervention of Foreign Minister Rauf Fico, who underlined that the disputes went against the instructions given by the Albanian government and that he was confident the Greek press would understand this viewpoint and put an end to the campaign.[182]

To gain international support for its cause, the Albanian Church published a French-language book in Geneva, titled *The Orthodox Autocephalous Church of Albania*. The book described the history of the ecclesiastical issue, from the talks between the Albanian government and His Grace Chrysanthos in 1926 all the way to the delay of recognition by the Patriarchate. It also included letters exchanged between the patriarch, the Albanian consulates in Istanbul and Athens, His Grace Joakim, King Zog, and Prime Minister Kota. The book concluded with an epilogue emphasizing the fact that Albanians lived in a secular country which respected all freedoms for its four religious communities.[183]

His Grace Theofan Noli had not been present for the attainment of the autocephaly he had pioneered. The position maintained by Noli's supporters within Albania was not entirely clear, although his loyal aides Agathangjel Çamçe and Vasil Marko were key members of the Synod. The Albanian diaspora in the United States strongly backed Noli, while many of his political supporters, in exile since his fall at the end of 1924, had resettled in Europe. On 16 March 1929, His Beatitude Visarion sent an open memorandum to the Albanian diaspora in Washington, Ankara, Alexandria, Bucharest, Sofia, and Athens, announcing the Synod's establishment and asking for the support of all Albanians.[184] In April, Noli published three articles in the Geneva-based Albanian-language newspaper, *Liria Kombëtare* (National Freedom), questioning the wisdom of basing the solution of the issue on Serbian help and having an archbishop like Visarion Xhuvani at the helm of the Church. Ultimately, however, Noli backed the chosen path as it prevented the Albanian Church from being placed under the Greek Patriarchate.[185] The Albanian Orthodox Church in the United States, based in Boston, did not reach a consensus, with three priests, early opponents of Noli, aligning themselves with King Zog and the Albanian Holy Synod, and the other churches remaining loyal to Bishop Noli.[186] The annual Orthodox Church meeting in the United States decided to await Noli's return from Europe before making a decision. In the end, only Saint Trinity's Church in Boston joined the OACA, on 14 June 1933.[187]

Among the Albanian diaspora, the strongest opponent was Koço Tasi, who had been the prefect of Gjirokastra during the Noli administration. Tasi, one of the most vocal representatives of the conservative part of Orthodox Albanian nationalists, was a staunch supporter of the Church's autocephaly, but he was also afraid of the Muslim majority having control over the Orthodox minority. After Zog's return to power, Tasi fled into exile, moving between Alexandria and Athens, and also came into conflict with his former friend Fan Noli. Tasi eventually became the most prominent adversary of the path chosen for establishing the Holy Synod, disagreeing even with his brother, Arqile Tasi, who at the time led the Albanian–American Vatra association.[188] On 16 April 1929, Tasi published a booklet in Athens titled *Christian Albanian Associates of the Mohammedans*. Tasi claimed that Albania was now being ruled by Muslims, a state of affairs for which he strongly blamed their Orthodox "associates" Prime Minister Kota, Assembly Speaker Evangjeli, the deposed and exiled Theofan Noli, and even Zoi Xoxa. Tasi asserted that it would be difficult for him to return to Albania since the majority of Muslims failed to realize that they were leading their nation blindly into a religious civil war. He placed most of the blame on Koço Kota and Pandeli Evangjeli, dismissing them as pawns who, for their own personal glory, were pushing Albania into the abyss.[189]

Albanians around the world immediately rebuked Tasi's booklet, noting that Tasi was using the same argument the Greeks had used when they said that a "Muslim government" had assumed control of the ecclesiastical issue. In his booklet, Tasi had concealed the vital fact that prominent Orthodox figures such as Kota and Evangjeli were the actual driving force in resolving the ecclesiastical issue and hardly anyone's pawns. The Albanian diaspora in Egypt was the first to react, on 10 May 1929, when Vasil Tako published his own booklet *The Replies from the Christian Albanians of Misir to Koço Tasi's Publications*. Tako blamed Tasi for backing Greece in this dispute in an effort to Hellenize even their shared birthplace, the southern Albanian town of Përmet. For Tako, this would be impossible as long as Albanians, and particularly the citizens of Përmet, remained staunch patriots. He wrote that any Albanian who used religion at the expense of his homeland was not an Albanian but an enemy of the nation and a traitor – the worst insult Tako could level at Tasi.[190]

Zoi Xoxa dedicated two issues of *Gazeta e Re* to Koço Tasi. He argued that opposition from foreigners was natural, but from compatriots it was unacceptable. The establishment of the Synod was in the nation's best interests and honoured the work and sacrifices of Albanian patriots, and the Patriarchate should have accepted it long ago. Xoxa noted that, had Tasi not been blinded by Greece's 30 pieces of silver, he would have witnessed Albania's Western progress.[191] Xoxa challenged Tasi to name even one occasion when Albania's Muslims had persecuted Albanian Christians, noting that most employees in the Tirana government were Orthodox and praising the religious coexistence of all the country's citizens.[192]

Almost all Albanians, wherever they lived, embraced the Albanian ecclesiastical movement. The Albanians in Albania and in the diaspora, including His Grace Theofan Noli and his political supporters, all hailed the establishment of the Holy Synod – the sole opposition was Koço Tasi.[193] Besides the Albanian majority among the Orthodox believers, the country's Greek minority also strongly backed the Synod's establishment, as they had actively participated in the elections for the Korça Church Congress. Foreign diplomats in Tirana, such as the British ambassador, Sir Robert Hodgson, noted and emphasized this overall support.[194]

Figure 5.1 Archbishop Visarion Entering Korça.

Figure 5.2 Bishop Joakim Martishti.

Figure 5.3 Congress of Korça.

Figure 5.4 Delegates at the Congress of Korça.

Figure 5.5 Visarion Xhuvani during his First Liturgy as Archbishop.

Notes

1 Zoi Xoxa, *Kujtimet e një gazetari [Memoirs of a Journalist]* (Tirana: 55, 2007), 121.
2 *Zëri i Korçës [Voice of Korça]*, 15 September 1928, 4.
3 AQSH, F. 152 "MIA", Y. 1928, f. 39, 46, Korça Prefecture to MIA, 3 October 1928.
4 AQSH, F. 152 "MIA", Y. 1928, f. 39, 53, Berat Prefecture to MIA, 9 October 1928.

5 AQSH, F. 152 "MIA", Y. 1928, f. 39, 58, Korça Prefecture to MIA, 10 October 1928.
6 *Zëri i Korçës [Voice of Korça]*, 12 October 1928, 4.
7 *Zëri i Korçës [Voice of Korça]*, 20 October 1928, 2.
8 *Zëri i Korçës [Voice of Korça]*, 23 October 1928, 1.
9 AMFA, Y. 1928, f. 333, 104, Istanbul Consulate to MFA, 16 October 1928.
10 Glavinas, *Documents 1929*, 44.
11 AQSH, F. 152 "MIA", Y. 1928, f. 39, 81, MIA to Korça Prefecture, 4 November 1928.
12 *Zëri i Korçës [Voice of Korça]*, 27 October 1928, 2.
13 AQSH, F. 152 "MIA", Y. 1928, f. 39, 82, MIA to Korça Prefecture, 5 November 1928.
14 AQSH, F. 152 "MIA", Y. 1928, f. 39 89, Korça Prefecture to MIA, 9 November 1928.
15 "Një shkresë e Kryeministrisë mbi çështjen e Kishës Autoqefale [A Letter from the Prime Minister on the Autocephalous Church Issue], *Gazeta e Re [New Gazette]*, 13 November 1928, 1.
16 AQSH, F. 152 "MIA", Y. 1928, f. 39, 95, MIA to Korça Prefecture, 14 November 1928.
17 *Zëri i Korçës [Voice of Korça]*, 17 November 1928, 2.
18 Kondis, *Elinismos III*, 403: IDAYE, f. A/22/1β, no. 3731, Korça Consulate to Greek MFA, 27 March 1929.
19 AQSH, F. 152 "MIA", Y. 1928, f. 39, 102, MIA to Korça Prefecture, 20 November 1928.
20 AQSH, F. 152 "MIA", Y. 1928, f. 39, 105, Korça Prefecture to MIA, 22 November 1928.
21 AQSH, F. 152 "MIA", Y. 1928, f. 39, 109, MIA to Korça Prefecture, 23 November 1928.
22 AQSH, F. 152 "MIA", Y. 1928, f. 39, 111, MIA to Korça Prefecture, 24 November 1928.
23 AQSH, F. 152 "MIA", Y. 1928, f. 39, 121, MIA to Korça Prefecture, 29 November 1928.
24 AQSH, F. 152 "MIA", Y. 1928, f. 39, 127, Korça Prefecture to MIA, 7 December 1928.
25 AQSH, F. 152 "MIA", Y. 1928, f. 39, 141, Korça Prefecture to MIA, 10 December 1928.
26 AMFA, Y. 1928, f. 333f. 114, MFA to Thessaloniki Consulate, 8 December 1928.
27 "Hirësi e Tij Visarion Xhuvani në Pallat [His Grace Visarion Xhuvani at the Palace]", *Zëri i Korçës [Voice of Korça]*, 1 December 1928, 2; "Imzot Kisi përsëri në Tirana [His Grace Kisi again in Tirana]", *Zëri i Korçës [Voice of Korça]*, 1 December 1928, 2.
28 AQSH, F. 152 "MIA", Y. 1928, f. 39, 143, MIA to Korça Prefecture, 28 December 1928.
29 AQSH, F. 152 "MIA", Y. 1928, f. 39, 148, Korça Prefecture to MIA, 30 December 1928.
30 AMFA, Y. 1928, f. 333, 112, MFA to Athens Embassy, 18 December 1928.
31 AMFA, Y. 1928, f. 333, 112, Athens Embassy to MFA, 29 December 1928.
32 AMFA, Y. 1928, f. 333, 113, MFA to Athens Embassy, 24 December 1928.
33 AMFA, Athens Embassy to MFA, 29 December 1928, quoted.
34 AMFA, Y. 1928, f. 333, 113, Athens Embassy to MFA, 5 January 1928.
35 AMFA, Y. 1928, f. 333, 114, MFA to Athens Embassy, 14 January 1928.
36 "Sovraniteti i Shtetit nuk cënohet! [State Sovereignty Cannot Be Infringed!]", *Gazeta e Re [New Gazette]*, 10 January 1929, 1.
37 AQSH, Metropolitan Kristofor to Kota, 15 March 1929, quoted.
38 Ibid.

39 AQSH, F. 152 "MIA", f. 119/2, Metropolitan Kristofor to Reverend Josif Qirici, 28 March 1929.
40 Xoxa, *Memoirs*, 126.
41 "Çështja e Kishës Autoqefale u-zgjith: Arqimandrit Çamçeja u-dorëzua episkop [The Issue of the Autocephalous Church Resolved: Archimandrite Çamçe Was Ordained Bishop]", *Gazeta e Re [New Gazette]*, 12 February 1929, 1.
42 AQSH, F. 152 "MIA", Y. 1929, f. 119/1, Church High Council Decision, 3 February 1929.
43 AQSH, F. 152 "MIA", Y. 1929, f. 119/1, MIA to All Prefectures, 2 February 1929.
44 AQSH, F. 152 "MIA", Y. 1929, f. 119/1, Shkodra Prefecture to MIA, 13 February 1929.
45 Xoxa, *Memoirs*, 126–127.
46 "The Matter of the Autocephalous Church", 1.
47 "Dje u konsakrua episkop dhe Atë Efthim Hoshteva [Reverend Efthim Hoshteva Was Ordained Bishop Yesterday]", *Gazeta e Re [New Gazette]*, 13 February 1929, 1; Alqi Jani, "Të njohim dhe nderojmë klerikët e Kishës Ortodokse të Shqipërisë: Episkopi Eugjen Hoshteva [To Acknowledge and Honor the Clerics of the Orthodox Church of Albania: Bishop Eugjen Hoshteva]", *Republika [Republic]*, 27 May 2009.
48 AQSH, F. 152 "MIA", Y. 1929, f. 119/1, MIA to Gjirokastra Prefecture, 13 February 1929.
49 "Sinodhi Kishtar i Shqipëris uformua dhe udeklarua dje [The Church Synod of Albania Established and Announced Yesterday]", *Gazeta e Re [New Gazette]*, 19 February 1929, 1.
50 AQSH, F. 152 "MIA", Y. 1929, f. 262, 1, OACA to PMO, no date.
51 "Meditim rreth dy fotografive [Meditation about Two Photos]", *Autoqefalia Ortodokse Shqiptare [Albanian Orthodox Autocephaly]*, 1994, 3.
52 AQSH, F. 152 "MIA", Y. 1929, f. 119/1, Church Eldership Decision, 18 February 1929.
53 "Church Synod of Albania", 1.
54 "Sinodhi i Shenjtë përpara Lartmadhnisë së Tij Mbretit [The Holy Synod before His Majesty the King]", *Gazeta e Re [New Gazette]*, 27 February 1929, 1.
55 *Zëri i Korçës [Voice of Korça]*, 5 March 1929, 4.
56 AQSH, F. 152 "MIA", Y. 1929, f. 119/1, MIA to All Prefectures, 27 February 1929.
57 AQSH, F. 152 "MIA", Y. 1929, f. 119/1, MIA to Berat Prefecture, 6 March 1929.
58 AQSH, F. 152 "MIA", Y. 1929, f. 119/1, Lushnja sub-prefecture to MIA, 11 March 1929; "Pritja e Emz. Agathangjelit në Lushnjë [His Grace Agathangjel's Reception in Lushnja]", *Gazeta e Re [New Gazette]*, 14 March 1929, 1.
59 V. K., "Kryetari i Synodhit të Shenjtë në Shkodër [Chairman of the Holy Synod in Shkodra]", *Gazeta e Re [New Gazette]*, 16 March 1929, 4.
60 "Imzot Visarioni uprit me nderime të mëdha në Durrës [His Grace Visarion Welcomed with Great Honors in Durrës]", *Gazeta e Re [New Gazette]*, 17 March 1929, 6.
61 "Pritja madhështore e Kryetarit të Sinodhit në Kavajë [Magnificent Reception for the Synod Chairman in Kavaja]", *Gazeta e Re [New Gazette]*, 20 March 1929, 1; "Elbasani dhe Kisha Autoqefale [Elbasan and the Autocephalous Church]", *Gazeta e Re [New Gazette]*, 14 March 1929, 2; "Populli Pogradecit falënderon Z-it Kota [The People of Pogradec Thank Mr Kota]", *Gazeta e Re [New Gazette]*, 23 March 1929, 4.
62 Shkalla, Vrina, Mursi, Xarra, Sopik, Muzina, Peca, Senica, Nivica, Saint Vasil, Lukova, and Piqeras.
63 Arqile Bërxholli, *Bashkësia shoqërore ortodokse në Shqipëri [The Orthodox Social Community in Albania]* (Tirana: Julvin, 2013), 48–52.

64 AQSH, F. 152 "MIA", Y. 1929, f. 119, 7, Gjirokastra Prefecture to MIA, 7 March 1929.
65 Kondis, *Elinismos III*, 399: IDAYE, f. A/22/1β, no. 3383, Saranda Consulate to Tirana Embassy, 10 March 1929.
66 "Episkopi i Gjinokastrës do të meshojë në Tiranë [Bishop of Gjirokastra to Hold Liturgy in Tirana]", *Gazeta e Re [New Gazette]*, 8 March 1929, 2.
67 "Ardhja e Dhespotit të Gjirokastrës Pritja e tij triumfale në Sarandë, Delvinë e Gjirokastrë. Fjalët e mbajtura [The Arrival of the Gjirokastra Bishop, His Triumphal Reception in Saranda, Delvina and Gjirokastra. The Speeches]", *Gazeta e Re [New Gazette]*, 19 March 1929, 3; "Populli i Sarandës rëfen ndjenjat e tij patriotike [The People of Saranda Show Their Patriotic Feelings]", *Gazeta e Re [New Gazette]*, 17 March 1929, 6.
68 AQSH, F. 152 "MIA", Y. 1929, f. 119/1, Delvina Subprefecture to MIA, 13 March 1929.
69 "Populli i Delvinës falënderon Z-in Kryeministër [The People of Delvina Thank Mr Prime Minister]", *Gazeta e Re [New Gazette]*, 15 March 1929, 1.
70 "Pritja e Episkop Ambrozit në Gjinokastër [Reception of Bishop Ambroz in Gjirokastra]", *Gazeta e Re [New Gazette]*, 19 March 1929, 1.
71 "E para meshë Episkopale në Gjirokastrë [The First Episcopal Liturgy in Gjirokastra]", *Gazeta e Re [New Gazette]*, 24 March 1929, 3.
72 AQSH, F. 152 "MIA", Y. 1929, f. 119, 35, Gjirokastra Prefecture to MIA, 14 March 1929.
73 AQSH, F. 152 "MIA", Y. 1929, f. 119, 124, Gjirokastra Prefecture to MIA, 4 April 1929.
74 Ibid.; AQSH, F. 152 "MIA", Y. 1929, f. 119, 57, Gjirokastra Prefecture to MIA, 26 March 1929.
75 AQSH, F. 152 "MIA", Y. 1929, f. 119, 64, MIA to OACA, 2 April 1929.
76 AQSH, F. 152 "MIA", Y. 1929, f. 119/1, OACA to MIA, 13 July 1929; AQSH, F. 152 "MIA", Y. 1929, f. 119, 91, MIA to Korça Prefecture, July 1929.
77 AQSH, F. 152 "MIA", Y. 1929, f. 119, 98, MIA to Korça Prefecture, September 1929.
78 "A Grand Reception", 3.
79 "Mbledhja e parë e Sinodhit [The First Meeting of the Synod]", *Zëri i Korçës [Voice of Korça]*, 30 March 1929, 1.
80 "Sinodhi i Shejtë e plotësoi Statutin Kishëtar [The Holy Synod Completes the Church Statute]", *Gazeta e Re [New Gazette]*, 10 April 1929, 1.
81 "Mbledhjet e Sinodhit të Shenjtë Kishtar [Church Holy Synod Meetings]", *Gazeta e Re [New Gazette]*, 18 April 1929, 2.
82 "Holy Synod Completes the Church Statute", 1.
83 "Manifestim madhështorë për Kishën Autoqefale [Glorious Manifestation for the Autocephalous Church]", *Gazeta e Re [New Gazette]*, 12 May 1929, 3.
84 *Gazeta e Re [New Gazette]*, 14 May 1929, 4; "Hirësia e Tij Kryepiskopi Visarion [His Grace Archbishop Visarion]", *Gazeta e Re [New Gazette]*, 30 May 1929, 2; "Aktivitet dhe reforma të çuditëshme në çështjet kishëtare [Activities and Strange Reforms in the Ecclesiastical Issue]", *Gazeta e Re [New Gazette]*, 25 May 1929, 3.
85 "Populli i Përmetit për Kishën Autoqefale [People of Përmet for the Auto-cephalous Church]", *Gazeta e Re [New Gazette]*, 5 June 1929, 1; "Hirësia e Tij Imz. Xhuvani u nis për në Korçë [His Grace Xhuvani Sets Off for Korça]", *Gazeta e Re [New Gazette]*, 25 May 1929, 1; "Imzot Visarioni u kthye në Korçë [His Grace Xhuvani Returns to Korça]", *Gazeta e Re [New Gazette]*, 4 June 1929, 3.
86 "Kthimi i episkopit [Return of the Bishop]", *Gazeta e Re [New Gazette]*, 28 April 1929, 6.

87 "Pritja madhështore që i u bë Episkop Ambrozit në Himarë [Magnificent Reception for Bishop Ambroz in Himara]", *Gazeta e Re [New Gazette]*, 17 May 1929, 4.

88 "Axhentat grekë kanë dashur të nxjerrin turbullime në Delvinë [Greek Agents Wanted to Bring Disturbances in Delvina]", *Gazeta e Re [New Gazette]*, 29 May 1929, 1.

89 AQSH, F. 152 "MIA", Y. 1929, f. 119/1, Army Company I Command to Battalion IV Command, 4 June 1929.

90 AQSH, F. 152 "MIA", Y. 1929, f. 119/1, Gjirokastra Prefecture to MIA, 15 June 1929.

91 AQSH, F. 152 "MIA", Y. 1929, f. 119, 61–63, Korça's Prefecture to MIA, 1 April 1929.

92 AQSH, F. 136 "Durrës Deanery", f. 34, 1–2, Holy Synod Memo no. 4 and no. 5, 30 May 1929.

93 AQSH, F. 152 "MIA", Y. 1929, f. 119/2, Korça Prefecture to MIA, 10 June 1929.

94 "Kisha Autoqefale po ecën me çape të forta në udhën e pregatitur prej Sinodhit të Shenjtë [Autocephalous Church Progressing with Strong Steps on the Path Paved by the Holy Synod]", *Zëri i Korçës [Voice of Korça]*, 1 June 1929, 1.

95 AQSH, F. 155 "MJ", Y. 1929, f. VIII-94, 3, OACA to MIA, 20 June 1929.

96 AQSH, F. 155 "MJ", Y. 1929, f. VIII-91, 1, MJ to Vasil Bidoshi, 15 June 1929.

97 See following section.

98 "Kongresi panorthodoks mori fund [Pan-Orthodox Congress Ends]", *Gazeta e Re [New Gazette]*, 2 July 1929, 1.

99 "Mbreti i drejton letër falënderimi Z. Kryeministër për triumfin Kishëtar [The King Sends Appreciation Letter to Mr Prime Minister on the Church Triumph]", *Gazeta e Re [New Gazette]*, 20 June 1929, 1.

100 "Letra Falenderimie N. M. T Mbretit për Z. Kryeministër [Appreciation Letter from His Majesty the King to Mr Prime Minister]", *Gazeta e Re [New Gazette]*, 23 June 1929, 1.

101 OACA, *Statuti i Kishës Orthodhokse Autoqefale të Shqipris [The Statute of the Orthodox Autocephalous Church of Albania]* (Korça: Korça, 1929).

102 Beqir Meta, "Debati shqiptaro-grek për problemet e minoriteteve dhe të Kishës Autoqefale Shqiptare në organizmat ndërkombëtarë në vitet 1929–1934 [Albanian-Greek Debate on Minority Issues and the Albanian Autocephalous Church in International Organizations in 1929–1934]", *Studime historike [Historical Studies]* 3–4 (2011):37–61.

103 Valentina Duka, "Institucionet fetare gjatë mbretërimit të Ahmet Zogt: një vështrim të legjislacionit të kohës (1928–1939) [Religious Institutions during the Reign of Ahmet Zog: An Overview of Legislation during that Period (1928–1939)]", *Studime Albanologjike [Albanological Studies]* 11:1 (2008):48–54.

104 Kondis, *Elinismos III*, 125: IDAYE, Durrës Embassy to Greek MFA, 7 January 1924, quoted.

105 Kondis, *Elinismos III*, 196–207: IDAYE, Greek MFA Third Political Office to Greek MFA First Political Office, 16 February 1925, quoted.

106 AQSH, F. 155 "MJ", Y. 1927, f. 57, Durrës Metropolitanate to MJ, 26 January 1927.

107 P.S., *Zëri i Korçës [Voice of Korça]*, 18 August 1928, 2; AQSH, F. 152 "MIA", Y. 1928, f. 39, 73, MIA to Korça Prefecture, 22 October 1928.

108 AQSH, F. 152 "MIA", Y. 1928, f. 39, 173, MIA to Shkodra Prefecture, 25 October 1928.

109 AQSH, F. 152 "MIA", Y. 1928, f. 119/1, Korça Prefecture to MIA, 7 December 1929.

110 AMFA, Y. 1929, f. 850, 20, Belgrade Embassy to MFA, 23 February 1929.

111 Antonios Koulas, "Ελληνογιουγκοσλαβικές σχέσεις άπο το 1923 εώς το 1928 [Greek-Yugoslav Relations from 1923 to 1928]", (PhD Dissertation, Thessaloniki University, 2007), 102–117. Belgrade declared that there were 450,000 Serbs in Greece, referring to the Slavs residing there as Serbs. The first request for the liturgy to be performed in the Slavic language was made on 6 May 1925.

112 Ibid, 189–242.

113 AMFA, Y. 1929, f. 850, 257, Appointment Decision, 28 February 1929.

114 "Imz. Viktori zëv. Mitropolit i Shkodrës [His Grace Viktor, Dean of Shkodra]" *Gazeta e Re [New Gazette]*, 2 March 1929, 1.

115 AQSH, F. 152 "MIA", Y. 1929, f. 119/1, Cetinje Metropolitanate to Bishop Viktor, 3 March 1929.

116 Tasoudis, *Biographical Memoirs*, 56–59. Chrysanthos later met Patriarch Miron in Bucharest and Metropolitan Dionysius in Warsaw who pledged not to recognize the Albanian Church.

117 AMFA, Y. 1929, f. 850, 40, Belgrade Embassy to MFA, 5 March 1929.

118 AMFA, Y. 1929, f. 850, 68, Belgrade Embassy to MFA, 21 March 1929.

119 Koulas, "Greek-Yugoslav relations", 189–242.

120 AQSH, F. 152 "MIA", Y. 1929, f. 119/2, Istanbul Consulate to MFA, 6 April 1929.

121 AQSH, F. 152 "MIA", Y. 1929, f. 119/1, Shkodra Prefecture to MIA, 24 June 1929. Viktor was not the only bishop not invited to the Korça Congress. His Grace Eugjen remained behind in Elbasan, since he was not elected as a representative.

122 AQSH, F. 152 "MIA", Y. 1929, f. 119/1, MIA to Elbasan Prefecture, 16 June 1929; Xoxa, *Memoirs*, 133.

123 AQSH, F. 152 "MIA", Y. 1929, f. 119/1, Korça Prefecture to MIA, 22 June 1929.

124 AQSH, F. 155 "MJ", Y. 1929, f. VIII-86, 49, Vasil Bidoshi to MJ, 22 June 1929.

125 AQSH, F. 155 "MJ", Y. 1929, f. VIII-86, 49, Vasil Bidoshi to MJ, 1 July 1929.

126 AQSH, F. 152 "MIA", Y. 1929, f. 119/1, Shkodra Prefecture to MIA, 28 August 1929.

127 AQSH, F. 152 "MIA", Y. 1929, f. 119/1, Shkodra Prefecture to MIA, 10 September 1929.

128 "Zgjedhja e Emzot Eugjenit për Episkop të Shkodrës dhe shvillimi fetar i komunitetit Orthodoks të këtushëm [Election of His Grace Eugjen as Bishop of Shkodra and the Religious Development of the Local Orthodox Community]", *Gazeta e Re [New Gazette]*, 20 October 1929, 3.

129 AQSH, F. 152 "MIA", Y. 1929, f. 119/1, OACA to MIA, 21 July 1929.

130 AQSH, F. 152 "MIA", Y. 1929, f. 119/2, Reverend Stavro Kanxheri to PMO, 8 November 1929.

131 Dimitrije M. Kalezić, "Srpske škole u Albaniji [Serbian Schools in Albania]", (paper presentation at "Population of Slavic Origin in Albania" Scientific Conference, Cetinje, Montenegro, 21–23 June 1990).

132 AQSH, F. 155 "MJ", Y. 1930, f. VIII-127, 11–15, OACA to MIA, May 1930.

133 "Episkopi Imzot Viktori u kthye përsëri n'Atdhen'e vet [Bishop His Grace Viktor Returns to His Homeland]", *Zëri i Korçës [Voice of Korça]*, 18 October 1930, 1.

134 AQSH, F. 155 "MJ", Y. 1930, f. VIII-315, 1, Shkodra Prefecture to MIA, 28 December 1934.

135 AMFA, Y. 1929, f. 850, 99, Istanbul Consulate to MFA, 6 April 1929.

136 AMFA, Y. 1929, f. 850, 201–206, Proclamation to the Orthodox People of Albania, 25 February 1929.

137 Glavinas, *Documents 1929*, 21–23.

138 AMFA, Y. 1929, f. 850, 165–167.

139 Glavinas, *Documents 1929*, 26–27. AMFA, Y. 1929, f. 851, 181–199, Orthodoxy Journal.
140 AMFA, Y. 1929, f. 851, 77, "Progress" Newspaper, 9 March 1929.
141 Glavinas, *Documents 1929*, 31–37.
142 Glavinas, *Documents 1929*, 25.
143 Tasoudis, *Biographical Memoirs*, 56–59.
144 AMFA, Y. 1929, f. 851, 118, Istanbul Consulate to MFA, 17 April 1929.
145 *Zëri i Korçës [Voice of Korça]*, 5 March 1929, 4.
146 AQSH, F. 152 "MIA", Y. 1929, f. 119, 4, Korça Prefecture to MIA, no date.
147 AQSH, F. 152 "MIA", Y. 1929, f. 119, 34, Ierothe to Zog, no date.
148 Glavinas, *Documents 1929*, 52–54: Ierothe to the Patriarch, 20 March 1929.
149 Ilia Spiro Vasili, "Si e gjeta Episkop Jerotheun [How I Found Bishop Ierothe]", *Ngjallja [Resurrection]*, August 1996, 9.
150 Glavinas, *Documents 1929*, 50: Ierothe to the Patriarch, 13 March 1929.
151 AMFA, Y. 1929, f. 852, 1, "Korça's Archbishop" to the League of Nations, 6 March 1929.
152 AMFA, Y. 1929, f. 852, 3, MFA to the League of Nations, 12 April 1929.
153 AMFA, Y. 1929, f. 852, 5, "Korça's Archbishop" to the League of Nations, 17 April 1929.
154 AMFA, Y. 1929, f. 852, 7, MFA to the League of Nations, 19 April 1929.
155 AMFA, Y. 1929, f. 852, 16, "Korça's Archbishop" to the League of Nations, 20 May 1929; AMFA, Y. 1929, f. 852, 18; "Korça's Archbishop" to the League of Nations, 27 May 1929.
156 AMFA, Y. 1929, f. 852, 34–36, MFA to the League of Nations, 5 June 1929; AMFA, Y. 1929, f. 852, 41–42, MFA to the League of Nations, 8 June 1929.
157 AMFA, Y. 1929, f. 852, 54, The League of Nations to MFA, 28 October 1929.
158 AMFA, Extra F. 1, f. 178, 1, Talo, Marangos etc., to the League of Nations, no date. The signatories included Panajot Talo, Kostas Marangos, Ilia Dalla, Kosta Pilo, and others.
159 AMFA, Y. 1929, f. 850, 42, Athens Embassy to MFA, 2 March 1929.
160 AMFA, Y. 1929, f. 850, 50, Athens Embassy to MFA, 9 March 1929.
161 AMFA, Y. 1929, f. 850, 97, *Eleftheria [Freedom]*, 4 April 1929.
162 AMFA, Y. 1929, f. 850, 124, Athens Embassy to MFA, 20 April 1929.
163 AMFA, Y. 1929, f. 850, 35, Athens Embassy to MFA, 14 February 1929.
164 AMFA, Y. 1929, f. 850, 19–21, *Elinikos Tahidromos [The Greek Courier]*, 14 February 1929.
165 AMFA, Y. 1929, f. 850, 30, *Ethnos [Nation]*, 5 March 1929.
166 AMFA, Y. 1929, f. 851, 58, *Elinikos Kathimerini [The Greek Daily]*, 14 March 1929.
167 AMFA, Y. 1929, f. 851, 15, *Imerisios Tipos [Daily Press]*, 15 February 1929.
168 AMFA, Y. 1929, f. 851, 12, *Estia [Focus]*, 15 March 1929.
169 "Çpifjet e një gazete greke të Janinës [The Slander of a Greek Gazette from Ioannina]", *Gazeta e Re [New Gazette]*, 4 April 1929, 3.
170 See AMFA, Y. 1929, f. 851.
171 AMFA, Y. 1929, f. 851, 21, *Kairon [The Times]*, 25 February 1929.
172 AMFA, Y. 1929, f. 851, 44, *Proia [Morning]*, 8 March 1929.
173 AMFA, Y. 1929, f. 851, 28, Press Directorate Memo, 2 March 1929.
174 AMFA, f. 850, 10–12, *Elefthero Vima*, 5 March 1929.
175 "Shtypi grek dhe Kisha Autoqefale [The Greek Press and the Autocephalous Church]", *Gazeta e Re [New Gazette]*, 2 March 1929, 1.
176 "Realizimi i një vepre kombëtare [The Accomplishment of a National Work]", *Gazeta e Re [New Gazette]*, 23 March 1929, 1.
177 AMFA, Y. 1929, f. 851, 7, Albanian Telegraphic Agency Daily Bulletin, 7 March 1929; "Nji deklaratë me randsi e Hirësis së Tij Imzot Visarion [An Important Statement by His Grace Visarion]", *Gazeta e Re [New Gazette]*, 8 March 1929, 4.

178 AMFA, 25 March 1929, Y. 1929, f. 852, 92, Istanbul Consulate to MFA.
179 AMFA, Y. 1929, f. 851, 43, *Le Temps [The Times]*, 14 March 1929; AMFA, Y. 1929, f. 851, 44, *Journal des Debates [Journal of Debates]*, 18 March 1929.
180 Ç'shkruan "The Near East and India" për Kishën Orthodhokse Shqiptare [What "The Near East and India" Writes about the Albanian Orthodox Church]", *Gazeta e Re [New Gazette]*, 23 March 1929, 1.
181 AMFA, Y. 1929, f. 851, 23–24, *The Times*, March 1929.
182 Zoi Xoxa, "Intervista e jonë me Z-in Ministër të Punëvet të Jashtme [Our Interview with the Minister of Foreign Affairs]", *Gazeta e Re [New Gazette]*, 30 May 1929, 1.
183 OACA, *The Church*.
184 AMFA, Y. 1929, f. 850, 47, OACA to Albanian Embassies in Washington, Ankara, Alexandria, Bucharest, Sofia, and Athens, 16 March 1929.
185 Rama, "The State and Recognition", 76–77.
186 "Peshkopata e Kishës Shqiptare në Boston Uron Guvernën për zgjid hjen e çështjes kishëtare [Albanian Church Diocese in Boston Congratulates the Government for the Solution of the Ecclesiastical Issue]", *Gazeta e Re [New Gazette]*, 26 July 1929, 1.
187 AMFA, Y. 1933, f. 483, 13–18, Boston Consulate to MFA, 21 April 1933.
188 *Gazeta e Re [New Gazette]*, 20 August 1929, 2.
189 Koço Tasi, *Shqiptarvet të Krishtern bashkëpunëtore të Muhamedanëvet [Christian Albanians Associates of the Mohammedans]* (Athens, 1929), found in AMFA, Y. 1929, f. 850.
190 Vasil J. Tako, *Përgjigje e Shqiptarëvet Krishten të Misirit për Botimet e Koço Tasit [The Replies from Christian Albanians of Misir [Egypt] to Koço Tasi's Publications]* (Egypt, 1929), found in AMFA, Y. 1929, f. 850, 210–213; AQSH, F. 152 "MIA", Y. 1929, f. 119/1, Gjirokastra Prefecture to MIA, 6 July 1929.
191 "Një zë i shitur! [A Bought Blabbermouth]", *Gazeta e Re [New Gazette]*, 11 August 1929, 1.
192 Laonikus, "Fushata e një të shituri [Campaign of a Turncoat]", *Gazeta e Re [New Gazette]*, 12 August 1929, 3.
193 Koço Tasi would continue his political activities after King Zog was exiled from Albania, following the Italian invasion in 1939. During the Second World War, Tasi took over the governance of the Axis-occupied Kosovo region, facilitating the union of the Prizren Diocese with the OACA. Tasi pledged that he did not lack patriotic fervour, even in the ecclesiastical issue. See the last section in Chapter 6 of this book.
194 Meta, *The Greek-Albanian Tension*, 39.

6 Consolidation, recognition, and expansion to Kosovo, 1929–1945

New negotiations with the Ecumenical Patriarchate, 1929–1931

The metropolitan of Corfu, Athenagoras Spyrou (later archbishop of North and South America, 1930–1948, and the ecumenical patriarch, 1948–1972), was born in an ethnic Albanian family, in a Greek village near the Albanian border. Blaming the Greek government for the establishment of the Albanian Holy Synod, he reported to the Holy Synod of the Church of Greece that the new developments were purely an Albanian victory stemming from King Zog's personal goals. Athenagoras requested the establishment of a new Greek Church in Albania, separate from the one led by Visarion, with the expectation that the majority of Albanians would side with the Greek Church. The metropolitan feared that if Greece had no say in the Albanian Church, it would lose all its influence there, leading to uprisings in the parts of Greece inhabited by Albanians. He concluded that Albania would not retreat from its position as there was no Greek or international pressure to do so.[1]

In an interview given to the Albanian press on 10 August 1929, Greek Prime Minister Eleftherios Venizelos said he viewed the ecclesiastical issue as a black cloud that had destroyed the friendly politics between the two countries. He pointed out that he liked Albanians, as he had always worked with Greek politicians of Albanian descent, such as Kountouriotis, Repoulis, Miaoulis, and Diomidis. While agreeing that the issue was Albania's internal affair, Venizelos attributed Greece's involvement to the historic bond between the Greek people and the Patriarchate.[2] Athenagoras's proposals for a new Greek Church and Venizelos's plea for peaceful coexistence between the two nations were both inconceivable without new talks between the two countries.

As soon as the Korça Church Congress concluded in the summer of 1929, the press spread the news that Albania would be seeking an agreement with the Ecumenical Patriarchate. Although the Albanian government had emphasized that it would accept no solution less than full recognition of the new Holy Synod, both Albania and Greece agreed to resume talks.[3] Leon

Melas, the Greek ambassador in Albania, assured Tirana that it would find goodwill in Athens.[4] On 19 October, the Albanian government put Vasil Avrami, the mayor of Korça, in charge of an important mission to Athens to reach a new agreement. Avrami, a prominent Albanian patriot and a fierce supporter of autocephaly, was widely accepted by all Orthodox Albanians.[5] He arrived in Athens in early November with authorization to hold talks with Metropolitan Chrysanthos in order to "repair the brotherly ecclesiastical relations between the Great Church of Christ of Constantinople and its daughter in Christ, the Albanian Orthodox Church".[6]

His Grace Chrysanthos bluntly blamed Albania for its insistence on implementing the Tirana Church Protocol of 1926. Avrami replied that the current situation could not be reversed and that the talks were not compulsory but only an exchange of opinions. The tangible supremacy of Albania's position enabled Avrami to obtain several changes to the 1926 Tirana Church Protocol, and he and Chrysanthos reached an agreement on 9 December. Despite Chrysanthos's initial strong objections, they agreed that the Greek language would be used only by the Greek minority and in no case by Albanian Orthodox communities. The Patriarchate finally accepted the provisions in the Statute of the Albanian Church that the Albanian Holy Synod would comprise one metropolitan and three bishops, and not five metropolitans, as had been decided three years earlier in the Tirana Church Protocol.[7] Both parties agreed that Evlogji Kurilla would be the new archbishop, His Grace Kristofor Kisi would be the new bishop of Korça, and Pandeli Kotoko would be elected as bishop of Gjirokastra. His Grace Agathangjel would continue to lead the diocese of Berat. His Grace Ambroz and His Grace Eugjen would resign, citing old age as the reason, while His Beatitude Visarion would leave his position and retreat in a monastery.[8] To preserve their dignity, Visarion, Ambroz, and Eugjen would be granted patriarchal forgiveness and recognition.

His Grace Chrysanthos told Avrami that this was the Patriarchate's final offer.[9] The Albanian foreign minister, Rauf Fico, backed the agreement and promised the Greek ambassador in Tirana that he would do his best to convince the government to quickly endorse it.[10] Unlike Fico, however, Prime Minister Koço Kota believed that Albania should not step back from its position at all: he convinced his government and the Orthodox elite to firmly reject and criticize the agreement.[11] The government justified its rejection by saying that changes to the ecclesiastical order would result in strong protests from Orthodox Albanian patriots.[12]

King Zog told Ambassador Melas that Albania was unwilling to accept any provision in the deal with Chrysanthos that related to ethnic minorities, since this was a political matter and, as such, could be dealt with only by the Albanian and Greek governments, not the Church. In addition, Zog requested that either Joakim or Kristofor be elected archbishop, after Visarion resigned in favour of Ambroz, who would lead the Holy Synod during the transition.[13] The king ruled out any mention of Evlogji Kurilla, who was extremely interested in politics and so, he feared, might follow in Bishop Noli's path by using his religious influence to interfere in matters of government.[14] The press wrote straightaway about the return of Joakim and Kristofor, but the Albanian government denied this news and ordered complete silence on the issue until a final settlement.[15]

Within a week, the Patriarchate sharply objected, writing that the agreement of 9 December 1929 was its final offer.[16] It took two months for Albania to respond, as the country was undergoing political turmoil, which culminated in the resignation of Prime Minister Kota. He was succeeded by Pandeli Evangjeli. Within days, Vasil Avrami, who had led the talks with Chrysanthos in Athens, was appointed the new minister of justice, who was also responsible for religious affairs. The change in government revived hopes in Athens for a different outcome to the talks, since the Greeks believed that Avrami would now drop the government's objections to the 9 December agreement. To their disappointment, however, both Prime Minister Evangjeli and Minister Avrami continued Kota's unyielding stance on the issue.

Although Ambassador Melas expressed Greece's genuine desire to solve the impasse on friendly terms, he threatened that Athens would refuse to compensate any Albanian for property seized during Greece's recent land reform if Tirana did not accept the 9 December deal.[17] In June 1930, the Albanian government announced that it would accept the deal's provision on ethnic minorities provided that the Patriarchate agreed to limit its scope only to the Greek minority.[18] The Albanian government would accept either His Grace Kristofor or His Grace Joakim as the future archbishop, while Pandeli Kotoko had to wait no more than three months to be ordained bishop.[19]

If the Patriarchate accepted these changes, Avrami was willing to travel to either Athens or Istanbul to sign the new agreement. The postponement of Kotoko's ordination was justified on the grounds that he would need to go through several stages in order to become a bishop: Kotoko would have to be ordained first as a deacon, then as a priest, and finally as a bishop. Even so, the Albanian government provided no further assurance that, in the end, Kotoko would be ordained, which led Greece to suspect some hidden plan behind the delay. The ordination was important for Athens, since – unlike Joakim, Kristofor, Ambroz, and Kurilla, whom Greece had never trusted – Kotoko was a loyal Hellenist. Hoping to thwart this Albanian scheme, Greece asked for a written pledge that Kotoko would indeed be ordained, but Prime Minister Evangjeli refused.[20]

The new talks failed, but the press did not report the stalemate and leaders in both countries kept the doors open for future talks. King Zog told the Greek ambassador that Greece should understand that, in the twentieth century, religious affairs did not affect people as they had in the past, especially in a country with a rare, peaceful religious coexistence such as Albania. Zog demanded the Patriarchate not to set conditions that were offensive to the dignity of the Albanian people, to which the ambassador replied that Greece could not ask the Patriarchate to breach the Holy Canons.

Zog asserted that, unlike Greece, Albania was a secular state, adding that he was willing to send a delegation to Istanbul or Athens to speak to the religious leaders on equal terms, in full respect of the Holy Canons.[21]

The Greek ambassador wrote to his government in Athens asking to delay any developments on the matter until Rauf Fico left the Albanian Foreign Ministry since, in his opinion, Fico was anti-Greek. Everything would be easier, he said, if the Hellenophile Hysni Vrioni became the new foreign minister, as the Albanian press had reported. The ambassador thought that Greece should accept the Albanian proposition and stressed that no one could deny the Albanian state's right to intervene in the Church leadership, as this was an old tradition in the Orthodox Church.[22]

In the meantime, the Albanian Foreign Ministry, in a confidential memo to the king and his government, wrote that Albania should not accept any Greek demands, since it would be a humiliation to the country to relinquish the newly elected bishops. The three Albanian hierarchs had served when necessary and Albania should not give the impression that "the Patriarchate was able to overthrow" and replace them. The recognition of autocephaly was important to Albania in order to improve relations with Greece and resist any Serbian and Catholic attempts to interfere in Albania. In this light, the memo proposed that Zog secretly summon Kristofor and Joakim and make an agreement with them to replace the Church's hierarchs before any new deal with the Patriarchate. After this, new talks with the Patriarchate could be held to reach other changes, including the election of Agathangjel as bishop of Berat and providing the right of the king to remove bishops by royal decree.[23]

For the first time in this saga, Greece took the step of becoming the official mediator between the Albanians and the Patriarchate. Greece justified its new role by stressing that it was an "Orthodox state" and a nation that took care of its fellow believers, while intentionally ignoring the fact that the Orthodox in Albania were overwhelmingly Albanian. Albania, meanwhile, saw Greece's involvement as a way to help persuade the Patriarchate without treating the Albanian Church as an Albanian–Greek issue.

Disheartened by these developments, each party blamed the other for the implicit failure of the talks. Greece said that Albania was reneging on its commitments of 9 December, while Albania viewed the Greek demands as interference in its internal affairs. The British ambassador to Tirana, Sir Robert Hodgson, thought that Greece was the only one to blame, as Athens had been using the Patriarchate as a tool to achieve its own political gains. He was of the opinion that Greece had confirmed the general suspicion that the Patriarchate was Greece's instrument for increasing its political leverage in Albania.[24]

On 14 April 1931, Zog told the Greek ambassador that his country's governmental crisis had made it impossible to send a delegation to Athens to solve the outstanding issues. He promised the ambassador that there would be a fresh approach to the matter once the crisis had ended.[25] Greece, for its part, was also ready for renewed negotiations, and in early September it ordered the Greek press not to publish any articles against either Albania or King Zog.[26] The Albanian government, too, did not wish to give up on this chance for further talks.[27]

Consolidation of the Orthodox Autocephalous Church of Albania (OACA)

The Holy Synod of the Albanian Orthodox Autocephalous Church faced a number of challenges, but for the first time in 20 years the Church now had a formal leadership in place. To deal with the various pressing ecclesiastical matters, the Synod set up several working committees. These groups included some of Albania's most prominent intellectuals, such as Aleksandër Xhuvani, Mihal Sherko, Zoi Xoxa, Kostaq Cipo, Sotir Papahristo, Agathokli Xhitoni, and Thoma Turtulli, among many others. This strategy helped the Church achieve rapid internal consolidation. For example, the Permanent Economic Council involved a number of prominent Orthodox believers, with the MPs Andon Beça and Stavro Stavri, the former minister Dhimitër Kacimbra, and Mihal Shani elected as full-time members.[28]

Tirana became the official seat of the Church, although choosing the location had led to fierce clashes during the Korça Congress, especially between the Korça and Tirana delegates. The government intervened and persuaded the parties to find common ground, with the final solution being left in the hands of King Zog. Article 14 of the Church Statute stipulated that until the king's decision the Church would be based in Korça.[29] In early April 1930, Zog issued his decree, making Tirana the official seat, which was justified by the need to connect the Church leadership with government officials.[30] The capital had never been a diocesan centre and, as a result, it had very few church buildings. Even the deanery had served as a temporary residence for the prime minister ever since His Grace Theofan Noli came to power in June 1924. The Albanian state returned the building to the Orthodox Autocephalous Church of Albania (OACA) at the end of 1930.[31]

The archbishop oversaw the establishment of church elderships in the four dioceses, with Tirana being the last to vote in January 1930. The eldership elected Dr Athanas Shundi, one of the first teachers in Tirana's Albanian School, as dean of Tirana.[32] The Korça eldership elected Reverend Josif Qirici as its dean, while the Holy Synod appointed Reverend Vasil Marko as vicar of the diocese of Korça during the archbishop's absences.[33]

During Albania's second national census, held in 1930, Archbishop Visarion urged Orthodox believers to disclose their personal data honestly and in good faith. He judged that it was a sacred Christian duty for any good believer to tell the truth, even if it might harm them.[34] The increase in Albanian patriotism led to an increase in the official number of Orthodox believers: in 1922, Orthodox followers counted for 20.1 per cent of the population, rising to 21.4 per cent five years later. In the 1930 census, the numbers continued to grow, with fully 22 per cent of Albanians declaring their affiliation as Orthodox – 2 per cent more than before the Church's declaration of autocephaly.[35] The Albanian Orthodox Autocephalous Church had 400 priests and 722 sanctuaries, which consisted of 384 churches, 38 monasteries, and 300 chapels.[36]

For the first time in its history, the Albanian Holy Synod drafted and approved by vote a centralized budget, based on income derived mainly from gifts and revenue from churches and monasteries, with no special tax imposed on believers.[37] The Mixed Council – composed of the bishops and one lay member of each diocese with the authority to run the economic affairs of the Church – had drafted a budget of 216,000 gold francs, of which 50,000 gold francs would be subsidized by the government.[38] The Holy Synod and the Mixed Council logged several achievements in less than a year, including, for the first time, the creation of a register for the assets of monasteries, churches, communities, married believers, and volunteers. Priests had their relevant personal files, with photographs and biographies, and the Church secured and clarified the ecclesiastical order.[39] The OACA prohibited its priests from spending long hours in shops and bars, which it considered undignified; the clergy must be examples of human purity as well as fatherly and noble behaviour.[40]

The Holy Synod established four charitable institutions, one for each diocese.[41] St John the Baptist's Monastery in Voskopoja, in the diocese of Korça, sheltered the elderly. The diocese of Gjirokastra hosted an orphanage at the Holy Trinity Monastery in the village of Pepel, while St Mary's Monastery in Zvërnec near Vlora – part of the diocese of Berat – became a shelter for the "mentally and morally ill". The metropolitanate of Tirana and Durrës established a shelter for old and indigent priests, as well as another shelter in St Jovan Vladimir's Monastery in the area of Shpat, near Elbasan, for believers called to monastic solitude.[42]

For the first time, the priests' full salaries were included in a centralized budget, in contrast to previously, when local communities paid the Orthodox clergy from the income of the individual churches. The Greek embassy in Tirana noted with sadness that the resulting damage was self-evident since these priests would now lose their allegiance to the Patriarchate.[43] A large part of the Albanian Church budget went towards establishing an Orthodox seminary and providing for theology scholarships, translations, publications, celebrations, charity, new church construction, and national religious choirs. However, when the Holy Synod met in August, the balance sheet was disappointing.[44] The Church had only partially achieved its projected income and would reach, with difficulty, only about 70 per cent of its forecast budget by the end of the year. To reach the anticipated budget for 1931, the Holy Synod and the Mixed Council appealed to all believers, from richest to poorest, not to stint on their financial donations.[45] Nonetheless, the Church leadership decided to tighten the budget accordingly.[46] Over the next few years, the balance sheet became more in line with the overall economic growth of the Church, with capital deriving mainly from direct contributions and special donations.

Another challenge the Church faced was uprooting outdated and medieval traditions, especially with regard to funerals. Archbishop Visarion ordered that, to avoid health risks, the bodies of the departed must be covered during processions to the cemetery.[47] He also decreed that, in the cities, church bells should not toll for each and every death, since this could cause public annoyance. This was especially true in Korça, where several deaths occurred daily due to the city's large number of Orthodox believers.[48] Visarion also announced that a tradition among Orthodox believers in Shkodra, in which people screamed and shouted during vigils and funerals, was incompatible with the norms of Orthodox rites and ordered its immediate ban.[49] Also, weddings in Orthodox communities where there was only a small number of guests should limit the festivities to a single night rather than going on for days, as was the general custom. The archbishop also banned throwing various good luck items at the newlyweds during the wedding ceremony, as this diminished the importance of the service and disturbed the sacred mystery.[50] His Beatitude Visarion had strongly opposed bringing the Russian choir to the Church – a holdover from the time of His Grace Theofan Noli – but after discussions on 25 May 1929, Tirana's church eldership, under Visarion's leadership, set up a commission to re-establish the choir.[51]

Religious education was seen as a priority, and the Church took particular care in this area. The Mixed Council decided to create a special fund for religious instruction in the schools and assigned Josif Qirici to draft a prayer booklet for children.[52] Over the next few years, the Holy Synod published an impressive number of school textbooks, including *The History of the Old Testament*, *The History of the New Testament*, and *The Orthodox Christian Catechism*.[53] Visarion prepared the first group of Albanian theology students and, in August 1930, requested through the Romanian ambassador that such students be accepted into Romanian seminaries.[54] A few years later, Yugoslavia would also accept Orthodox Albanian theology students,[55] including some who would later rise to prominence, such as the poet Migjeni, the future priest Petro Doçi, Branko Kadia, and Theofan Popa, who were all educated at the seminary in Bitola.[56] Following in their footsteps, the future Bishop Irine Banushi attended the seminary in Cetinje and the Theological Faculty in Belgrade.[57] One of the Albanian Church's greatest achievements in religious education was the establishment of the National Orthodox Seminary, which was inaugurated by the Holy Synod in Durrës on 1 March 1931.[58]

The Greek embassy in Tirana saw clearly that all the Orthodox priests in the country supported the Autocephalous Albanian Church, which by now was fully Albanized.[59] With rare exceptions, Albanian had become the only language used in Albanian churches, with only a few complaints in Gjirokastra. Gjirokastra's bishop and the representatives who had attended the Church Congress in Korça faced few objections when they returned to the city on 29 July 1929.[60] In a number of villages, Reverend Thanas from the village of Labova e Kryqit started preaching against the Autocephalous

Church.[61] The Holy Synod moved to ban bilingualism in this diocese, except for the Greek minority villages[62]; mostly they were worried about secret instructions being conveyed from the Greek consulate in Gjirokastra.[63]

Korça, the major hub of the ecclesiastical question, faced no difficulties in the complete Albanization of the Church other than two attempts to challenge the new ecclesiastical order. The Greek consulate in Korça dispatched a Greek employee to the villages of Hoçisht, Ziçisht, Grapsh, and three other nearby villages to organize ways to prevent holding the liturgy entirely in Albanian. On 14 September 1930, the psalm-singers in Bilisht, on orders from the Greek consulate, refused to accept the use of the Albanian language, claiming that they did not know the psalms in Albanian. Dhimitër Tushemishti, the deputy prefect and a known Hellenist, ordered the altar boys to sing the psalms in Greek, but only those verses they did not know in Albanian. Upon hearing of this, the Tirana government fired Tushemishti and the church again established Albanian as the only language in services.[64] The only other incident occurred in Korça at the initiative of Professor Sotir Papahristo and Pandeli Kotoko. Reverend Josif Qirici conducted the liturgy in Albanian during the first days of Easter in 1931. Circumstances changed, however, after the third day of Easter, when Reverend Sotir Ilia officiated in the St Athanasius Church. On that Saturday, Reverend Sotir, an opponent of autocephaly, conducted the liturgy entirely in Greek, while the choir sang the psalms in both languages. The following day, a new excuse was found when a football team from Ioannina, Greece, came to Korça to play the local team. Reverend Sotir decided that, in order to serve the spiritual needs of the players, he had the right to hold the liturgy in Greek.[65] The last liturgy in the Greek language in Korça was held on 17 April 1931,[66] which led the OACA to take action. The following year, the archbishop ordered the diocese of Korça to distribute a memo prohibiting Greek in the liturgy, including the singing of psalms. It was agreed that Albanian churches could use Greek only in reading from the *Book of Daniel*, which the OACA had not yet translated into Albanian.[67] In 1932, Albania's secret services identified 82 Hellenists in Korça, whom they divided into 3 groups. The first was made up of 11 "Hellenists from 1914"; in the second there were 8 "people with Hellenist feelings", while the remaining 63 Hellenists operated "under the guise of Albanianism, but in reality had completely Greek feelings", with Pandeli Kotoko standing out as a prominent member of this last group.[68] Nevertheless, such small numbers indicated just how few Hellenists were to be found in Korça.

The other two dioceses, those of Tirana and Berat, faced no difficulties either. In the only incident recorded in the diocese of Berat, Archimandrite Isaia, the dean of Vlora, made sure that the Greek consul's interference failed. The Greek consulate in Vlora had distributed 3,000 gold francs, taken from Jovan Banga's inheritance fund, among the Hellenists there. The consul in charge, when he heard the liturgy held in Albanian, had called the Albanian Church "a brothel", which resulted in demands for his expulsion from native Orthodox believers. An attempt from the same consulate to promote the liturgy in Greek failed because the church choir was composed of Albanian patriots.[69]

The Himara region, in the diocese of Gjirokastra, was precariously divided between pro-Albanian and pro-Greek factions. Except in the town of Himara itself and a small part of nearby Dhërmi, the pro-Albanian side inhabited all the surrounding villages. The pro-Albanians threatened to convert en masse to Uniatism if the deanery did not embrace the Autocephalous Church. The pro-Greek elite in Himara refused to hand over the local church to the dean appointed by the bishop of Gjirokastra, which created uneasy friction between the opposing factions.[70] The situation remained unresolved until the elections for the church eldership, which took place on 19 October, with the majority of votes going to the pro-Albanian side.[71]

The final blow for the Hellenists in southern Albania was the closure of the private schools that had been established for the Greek minority with financial support from Greece. His Beatitude Visarion rushed to congratulate King Zog for deciding to do this.[72] Greek objections to this measure brought an official complaint from the secretary-general of the League of Nations, Eric Drummond, who asked Albania to restrain from interfering in the country's Greek-speaking areas.[73]

Another concern for the Albanian Orthodox Church was the matter of the Vlach minority in the city of Elbasan, in central Albania. The Vlachs, who lived in the city's St Nicholas quarter, had requested to hold the liturgy in their own language in a Uniate church. The Holy Synod of the OACA asked the government to intervene, and the Tirana authorities expelled the Uniate priest, Archimandrite Serbojan, on 1 December.[74] However, his expulsion did not eliminate the threat of Uniatism, and Archbishop Visarion, wishing to avoid intervention from the Vatican, asked the Albanian government to allow a bilingual liturgy in Elbasan's Vlach quarter.[75] Prime Minister Evangjeli, however, was unwilling to make this concession and informed Visarion that he would be held responsible for any change in the status quo.[76] It was not until 1935 that the church eldership was able to persuade the Vlachs to hold the liturgy in Albanian as the Orthodox Albanian majority living in this quarter objected to hold the liturgy in the Aromanian language.[77]

The full cooperation between the government and the leadership of the OACA had resulted in the Church's swift Albanization. The government informed the archbishop of every case in which it considered it necessary to expel a priest, with state officials having the right to intervene only after they received the opinion of the Church.[78] This concession was similar to the Patriarchate's requests in 1927, which the government had considered extreme. But in a stark contrast with the past, these provisions were not the result of foreign pressure, but of the ever-growing mutual confidence between the Albanian state and the country's Orthodox Church. This collaboration was an application in real-life circumstances of the *symphony* principle.

Uniatism was the common denominator in the problems encountered both in Himara and, with the Vlachs, in Elbasan. When Albania achieved

independence in late 1912, the movement did not have many actual supporters in the country. Orthodox Albanians were, however, regularly threatening to turn to Uniatism – a threat that was closely linked to the Albanian
ecclesiastical question. Even as far back as the late nineteenth century,
some Albanian believers had threatened to place themselves under the
jurisdiction of the pope if the liturgy in Albanian was not accepted.[79] In
Elbasan, a Uniate church had existed since the 1890s; it had been established by Archimandrite Germanos, the nephew of the former metropolitan of Durrës, Visarion. But the number of Uniates shrunk after the Berat
Congress, and Germanos was the only Uniate priest left in Albania.[80] The
Uniate issue returned again in late 1928, shortly before the establishment
of the Autocephalous Church. The international press reported that many
Albanian Orthodox priests had accepted Catholicism due to the lack of an
ecclesiastical order and hierarchy.[81] Archbishop Visarion was an extreme
opponent of Uniatism. In late August 1929, he objected to the opening of
the Uniate church in Elbasan, declaring that there could be no Orthodox
church in Albania outside the jurisdiction of the Autocephalous Church.[82]
The Uniates opened their church anyway and brought over a priest from the
Arbëreshë community in Italy, Reverend Petro Skarpeli, to conduct the
liturgy in Greek. It appears that the Uniate priests were hoping to lure away
the Hellenists now that the Albanian Church was firmly established on national foundations. This was different from the situation only a few years
earlier, when the Uniates targeted Albanian patriots for conversion. Visarion officiated at the liturgy for Orthodox believers in Saint Mary's Church
in Elbasan's Kala (Castle) quarter on the same day the Uniate church
opened. He threatened to excommunicate any Orthodox who went to the
Uniate church, which he described as "the devil's work and a cancer that
seeks to undermine Albanian autocephaly".[83] Visarion asked the government to expel Reverend Petro and every other Uniate member or clergyman,
arguing that the Uniates were trying to increase their ranks through corruption since they had no true followers.[84] Taking advantage of the state's
willingness to protect the Autocephalous Church, Visarion managed to
convince the government that it must stop the growth of Uniatism. King
Zog promised the archbishop to ban all Uniate liturgies in Elbasan, and
the government intervened by closing the Uniate church barely one month
after its opening.[85] Greek officials, meanwhile, were not afraid of any mass
conversion of Orthodox Albanians to Uniatism. In January 1935, they argued, that the vast majority of believers would not fall prey to the siren calls
of Uniate priests, since the Albanian government was opposed to them.[86]
Upon hearing that the Albanian government had distributed a memo label-
ling the Uniates as "enemies of the Motherland and tools of the Vatican and
Italy", the Greek embassy in Tirana reported that it considered the tough
Albanian stance sincere and credible.[87] It also noted that there were two
factions: Italophiles, including such important figures as Eqrem Libohova
and Abdurrahman Krosi, and fierce opponents of Uniatism, such as Vasil

Avrami, Abdurrahman Dibra, Xhafer Vila – all with high-ranking positions in Albanian politics – as well as Archbishop Visarion. In the end, the latter faction had prevailed.[88]

Despite its internal consolidation, the Albanian Church was still not recognized as independent by any other Orthodox Church. Although all the non-Greek Churches sympathized the Albanian cause, the Ecumenical Patriarchate had succeeded in blocking them from recognizing the new Albanian Holy Synod. In 1931, hoping to by-pass such obstacles, the Albanian Church accepted the invitation to join the World Alliance for International Friendship through the Churches and took part in the Alliance's meeting in September of that year, in Cambridge, England; it was represented by Archbishop Visarion and Stavro Stavri. The envoy of the Ecumenical Patriarchate left the meeting in protest, while the envoy of the Serbian Church, still bitter over Bishop Viktor's expulsion from Shkodra, questioned Visarion's title as an archbishop. The Bulgarian and the Romanian patriarchs, however, sided with the Albanians, threatening to leave Cambridge if Visarion was not accepted with full rights. Visarion spoke on the rights enjoyed by Albania's ethnic minorities and, at the end of his talk, requested equal treatment for the Albanian minorities in Greece and Yugoslavia.[89]

The OACA also took part in the meeting of the Alliance the following year in Romania.[90] King Carol II of Romania received Archbishop Visarion and assured him of his support for the Albanian Church. According to the king, Prime Minister Nicolae Iorga had conveyed to the Romanian patriarch his wish for a speedy recognition of Albanian autocephaly. The patriarch had promised that, although he could not overrule the Ecumenical Patriarch, he would intervene in favour of the Albanian Church if the occasion arose.[91] True to his word, Patriarch Miron did in fact lobby for the Albanian Church and stated that the Romanian Orthodox Church would not accept any decision against the Albanian hierarchs either now or in the future.[92]

In 1933, it was Bulgaria's turn to welcome the delegations of the World Alliance. King Zog awarded the Grand Cordon of the Order of Skanderbeg to Sofia's Patriarch Stefan[93] as Bulgaria had been the Albanian Church's most loyal supporter. His Beatitude Visarion decided to travel through Yugoslavia to attend the conference. The Serbian Patriarchate, meanwhile, had reconsidered its position on the Albanian issue after new clashes with Greece. Orthodox priests from the Yugoslav city of Bitola (which had a significant Albanian minority) sang the liturgy alongside Visarion and referred to him as a canonical archbishop. The World Alliance conference began on 15 September 1933. After the opening, Visarion was received by Bulgaria's Tsar Boris III, who spoke Albanian fluently. The Bulgarian monarch expressed his support to the Albanian nation, King Zog, and the Albanian Church, and at his urging the Bulgarian Church officially recognized the OACA and blessed its Holy Synod.[94] The Bulgarian patriarch asked His Beatitude Visarion to co-officiate with the Bulgarian bishops at a liturgy in both Bulgarian and Albanian.[95]

In his mission, Visarion succeeded in receiving at least indirect recognition for the OACA from all the autocephalous Churches except the Greek ones. From then on, representatives from the Yugoslav, Bulgarian, and Romanian embassies in Tirana would attend all the major Orthodox celebrations in Albania.[96] Visarion also tried to use personal friendships to internationalize the autocephaly issue, as two of his former classmates, Ioannis Theotokis and Alexandros Hatzikyriakos, became ministers in the Greek government in 1932.[97] Both ministers received congratulations from the Albanian archbishop and hurried to reply, thanking him for his blessings.[98] The Albanian press office characterized the telegrams as ice-breakers in the deadlock between the Albanian Church and Hellenism,[99] but this turned out not to be true. Only a month after the exchange of courtesies, the Greek press launched a fresh campaign against the Albanian Church,[100] spreading news of an eventual replacement for Visarion.[101]

Albania knew that the support of the Greek government was necessary for official recognition from the Ecumenical Patriarchate. In July 1932, Leon Melas, the former Greek ambassador in Tirana, told the Albanian envoy in Athens, Ali Asllani, that Albania had the right to choose the leaders of the Albanian Church. He added, however, that the Patriarchate would grant the tomos only if His Beatitude Visarion left his position.[102]

Visarion's resignation and the recognition of autocephaly

Visarion Xhuvani was no longer the undisputed leader of the Church of Albania when Kristofor Kisi returned to the scene in 1933, after spending four years in monasteries. The Albanian government had refused Visarion's request to expel him from the country, considering His Grace Kristofor loyal to both the state and the nation. Greece was well aware of this appraisal and subsequently called Kisi a tool of the Albanian government.[103]

On 4 January 1933, Bishop Kristofor informed Visarion of his willingness to serve the Church, implying that, if asked, he would lead the diocese of Korça, which had no ruling bishop, but Visarion did not reply.[104] However, through the mediation of Koço Kota, His Grace Kristofor arranged a meeting with King Zog and requested that the Albanian state officially acknowledge his return as a ruling bishop in the OACA. Visarion hurried to disparage the royal reception of the bishop, calling it a three-minute courtesy meeting. Ironically, Visarion claimed that Kristofor had, for the last four years, been begging for such a meeting, which took place just a few days after Visarion's own hour-long meeting with the king.[105] Visarion said that the diocese of Korça would continue to be vacant, spreading rumours that Kristofor had left behind grudges among Albanian patriots.[106] After spending 33 days in the capital, the bishop again departed for the monastery. Still seething, Visarion drew attention to the fact that Kristofor had left for the monastery by bus and not by car – as would have been the case if he were an honoured official.[107]

The archbishop's description of the situation, however, did not match its complex reality, and in November 1933, the Holy Synod appointed Kristofor Kisi as the new ruling bishop of Korça. Greek officials and the Ecumenical Patriarchate threatened Kristofor with excommunication if he again became involved with OACA affairs, but the bishop was not afraid of their threats.[108] For its part, the Albanian government was trying to implement the plan drafted two years earlier when talks with Athens had failed, and Kristofor agreed to be part of it. Removing Bishop Ambroz and Eugjen proved to be easy: Eugjen resigned and returned to his birthplace, Hoshteva, in 1934,[109] while Ambroz continued his duties until he passed away on 20 May 1934. Bishop Kristofor now considerably strengthened his position, as the Holy Synod entrusted him also with supervising the Gjiro-kastra diocese.[110] The Greek newspapers called the move illegal, but the Albanian press office stressed that the Orthodox of Gjirokastra had received Kristofor's appointment with joy, as he was as among the Albanian Church's most eminent hierarchs.[111]

Kristofor had not easily forgotten Visarion's strong objection to his election, but the conflict between the two men heralded a sudden clash with the Tirana government. In 1934, the government unexpectedly banned religious education from school hours on the grounds that it did not accord with the desired curriculum of public schools in a secular state.[112] Archbishop Visarion objected to the measure, stressing that religious education was necessary for the spiritual growth of all believers. In April of that year, he sent King Zog a memorandum accusing the government of persecuting the Orthodox Church by illegally acquiring its properties and complained that some Albanian diplomats were not doing enough to promote recognition of the Holy Synod. Visarion wrote that he was addressing the king directly because he considered the Church's situation serious and urgent.[113] The Interior Ministry, however, ordered the regional post and telegraph offices not to send any of the archbishop's telegrams to the king if they considered the content to be harmful.[114]

In the meantime, the situation in the Balkans was changing, and the Greek government revised its position on the Albanian Church. In a meeting with prominent Greek diplomats and His Grace Chrysanthos, the Greek ambassador in Tirana proposed that the Ecumenical Patriarchate grant autocephaly to the Albanian Church, but on the sole condition that Visarion be removed from the Holy Synod. The Greek Foreign Ministry accepted this proposal but delayed implementation, not wishing to raise Italian hopes for the Dodecanese Church.[115] In late 1934, Koço Kota, now the speaker of Albania's National Assembly, met with Pandeli Kotoko and expressed his willingness to remove Visarion if the Patriarchate granted the tomos.[116]

Both domestic developments and the expected agreement between the Albanian government and the Ecumenical Patriarchate implied that the archbishop's dismissal from the Church leadership was a foregone conclusion. In a desperate move to hold onto his position, Visarion tried to win official recognition for Albanian autocephaly from the Serbian and Greek Churches, promising to allow the liturgy in either Slavic or Greek in certain parts of Albania. Making good on his promise, Visarion personally conducted the liturgy in Albanian, Greek, and Slavonic on Christmas in 1935.[117] The Greek consulate in Korça, trying immediately to take advantage of the sudden development, requested that a liturgy be held in Greek for its employees in one of the city's churches.[118] The Albanian government denied the request as incompatible with the Albanian Church Statute.[119] Kristofor, recognizing this as an opportune moment to strike a final blow against Visarion, organized a petition for his removal and, at the same time, called for a new ecclesiastical congress.[120] The Orthodox believers of Përmet drafted the official request, expressing their sadness over the situation the Church found itself in and argued that a new congress would resolve the issues of the Church's international recognition and its leadership.[121] The draft of the petition soon arrived in Korça, where it was signed by a large number of prominent Orthodox faithful, with the discreet encouragement of Bishop Kristofor.[122] As the signatories had asked all dioceses to elect representatives for a new congress, Korça's eldership gathered on 4 May 1936 to discuss the petition. Kristofor did not rush to support the initiative but first asked lawyers to assess the petition from the legal point of view.[123] The Albanian government feared that a new congress might bring up other issues, such as the election of MPs based on religious affiliation or the removal of the royal prerogative to dismiss bishops. This fear was due to the fact that, although the vast majority of the petition's signatories were staunch Albanian patriots, they also included two known Hellenists.[124] The Tirana government instructed all prefectures to reject the request,[125] declaring that, if need be, it was willing to remove Visarion if he refused to resign.[126]

The Gjirokastra eldership rejected the petition for a new congress[127] and requested only Visarion's removal,[128] a request that, in the days that followed, was joined by all the other dioceses. Reverend Pano Çuçi, the pioneer of the Albanian Church's independence in the region, was against Visarion's removal, considering it to be the death knell of the national language.[129] The government, meanwhile, had convinced the archbishop to resign and played a subtle game to present the removal as Visarion's own decision and not the result of machinations. On 27 May, Visarion convened the Holy Synod in order to hand in his resignation.[130] He explained that he considered it necessary to resign from the Church leadership because of fatigue and a need for peace and quiet. He claimed that he had wished to resign before an all-Orthodox congress, as such a body had elected him, but this was not possible. He went on to announce that neither the Albanian state nor its people had forced him to resign and that his decision was not due to any fear that foreign enemies might kill him. The archbishop said that he had been thinking about his resignation since 1932 but was worried about being misunderstood, so he had decided to wait for an opportune time. Visarion explained that his decision would facilitate recognition of the OACA by the Ecumenical Patriarchate and expressed the hope that the government would support the new archbishop, probably even more than he had been supported. Archbishop Visarion entrusted the Church leadership to Kristofor Kisi, the bishop of Korça, assuring him that he would provide all the help and support he could muster. He also promised that he would stay far away from any political or religious affairs.[131]

Bishop Kristofor expressed his sadness about the resignation and assured Visarion that the Synod would always call him a brother and colleague on all matters concerning the welfare of the Church.[132] Visarion delivered his notice of resignation to the Ministry of Justice the very next day,[133] and King Zog decreed it official on 2 June 1936, thus ending Visarion Xhuvani's seven-year leadership of the Church.[134] The Greek press duly noted that the path was now clear and open for granting the tomos of autocephaly.[135]

Although Visarion's resignation was disguised as an uprising led by his fellow bishops, it was, in fact, the direct result of the new period in Albanian–Greek relations that had started in early 1933, just months after power changed hands in Athens. Panagis Tsaldaris was sworn in as the prime minister of Greece, marking the end of Eleftherios Venizelos's career and opening the path towards improved relations with Albania. The ecclesiastical issue, however, was not the only political sticking point between the two countries; the main problem related to the ethnic minorities. In Albania, there were Greeks living in the Pogoni, Dropulli, and Vurgu areas, but a much larger number of Albanians lived in Greece. Albanians had a permanent presence in central Greece, including Athens, where they had lived since the Middle Ages, and were fully integrated into the fabric of Greek society. In the Chameria region, which stretched from the city of Preveza in north-western Greece all the way north to the Albanian border, Albanians constituted the majority. In 1932, in the Chameria region alone, Greek officials reported 86 Greek villages and 99 Albanian villages; of the latter, 49 were Orthodox, 30 were Muslim, and 20 were religiously mixed.[136] Some rights enjoyed by the Albanian minority during the short-lived Pangalos regime had disappeared soon after Pangalos fell from power. Local Greek officials noted that Cham Albanians sought only spiritual bonds with Albania and the preservation of their national language and identity, but to Greek ears even these demands sounded excessive.[137] After it became a kingdom in 1928, Albania sought on several occasions to address the question of the educational rights of Cham Albanians, but Greece had always rejected Albanian requests and constantly avoided the issue. In the 1930s, Albania believed that in order for the two countries to have good relations, it was imperative that Albanians in Greece enjoyed the same rights as Greeks in Albania and received fair compensation for properties seized by Greece. Thus, the issue of the Albanian Orthodox Church was an inseparable part of a wider diplomatic tango, which the two countries had to dance regardless. Anti-Venizelists began to see only one solution: a third Albanian–Greek rapprochement, which reached its peak from mid-1934 to 1937.[138]

Since 1933, relations between the countries had been thawing, with a new trade agreement as the vanguard of stronger bilateral relations. A few months later, Greece approved a plan for compensating Albanian landowners, leaving only two issues unresolved: the rights of the ethnic minorities and the recognition of the Albanian Church. Albania had fulfilled its commitments as far as ethnic minorities were concerned and now it was Greece's turn. In 1935, Greece permitted the teaching of Albanian in Muslim-majority schools in the Chameria region, although not in villages with an Orthodox Albanian population.[139]

Given these circumstances, resolving the ecclesiastical issue was the last move needed to complete the third Albanian–Greek rapprochement. Official talks resumed after November 1936, when Koço Kota was again sworn in as prime minister and made the Patriarchate's recognition of the Albanian Church a key goal of his government. On 6 March 1937, Tirana sent a two-member delegation to Athens to negotiate with His Grace Chrysanthos.[140] The Greek hierarch accepted all Albanian conditions and the parties reached a final agreement on 18 March 1937. The agreement stated that the Church of Albania consisted of four dioceses, as in the present, but only the diocese of Tirana, Durrës, and Elbasan would be a metropolitanate, while the other three would be bishoprics. The hierarch of the capital would be the metropolitan of Tirana, Durrës, and Elbasan, who was also the archbishop of all Albania, while the other three hierarchs would be bishops of the central city of their diocese. The parties appointed His Grace Kristofor Kisi as the new archbishop of all Albania, Evlogji Kurilla as the new bishop of Korça, and Pandeli Kotoko as the new bishop of Gjirokastra. Before His Grace Agathangjel Çamçe could again be appointed bishop of Berat, he was obliged to ask forgiveness of the Patriarchate.[141] Chrysanthos objected to Reverend Vasil Marko's participation in the Holy Synod[142]; Prime Minister Kota, however, insisted that the agreement note that the Church was establishing the Holy Synod on the basis of the existing statute – he did not want to give the impression that Greece had compelled Reverend Vasil's removal.[143] In the final agreement, Greece failed to force through any of its preconditions for talks and had to be satisfied only with the election of Pandeli Kotoko to the Synod, thus leaving the majority of the Synod in the hands of Albanian patriots. The Greek foreign vice-minister, Nikolaos Mavroudis, claimed that this agreement ended all outstanding bilateral issues between the two countries.[144]

However, the internal clashes within the Albanian Orthodox Church had not disappeared. Just prior to Visarion's resignation, Kota had promised the archbishop's seat to Evlogji Kurilla. The Holy Synod, however, elected Kisi as the leader of the Church – a reward for him remaining in Albania during this trying period and reinvolving himself in church affairs. Kota used all his powers of persuasion to get Kurilla to accept the bishopric of

Korça. Appealing to the cleric's patriotism, Kota made him take an oath to Albanian nationalism. At the same time, he subtly left open the possibility that the Church might elect another archbishop once the Patriarchate granted the tomos. Not long after relinquishing the possibility of becoming the leader of the Church, Kurilla wrote to the prime minister claiming that he wished to avoid being an additional obstacle to the resolution of the ecclesiastical issue, which, once the tomos was granted, would be the greatest triumph of Kota's political life.[145] The last matter to be addressed before the tomos could be granted was the official pardon of the Albanian hierarchs. His Grace Agathangjel officially submitted his plea for forgiveness to the Patriarchate on 10 March.[146] Ten days later, the Albanian government sent Reverend Vasil Marko's request for forgiveness to Istanbul by airmail.[147]

Everything was now in place for granting the tomos of autocephaly. The Albanian delegation consisted of the government's representative, Josif Kedhi, and three designated Synod members: Kristofor Kisi, Evlogji Kurilla, and Pandeli Kotoko. All arrived in Istanbul on 28 March, welcomed by the Albanian diaspora there and representatives of the Patriarchate.[148] The talks in Istanbul were purely a formality; on the very day of the delegation's arrival, the Patriarchate's representative and Kedhi signed the agreement that had been drafted in Athens just ten days earlier. The Ecumenical Patriarch, Benjamin I (Veniamin Kyriakou, in office 1936–1946), expressed his satisfaction with what he described as the proper solution to the ecclesiastical question of a newly independent state, which was ruled by a monarch of rare qualities. Benjamin prayed for the country, King Zog, and the noble Albanian nation. The Albanian delegation stressed that Benjamin's name would remain unforgettable in Albanian religious history.[149]

The following day, the Holy Synod of the Ecumenical Patriarchate, acting in accord with the agreement, renamed the Albanian dioceses and placed them under the direct authority of the ecumenical patriarch until the tomos was granted. The Patriarchate delayed granting the tomos for a few days more, to allow time for Kurilla and Kotoko to be ordained. They became deacons on 2 April and, the following day, the Holy Synod of the Patriarchate elected them as bishops. Pandeli Kotoko assumed the name Pandelejmon. Three metropolitans of the Patriarchate ordained both men as priests and archimandrites on 4 April, and as bishops on 11 April.[150] On 12 April, the Holy Synod convened again to approve unanimously *The Patriarchal and Synodical Tomos on the Blessing of the Autocephaly of the Orthodox Church in Albania*. The tomos affirmed the Patriarchate's compassion, care, and willingness to fulfil the needs of Albania's faithful. The Synod accepted the request of Orthodox Albanians based on assurances provided by the state for the full freedom of the Church in Albania. The Albanian consul was seated next to the patriarch during the meeting of the Synod, while the 11 metropolitans of the Holy Synod sat next to the Albanian hierarchs and prominent members of the Albanian Orthodox diaspora in Istanbul. Patriarch Benjamin handed the tomos to Archbishop Kristofor Kisi, who thanked the patriarch and expressed the gratitude of all Albanian Orthodox believers. The Holy Synod of the Ecumenical Patriarchate then issued an official "Letter of Notification to all Orthodox People of Albania", calling for their obedience and submission to the Holy Synod of the OACA.[151]

Visarion, the former archbishop, although he had been willing to reach a conclusive agreement with the Patriarchate, objected bitterly when he learned about the conditions of the tomos. He sent a memo to the Albanian government objecting to the ordination of the bishops in Istanbul and the pardon the Patriarchate had granted to the members of the Albanian Holy Synod. Visarion was afraid that such moves would mislead foreign nations into thinking that the Albanian government had indeed been oppressing Orthodox Albanians since 1929 and could possibly open the door to later conspiracies.[152] However, the insistence of the Albanian government prompted Visarion to apologize to the Patriarchate, which then recognized him as a metropolitan, but only on the condition that he would not lead any Albanian diocese in the future.

Albania's Orthodox elite had been looking forward to the recognition of the Church's autocephaly. Dozens of congratulation letters were exchanged with King Zog, Prime Minister Kota, and Archbishop Kristofor. In addition, Bishop Theofan Noli sent congratulations on the achievement to Prime Minister Kota, his former political rival. Kota responded at once, praising Noli's efforts, "by which the historic work initiated by Your Grace received a happy ending".[153] The Ecumenical Patriarchate informed all the other patriarchates and autocephalous Churches around the world that the tomos of autocephaly had been granted to the Albanian Church. The last paragraph of the letter sent to the patriarchates of Serbia and Romania was, however, different from the others, and for specific reasons. This paragraph stressed that the Church of Constantinople had organized the Church of Albania without regard to ethnic differences and that all ethnic minorities within Albania would enjoy full rights and freedoms, especially in the matter of using their mother tongue in religious services. The Churches of Greece, Cyprus, Alexandria, and Antioch all hailed the tomos.[154]

The Albanian Church, it seemed, had been created along two different yet parallel paths, which eventually converged into one. In the view of the Ecumenical Patriarchate, the OACA was created with the granting of the tomos, even though the tomos was merely confirming a status quo that had existed since 1929. Conversely, the Holy Synod of the Church of Albania viewed the tomos as official recognition of an already existing autocephaly and considered itself the continuation of the previous Holy Synod, which had been established in 1929. Regardless of these doctrinaire internal concerns, on 24 April, King Zog appointed His Grace Kristofor Kisi as metropolitan of Tirana and Durrës and archbishop of all Albania, Evlogji Kurilla as bishop of Korça, and Pandelejmon Kotoko as bishop of Gjirokastra. There was no need for a royal decree for His Grace Agathangjel because his appointment had been announced since 1929.[155] The king signed the decrees the same day the hierarchs returned from Istanbul to the port of Durrës. The following day, which was also Palm Sunday, a liturgy presided over by the Holy Synod took place in Tirana. Bishop Pandelejmon read the tomos of autocephaly and the hierarchs present delivered impassioned speeches to mark the historic moment.[156] Once they had finished in Tirana, the bishops went to care for their respective dioceses during the Holy Week, where thousands of believers welcomed their arrival with special ceremonies and festivities.[157]

The question of the independence of the Albanian Church had been resolved in the best interests of the Albanian state, which had made no concession at all to Greece. Thus, on paper, consolidating the OACA seemed an easy task. However, the actual situation was clearly different for two reasons. First, three out of the four members of the Holy Synod were prominent Albanian nationalist figures, but Pandelejmon Kotoko, although an ethnic Albanian, was a supporter of the Greek government. Furthermore, Kotoko was the leading cleric in the Gjirokastra diocese, the only region in Albania where there was an ethnic Greek minority, which made up a third of the Orthodox population in the diocese. Second, the four leading hierarchs all came from different backgrounds and would inevitably clash with each other. When Kristofor Kisi abandoned the Ecumenical Patriarchate to join the Albanian ecclesiastical movement, he was labelled the first "traitor" of the Patriarchate. Bishop Agathangjel was a Noli supporter who, when it was necessary to side against Visarion or to unite both sides in the interest of the national cause, he sincerely cooperated with Kristofor Kisi. But Kristofor and Agathangjel had never established a solid bond. Bishop Evlogji, although considered a Hellenophile, was in fact an Albanian nationalist who did not wish to harm the Albanian national movement. Nonetheless, the Albanian authorities viewed him as stubborn and he frequently had quarrels with the other Albanian hierarchs. Of all the members of the Holy Synod, only Bishop Agathangjel and Reverend Vasil Marko shared a genuine collaborative relationship.

The effects of Pandelejmon Kotoko's leadership in the diocese of Gjirokastra were evident from the start, despite his pledge to do his best for the Albanian nation.[158] Pandelejmon was widely acknowledged to be on the payroll of the Greek authorities, and his pro-Greek sentiments grew over time, culminating in open propaganda by 1938. In Albanian villages with a Greek ethnic minority Kotoko held the liturgy and delivered sermons only in Greek, which was unacceptable for the local Albanian authorities, who told him quite clearly that the official language of both the state and the Church was Albanian. In these areas, only the liturgy itself could be held in the Greek language; the rest of the service had to be bilingual. This clash encouraged members of the Greek ethnic minority to despise the local authorities and place offensive billboards all over the region without permission. A liturgy in Saranda stirred particular enmity towards the bishop. Saranda's residents were Orthodox Albanians, and the liturgy and sermons held in Greek led to a general outcry against Pandelejmon's *volte-face*.[159]

In May 1938, Bishop Pandelejmon appointed a Greek priest to serve in the Orthodox Albanian village of Saraqinisht, in the Libohova region.[160] The prefect of Gjirokastra (and former prefect of Korça), Nikollaq Zoi, demanded that the Albanian government intervene immediately to appoint an Albanian priest, as the villagers had very clearly requested.[161] Archbishop Kristofor summoned Pandelejmon to Tirana in late July to explain his actions.[162] Zoi reported that, after this visit, the bishop changed his tactics, publicly expressing the need for unity between Orthodox Albanians and Greeks. In secrecy, however, he was working to establish groups and associations that disseminated Greek nationalism among Orthodox Albanian villages. Pandelejmon arranged a meeting with a group of Albanian Orthodox patriots, who he suspected had reported such violations to the authorities, and threatened to curse them if they recounted what they saw or heard.[163] The Albanian Holy Synod had ordered the transferral and even dismissal of several priests involved in anti-Albanian propaganda, and yet, despite this sanction, the Gjirokastra bishop refused to implement these decisions and openly protected the clerics.[164]

In December 1938, Pandelejmon denied allegations from the Holy Synod that he was on the payroll of the Greek consulate in Gjirokastra, claiming that the money he had received through diplomatic channels was an inheritance from a relative who had died in Greece. Kotoko further defended himself by saying that the liturgy in Greek in Albanian villages was performed by priests whose old age prevented them from learning how to conduct the liturgy in Albanian. The Gjirokastra prefecture vehemently denied this, stressing that it was Pandelejmon himself who, with threats, had ordered a number of priests not to officiate in Albanian. The standoff between the local civil authorities and the bishop continued until Italy invaded Albania in April 1939; until then the Albanian government kept him under surveillance and curtailed his efforts to align Orthodox Albanians with Greece.[165]

Another fierce battlefront was the various clashes between the other three bishops of the Holy Synod. During his first meeting as the head of the Korça eldership, on 6 May 1937, Evlogji Kurilla stressed the need to revive the diocese, which he said was in a desperate state.[166] His open contempt and criticism for the manner in which the former bishop of Korça, Archbishop Kristofor, had run the diocese before his arrival, became the flashpoint of an angry clash between Evlogji and the new archbishop. His Grace Evlogji asked time and again for an increase in the Church's budget, which he considered ridiculously low, but Archbishop Kristofor continuously denied his requests.[167] In September 1937, Bishop Evlogji asked Prime Minister Kota to "protect" him from Kristofor's reprisals. The archbishop, to exact revenge, had gone as far as to reduce Evlogji's salary after he took over the Korça diocese.[168] In a stream of letters to Albania's political and religious leadership, His Grace Evlogji accused His Beatitude Kristofor and His Grace Agathangjel of attempting to diminish Korça's reputation and remove him. Waiting in vain for a reply, Evlogji wrote to the king himself in 1938, asking him to personally show greater care and return a number of buildings to the Church, all located within the yard of the Korça Metropolitanate, as religious property. The bishop promised Zog that if the government returned the properties, he would build a Mausoleum of the Great Patriots and Benefactors of Korça, in order to set a good patriotic example.[169]

The local authorities received a number of complaints against Evlogji Kurilla. Although he had made a number of enemies within the Church, including his fellow bishops, the complaints against him were in fact initiated by the Greek consulate in Korça. In 1939, former Archbishop Visarion revealed that Greece had been plotting to have Pandelejmon Kotoko transferred from Gjirokastra to lead the Korça diocese. It was thought that this would ensure that a loyal Hellenist was running Korça. In the eyes of the Greek authorities, Kotoko was no longer necessary in Gjirokastra, where the Greek minority was already large enough.[170] Also, Greece was unhappy with the way Bishop Evlogji had been running the diocese of Korça. Evlogji had not in the slightest acted in favour of Greece; he had conducted the liturgy solely in Albanian and banned the use of Greek in the churches of Korça, thus keeping the patriotic feelings of Albanians very much alive. In addition, he had blocked any attempt by the Greek consulate to place Hellenists on the church eldership and managed to have only conservative, nationalist Albanians elected to it. Yet Evlogji was also in constant conflict with the local Albanian authorities, as his conservative stance dissatisfied some of the Albanian faithful, who desired a more liberal leadership.

Considering his acrimonious relationship with Archbishop Kristofor, as well as Bishop Agathangjel's public aspiration to become the bishop of Korça, Evlogji Kurilla found himself in a difficult position with no apparent supporters either in Korça or anywhere else in the country. The final act in these clashes came in March 1939 at an extraordinary session of the Holy Synod and the Mixed Council of the OACA, which Bishop Evlogji did not attend, citing a lack of financial means. Vasil Mani and Petro Kotoko (Pandelejmon's brother) presented a petition with 200 signatures requesting Evlogji's dismissal. However, the lay representative of Korça on the Mixed Council objected to continuing the meeting without Evlogji, who in turn informed Koço Kota. Kurilla took part in the next meeting of the Holy Synod and replied to all the allegations made against him. In an unusual address to the meeting, His Grace Evlogji accused Pandelejmon Kotoko of being in constant communication with the Greek Foreign Ministry, citing evidence that Kotoko had reported to his Greek superiors during his frequent travels to Athens under the guise of studying law. Kurilla ended his speech by directly addressing Kotoko with an ironic remark: "You want Korça, I know. I will give it to you, but you do not have to insult the science of the law". After the Synod's meeting ended, Evlogji Kurilla was received by King Zog, to whom he presented all the problems he had faced in his struggle to establish a strong national Albanian Church. The king, expressing his full support of the bishop, promised he would take all necessary measures to deal with the situation.[171]

Greece, for its part, almost succeeded in having the trusted Pandelejmon Kotoko enthroned in Korça. Had this occurred, it might have completely changed the balance set by the Albanian nationalist Evlogji Kurilla. The promises of Zog to Bishop Evlogji Kurilla never became a reality, due to the fact that, for Ahmet Zog and Koço Kota, the two undisputed political protagonists of the ecclesiastical issue, their time as rulers of Albania was in its last days. Italy, one of Europe's Great Powers, which had once promised its protection to Albania, had significantly changed its strategy towards the Balkan country. Just a few days after receiving His Grace Evlogji Kurilla, the king received a humiliating ultimatum from their neighbour: Albania had to surrender unconditionally to Fascist Italy. Zog refused. On the morning of 7 April 1939, Italian troops entered Albania, overcoming a small yet resolute Albanian nationalist resistance. In order to keep the Albanian government alive, Zog went into exile, crossing the Albanian–Greek border at Kapshtica. The first day of the invasion was also Good Friday, but not a single religious service was held that day.

The Second World War: Uniatism, Communism, and expansion towards Kosovo

Italy's invasion of Albania had been triggered by rivalry between Rome and Berlin. Five months earlier, without warning, Adolf Hitler had ordered the invasion of Czechoslovakia. His Axis ally, Benito Mussolini of Italy, felt neglected. So in order to restore the prestige of the Italian Empire, Mussolini decided to carry out a similar attack, and Albania was the easiest victim. European governments had long recognized Italy's special position vis-à-vis Albania, which had been cemented by the bilateral pacts signed in Tirana in 1926 and 1927. After the invasion of 1939, King Zog sought the support of the Great Powers, but, as Mussolini had foreseen, they turned him down. Thus, under the instructions of the Albanian parliament – which convened in Korça as Tirana was now under occupation – King Zog, Queen Geraldine, their two-day-old son, Leka, and the royal entourage left Albania via the Kapshtica border crossing, going first to Greece and then to Turkey. The Albanian government's regular forces organized a small resistance at all ports, but, given the military superiority of Fascist Italy, they had little chance of success. Italian troops entered Tirana on the morning of 8 April, Holy Saturday, and on Easter Day organized a lavish reception to mark "the beginning of the Fascist era" in Albania. A few days later, a general Albanian assembly convened by the Fascist invaders dethroned King Zog and conferred the title king of Albanians to King Victor Emmanuel III of Italy. The assembly also established a new, puppet government led by Shefqet Vërlaci, while Victor Emmanuel appointed as viceroy Francesco Jacomoni, who until then had been Italy's ambassador to Albania.

The affairs of the OACA were of little interest to the new rulers during the first few months of occupation. The Fascists forced the leaders of the four major religious communities to hail the invasion. Among them, His

Beatitude Kristofor Kisi gave an interview for *Giornale d'Italia*, in which he said that the decision to unite the two crowns "was living proof that the Albanians welcomed Italy's glorious armies as brothers and friends, not as invaders".[172] A small segment of the Albanian clergy, especially among the Catholic community, heartily welcomed the occupation. His Grace Visarion Xhuvani was one of the very few Orthodox clerics to approve the Fascist invasion. He met with Francesco Jacomoni and was a member of the delegation that handed King Zog's Crown of Skanderbeg to Victor Emmanuel. By contrast, His Grace Evlogji Kurilla was a fierce opponent of the invasion and urged armed resistance against the Italians. After King Zog left Albania and the Italian troops progressed towards Korça, Kurilla asked the Greek consulate to call on the Greek army to cross the border to fight the Fascists and liberate Korça and Albania.[173] At the time of the invasion, however, Kurilla sent a congratulatory telegram to Mussolini, writing that Orthodox Albanians were excited to see the two flags waving side by side.[174] Nonetheless, Bishop Evlogji was the first "victim" of the new regime. In September 1939, he travelled to Athens for health reasons, as he had fractured his leg during a tour of the diocese. The Holy Synod granted him permission to travel, but after he crossed the border, the puppet government in Tirana informed him that he could no longer return.[175] This abrupt removal of Evlogji from Albania's religious scene was the result of clashes he had had with certain members of the Holy Synod before the Fascist invasion. Now, with the occupation, these hierarchs found the perfect opportunity to achieve what they had planned since March: Evlogji Kurilla's permanent expulsion from Albania. The Italian government tried to persuade Bishop Evlogji to resign his post, and even promised him the leadership of the Church of Dodecanese, but he refused.[176]

The Second World War officially began in September 1939, with Germany's invasion of Poland and Hitler's declaration of war against France and Great Britain. These international developments made Fascist Italy greedy for further expansion in the Mediterranean region. In late 1940, with the support of the puppet government in Tirana and attempting to involve as many Albanians in its military as possible, Fascist Italy used the violated rights of the Chameria Albanians as a pretext for invading Greece. The Italian–Greek war began officially on 28 October 1940, when Greece rejected Mussolini's ultimatum, just as King Zog had done a year and a half earlier. The Fascists' plan failed, however, and an overwhelming majority of the drafted Albanian foot soldiers defected. The Greek troops not only repelled the Italians but also occupied a large part of southern Albania in just a few weeks. Greece invaded Korça on 22 November, and captured Pogradec, Gjirokastra, and Himara within a month. A major, but unsuccessful, Italian counteroffensive began in March 1941, with Italian troops only managing to recover Himara. The situation changed completely after Germany attacked Greece on the Greek–Bulgarian frontier. Italian troops re-entered Korça on 14 April 1941, and a week later, crossed the Albanian border into Greece.

In the midst of these disorienting events, the brief invasion of Albanian territory by Greek forces in an area Greece considered Northern Epirus was of telling importance. First, it clearly showed that Greece's permanent goal was the area's annexation, a target that its interwar foreign policy had cunningly managed to conceal. Second, it confirmed that after nearly 30 years of Albanian independence the Hellenist movement was insignificant. Orthodox Albanians refused to cooperate with the idea of Greece's annexation of "Northern Epirus", even if they continued to sympathize with the Greek nation.[177] Pandelejmon Kotoko, the bishop of Gjirokastra, was an exception and held a religious service to welcome the Greek troops.[178] A few days later, on 8 December 1940, he sent a telegram to Chrysanthos, who had now become the archbishop of Athens, congratulating him "with fiery enthusiasm" on the "liberation of the diocesan centre and the surrounding districts". Chrysanthos replied that he was deeply touched. So when Italy reoccupied Gjirokastra in April 1941, it was no surprise that Kotoko fled with the retreating Greek army, ending up in Athens.[179] Kotoko was one of only two Albanian Orthodox priests who welcomed the Greek troops, the other being Reverend Sotir Ilia, a 65-year-old priest from the village of Dardha in the Korça region. When his parish's Albanian congregation started criticizing his actions, Ilia declared that the churches in Korça were now Greek.[180]

These were the only two cases of open pro-Greek propaganda during the time of Greece's control over southern Albania. The fact that, of the nearly 400 priests in Albania, only 2 betrayed the nation by holding welcoming ceremonies for an invading army or cooperating with occupiers shows that national consciousness in the Albanian Church was solid. It also shows that, overall, the Albanian clergy perceived Greek attempts to influence ecclesiastical matters as a greater threat to their national identity than Italy's military invasion. At the Holy Synod's meeting of May 1941, Archbishop Kristofor hailed the "the brave, manly, and patriotic attitude of the Orthodox element in Albania during the Greek invasion".[181]

The Albanian Orthodox Church faced yet another serious threat during this turbulent time. Archbishop Kristofor tried in every possible way to protect the Orthodox Church from foreign influences and especially from Uniate propaganda, which gained noticeable ground after the Italian invasion. The influence of the Uniate movement had been sporadic before the recognition of autocephaly, but, from 1940 onwards, Italy began to give substantial support to yet another schism. From Italy's perspective, it would be politically beneficial if the OACA was placed under the Vatican's authority. The Albanian General Directorate of Police, now under Fascist leadership, ordered all local authorities to work towards this goal slowly and carefully, using the right lay people but bypassing Albanian public figures.[182]

The diocese of Gjirokastra was an opportune place for Italian officials to test the new policy. The local authorities declared that by depriving Orthodox believers of their religious services, the diocese had ecclesiastically abandoned the Christians in the area.[183] Pandelejmon Kotoko's insolent and biased political activity, almost completely evading his religious obligations in the process, had led his unguided flock towards Uniatism. On 16 August 1939, Viceroy Francesco Jacomoni reported that there was a discernible effort in the Orthodox Church to lean towards Uniatism, a drive found mainly among those Church leaders with a good understanding of the country's multifaceted political situation. Jacomoni asked for Archbishop Kristofor's opinion on the matter. His Beatitude replied delicately that Uniatism was a long-standing goal for Orthodox Albanians.[184] In September 1939, the archbishop reported that three of the five members of the Albanian Holy Synod were in favour of Uniatism, namely, the archbishop himself, His Grace Agathangjel, and Reverend Vasil Marko, while Evlogji Kurilla and Pandelejmon Kotoko opposed it. Despite the latter two bishops' opposition, relentless pressure from the Italian authorities forced both Kurilla and Kotoko to promise to review their reasoning on the matter.[185] In 1941, a delegation of the OACA, led by the Bishop Agathangjel of Berat, took part in the meeting of the Synod of Arbëreshë Uniate bishops at the Abbey of Grottaferrata near Rome.[186] This was the first time an Albanian Orthodox bishop had been a guest of this Uniate monastery.[187]

Nevertheless, the actions of the Orthodox hierarchs show clearly that they tried at all costs to avoid putting themselves under the Vatican's jurisdiction. In an attempt to appease his superiors, Jacomoni had listed even Bishop Evlogji as a supporter of Uniatism, despite him being a fierce opponent when he was bishop of Korça. In order to postpone and obstruct Italian efforts to accelerate the process of Orthodox Albanians conversion to Uniatism, the Albanian hierarchs put extravagant conditions on the negotiation table. Archbishop Kristofor explained to the Italian authorities that for such a move to succeed the Orthodox Church would need an annual subsidy of 450,000 gold francs, or 2.8 million Italian lira. This astonishing sum was in fact five times the annual subsidy received by the Roman Catholic Church in Albania, while the most the Italians were willing to offer the OACA was only 850,000 lira per year. Kristofor replied that he would discuss the numbers again with the Holy Synod, thus gaining valuable time and even further postponing the decision. Several Uniate missions spread throughout Albania trying to gain as many followers as possible. Yet despite the cat-and-mouse game, the Vatican's representatives in the country continued to maintain good relations with the Orthodox leaders. And it is clear why: at their peak, the Uniates in Albania did not exceed 400 believers, or 0.15 per cent of the Orthodox.[188]

By early 1941, the OACA had only two bishops left: Archbishop Kristofor and Bishop Agathangjel. Both the Italian government and the Albanian puppet government pressured the OACA to appoint Uniate clerics from Italy to the dioceses of Gjirokastra and Korça, in the hope of facilitating the spread of Uniatism. The three remaining members of the Albanian Holy Synod – Archbishop Kristofor Kisi, Bishop Agathangjel Çamçe, and Reverend Vasil Marko – decided to act quickly.[189] In order to secure and protect Albanian Orthodoxy in one of its most important dioceses, representing two-thirds of the country's Orthodox believers, they appointed Agathangjel

Çamçe, the bishop of Berat, to lead the diocese of Korça.[190] Then in November, in an unexpected move, the Holy Synod appointed Visarion Xhuvani as metropolitan of Berat, Vlora, and Kanina. In this way, despite his promise four years earlier, when he resigned as archbishop, not to take any political or religious position in the future, Xhuvani again became a member of the Holy Synod. His initial support for the Italians, however, should not be seen as approval of their promotion of Uniatism. In his battle against the spread of Uniatism, Visarion remained the same old fighter he had been when he led the Orthodox Church. In July 1941, in an effort to complete the Synod with four devoted Orthodox members and put an end to Italian pressure to appoint Uniate clerics in the vacant bishoprics, the Holy Synod elected Ilia Banushi, a theologian from Shkodra, for the last available seat. Just a few days before his election, Kristofor told Banushi that Jacomoni had been pressuring him to fill the vacant seat in Gjirokastra with a Uniate bishop. But by electing Banushi instead, the archbishop felt that his ordination would "save Orthodoxy from Uniatism". The Italian authorities instantly rejected this move. But after Kristofor's convincing persistence, they relented, agreeing to Banushi's election on the condition that the Holy Synod appoint him only as an assistant bishop and not as the ruling bishop of Gjirokastra. Kristofor and Agathangjel ordained Ilia Banushi as a deacon on 30 January 1942, the following day as a priest and archimandrite, and on 1 February 1942, he was elected as assistant bishop of Apollonia under the ecclesiastical name Irine.[191]

By such manoeuvres the leaders of the OACA were able to protect their hard-won institution, not only from Greece's assertive aims during the Greco-Italian war, but also from the much-despised Italian designs throughout the occupation of Albania. The new hierarchy of Albania's Orthodox Church, composed of Archbishop Kristofor, Bishops Visarion, Agathangjel, and Irine, and Reverend Vasil Marko, resourcefully resisted Uniate pressure right up to Italy's capitulation in September 1943 and its subsequent withdrawal from Albania.

Another major change had occurred in the region by the time Italy reoccupied Albania after the Greco-Italian war of 1941. The invasion of the Balkans by German and Italian troops brought about a shift in the peninsula's volatile political configuration. Reshaping boundaries to serve their own interests, the two Axis powers expanded the national borders of Albania to include parts of Yugoslavia inhabited largely by ethnic Albanians. These areas included most of the Kosovo region (excluding the towns of Mitrovica, Podujeva, Kaçanik, and Ferizaj); the towns of Ulqin, Hoti, Gruda, Plav, and Guci, from Montenegro; the towns of Rozhaje and Novi Pazar in the Sandžak region; and the towns of Tetovo, Gostivar, Dibra, Kërçova, Struga, and Prespa, from Yugoslav Macedonia. Skopje, in Macedonia, and Kaçanik, in Kosovo, and the surrounding territories were annexed by Bulgaria, while Mitrovica remained a self-administered entity under German occupation. Chameria did not join Albania but was administered by the German authorities based in Athens. Albania officially named its newly annexed territories "the Free Lands". While these territories were overwhelmingly populated by Albanian Muslims and Catholics, there were a small number of Orthodox Albanians living in the Reka area near Gostivar. However, with the 150,000 Orthodox Serbs, Montenegrins, Vlachs, and Bulgarians living in these Free Lands as ethnic minorities, the overall number of Orthodox believers in the newly defined Albania increased considerably.[192] Fejzi Alizoti, the Albanian minister responsible for the administration of the Free Lands, ordered on 28 August 1941 that the authorities must seek the opinion of the OACA on all issues related to Orthodox churches and monasteries and, for the time being, must maintain the status quo with regard to these religious institutions.[193]

The Orthodox priests of Dibra and Tetovo, who declared themselves to be Bulgarians, expressed their willingness to join the OACA as soon as possible.[194] Nor did the Albanian government have any problems integrating the other ethnic minorities, with the sole exception of the Serbian population in Kosovo. Even among the Serbs, however, the Albanian authorities soon found supportive priests who were willing to cooperate with the OACA and the Albanian government. From the very beginning of the Fascist Italian occupation, Reverend Simon, from Rahovec in Kosovo, as well as a number of other priests in the area, expressed their loyalty to Albania and preached the need for peaceful coexistence with the Albanians and obedience to the state authorities. Reverend Simon, citing his humble efforts for Albania and the Albanian Orthodox Church, petitioned the Albanian authorities to appoint him as the abbot of the Gračanica Monastery in Prishtina, a request the OACA fulfilled.[195]

The Albanian government appointed Koço Tasi as high inspector of the Kosovo region, for two main reasons: Tasi was not only a staunch Albanian nationalist who could oversee Kosovo's integration with the rest of Albania; he was a well-known conservative Orthodox believer, who could make a genuine attempt to integrate the Serbian Orthodox minority into the OACA. Tasi managed to convince Bishop Serafim Jovanović of the diocese of Prizren, which included all of Kosovo, to put the diocese under the authority of the Albanian Orthodox Church. His Grace Serafim arrived in Tirana in early June 1942, accompanied by Milan Trifunović, a priest based in Prizren. During his participation in the meetings of the Holy Synod as its newest member, His Grace Serafim expressed his obedience to both the Albanian state and the Albanian Church.[196] He also presented some ideas about improving relations between the different religious groups in the Free Lands.[197]

The expansion of Albania's territory required a new organization of the OACA.[198] On 13 July 1942, only six months after his ordination, the Holy Synod appointed Irine Banushi as the new bishop of Struga.[199] The diocese of Prizren was also expanded to include the provinces of Rozhaje, Plav, Guci, Tuz, and Ulqin. In addition, the Holy Synod established the diocese of Peshkopia, created by uniting the deaneries of Dibra, Rostusha, Gostivar,

Kërçova, and Tetovo. On 7 April 1944, after a long delay, the Albanian parliament finally approved a new religious law to reflect these territorial rearrangements, a law the Orthodox Church had drafted in early 1943. It allowed the OACA to oversee the pastoral care of seven dioceses. The metropolitanate of Tirana and Durrës included the deaneries of Tirana, Durrës, Elbasan, Pogradec, Gora-Mokra, Kavaja, and Shkodra. The diocese of Korça was composed of the deaneries of Korça, Devoll, Kolonja, Përmet, and Voskopoja. The diocese of Gjirokastra saw no change in its organization, and, as before, included the deaneries of Gjirokastra, Libohova, Delvina, Saranda, and Himara. The same was true for the diocese of Berat, which continued to comprise the deaneries of Berat, Vlora, Levan, and Lushnja. The diocese of Prizren had no deaneries, while the newly established diocese of Peshkopia was composed of the deaneries of Peshkopia and Golloborda, Dibra and Rostusha, Gostivar, Tetovo, and Kërçova. Finally, the Diocese of Struga had two deaneries: Struga and Prespa. The expanded Albanian Holy Synod was now composed of Archbishop Kristofor, the metropolitan of Tirana; Visarion, the metropolitan of Berat; Agathangjel, the bishop of Korça; Serafim, the bishop of Prizren; Irine, the bishop of Struga; and Reverend Vasil Marko. This wartime period also saw an increase in clerical publishing, including journals, translations, children's publications, and religious periodicals.[200]

After Fascist Italy's capitulation in September 1943, Nazi Germany invaded and swiftly occupied all of Albania. The Albanian nationalist forces now ended the armed resistance in which they had been engaged during the Italian occupation. With the approval of the new Nazi occupiers, several prominent Albanian nationalists began governing Albania, alongside the Germans. Although German troops were stationed throughout the country, the Albanian nationalists in power declared Albania a de jure neutral and independent state, hoping that this would guarantee an independent, ethnic Albania within the enlarged borders set in 1941. Meanwhile, a faction of the Albanian National Front remained silently opposed to the Nazi-supported regime and the Albanian Legalists, who still supported King Zog even though he was in exile, continued to fight among the nationalist ranks. The main armed resistance in Albania against the Nazis was the Anti-Fascist National Liberation Front, organized by Communist forces. The Communists were fighting not only against German troops but also against the forces of the Albanian puppet government.

The Albanian Orthodox Church leaders viewed Communism as a genuine threat, assuming that if the Albanian Communists came to power after the war, they would follow the Marxist principle, "Religion is the opium of the people". For the Orthodox leaders, the Soviet Union was a frightening example of this, as it had expelled dozens of priests and replaced the Holy Synod of the Moscow Patriarchate with a group of pro-Communist clerics. The Soviet Union had nationalized all the properties of the Church, persecuted huge numbers of believers because of their religious affiliation, and virtually destroyed the Church's influence in society. Thus, if the Communists came to power, the OACA would be facing the challenge of survival; the question would no longer be how to preserve the Church's Albanian patriotic nature, but how to preserve Orthodoxy itself.

Nonetheless, there were also some Orthodox clerics within the ranks of the Albanian Communists. The former abbot of the St Marina's Monastery in Llëngë, Reverend Dhimitër Kokoneshi, a widowed priest, joined the Communist partisans.[201] During the reign of King Zog, the Albanian authorities suspected that Kokoneshi was spying on behalf of the Yugoslavs but never had enough proof to charge him. Kokoneshi joined the Albanian Communists during the anti-fascist resistance, taking an active part in battles, which earned him the nickname "the priest with a gun in his belt".[202] Another cleric who took part in the anti-fascist resistance was Archimandrite Pais Vodica, the former dean of Kolonja. Vodica, a clergyman with a renowned religious and patriotic reputation, was chosen as a delegate to the Congress of Përmet in 1944, which established the controlling Anti-Fascist National Liberation Council as the future Communist government of Albania.[203]

Communism's anti-religious stance, however, led most clergy and hierarchs to support the fiercely the anti-Communist nationalist forces. For some, such as Kristofor Kisi and Visarion Xhuvani, the ideals and goals of the nationalist forces represented the same ideology they themselves had espoused their entire lives. But, except for a very few cases in the Greek-minority villages, where some clerics supported the Greek nationalist forces, the overwhelming majority of Orthodox priests in Albania either remained impartial during the Second World War or supported the Albanian puppet government and other nationalist troops.[204] By 1944, instead of a war of liberation, the anti-fascist struggle was turning into an all-out Albanian civil war. In the midst of this carnage between his fellow Albanians, His Beatitude Kristofor Kisi sent out a special homily to all believers, in which he referenced a letter from the Albanian minister of culture, Rexhep Mitrovica, who appealed for the preservation of the national conscience against the evil tide of civil war. Kisi wrote: "Our religious capacity and love for the homeland impels us to preach on behalf of brotherhood and cooperation between all our fellow compatriots against the rule of anarchy, which is to the detriment of our interests".[205] His Grace Visarion Xhuvani, the metropolitan of Berat, appealed to all believers for full cooperation and urged them to oppose the civil war. Visarion campaigned against the tragic discord among his people in the 16 meetings he held in December 1943 in Berat, Vlora, Narta, and Fier. He stressed the need for national unity, progress in the country, and obedience to the Albanian government authorities. Visarion described his extensive tour against the civil war as his personal duty,

"...as a human being, an Albanian, a theologian, and a prelate, but also as the spiritual shepherd in Berat, Vlora, and their surroundings and, at the same time, because I feel the pain of all Albanians who are caught in this war".[206]

The OACA had expanded into the new territories, even holding the liturgy in two languages in areas inhabited by Serbs or Bulgarians. By the end of 1944, the OACA was more consolidated than ever before, and the ecclesiastical struggle of nearly three decades seemed to have ended in triumph. However, just as Visarion Xhuvani and Kristofor Kisi had feared, once the Nazi invaders had been defeated, Albania shrunk again as Yugoslavia reoccupied Kosovo, and the Communist forces succeeded in winning the civil war in Albania. Now, the OACA would be facing a new danger: Communist atheism.

Figure 6.1 Bishop Agathangjel Çamçe.

Figure 6.2 Bishop Evlogji Kurilla.

Figure 6.3 Prime Minister Koço Kota, the Political Leader of the Albanian Orthodox Movement.

Figure 6.4 Prime Minister Mustafa Merlika Kruja at the Deçani Monastery, after the Incorporation of Kosovo into Albania, and the Expansion of the Albanian Church to it.

Figure 6.5 Holy Synod after the Recognition of Autocephaly – Archbishop Kisi and Bishops Çamçe, Kurilla, and Kotoko.

Notes

1 Kondis, *Elinismos III*, 167: IDAYE, f. A/22/1β, no. 4845, Metropolitan Athenagoras to the Holy Synod of Greece's Church, 27 May 1929.
2 *Gazeta e Korçës [Korça Gazette]*, 29 August 1929, 1.
3 "Qeveria s'ka bërë asnjë ndërhyrje për marrëveshje me Patriarkanën [The Government Has Made No Intervention for an Agreement with the Patriarchate]", *Zëri i Korçës [Voice of Korça]*, 6 August 1929, 1.
4 AMFA, Y. 1929, f. 850, 247–249, Athens Embassy to MFA, 26 November 1929.
5 AQSH, F. 152 "MIA", Y. 1929, f. 119/1, Authorization, 19 October 1929.
6 Tasoudis, *Biographical Memoirs*, 61–63.
7 AMFA, Athens Embassy to MFA, 26 November 1929, quoted.
8 Tasoudis, *Biographical Memoirs*, 61.
9 Kondis, *Elinismos IV*, 54–64: IDAYE, Y. 1930–1931, f. A/4/I, no. 1083, Tirana Embassy to Greek MFA, 12 July 1930.
10 Kondis, *Elinismos IV*, 49–53: IDAYE, Y. 1930–1931, f. A/4/I, without number, Note of the First Political Office of the Greek MFA regarding the Albanian Church issue, 12 June 1930.
11 Meta, "The Greek-Albanian Debate", 37–61. Kondis, *Elinismos IV*, 49–53: IDAYE, Note.
12 Kondis, *Elinismos IV*, 54–64: IDAYE, Tirana Embassy to Greek MFA, 12 July 1930, quoted.

13 Kondis, *Elinismos IV*, 49–53: IDAYE, Note.
14 Kondis, *Elinismos IV*, 54–64: IDAYE, Tirana Embassy to Greek MFA, 12 July 1930, quoted.
15 AQSH, F. 152 "MIA", Y. 1929, f. 119/1, MIA to Prefectures, 24 December 1929.
16 Kondis, *Elinismos IV*, 49–53: IDAYE, Note.
17 Kondis, *Elinismos IV*, 44–46: IDAYE, Y. 1930–1931, f. A/4/I, no. 3461, Greek MFA to Tirana Embassy, 19 March 1930.
18 Kondis, *Elinismos IV*, 54–64: IDAYE, Tirana Embassy to Greek MFA, 12 July 1930, quoted.
19 Kondis, *Elinismos IV*, 49–53: IDAYE, Note.
20 Kondis, *Elinismos IV*, 54–64: IDAYE, Tirana Embassy to Greek MFA, 12 July 1930, quoted.
21 Kondis, *Elinismos IV*, 71–82: IDAYE, Y. 1930–1931, f. A/4/I, no. 11781, Tirana Embassy to Greek MFA, 9 September 1930.
22 Ibid.
23 AMFA, Extra F. 3, f. 300, 1–2, MFA Memo, no date.
24 Meta, "The Greek-Albanian Debate", 37–61.
25 Kondis, *Elinismos IV*, 103: IDAYE, Y. 1930–1931, f. A/4/I, no. 5336, Tirana Embassy to Greek MFA, 14 April 1931.
26 Kondis, *Elinismos IV*, 115: IDAYE, Y. 1930–1931, f. A/4/I, no. 11220, Greek MFA to Press Office, 3 September 1931.
27 AMFA, Y. 1931, f. 70, 1–11, Memo for Vasil Avrami.
28 "Deklarata VI [Declaration VI]", *Kisha Kombëtare [The National Church]*, 9 November 1930, 1.
29 OACA, *1929 Statute.*
30 "Qendra e Kishës Orthodhokse Autoqefale Vendoset në Tiranë [Tirana Becomes the Center of the Autocephalous Orthodox Church]", *Zëri i Korçës [Voice of Korça]*, 8 April 1930, 1.
31 "Kryesia e Kishës Orthodhokse në Mitropolin e Shenjtë [The Orthodox Church's Leadership in the Holy Metropolitanate]", *Zëri i Korçës [Voice of Korça]*, 23 December 1930, 1.
32 The other members were Leonidha Nishku, Kristo Luarasi, Krisanth Janku, Marko Hobdari, and Gavril Lasku. "Dhimogjerondia e re e Komunitetit Orthodhoks të Tiranës [The New Eldership of Tirana's Orthodox Community]", *Zëri i Korçës [Voice of Korça]*, 21 January 1930, 2.
33 "Transferimi i Kryesis së Kishës Orthodhokse Autoqefale në Kryeqytet [The Leadership of the Autocephalous Orthodox Church Transfers to the Capital]", *Zëri i Korçës [Voice of Korça]*, 12 April 1930, 1.
34 "Një apel për regjistrimin popullit orthodhoks shqipëtar [An Appeal towards the Albanian Orthodox People to Complete the Census]", *Zëri i Korçës [Voice of Korça]*, 20 May 1930, 1.
35 Bërxholli, *The Orthodox Social Community in Albania*, 48–52.
36 AMFA, Y. 1932, f. 268, 2, OACA to MIA, 15 April 1932.
37 "Declaration VI", 1.
38 AQSH, F. 155 "MJ", f. VIII-93, 1, OACA Budget, no date.
39 "Declaration VI", 1.
40 Xhuvani, *Works*, 97–98.
41 *Zëri i Korçës [Voice of Korça]*, 5 November 1929, 4.
42 "Sinodhi i Shenjtë dhe vepërimet e tij [The Holy Synod and Its Actions]", *Zëri i Korçës [Voice of Korça]*, 12 November 1929, 4.
43 Kondis, *Elinismos IV*, 43–44: IDAYE, Y. 1929–1930, F. A/22/iβ, no. 2665, Tirana Embassy to Greek MFA, 17 February 1930.
44 Xhuvani, *Works*, 93–102.
45 "Qarkore [Memo]", *Kisha Kombëtare [The National Church]*, 9 November 1930, 2.

46 Xhuvani, *Works*, 75–76.
47 "Një mas'e urtë e Sinodhit të Shenjtë [The Holy Synod's Wise Move]", *Gazeta e Re [New Gazette]*, 22 May 1929, 2.
48 "The Holy Synod Ends its Congregation", 3.
49 Xhuvani, *Works*, 129–130.
50 Xhuvani, *Works*, 75–99.
51 "Formohet një kor kishëtar në Tiranë [A Church Choir Established in Tirana]", *Gazeta e Re [New Gazette]*, 25 May 1929, 1.
52 Xhuvani, *Works*, 75–76.
53 Beduli, *Church and Culture*, 37–59.
54 AMFA, Y. 1930, f. 327, 9, MIA to MFA, August 1930.
55 Kristofor Beduli, *Dhimitër Beduli* (Tirana: OACA, 1999).
56 Kristofor Beduli, *Saqellar Atë Petro Doçi [Reverend Petro Doçi]* (Tirana: Neraida, 2006), 10–11.
57 Kristofor Beduli, *Episkop Irine Banushi: Martir i Kishës Orthodhokse Autoqefale të Shqipërisë [Bishop Irine Banushi: A Martyr of the Orthodox Autocephalous Church of Albania]* (Tirana: OACA, 2000), 10.
58 Xhuvani, *Works*, 119–120.
59 Kondis, *Elinismos IV*, 43–44: IDAYE, Tirana Embassy to Greek MFA, 17 February 1930, quoted.
60 "Kthimi i Episkopit dhe i Delegatëve të Korçës [The Return of Korça's Bishop and Delegates]", *Gazeta e Re [New Gazette]*, 30 July 1929, 3.
61 AQSH, F. 152 "MIA", Y. 1929, f. 119/1, Gendarmerie Command to MIA, 17 September 1929.
62 Meta, "Efforts to Consolidate", 100.
63 AQSH, F. 152 "MIA", Y. 1930, f. 187, f. 110, OACA to MJ, 22 July 1930.
64 Kondis, *Elinismos IV*, 82–84: IDAYE, Y. 1930, f. A/22/Ìβ, no. 11508, Korça Consulate to Tirana Embassy, 22 September 1930.
65 AQSH, F. 152 "MIA", Y. 1931, f. 193, 31, Records, 24–26 July 1931.
66 AQSH, F. 152 "MIA", Y. 1931, f. 193, 1, Korça Prefecture to MIA, 2 May 1931.
67 Kondis, *Elinismos IV*, 148–150: IDAYE, Y. 1931–1932, f. A/4, no. 5800, Korça Consulate to Tirana Embassy, 10 May 1932.
68 Kastriot Dervishi, *Shërbimi Sekret Shqiptar 1922–1944 [The Albanian Secret Service 1922–1944]* (Tirana: 55, 2007), 146.
69 AQSH, F. 152 "MIA", Y. 1931, f. 848, 3–4, Vlora Prefecture to MIA, 16 May 1931.
70 AQSH, F. 152 "MIA", Y. 1934, f. 164, 133, Himara Subprefecture to Vlora Prefecture, 6 October 1934.
71 AQSH, F. 152 "MIA", Y. 1934, f. 164, 138, Himara Subprefecture to Vlora Prefecture, 19 October 1934.
72 AMFA, Y. 1933, f. 485, 12, the OACA to King Zog I, 12 May 1933.
73 Beqir Meta, "Çështja e minoriteteve në Shqipëri, në Lidhjen e Kombeve në vitet '30 [The Issue of Minorities in Albania in the League of Nations in the 1930s]", *Studime historike [Historical Studies] 3–4* (2006):150.
74 AQSH, F. 152 "MIA", Y. 1929, f. 119/1, Korça Prefecture to MIA, 19 September 1929.
75 AQSH, F. 155 "MJ", Y. 1931, f. 172, OACA to MJ, 16 May 1931.
76 AQSH, F. 155 "MJ", Y. 1931, f. 172, MJ to OACA, 18 May 1931.
77 AQSH, F. 152 "MIA", Y. 1935, f. 471, 4, Elbasan Prefecture to MIA, 2 May 1935.
78 AQSH, F. 155 "MJ", Y. 1931, f. 170, 1–3, OACA to MJ, 17 December 1931.
79 During this period, the Roman Catholic pope increased efforts to spread Uniatism throughout the Balkans, including Greece, where some churches became Uniate in 1925. "Η Ορθόδοξος Ανατολική Εκκλησία και οι Ουνιταί [The Eastern Orthodox Church and the Uniates]", *Απόστολος Ανδρέας [Apostle Andrea]*, 1 May 1925, 1–2.

80 Murzaku, *The Basilian Monks*, 138–140.
81 AMFA, Y. 1928, f. 335, 1, "Le Temps" Newspaper, 6 November 1928; "Mbi desertimin e priftnavet të Shën Kollit [On the Desertion of Saint Nicholas Sanctuary Priests]", *Gazeta e Re [New Gazette]*, 2 November 1928, 3.
82 "Një deklaratë e Kryepiskopit [A Statement from the Archbishop]", *Gazeta e Re [New Gazette]*, 28 August 1929, 2.
83 Murzaku, *The Basilian Monks*, 141–142.
84 AQSH, F. 152 "MIA", Y. 1929, f. 119/1, OACA to MIA, 17 September 1929.
85 AQSH, F. 152 "MIA", Y. 1929, f. 119/1, MIA to Elbasan Prefecture, 18 September 1929. AQSH, F. 152 "MIA", Y. 1929, f. 119/1, OACA to MIA, 3 October 1929.
86 Kondis, *Elinismos IV*, 222–223, IDAYE, Tirana Embassy to Greek MFA, 13 November 1934; and Kondis, *Elinismos IV*, 224–225, IDAYE, f. A/4/2, no. 20245, Embassy to Greek MFA, 22 January 1935.
87 Kondis, *Elinismos IV*, 226–227, IDAYE, f. A/4/2, 20312, Tirana Embassy to Greek MFA, 3 April 1935.
88 Kondis, *Elinismos IV*, 226–227, IDAYE, f. A/4/9/I, 9421, Epirus Governor to Greek MFA, 17 May 1935.
89 AMFA, Y. 1931, f. 219, 44, London Embassy to MFA, 10 September 1931.
90 AMFA, Y. 1932, f. 271, 4, MFA to Bucharest Consulate, 11 May 1932.
91 AMFA, Y. 1932, f. 271, 6, Bucharest Consulate to MFA, 27 May 1932.
92 AQSH, F. 136 "Durrës Deanery", f. 93, 1, Memo, 9 March 1933.
93 AMFA, Y. 1932, f. 271, 23–24, Sofia Embassy to MFA, 7 June 1932.
94 Xhuvani, *Works*, 120–127.
95 AMFA, Y. 1933, f. 487, 3, Sofia Embassy to MFA, 25 September 1933.
96 "Ministrat e Huaj [The Foreign Ministers]", *Predikimi [Preaching]*, 7 May 1934, 1.
97 AMFA, Y. 1933, f. 496, 2, Press Office, "Kisha shqiptare dhe marrëdhëniet greko-shqiptare [The Albanian Church and Greek-Albanian Relations]", 1 March 1933.
98 AMFA, Y. 1933, f. 496, 3, Hatzikyriakos to His Grace Visarion, 28 March 1933.
99 AMFA, "The Albanian Church and Greek-Albanian Relations", 1 March 1933, quoted.
100 AMFA, Y. 1933, f. 496, 11, Refutation from the OACA, 5 May 1933.
101 AMFA, Y. 1933, f. 496, 12, *Athinaika Nea [Athens News]*, 31 May 1933.
102 AMFA, Y. 1932, f. 99, 1, Athens Embassy to MFA, 9 July 1932.
103 Kondis, *Elinismos IV*, 49–53: IDAYE, Note, quoted.
104 AQSH, F. 136 "Durrës Deanery", f. 71, 1, Memo, 21 January 1933.
105 AQSH, F. 136 "Durrës Deanery", f. 71, 3, Memo, 23 January 1933.
106 AQSH, F. 136 "Durrës Deanery", f. 71, 4, Memo, 24 January 1933.
107 AQSH, F. 136 "Durrës Deanery", f. 71, 5, Memo, 25 January 1933.
108 Glavinas, "Kristofor of Synadon", 99.
109 Xhuvani, *Visarion Xhuvani*, 142–144.
110 AQSH, F. 152 "MIA", Y. 1934, f. 164, 170, MIA to Gjirokastra Prefecture, 7 November 1934.
111 AMFA, Y. 1934, f. 479, 20, Refutation, 5 December 1934.
112 See AQSH, F. 155 "MJ", Y. 1934, f. VIII-273.
113 Xhuvani, *Works*, 129–141.
114 AQSH, F. 152 "MIA", Y. 1935, f. 473, 1, MIA to Lezhë Post-Telegraph Directorate, 27 April 1935.
115 Kondis, *Elinismos IV*, 222–223, IDAYE, f. A/22/Iβ, no. 12159, Tirana Embassy to Greek MFA, 13 November 1934.
116 Kondis, *Elinismos IV*, 224–225, IDAYE, f. A/4/2, no. 20245, Tirana Embassy to Greek MFA, 22 January 1935.

117 "Krishtlindja në gjuhën helenike dhe sllavishte [Christmas in Hellenic and Slavonic Languages]", *Predikimi [Preaching]*, 16 January 1936, 8.
118 AQSH, F. 149 "PMO", Y. 1936, f. VI-578, 2, Korça Prefecture to MIA, 9 January 1936.
119 AQSH, F. 149 "PMO", Y. 1936, f. VI-578, 3, PMO to Korça Prefecture, 18 January 1936.
120 AQSH, F. 152 "MIA", Y. 1936, f. 317, 7, Korça Prefecture to MIA, 15 April 1936.
121 AQSH, F. 141 "Metropolitanate of Korça", Y. 1936, f. 567, 1, A Request from Përmet's Orthodox Followers, no date.
122 AQSH, F. 152 "MIA", Y. 1936, f. 317, 13, Korça Prefecture to MIA, 29 April 1936; AQSH, F. 152 "MIA", Y. 1936, f. 317, 15, Korça Prefecture to MIA, 30 April 1936.
123 AQSH, F. 152 "MIA", Y. 1936, f. 317, 19, Korça Prefecture to MIA, 5 May 1936.
124 AQSH, F. 152 "MIA", Y. 1936, f. 317, 38, Korça Prefecture to MIA, 9 May 1936.
125 AQSH, F. 152 "MIA", Y. 1936, f. 317, 23, MIA to Elbasan, Vlora, Durrës, and Berat Prefectures, 7 May 1936.
126 AQSH, F. 152 "MIA", Y. 1936, f. 317, 22 MIA to Gjirokastra Prefecture, 6 May 1936.
127 AQSH, F. 152 "MIA", Y. 1936, f. 317, 40, Gjirokastra Prefecture to MIA, 8 May 1936.
128 AQSH, F. 150 "Royal Court Ministry", Y. 1936, f. VI-287, 13, Gjirokastra Prefecture to Royal Court Chief Inspector, 2 May 1936.
129 AQSH, F. 149 "PMO", Y. 1936, f. VI-576, 1, Reverend Pano Gjirokastra to PMO, 18 May 1936.
130 AQSH, F. 152 "MIA", Y. 1936, f. 317, 72, Korça Prefecture to MIA, 21 May 1936.
131 AMFA, Y. 1936, f. 305, 20, Resignation Act, no date.
132 Xhuvani, *Works*, 165–167.
133 AQSH, F. 149 "PMO", Y. 1936, f. VI-576, 3, Visarion to MFA, 28 May 1936.
134 AQSH, F. 149 "PMO", Y. 1936, f. VI-576, 6, Resignation Decree, 2 June 1936.
135 AMFA, Y. 1936, f. 304, 4, *Nei Kairi [New Times]*, 4 April 1936.
136 Kondis, *Elinismos IV*, 147: IDAYE, Y. 1935, f. A/4/9, no. 55, Thiamidos Deputy Prefect to PMO, 16 April 1932. These "mixed" villages were mainly populated by Albanians but were referred to as "mixed" since they were inhabited by both Muslim and Orthodox Albanians.
137 Kondis, *Elinismos IV*, 147: IDAYE, Y. 1935, f. A/4/9/I, no. 9365, Gendarmerie Command to Greek MFA, 10 October 1933.
138 Rigos, *Second Greek Republic*, 223–251.
139 Puto, *Political Albania*, 350–450.
140 "Komisjoni për rregullimin e çështjes kishtare [Commission on Regulation of the Ecclesiastical Issue]", *Predikimi [Preaching]*, March 1937, 8.
141 AMFA, Y. 1937, f. 307, 4, MFA to Athens Embassy, 6 March 1937.
142 AMFA, Y. 1937, f. 307, 6, Archbishop Kristofor to MFA, 8 March 1937.
143 AMFA, Y. 1937, f. 307, 7, MFA to Athens Embassy, 9 March 1937.
144 AMFA, Y. 1937, f. 307, 12, Athens Embassy to MFA, 5 April 1937.
145 AQSH, F. 141 "Metropolitanate of Korça", Y. 1937, f. 581, 2. Kurilla to Kota, 14 September 1937.
146 Tasoudis, *Biographical Memoirs*, 81.
147 AMFA, Y. 1937, f. 307, 9, MFA to Athens Embassy, 20 March 1937.
148 Glavinas, *The Orthodox Church*, 59.
149 AMFA, Y. 1937, f. 307, 19–25, Istanbul Consulate to MFA, 16 April 1937.
150 Ibid.
151 Glavinas, *The Orthodox Church*, 68–70.
152 AQSH, F. 536 "OACA", f. 1435, 1–18, Visarion's Report, 18 January 1937.

153 AQSH, F. 149 "PMO", f. VI-6421, Noli to Kota on 13/5.
154 Glavinas, *The Orthodox Church*, 73–95.
155 AQSH, F. 155 "MJ", f. VIII-366, 1, PMO to MIA, 24 April 1937.
156 Glavinas, *The Orthodox Church*, 77–78.
157 AQSH, F. 152, Y. 1937, "MIA", f. 158, 4, Korça Prefect to MIA.
158 AQSH, F. 152, Y. 1937, "MIA", f. 158, 8, Pandelejmon to Gjirokastra Prefecture.
159 AQSH, F. 155 Y. 1938, "MJ", f. VIII-432, 1, Gjirokastra Prefecture to MJ, 26 March 1938.
160 AQSH, F. 152, Y. 1938, "MIA", f. 25, 15, Gjirokastra Prefecture to MIA, 24 May 1938.
161 AQSH, F. 152, "MIA", Y. 1938, f. 25, 23, Gjirokastra Prefecture to MIA, 1 July 1938.
162 AQSH, F. 152, "MIA", Y. 1938, f. 25, 28, Kristofor to MIA, 15 July 1938.
163 AQSH, F. 152, "MIA", Y. 1938, f. 990, Captain Xhafer Shkëmbi to MIA, 24 September 1938.
164 AQSH, F. 155 "MJ", Y. 1938, f. VIII-406, 12, MIA to MJ, 4 November 1938.
165 AQSH, F. 155 "MJ", Y. 1938, f. VIII-406, Kotoko to Kristofor, 15 December 1938.
166 AQSH, F. 141 "Metropolitanate of Korça", Y. 1937, f. 570, 5, Evlogji's Speech, 24 May 1937.
167 AQSH, F. 141 "Metropolitanate of Korça", Y. 1937, f. 572–575.
168 AQSH, Kurilla to Kota, 14 September 1937, quoted.
169 AQSH, F. 150 "Royal Court Ministry", Y. 1939, f. VI-391.
170 AQSH, Visarion's Report, 18 January 1937, quoted.
171 This is reported in Kurilla's autobiography; see Evlogji Kurilla (Eulogios Kourilas), Δεκεμβριανή τραγωδια των ομηρων *[The Tragedy of the December Hostages]* (Athens: Eleftheris Skepsis, 2003), 246–248.
172 "Situata e re [The New Situation]", *Predikimi [Preaching]*, March–April 1939, 1.
173 Kurilla, *The Tragedy*, 246–248.
174 AQSH, F. 163 "Italian Embassy", Y. 1939, f. 266, 3.
175 AQSH, F. 379 "Tirana Prefecture", f. 120, 2, Order, 1 December 1939.
176 Kurilla, *The Tragedy*, 246.
177 Anastasopoulou, *The Albanian Orthodox*, 25–27.
178 AQSH, F. 152 "MIA", Y. 1941, f. 105, 1, MIA to OACA, July 1941.
179 Glavinas, *The Orthodox Church*, 111.
180 AQSH, F. 152 "MIA", Y. 1941, f. 105, 28, MIA to OACA, 20 October 1941.
181 AQSH, F. 167 "Kosova-Dibra-Struga Commission", Y. 1941, f. 151, 15.
182 AQSH, F. 153 "Police Directorate", Y. 1940, f. 101, 2.
183 AQSH, F. 153 "Police Directorate", Y. 1940, f. 101, 3, Gjirokastra Police Director to the General Director, 29 March 1940.
184 Della Rocca, *Nationality and Religion*, 214.
185 AQSH, F. 153 "Police Directorate", Y. 1940, f. 101, 2.
186 Glavinas, *The Orthodox Church*, 112.
187 Such a visit would be repeated again in 2009, when a group of five bishops of the Albanian Orthodox Church, led by the archbishop, held a meeting in Grottaferrata Monastery (Anastas Bendo, "Takim historik i Kryepiskopit të Tiranas, Durrësit dhe të gjithë Shqipërisë, Anastasit me Papën Benedikti XVI [An Historical Meeting of Anastas, Archbishop of Tirana, Durrës and all Albania, with Pope Benedict XVI]", *Ngjallja [Resurrection]*, December 2009, 1–8).
188 Della Rocca, *Nationality and Religion*, 215–217.
189 AQSH, F. 141 "Metropolitanate of Korça", f. 611, 8, Eldership Meeting, 8 July 1940.
190 AQSH, F. 141 "Metropolitanate of Korça", f. 611, 26.

191 Beduli, *Irine Banushi*, 23–31.
192 AQSH, F. 155 "MJ", f. VIII-4916, Kristofor to MJ, 4 October. As regards to the population of Macedonia, the documents found in Albania's Central State Archives refer to the "Bulgarian" population. This book uses the same terms found in the archival sources without bias as regards the historical disputes surrounding the linguistic and ethnic identity of Macedonians.
193 AQSH, F. 167 "Kosova-Dibra-Struga Commission", Y. 1941, f. 151, 3.
194 AQSH, F. 167 "Kosova-Dibra-Struga Commission", Y. 1941, f. 151, 7.
195 AQSH, F. 167 "Kosova-Dibra-Struga Commission", Y. 1941, f. 151, 62, Reverend Simon's Letter.
196 AQSH, F. 149 "PMO", Y. 1942, f. VI-153, 1. Koço Tasi's Report.
197 AQSH, F. 155 "MJ", Y. 1942, f. VIII-517, 5. OACA to MJ, 13 July 1942.
198 AQSH, F. 149 "PMO", Y. 1941, f. VI-53, 2. Kristofor to MJ, 31 July 1941.
199 AQSH, F. 155 "MJ", Y. 1942, f. VIII-517, 36, Appointment of Irine Banushi, 13 July 1942.
200 Beduli, *Church and Culture*.
201 "Një festim madhështor në Manastirin e Shën Marinës [A Magnificent Celebration in Saint Marina's Monastery]", *Kisha Kombëtare [The National Church]*, 17 August 1930.
202 Artan Hoxha, *Kisha Ortodokse nën komunizëm [The Orthodox Church Under Communism]* (Tirana: UET Press, 2017), 63–64.
203 Thanasi, *Pais Vodica*, 88–125.
204 The Greek nationalist guerilla force EDES (the National Republican Greek League) had a small base in Albania, while the Communists had support in the Dropulli region. (Sonila Boçi, *Minoritetet në Shqipëri midis identitetit dhe integrimit (1939–1949) [The Minorities in Albania between Identity and Integration (1939–1949)]* (Tirana: QSA, 2012), 124.)
205 AQSH, F. 136 "Durrës Deanery", f. 223, 1. Archbishop Kristofor's Memo, no date.
206 AQSH, F. 149 "PMO", Y. 1944, f. VI-282, 1–2. Visarion's Report, 13 February 1944.

Bibliography

Archival sources

- Central State Archives of Albania (AQSH)
    - F. 2 "Asdreni"
    - F. 14 "Fan Noli"
    - F. 55 "Sotir Peçi"
    - F. 70 "25th Anniversary of Self-Governance"
    - F. 99 "Albanian Colony in Romania"
    - F. 136 "Durrës Deanary"
    - F. 141 "Metropolitanate of Korça"
    - F. 142 "Shkodra Orthodox Community"
    - F. 143 "Documents Collection"
    - F. 149 "Prime Minister's Office"
    - F. 150 "Royal Court Ministry"
    - F. 152 "Ministry of Interior Affairs"
    - F. 153 "Police Directorate"
    - F. 155 "Ministry of Justice"
    - F. 156 "The Dictation Court"
    - F. 163 "Italian Embassy"
    - F. 167 "Kosova-Dibra-Struga Commission"
    - F. 317 "Prefecture of Korça"
    - F. 379 "Tirana Prefecture"
    - F. 536 "Orthodox Autocephalous Church of Albania"

- Archives of the Ministry of Foreign Affairs of Albania (AMFA)
- Central State Archives of Greece (GAK)
    - F. "Prime Minister's Political Office"

- Greek Historical and Logotechnical Archives (ELIA)
    - F. "Eleftherios Venizelos"
    - F. "Chrysanthos, Archbishop of Athens"

- Northern-Epirotan Research Foundation (IBE)
    - F. "Metropolitan Ierothe"

Periodicals

- Albania, years 1908–1918.
- Apostolos Andreas, year 1925.

- Dajti, year 1926.
- Dituria, year 1927.
- Empros, years 1912–1918.
- Gazeta e Korçës, years 1924–1929.
- Gazeta e Re, years 1928–1929.
- Gjergj Kastrioti, year 1924.
- Kisha Kombëtare, year 1930.
- Koha, years 1911–1926.
- Korça, year 1909.
- Liria, year 1925.
- Lidhja Ortodokse, year 1908.
- Makedonia, years 1912–1918.
- Posta e Korçës, year 1921.
- Predikimi, years 1934–1938.
- Skënderbeu, year 1925.
- Skrip, years 1912–1918.
- Tirana, years 1924–1925.
- Zëri i Gjirokastrës, year 1923.
- Zëri i Korçës, years 1925–1929.

Published archives

Çami, Muin, ed. *Lufta e popullit shqiptar për çlirimin kombëtar 1918–1920 [The War of the Albanian People for National Liberation1918–1920].* 2 vols. Tirana: Mihal Duri, 1975 and 1978.

Duka, Valentina. *Dokumente britanike për Shqipërinë dhe Shqiptarët, Vëllimi II, 1914 [British Documents of Albania and Albanians, Volume II, 1914].* Tirana: Toena, 2012.

Glavinas, Apostolos. *Εγγραφα περί της πραξικοπηματικής συγκροτήσεως της συνόδου της Ορθοδόξου Εκκλησίας της Αλβανίας (1929) [Documents on the Coup d'État Organization of the Orthodox Church Synod of Albania (1929)].* Ioannina: The Foundation of Ionian and Adriatic Space, 1981.

Kondis, Vasilios and Eleftheria Manda, eds. *The Greek Minority in Albania: A Documentary Record (1921–1993).* Thessaloniki: Institute of Balkanic studies, 1994.

Kondis, Vasilios., ed. *Ελληνισμός της Βορείου Ηπείρου και ελληνοαλβανικές σχεσείς, έγγραφα άπο το ιστορικό αρχείο του Υπουργείου Εξωτερικών, [Hellenism of Northern Epirus in Greek-Albanian relations: Documents from the Historical Archives of the Foreign Ministry].* 4 vols. Athens: Estia, 1995.

Naska, Kaliopi. *Dokumente për Çamërinë: 1912–1939 [Documents on Chameria: 1912–1939].* Tirana: Dituria, 1999.

Publications

Academy of Sciences, ed. *70 Vjet të Kishës Ortodokse Autoqefale Shqiptare [70 Years of the Albanian Autocephalous Orthodox Church].* Tirana: Institute of History, 1993.

Academy of Sciences, ed. *Historia e Popullit Shqiptar [History of the Albanian People].* 2 vols. Tirana: Toena, 2007.

Anastasopoulou, Garoufalia. *Αλβανοί Ορθόδοξοι και Έλληνες της Αλβανίας και ο ρόλος της Ορθόδοξης Εκκλησίας της Αλβανίας [Orthodox Albanians and the Greeks of Albania and the Role of the Orthodox Church of Albania]*. Athens: Vivliorama, 2013.

Armstrong-Heaton, Duncan. *Gjashtë muaj mbretëri: Shqipëria 1914 [The Six Month Kingdom: Albania 1914]*. Tirana: Onufri, 2011.

Beduli, Dhimitër. *Gjuha Shqipe në Kishë [The Albanian Language in the Church]*. Tirana: AOCA, 1997.

Beduli, Dhimitër. *Kisha Ortodokse Autoqefale e Shqipërisë gjer në vitin 1944 [The Orthodox Autocephalous Church of Albania until 1944]*. Tirana: OACA, 2006.

Beduli, Dhimitër. *Kishë dhe kulturë [Church and Culture]*. Tirana: Institute of Dialogue and Communications, 2006.

Beduli, Dhimitër. *Shënime për bashkësinë ortodokse të Tiranas [Notes on the Orthodox Community in Tirana]*. Tirana: Neraida, 2007.

Beduli, Kristofor. *Dhimitër Beduli*. Tirana: AOCA, 1999.

Beduli, Kristofor. *Episkop Irine Banushi: Martir i Kishës Orthodhokse Autoqefale të Shqipërisë [Bishop Irine Banushi: A Martyr of the Orthodox Autocephalous Church of Albania]*. Tirana: AOCA, 2000.

Beduli, Kristofor. *Ortodoksët e Gollobordës [The Orthodox of Golloborda]*. Tirana: Neraida, 2008.

Beduli, Kristofor. *Saqellar Atë Petro Doçi [Reverend Petro Doçi]*. Tirana: Neraida, 2006.

Bërxholli, Arqile. *Bashkësia shoqërore ortodokse në Shqipëri [The Orthodox Social Community in Albania]*. Tirana: Julvin, 2013.

Boçi, Sonila. *Minoritetet në Shqipëri midis identitetit dhe integrimit (1939–1949) [The Minorities in Albania between Identity and Integration (1939–1949)]*. Tirana: QSA, 2012.

Bourchier, James David. "Albania". In *Encyclopædia Britannica*. 11th ed., edited by Hugh Chrisholm Cambridge: Cambridge University Press, 1911.

Çami, Muin. *Shqipëria në rrjedhat e historisë 1912–1924 [Albania in the Course of History 1912–1924]*. Tirana: Onufri, 2007.

Daskarolis, Ioanis. *Στρατιωτικά κινήματα στην Ελλάδα του Μεσοπολέμου 1922–1935) [Military Movement in Mid-War Greece (1922–1935)]*. Athens: Gnomon, 2012.

"Declaration Concerning the Protection of Minorities in Albania". *League of Nations Treaty Series 51*. Geneva: League of Nations, 1922.

Della Rocca, Roberto Morozzo. *Kombësia dhe feja në Shqipëri 1920–1944 [Nationality and Religion in Albania 1920–1944]*. Tirana: Elena Gjika, 1994.

Deringil, Selim. *Conversion and Apostasy in the Late Ottoman Empire*. Cambridge: Cambridge University Press, 2012.

Dervishi, Kastriot. *Historia e Shtetit Shqiptar [History of the Albanian State] 1912–2005*. Tirana: 55, 2006.

Dervishi, Kastriot. *Shërbimi Sekret Shqiptar 1922–1944 [The Albanian Secret Service 1922–1944]*. Tirana: 55, 2007.

Duka, Valentina. *Histori e Shqipërisë 1912–2000 [History of Albania 1912–2000]*. Tirana: SHBLU, 2007.

Durham, Edith. *High Albania*. London: Edward Arnold, 1909.

Durham, Edith. *Twenty Years of Balkan Tangle*. London: Allen and Unwin, 1920.

Dushku, Ledia. *Kur historia ndau dy popuj miq: Shqipëria dhe Greqia (1912–1914) [When History Divided Two Friendly Peoples: Albania and Greece (1912–1914)]*. Tirana, QSA, 2012.

Enosis Smyrneon. *Ο Μητροπολίτης Μυτηλήνης Ιάκωβος, ο άπο Δυρραχίου [Metropolitan of Mytilene Iakovos, the One from Durrës]*. Athens: Enosis Smyrneon, 1965.

Estrefi, Diana. *Ligjvënësit shqiptarë 1920–2005 [Albanian Lawmakers 1920–2005]*. Tirana: Albanian Parliament, 2005.

Floqi, Thanas. *Fytyra e vërtetë e Haxhi Qamilit: Kujtime për vitet e mbrapshta 1914–1915 [The True Face of Haxhi Qamili: Memories of the Evil Years 1914–1915]*. Tirana: 55, 2008.

Frashëri, Mehdi. *Kujtime [Memoirs] 1913–1933*. Tirana: OMSCA-1, 2005.

Glavinas, Apostolos. *Ορθόδοξη Αυτοκέφαλη Εκκλησία της Αλβανίας [The Orthodox Autocephalous Church of Albania]*. Thessaloniki: AISF, 1992.

Glavinas, Apostolos. *Το αυτοκέφαλον της εν Αλβανία Ορθοδόξου Εκκλησίας επί τη βάσει ανεκδότων εγγράφων, [The Autocephaly of the Orthodox Church in Albania, Based on Unpublished Documents]*, Ioannina: Ioanian Foundation, 1978.

Grandits, Hannes, Nathalie Clayer, and Robert Pichler. *Conflicting Loyalties in the Balkans: The Great Powers, the Ottoman Empire and Nation-Building*. London: I.B. Tauris, 2011.

Gurakuqi, Romeo. *Principata e Shqipërisë dhe Mbretëria e Greqisë 1913–1914 [The Principality of Albania and Kingdom of Greece 1913–1914]*. Tirana: UET Press, 2011.

Hoxha, Artan. *Kisha Ortodokse nën komunizëm [The Orthodox Church Under Communism]*. Tirana: UET Press, 2017.

Iakovos (Metropolitan). *Asmatiki akolouthia tou Agiou endoxou ieromartyros Astiou: episkopou Dyrrachiou [Akolouthia of the Saint and Hieromartyr Astius, Bishop of Dyrrachium]*. Istanbul, 1918.

Ikonomou, Fotios G. *Η Ιστορια των τοπικων εκκλησιων της Ηπειρου Τομος Β' [History of the Churches of Epirus, Volume 2]*. Athens, 1969.

Ikonomou, Fotios G. *Η Ορθόδοξος Εκκλησια της Αλβανίας και η συμβολή της εις την διατήρησιν του ελληνισμού της Βορείου Ηπείρου [The Orthodox Church in Albania and Its Contribution to Safeguarding the Hellenism of Northern Epirus]*. Athens: Nees Theseis, 1988.

Jelavich, Barbara. *Russia and the Formation of the Romanian National State, 1821–1878*. Cambridge: Cambridge University Press, 1984.

Jelavich, Charles and Barbara Jelavich. *The Establishment of the Balkan National States, 1804–1920*. Seattle and London: University of Washington Press, 2000.

Jorgaqi, Nasho. *Jeta e Fan S. Nolit [Life of Fan. S. Noli] V. 1*. Tirana: Ombra GVG, 2006.

Kalkandijeva, Daniela. "The Bulgarian Orthodox Church". In *Orthodox Christianity and Nationalism in Nineteenth Century South-Eastern Europe*, edited by Lucian Leustean, 164–203. New York: Fordam University Press, 2014.

Kitromilides, Paschalis M. "The Ecumenical Patriarchate". In *Orthodox Christianity and Nationalism in Nineteenth Century South-Eastern Europe*, edited by Lucian Leustean, 14–33. New York: Fordam University Press, 2014.

Kola, Sifi. *Ο Αργυροκάστρου Παντελεήμων: Ο Αγωνιστής Ιεράρχης της Β. Ηπείρου [Pandelejmon of Gjirokastra: The Archpriest Fighter of Northern Epirus]*. Athens: Nei Palmi, 1970.

Kondiaris, Gerasimos. *Η Ελληνική Εκκλησία ως Πολιτιστική Δύναμις εν τη Ιστορία της Χερσονήσου του Αίμου [The Greek Church, as a Cultural Power in the History of the Peninsula of Haimos]*. Athens, 1948.

Kondis, Vasilios. *Albania and Greece 1908–1914*. Thessaloniki: Institute of Balkanic studies, 1976.

Kondis, Vasilios, "The Northern Epirus Question (1881–1921)". In *Epirus, 4000 years of Greek History and Civilization*, edited by Mixail B. Sakellariou. Athens: Ekdotike Athinon, 1997.

Kostandinides, Emmanuel. *Η ανακηρυξις του αυτοκεφαλου της εν Ελλαδι Εκκλησιας (1850) και η θεσις των μητροπολεων των Νεων Χωρων (1928) [Declaration of the Church's Autocephaly in Greece (1850) and the Place of Metropolitanates in New Countries (1928)]*. Athens: Parrhsea, 1974.

Kotnani, Apostol. *Kapedan At Stath Melani me shokë [Captain Father Stathi Melani with Friends]*. Tirana, 2007.

Krisafi, Ksenofon. *Për tokën dhe detin e Shqipërisë [On Albania's Land and Sea]*. Tirana: UET Press, 2014.

Kurilla Lavrioti, Evlogji (Eulogios Kourilas). *Δεκεμβριανη τραγωδια των ομηρων [The Tragedy of the December Hostages]*. Athens: Eleftheris Skepsis, 2003.

Kurilla Lavrioti, Evlogji (Eulogios Kourilas). *Grigorios, o Argirokastritis [Gregory, the Gjirokastran]*. Athens: Foinikos, 1933.

Kurilla Lavrioti, Evlogji (Eulogios Kourilas). *Η Μοσχόπολης και η Νέα Ακαδημία αυτής [Voskopoja and Its New Academy]*. Athens, 1935.

Leustean, Lucian., ed. *Eastern Christianity and the Cold War, 1945*. London: Routledge, 2010.

Leustean, Lucian., ed. *Orthodox Christianity and Nationalism in Nineteenth Century South-Eastern Europe*. New York: Fordam University Press, 2014.

Luarasi, Petro Nini. *Maλkimi i Ckroηavet Cqipe de çperfoja e Cqipεtarit [The Curse of Albanian Letters and the Slander of Albanian]*. Monastir: International Trade Press, 1911.

Llukani, Andrea. *Kanonet dhe statutet e kishës ortodokse [Canons and Statutes of the Orthodox Church]*. Tirana: Trifon Xhagjika, 2011.

Llukani, Andrea. *Kisha Ortodokse Autoqefale e Shqipërisë: nga vitet apostolike deri në vitet tona [The Orthodox Autocephalous Church of Albania: From the Apostolic Time to Ours]*. Tirana: Trifon Xhagjika, 2005.

Malltezi, Luan and Sherif Delvina. *Mid'hat Frashëri Ministër fuqiplotë: Athinë (1923–1926) [Mid'hat Frashëri Plenipotentiary Minister: Athens (1923–1926)]*. Tirana: Lumo Skëndo, 2002.

Matalas, Paraskevas. *Εθνος και Ορθοδοξια [Nation and Orthodoxy]*. Iraklio: Panepistimiakes Ekdosis Kritis, 2003.

Meta, Beqir. *Tensioni greko-shqiptar 1939–1949 [Albanian-Greek Tensions 1939–1949]*. Tirana: Geer, 2002.

Murzaku, Ines. *Returning Home to Rome: The Basilian Monks of Grottaferrata in Albania*. Grottaferrata, Rome: Analekta Kryptoferris, 2009.

Nesimi, Qani. *Ortodoksizmi te shqiptarët [Orthodoxy among Albanians]*. Tetovo, North Macedonia, 2005.

Nikolaidou, Eleftheria. "Ξένες προπαγάνδες και εθνική αλβανική κίνηση στις Μητροπωλιτικές Επαρχίες Δυρραχιου και Βελεγράδων κατά τά τέλη του 19ου και τις αρχές του 20ου αιώνα *[Foreign Propaganda and the Albanian National Movement in the Metropolitan Eparchies of Durrës and Velegrad during the Late Nineteenth Century and Early Twentieth Century]*. Ioannina: University of Ioannina, 1978.

Nikols, Aidan. *Rome and the Eastern Churches: A Study in Schism*. Edinburgh: T&T Clark, 1992.

Noli, Fan S. *Autobiografia [Autobiography]*. Tirana: Elena Gjika, 1994.

Noli, Fan S. *Pesëdhjetëvjetori i Kishës Ortodokse Shqiptare 1908–1958 [The Albanian Orthodox Church's Fiftieth Anniversary 1908–1958]*. Boston: AOC, 1958.

Nosi, Lef. *Dokumente Historike 1912–1918 [Historical Documents 1912–1918].* Tirana: Nënë Tereza, 2007.

OACA. *L'Eglise Autocephale Orthodoxe d'Albanie [Orthodox Autocephalous Church of Albania].* Geneve: Imprimerie Albert Kundig, 1929.

OACA. *Statuti i Kishës Orthodhokse Autoqefale Kombëtare të Shqipërisë [The Statute of the National Orthodox Autocephalous Church of Albania].* Korça: Dhori Koti, 1923.

OACA. *Statuti i Kishës Orthodhokse Autoqefale të Shqipris [The Statute of the Orthodox Autocephalous Church of Albania].* Korça: Korça, 1929.

Papa, Kosta. *Greek Atrocities in Albania.* Framingham: Journal Press, 1917.

Peric, Dimso. *Srpska pravoslavna crkva i njena dijaspora [The Serbian Orthodox Church and Its Diaspora].* Belgrade, 1996.

Përmeti, Turhan P. *Shqipëria përballë Konferencës së Paqes Paris 1919 [Albania in Front of the Paris Peace Conference 1919].* Tirana: Eugen, 2007.

Pangalos, Theodoros. *Τα απομνημονεύματά μου 1897–1947 [My Memoirs 1897–1947].* Athens: Aetos, 1959.

Pano, Nicholas. "The Albanian Orthodox Church". In *Eastern Christianity and the Cold War, 1945–91,* edited by Lucian Leustean, 144–156. London: Routledge, 2010.

Pearson, Owen. *Albania and King Zog: Independence, Republic and Monarchy: 1908–1939.* London and New York: Centre for Albanian Studies and I. B. Tauris, 2004.

Perica, Vjekoslav. *Balkan Idols: Religion and Nationalism in Yugoslav States.* Oxford and New York: Oxford University Press, 2002.

Pitouli-Kitsou, Xristina. *Οι Ελληνοαλβανικές Σχέσεις και το Βορειοηπειρώτικο Ζήτημα κατα την Περίοδο 1907–1914 [Greek-Albanian Relations and Northern-Epirotes Issue during the Period 1907–1914].* Athens: Olkos, 1997.

Pollo, Stefanaq. *Në gjurmë të historisë shqiptare, Volumi II [In the Footsteps of Albanian History, Volume II].* Tirana: Institute of History, 2003.

Poradeci, Lasgush. *Vepra 2 [Works 2].* Tirana: Onufri, 1999.

Puto, Arben. *Shqipëria politike 1912–1939 [Political Albania 1912–1939].* Tirana: Toena, 2009.

Qiriazi, Dhori. *Krishtërimi në Shqipëri [Christianity in Albania].* Tirana: Argeta-LMG, 2000.

Ramet, Sabrina P., ed. *Eastern Christianity and Politics in the Twentieth Century.* Durham and London: Duke University Press, 1988.

Rich, Norman. *Great Power Diplomacy, 1814–1914.* New York: McGraw-Hill, 1991.

Rigos, Alkis. *Η Β΄ Ελληνική Δημοκρατία 1924–1935. [The Second Greek Republic 1924–1935].* Athens: Themelio, 1988.

Riis, Carsten. *Religion, Politics, and Historiography in Bulgaria.* Boulder: East European Monographs, 2002.

Runciman, Steven. *The Great Church in Captivity.* Cambridge: Cambridge University Press, 1968.

Runciman, Steven. *The Eastern Schism: A Study of the Papacy and the Eastern Churches during the XIth and XIIth Centuries.* Cambridge: Cambridge University Press, 1955.

Sadiku, Blerina. *Lindja e Çështjes Çame 1820–1943 [The Birth of the Cham Issue 1820–1943].* Tirana: Naimi, 2011.

Salleo, Ferdinando. *Shqipëria: gjashtë muaj mbretëri [Albania: The Six Month Kingdom].* Tirana: SHLK, 2000.

Spahiu, Avni. *Noli: Jeta në Amerikë [Noli: Life in America]*. Tirana: Toena, 2007.

Spahiu, Nexhmedin. *National Awakening Process among Orthodox Albanians.* Hamburg, 2006.

Stamatovic, Aleksandar. *Kratka istorija Mitropolije Crnogorsko-primorske (1219–1999) [A History of Montenegro's Metropolitanate (1219–1999)]*. Podgorica: Svetigora, 2000.

Stratigakis, Ioanis E. *Ο Μητροπολίτης Μυτιλήνης Ἰακωβος: ο άνθρωπος και η δράση του [Metropolitan of Mytilene Iakovos: The Man and His Action]*. Athens, 1956.

Sugar, Peter F. *Southeastern Europe under Ottoman Rule, 1354–1804.* Seattle: University of Washington Press, 1977.

Swire, Joseph. *Shqipëria: Ngritja e një mbretërie [Albania: The Rise of a Kingdom]*. Tirana: Dituria, 2005.

Schurman, Jacob Gould. *Luftërat Ballkanike [The Balkan Wars]*. Tirana: Uegen, 2006.

Shuteriqi, Dhimitër. *Shkrimet shqipe në vitet 1332–1850 [Albanian Writing in the Years 1332–1850]*. Tirana: Academy of Sciences, 1976.

Tako, Vasil J. *Përgjigje e Shqiptarëvet Krishten të Misirit për Botimet e Koço Tasit [The Replies from Christian Albanians of Misir [Egypt] to Koço Tasi's Publications]*. Egypt, 1929.

Tanner, Arno., ed. *The Forgotten Minorities of Eastern Europe: The History and Today of Selected Ethnic Groups in Five Countries.* Helsinki: East-West Books, 2004.

Tasi, Koço. *Shqiptarvet të Krishtern bashkëpunëtorë të Muhamedanëvet [Christian Albanians Associates of the Mohammedans]*. Athens, 1929.

Tasoudis, Georgios. *Βιογραφικαί αναμνήσεις του Αρχιεπισκόπου Αθηνών Χρύσανθου του από Τραπεζούντος: 1881–1949 [The Biographical Memoirs of the Archbishop of Athens, Chrysanthos from Trebizond: 1881–1949]*. Athens: Kostandinidi & Mihala, 1970.

Taylor, Alan J.P. *First World War.* London: Penguin Books, 1966.

Τραπεζούντος Χρύσανθος: Επίσημα έγγραφα περι της Εκκλησιαστικής και Εθνικής δράσεως του [Chrysanthos of Trebizond: Official Documents on His Ecclesiastical and National Activity]. Alexandria, 1925.

Tsalaxouris, Kostas. *Το Αυτοκέφαλο της Εκκλησίας της Δωδεκανήσου: από τα αρχεία του Υπουργείου των Εξωτερικών της Ελλάδος [Autocephaly of the Dodecanesean Church: From the Archives of the Greek Foreign Ministry]*. Athens, 1992.

Tsironis, Theodoris. *Εκκλησια Πολιτευομενη Ο Πολιτικός Λόγος και Ρόλος της Εκκλησίας της Ελλάδος (1913–1941) [Politicized Church: The Speech and Political Role of the Church of Greece (1913–1941)]*. Athens: Epikentro, 2011.

The Pan Albanian Federation of America Vatra, *Statement of the Christian Orthodox Albanians Natives of the Districts of Koritza and Kolonia in Reply to the Declaration of the Pan-Epirotic Union in America, of May, 1919*, Boston: Vatra, 1919.

Tritos, Mihail. *Η εκκλησία στο ανατολικό Ιλλυρικό και την Αλβανία [The Church in the Eastern Illyricum and in Albania]*. Athens: Kiriakidi Afi, 1999.

Thanasi, Vasil K. *Mëmëdhetari, luftëtar për paqe e progres, kleriku i shquar Paisi Vodica: 1882–1966 [The Patriot, a Warrior for Peace and Progress, the Outstanding Cleric Pais Vodica: 1882–1966]*. Tirana, 2004.

Veremis, Thanos. *Balkan Expansion of Greece.* Athens: Hellenic Foundation for Foreign and European Policy, 1995.

Verli, Mareglen., ed. *Shqipëria e viteve 1912–1964 në kujtimet e Spiro Kosovës, Vëllimi 1 [Albania in the Years 1912–1964 in Spiro Kosova's Memoirs, Volume 1]*. Tirana: Klean 2008.

Wied, Wilhelm. *Promemorie mbi Shqipërinë [Memorandum on Albania]*. Tirana: Skanderbeg Books, 2010.

Vllamasi, Sejfi. *Ballafaqime politike në Shqipëri [Political Confrontations in Albania]*. Tirana: Vllamasi, 2012.

Xhuvani, Nos. *Na flet Visarion Xhuvani [Visarion Xhuvani Speaks to Us]*. Tirana, 2008.

Xhuvani, Nos. *Visarion Xhuvani: Apostull i Atdhetarizmit dhe i Ortodoksisë Shqiptare [Visarion Xhuvani: An Apostle of Patriotism and Albanian Orthodoxy]*. Tirana, 2003.

Xhuvani, Visarion (Bishop). *Çashtje politiko-religjoze Kostandinopoli-Tiranë (Botohet me rastin e bisedimeve përkatëse që janë tyke u bamë kto dit në Tiranë) [Political and Religious Issues between Constantinople and Tirana (Published on the Occasion of the Relevant Talks Currently Being Held in Tirana)]*. Tirana: Tirana, 1926.

Xhuvani, Visarion (Bishop). *Kujtim vepre dhe intrige [Memory of Work and Intrigue]*. Tirana: Tirana, 1926.

Xhuvani, Visarion (Archbishop). *Vepra: Për Kishën Orthodhokse Shqiptare; Në Kuvendin e Shqipërisë; Për jetën dhe veprën [Works: On the Albanian Orthodox Church; at the Assembly of Albania; about His Life and Work]*. ed. Nos Xhuvani and Pavli Haxhillazi. Tirana: 55, 2007.

Tzortzatos, Varnavas (Metropolitan). *Η Αυτοκέφαλος Ορθόδοξος Εκκλησία της Αλβανίας και οι βασικοί θεσμοί διοικήσεως Αυτής [The Orthodox Autocephalous Church of Albania and Its Basic Managment Institutions]*. Athens, 1975.

Xoxa, Zoi. *Kujtimet e një gazetari [Memoirs of a Journalist]*. Tirana: 55, 2007.

Xoxi, Koli. *Shkolla ortodokse në Shqipëri dhe rilindësit tanë [The Orthodox School in Albania and Our Renaissance Men]*. Tirana: Mokra, 2002.

Unpublished dissertations

Gianakou, Maria. "Ο Μητροπολίτης Αργυροκάστρου Παντελεήμων και το Βορειοηπειρωτικό Ζήτημα [Metropolitan of Gjirokastra Pandelejmon and the Northern Epirotic Issue]". MA Thesis, University of Thessaloniki, 2009.

Karakitsios, Eleftherios. "Ο Ελληνισμός στην Μητροπολιτική Περιφέρεια Κορυτσάς [Hellenism in the Metropolitane of Korça]". PhD Dissertation, University of Thessaloniki, 2010.

Katopodis, Apostolos. "Ο Μητροπολίτης Δρυινουπόλεως Βασίλειος Παπαχρήστου στο Βοριοηπειρώτικο Αγώνα, [Metropolitan of Dryinopolis Vasil Papakristo in the Northern Epirotan Struggle]". PhD Dissertation, University of Thessaloniki, 2001.

Kondili, Pirro. "Η Ορθόδοξη Εκκλησία της Αλβανίας κατά τη διάρκεια της κομμουνιστικής δικτατορίας [The Orthodox Church of Albania during the Communist Dictatorship]". MA Thesis, University of Athens, 2002.

Koulas, Antonios. "Ελληνογιουγκοσλαβικές σχέσεις άπο το 1923 εώς το 1928 [Greek-Yugoslav Relations from 1923 to 1928]". PhD Dissertation, University of Thessaloniki, 2007.

Marmarinos, Ioustinios. "Η συμβολή του Μητροπολίτη Τραπεζούντος Χρύσανθου στην ανακήρυξη του αυτοκεφάλου της εν Αλβανία Ορθοδόξου Εκκλησίας [The Contribution of the Metropolitan of Trebizond, Chrysanthos in the Declaration of Autocephaly of the Orthodox Church in Albania]". MA Thesis, National and Kapodistrian University of Athens, 2003.

Articles in journals and newspaper

Anastasi, Aurela. "Statuti i Kishës Ortodokse Autoqefale Shqiptare dhe evoluimi i tij [The Albanian Autocephalous Orthodox Church Statute and Its Evolution]". *70 vjet të Kishës Ortodokse Autoqefale Shqiptare [70 Years of the Albanian Autocephalous Orthodox Church]*. Tirana: Institute of History, 1993.

Avakumovic, Mirko. "Pravoslavna Crkva u Albaniji [The Orthodox Church in Albania]." *Arhiv za pravno i drustvene nauke [Archive of Social and Judicial Studies]* 4 (1936): 41–67.

Bendo, Anastas. "Takim historik i Kryepiskopit të Tiranas, Durrësit dhe të gjithë Shqipërisë, Anastasit me Papën Benedikti XVI [An Historical Meeting of Anastas, Archbishop of Tirana, Durrës and All Albania, with Pope Benedict XVI]". *Ngjallja [Resurrection]*. December 2009.

Bidoshi, Petrit. "Një ngjarje e paharrueshme e vitit 1916 në Durrës [An Unforgettable Event of 1916 in Durrës]". *Autoqefalia Ortodokse Shqiptare [Albanian Orthodox Autocephaly]*. 7 June 1994.

Bihiku, Koço. "Themelimi i Kishës Ortodokse Kombëtare dhe roli i Nolit [The Establishment of the National Orthodox Church and the Role of Noli]". *70 vjet të Kishës Ortodokse Autoqefale Shqiptare [70 Years of the Albanian Autocephalous Orthodox Church]*. Tirana: Institute of History, 1993.

Çami, Muin. "Kleri i Lartë Ortodoks në Shqipëri dhe Lëvizja Kombëtare Shqiptare në vitet 1912–1921 [The Orthodox Hierarchs in Albania and the Albanian National Movement in 1912–1921]". *70 vjet të Kishës Ortodokse Autoqefale Shqiptare [70 Years of the Albanian Autocephalous Orthodox Church]*. Tirana: Institute of History, 1993.

Çami, Muin. "Ushtarakët francezë në Korçë, mbështetës të aspiratave kombëtare të popullsisë (1916–1920) [The French Military in Korça, Supporter of the People's National Aspirations]". *Studime Historike [Historical Studies]* 1–2 (2002):61–77.

Dilo, Vasil. "Psikoza e "Vorio Epirit" dhe marrëveshjet mbi protokollin e Korfuzit [The Psychosis of "Northern Epirus" and Agreements on the Corfu Protocol]". *Ndryshe [Different]*. 26 April 2007.

Dilo, Vasil. "Pushtimi italian dhe Shqipëria [The Italian Invasion and Albania]". *Ndryshe [Different]*. 22 April 2007.

Duka, Valentina. "Institucionet fetare gjatë mbretërimit të Ahmet Zogt: një vështrim të legjislacionit të kohës (1928–1939) [Religious Institutions during the Reign of Ahmet Zog: An Overview of Legislation during that Period (1928–1939)]". *Studime Albanologjike [Albanological Studies]* 11:1 (2008):48–54.

Duka, Valentina. "Veprimtaria e Kishës Ortodokse Shqiptare të Amerikës (1912–1920) [The Activity of the Albanian Orthodox Church in the United States (1912–1920)]". *70 vjet të Kishës Ortodokse Autoqefale Shqiptare [70 Years of the Albanian Autocephalous Orthodox Church]*. Tirana: Institute of History, 1993.

Dushku, Ledia. "Debatet shqiptaro-greke dhe Lidhja e Kombeve (1920–1922) [Albanian-Greek Debates in the League of Nations (1920–1922)]". *Studime Historike [Historical Studies]* 3–4 (2006):73–81.

Dushku, Ledia. "Greqia midis qeverisë së Vlorës dhe Pleqësisë së Shqipërisë së Mesme [Greece between the Vlora Government and the Central Albania Senate]". *Studime Historike [Historical Studies]* 3–4 (2008):79–88.

Glavinas, Apostolos. "Ιωακείμ Μαρτίστης η Μαρτινιανός [Joakim Martishti or Martiniani]". *Ηπειρωτικό Ημερολόγιο [Epirotan Calendar]* 3 (1981):44–53.

234   *Bibliography*

Glavinas, Apostolos. "Ο Μητροπολίτης Δυρραχίου Ιάκοβως και οι δραστηριότητες του για το εκκλησιαστικό ζήτημα της Αλβανίας [The Metropolitan of Durrës Iakovos and His Activity for the Ecclesiastical Issue in Albania]". *Ηπειρότηκο Ημερολόγιο [Epirotan Calendar]* 2 (1986):53–61.

Glavinas, Apostolos. "Ο Συναδών Χριστόφορος και οι δραστηριότητες του για το εκκλησιαστικό ζήτημα της Αλβανίας [Kristofor of Synadon and His Activity for the Ecclesiastical Issue in Albania]". *Ηπειρότηκο Ημερολόγιο [Epirotan Calendar]* 2 (1984):70–76.

Jani, Alqi. "Papa Pano Gjirokastra – Figurë e shquar e Kishës Shqiptare [Reverend Pano Gjirokastra – A Distinguished Figure of the Albanian Church]". *70 vjet të Kishës Ortodokse Autoqefale Shqiptare [70 Years of the Albanian Autocephalous Orthodox Church]*. Tirana: Institute of History, 1993.

Jani, Alqi. "Memorandumi i shqiptarëve ortodoksë dërguar Patrikanës së Stambollit [Orthodox Albanian Memorandum Sent to the Istanbul Patriarchate]". *55*. 6 June 1999.

Jani, Alqi. "Të njohim dhe nderojmë klerikët e Kishës Ortodokse të Shqipërisë: Episkopi Eugjen Hoshteva [To Acknowledge and Honor the Clerics of the Orthodox Church of Albania: Bishop Eugjen Hoshteva]". *Republika*. 27 May 2009.

Kalezić, Dimitrije M. "Srpske škole u Albaniji [Serbian Schools in Albania]". Paper presentation, "Population of Slavic Origin in Albania" Scientific Conference, Cetinje, Montenegro, 21–23 June 1990.

"Meditim rreth dy fotografive [Meditation About Two Photos]", *Autoqefalia Ortodokse Shqiptare [Albanian Orthodox Autocephaly]*, 1994.

Meta, Beqir. "Autoqefalia e Kishës Ortodokse Shqiptare në procesin e formimit të institucioneve kombëtare në vitet 1920–1924 [The Autocephaly of the Albanian Orthodox Church in the Proccess of Establishing National Institutions during 1920–1924]". *Studime Albanologjike [Albanological Studies]* 11:1 (2011):80–88.

Meta, Beqir. "Çështja e minoriteteve në Shqipëri, në Lidhjen e Kombeve në vitet '30 [The Issue of Minorities in Albania in the League of Nations in the 1930s]". *Studime Historike [Historical Studies]* 3–4 (2006):148–155.

Meta, Beqir. "Debati shqiptaro-grek për problemet e minoriteteve dhe të Kishës Autoqefale Shqiptare në organizmat ndërkombëtarë në vitet 1929–1934 [Albanian-Greek Debate on Minority Issues and the Albanian Autocephalous Church in International Organizations in 1929–1934]". *Studime Historike [Historical Studies]* 3–4 (2011):37–61.

Meta, Beqir. "Përpjekjet për konsolidimin e institucioneve kombëtare (1925–1935) [Efforts on Consolidation of National Institutions (1925–1935)]". *Studime Historike [Historical Studies]* 3–4 (2008):83–99.

Meta, Beqir. "Qëndrimi i shtetit shqiptar ndaj pakicës etno-kulturore vllehe dhe asaj malazeze në vitet 1920–1924 [The Albanian State Position towards the Vlach Ethno-Cultural Minority and the Montenegrins in 1920–1924]". *Studime Historike [Historical Studies]* 3–4 (2009):45–66.

Meta, Beqir. "Vështrim rreth kombëtarizimit dhe pavarësimit të Kishës Ortodokse [Overview of the Nationalization and Independence of the Orthodox Church]". *Studime historike [Historical Studies]* 1–2 (2006).

Naska, Kaliopi. "Kongresi themeltar i Kishës Ortodokse Autoqefale në Berat [Foundation Congress of the Autocephalous Orthodox Church in Berat]". *70 vjet të Kishës Ortodokse Autoqefale Shqiptare [70 Years of the Albanian Autocephalous Orthodox Autocephalous Church]*. Tirana: Institute of History, 1993.

Panev, Zhivko (reverend). "Some Remarks on the Notion of Autocephaly". *Sourozh* 63 (1996):125–133.

Pelushi, Joan (metropolitan). "Kisha Ortodokse dhe Konfliktet Etnike [The Orthodox Church and Ethnic Conflicts]". *Tempulli [Temple]* 9 (2004):1–9.

Pelushi, Joan (metropolitan). "Një vështrim i shkurtër historik mbi përkthimet fetare në Kishën Orthodhokse në Shqipëri [A Brief Historical Overview of Religious Translations in the Orthodox Church in Albania]". *Tempulli [Temple]* 2 (2000):4–25.

"Personalitet i dyfishtë, Ikonom Papapano atdhetar shqiptar dhe prift shqiptar [Dual Personality, Ikonom Papapano, an Albanian Patriot and Albanian Priest]", *Autoqefalia Ortodokse Shqiptare [Albanian Orthodox Autocephaly]*. 10 September 1994.

"Personalitet madhor i Kishës sonë Orthodhokse: Imzot Kristofor Kisi [Great Personality of Our Orthodox Church: Bishop Kristofor Kisi]". *Ngjallja [Resurrection]*. June 1996.

Psomas, Lambros. "Το πρόβλημα της άρνησης των Σέρβων για υποστήριξη των πρώτων προσπαθειών των Ορθοδόξων Αλβανών για αυτοκέφαλη Εκκλησία [The Problem of Serbian Refusal of the First Efforts of Albanian Orthodox for an Autocephalous Church]." *Theologia [Theology]* 77:2 (2006):645–655

Rama, Fatmira. "Sinodi i Parë Shqiptar dhe Kongresi i Dytë Panortodoks i Kishës Autoqefale Kombëtare [The First Albanian Synod and the Second Pan-Orthodox Congress of the National Autocephalous Church]". *70 vjet të Kishës Ortodokse Autoqefale Shqiptare [70 Years of the Albanian Autocephalous Orthodox Church]*. Tirana: Institute of History, 1993.

Rama, Fatmira. "Shteti dhe njohja e Kishës Autoqefale Shqiptare (1922–1929) [The State and the Recognition of the Albanian Autocephalous Church (1922–1939)]". *Studime Albanologjike [Albanological Studies]* 11:1 (2011):66–75.

Roudometof, Victor N. "From Rum Millet to Greek Nation: Enlightenment, Secularization, and National Identity in Ottoman Balkan Society, 1453–1821". *Journal of Modern Greek Studies* 16:1 (1998):11–48.

Sulstarova, Enis. "Lindja e kombeve dhe Naum Veqilharxhi [The Birth of Nations and Naum Veqilharxhi]". *Politika & Shoqëria [Politics & Society]* 2 (2004):91–103.

Tushi, Dion. "Joakim Martiniani". *Kërkim [Research]* 6 (2010):81–93.

Vasili, Ilia S. "Si e gjeta Episkop Jerotheun [How I Found Bishop Ierothe]". *Ngjallja [Resurrection]*. August 1996.

Xhufi, Pëllumb and Hajredin Isufi. "Aneksimi i dhunshëm i Çamërisë nga Greqia dhe lufta e shqiptarëve për mbrojtjen e saj [The Violent Annexation of Chameria by Greece and the Albanian Battle for Its Protection]". *Studime Historike [Historical Studies]* 1–4 (1996):3–27.

Photographies

Andrea Llukani's private collection
Niko Kotherja's private collection
Phothoteque of the General Directorate of Archives of Albania

Index

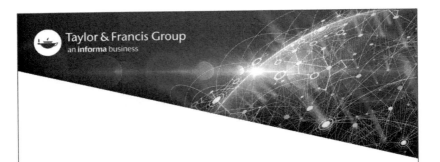